CREATIVE PRACTICE RESEARCH IN THE AGE OF NEOLIBERAL HOPELESSNESS

Edited by Agnieszka Piotrowska

EDINBURGH
University Press

Edinburgh University Press is one of the leading university presses in the UK. We publish academic books and journals in our selected subject areas across the humanities and social sciences, combining cutting-edge scholarship with high editorial and production values to produce academic works of lasting importance. For more information visit our website: edinburghuniversitypress.com

© editorial matter and organisation Agnieszka Piotrowska, 2020, 2022
© the chapters their several authors, 2020, 2022

Edinburgh University Press Ltd
The Tun – Holyrood Road
12 (2f) Jackson's Entry
Edinburgh EH8 8PJ

First published in hardback by Edinburgh University Press 2020

Typeset in 10/12.5 pt Sabon by
Servis Filmsetting Ltd, Stockport, Cheshire

A CIP record for this book is available from the British Library

ISBN 978 1 4744 6356 0 (hardback)
ISBN 978 1 4744 6357 7 (paperback)
ISBN 978 1 4744 6358 4 (webready PDF)
ISBN 978 1 4744 6359 1 (epub)

The right of the contributors to be identified as authors of this work has been asserted in accordance with the Copyright, Designs and Patents Act 1988 and the Copyright and Related Rights Regulations 2003 (SI No. 2498).

CONTENTS

List of Figures — vi
Notes on Contributors — viii
Acknowledgements — xiv
Preface: Life in the Post Pandemic Age — xvi

1. Introduction: Complexities, Compromises and Complicities — 1
   Agnieszka Piotrowska

2. Against the Grain: Women Film Practitioners and Theorists Talk Creative Practice and Theory — 19
   Jill Daniels, Rachel Velody and Eylem Atakav

3. *Married to the Eiffel Tower*: Notes on Love, Loss and Knowledge — 34
   Agnieszka Piotrowska

4. Creativity and Neoliberalism: Between Autonomy, Resistance and Tactical Compliance — 46
   Thomas Elsaesser

5. Tactical Compliance and the Persistence of Elsaesser — 70
   William Brown

6. Storytelling and Game Playing — 81
   Alexis Weedon

CONTENTS

7. Autonomy and the Other Woman: Queer Active Agency and Postcolonial Expectations   94
Jenny Barrett and Rosa Fong

8. From Neolithic to Neoliberal   107
Tony Clancy

9. First-person Expression on 'Non-Western' Screens: China as a Case Study   119
Kiki Tianqi Yu

10. Scholarly Exploration of the Creative Process: Integrating Film Theory and Practice   133
Warren Buckland

11. Teaching Practice as Theory: Guerrilla Filmmaking   150
William Brown

12. Baits of Falsehood: The Role of Fiction in Documentary or From Untheorised Practice to Unpractised Theory   164
Bruce Eadie

13. *Repented*: A Creative Intersemiotic Translation   183
Agnieszka Piotrowska

    Notes on *Repented*   197
Thomas Elsaesser

14. *How do you see me?* The Camera as Transitional Object in Diasporic, Domestic Ethnography   200
Nariman Massoumi

15. 'Shut Your Hole, Girlie. Mine's Making Money, Doll': Creative Practice-Research and the Problem of Professionalism   221
Roberta Mock

16. Feminist 'Pensive-creative Praxis' and Irigaray: A Porous, Dialogical Encounter   242
Judith Rifeser

17. The Paths of Creation, or How Can I Help my Dybbouk to Get Out of Me?   258
Isabelle Starkier

18. 'We Want to Kill Boko Haram': Reflections on the Photographic Representation of Children in a Displacement Camp   271
Tunde Alabi-Hundeyin

19. Between 'Counter-movement' (Ingold) and 'Living with Ghosts'
    (Demos) 288
    Mischa Twitchin

20. *Screen Memories*: A Video Essay on *Smultronstället/Wild
    Strawberries* 304
    Catherine Grant

Index 316

FIGURES

1.1	The team organising the conference	2
1.2	Thomas Elsaesser giving his talk during the conference	9
3.1	Screenshot *Married to the Eiffel Tower* (2008), dir. Agnieszka Piotrowska	35
3.2	Screenshot *Married to the Eiffel Tower* (2008), dir. Agnieszka Piotrowska	36
4.1	The incidental casualness of the Elsaesser family and friends on the Sun Island	49
4.2	The Sun Island as seen from the lake in 1940	57
4.3	Hans Peter Elsaesser, the author of the home movies, *The Sun Island* (2017)	62
4.4	Hans Peter Elsaesser, the author of the home movies, *The Sun Island* (2017)	63
4.5	Hans Peter Elsaesser, the author of the home movies, *The Sun Island* (2017)	64
8.1	From *The Plate Spinner* (2016), Tony Clancy	111
8.2	From *Stone Ghosts* (2018), Tony Clancy	114
9.1	From *Memory of Home* (2009), Kiki Tianqi Yu	121
9.2	Setting up a tombstone in *Children's Village* (2012), Zou Xueping	127
12.1	Folman's hallucination. From *Waltz with Bashir* (2009 [2008]), Ari Folman	171

13.1	Experimental film (2019) was based on the play *Finding Temeraire* (2017)	184
13.2	From the performance of *Finding Temeraire*, Harare International Festival of the Arts (2017)	187
13.3	The same scene as adapted for the screen for *Repented* (2019) using the split screen technique	187
13.4	Archive colonial footage in a split-screen display situates the love story in an actual historical moment	191
14.1	The author pictured with his mother and sister in 1985	202
14.2	A still frame from *How do you see me?* (2017)	209
15.1	Front cover of Pearl Williams's LP, *A Trip Around the World Is Not a Cruise* (1962)	222
15.2	Roberta Mock with Hazaar!, *A Trip Around the World Is Not a Cruise* (2016)	230
15.3	Roberta Mock, *A Trip Around the World Is Not a Cruise* (2016)	231
16.1	From *A Letter Of Love To You* (2016) (00:00:18)	246
17.1	From *Scrooge* (Avignon 2006) (Scrooge, the employee and the niece)	260
17.2	From *Quichotte* (Paris 2009) (Quichotte as a puppet and the actress as Pança)	261
17.3	From *Du côté d'Alice* (Avignon 2012) (Alice and the magic bottle)	262
17.4	From *Un gros grand gras Gargantua* (Avignon 2015)	263
17.5	*Kafka's dance*, Timothy Daly (Paris 2006) (the fiancée with Kafka's puppet)	266
18.1	Hauwa Ali (Photo: Tunde Alabi-Hundeyin)	275
18.2	Fatima Umoru (Photo: Tunde Alabi-Hundeyin)	275
18.3	'I share this matress with four of my siblings' (Photo: Fatima Umoru)	280
18.4	'This house is near our camp shelter' (Photo: Suleiman Nuhu)	280
18.5	'Star Boy, my pet cat' (Photo: Maimuna Umoru)	281
19.1	Exhibit at the 'European Ghosts' exhibition (2016), Kunstmuseum aan zee, Ostend	292
19.2	Exhibit at the 'European Ghosts' exhibition (2016), Kunstmuseum aan zee, Ostend	296
20.1	*Screen Memories*, A Video Essay	305

NOTES ON CONTRIBUTORS

Tunde Alabi-Hundeyin is a media creative whose passion lies in working on humanitarian narratives that contribute to improving human conditions in marginalised communities and disrupting existing hierarchies of power relations. He has carried out media projects for charity and corporate organisations, including exhibitions in Lagos, Enugu, Addis Ababa, Heidelberg, Friedrichshafen, Ulm, Karlsruhe, Brighton and in New York at the United Nations. His photos have also been used in UNICEF Nigeria advocacy materials. A doctoral researcher in Creative and Critical Practice at the University of Sussex, Tunde's research questions the objectification narratives of children of colour as victims of poverty and suffering. Through visual ethnography, participatory photography, and photo elicitation methodologies with children displaced by Boko Haram in Nigeria, it seeks to demonstrate contemporary representational practices of promoting ethical images of the distant 'other'.

Eylem Atakav is Professor of Film, Gender and Public Engagement at the University of East Anglia where she teaches courses on women, Islam and media; and Middle Eastern media. She is the Chair-Elect for the Teaching, Learning and Scholarship Knowledge Community of *NAFSA: Association of International Educators*. She is the recipient of the 2016 Society for Cinema and Media Studies Outstanding Contribution to Pedagogy Award, and is an HEA National Teaching Fellow (2016). She is the author of *Women and Turkish Cinema: Gender Politics, Cultural Identity and Representation* (2012) and editor of *Directory of World Cinema: Turkey* (2013). She recently completed an Arts and Humanities Research Council-funded project entitled 'British [Muslim] Values'. She is the director of *Growing Up Married* (2016) – an internationally acclaimed and award-winning documentary about forced marriage and child brides in Turkey.

Jenny Barrett is a Reader in Film and Popular Culture at Edge Hill University. Her research interests include ethnicity and racial representation in cinema and other forms of popular culture, Transatlantic slavery and historical narratives on screen. She is the Deputy Director of the International Centre on Racism based at Edge Hill.

William Brown is a Reader in Film at the University of Roehampton, London. He is the author of *The Squid Cinema from Hell: Kinoteuthis Infernalis and the Emergence of Chthulumedia* (with David H. Fleming, Edinburgh University Press, 2020), *Non-Cinema: Global Digital Filmmaking and the Multitude* (2018) and *Supercinema: Film-Philosophy for the Digital Age* (2013). He is also the editor, with David Martin-Jones, of *Deleuze and Film* (Edinburgh University Press, 2012). He is also a maker of no- to zero-budget films, including *En Attendant Godard* (2009), *Selfie* (2014), *The New Hope* (2015), *Circle/Line* (2016), *This is Cinema* (2019) and *The New Hope 2* (2019).

Warren Buckland is Reader in Film Studies at Oxford Brookes University. His recent publications include the monographs *Wes Anderson's Symbolic Storyworld* (2019) and *Film Theory: Rational Reconstructions* (2012), and the edited collections *Conversations with Christian Metz: Selected Interviews on Film Theory* (co-edited with Daniel Fairfax, 2017), *The Routledge Encyclopedia of Film Theory* (co-edited with Edward Branigan, 2014), *Hollywood Puzzle Films* (ed. 2014), and *Puzzle Films: Complex Storytelling in Contemporary Cinema* (ed. 2009).

Tony Clancy originally studied theatre and now works in photography, video and education. His practice research explores the space between the still and moving lens-based image as well as acoustics, and how they can re-present the familiar. His recent short films include *The Plate Spinner* and *Stone Ghosts*. As an educator he has worked for UCLAN, Falmouth and Gloucestershire universities, setting up, running and teaching courses both in practice and theory in photography and media.

Jill Daniels is an internationally renowned filmmaker and scholar. Over thirty years she has made numerous documentary films, including *Not Reconciled* (2009), *The Border Crossing* (2011), *My Private Life* (2013), *My Private Life II* (2014), *Journey to the South* (2017) and *Breathing Still* (2018). She has won many international awards including Jury Award for Best Experimental Film at Ann Arbor Experimental Film Festival, USA, in 2017 for *My Private Life II*. She is the author of *Memory, Place & Autobiography: Experiments in Documentary Filmmaking* (2019). She is co-editor of *Truth, Dare or Promise: Art and Documentary Revisited* (2013) and is a member of the editorial board of *Media Practice & Education*. She is Senior Lecturer at the University of East London where she teaches Film Practice and Theory.

Bruce Eadie has made documentaries on challenging subjects often involving state-sanctioned violence, from genocide to forced sterilisation to the death penalty. He won an Emmy for his 1996 film *Nuremberg* on the Nuremberg Trials. With an academic background in History at Cambridge and postgraduate work in Intellectual History at Sussex, he has returned to academia in recent years at Birkbeck, writing an MA thesis on the films of Patrick Keiller and is currently finishing a PhD on fictional films-within-the-film in recent documentaries that explore traumatic events in the life of an individual.

Thomas Elsaesser was an international film scholar and Professor of Film and Television Studies at the University of Amsterdam and the School of the Arts at Columbia University. His many books include *New German Cinema: A History* (1989), *Fassbinder's Germany: History Identity Subject* (1996), *Weimar Cinema and After* (2000), *Metropolis* (2000; 2nd edn 2012), *Studying Contemporary American Film* (with Warren Buckland, 2002), *Filmgeschichte und Frühes Kino* (2002), *European Cinema: Face to Face with Hollywood* (2005), *Film Theory: An Introduction through the Senses* (with Malte Hagener, 2010; 2nd edn 2015), *The Persistence of Hollywood* (2012), *German Cinema – Terror and Trauma: Cultural Memory since 1945* (2013), *Film History as Media Archaeology* (2018) and *European Cinema and Continental Philosophy: Film As Thought Experiment* (2018). He also wrote and directed *The Sun Island* (2017), a documentary essay film about his grandfather, the renowned architect Martin Elsaesser.

Rosa Fong is a filmmaker and academic. Her films have won awards from the British Film Institute and Arts Council of England. She has directed programmes for both the BBC and Channel 4. Rosa is also a Senior Lecturer in Film and Television Production at Edge Hill University. Her research practice explores transcultural identities and displacement. Her recent research focuses on memory, displacement, identity and performativity. This is explored through her documentary called *Deconstructing Zoe* (2016) about a transgender actor; a multimedia exhibition called *Dragons of the Pool* (2018) on the forced repatriation of Chinese seamen in Liverpool in 1946 and a series of short films called BEAST (2019), which uses verbatim dialogue to explore the lack of screen representation of East Asians in Britain. She has also worked as an Associate Producer on the feature length films *Cut Sleeve Boys* (2006), *Front Cover* (2015) and *Suk Suk* (2019) nominated for five Golden Horse Awards.

Catherine Grant is Professor of Digital Media and Screen Studies at Birkbeck, University of London, where she teaches and researches audiovisual cultures, audiovisual essay practices and digital forms of analysis and criticism. She is part of the programming group for the annual Essay Film Festival, run jointly with London's Institute of Contemporary Arts, and also Director of Birkbeck Institute for the Moving Image. A prolific experimental video-essayist, she runs the 'Film Studies For Free' blog and is a founding co-editor of *[in]Transition: Journal of Videographic Film and Moving Image Studies*.

Nariman Massoumi is a Lecturer in Film and Television at University of Bristol with a background in documentary television. His practice research focuses on family and displacement, with a wider interest in the role of film in the historical and cultural encounters between Britain and Iran.

Roberta Mock is Professor of Performance Studies and Director of the Doctoral College at the University of Plymouth. She was the founding co-Director of the AHRC-funded 3D3 Centre for Doctoral Training, which supported only practice-led research projects in digital art, design, culture and performance. Her own research focuses on gender, sexuality and bodies in performance, with a specific interest in live art and stand-up comedy by Jewish women. She is the author or editor of five books, including *Jewish Women on Stage, Film and Television* (2007), and is the current Chair of the Theatre & Performance Research Association (TaPRA). Championing and celebrating embodied knowledge at all stages of a research career, Roberta has written and spoken about and has led workshops across the UK, in Canada and Europe on practice-research methodologies.

Agnieszka Piotrowska is an award-winning filmmaker and a theorist. She is best known for her iconic documentary *Married to the Eiffel Tower* (2008). She obtained a PhD in Psychoanalysis and Film from Birkbeck, University of London, under Stephen Frosh and Laura Mulvey. She is a Reader in Film Practice and Theory at the University of Bedfordshire and Course Leader MA/MSc Digital Film. She is also a Visiting Professor in Film at the University of Gdansk, Poland. Her post-doctoral project has focused on (post) colonial trauma in Zimbabwe through the arts and literature. Piotrowska is the author of monographs *Psychoanalysis and Ethics in Documentary Film* (2014), *Black and White: Cinema, Politics and the Arts in Zimbabwe* (2016), and *The Nasty Woman and the Neo-Femme Fatale in Contemporary Cinema* (2019). She has edited *Embodied Encounters: New Approaches to Cinema and Psychoanalysis* (2015), and co-edited *Psychoanalysis and the Unrepresentable* (2016) and *Psychoanalysis and Femininity* (2019) (both with Ben Tyrer). Piotrowska made a number of collaborative film projects in Zimbabwe including an award-winning documentary *Lovers in Time or how we Didn't get arrested in Harare* (2015), an award-winning feature film *Escape* (2017), and a new experimental film *Repented* (2019), which screened internationally.

Judith Rifeser is a lecturer and audio-visual practitioner in the Department of Educational Studies at Goldsmiths University and a teaching fellow at UCL. A plurilingual scholar in language teaching and learning, as well as cultural studies, she is particularly interested in creative praxis, teaching with and through film, and in women's studies in relation to identity and diversity. She completed her Creative Practice Research PhD at the University of Roehampton where she taught on the cultural studies and film programmes. She was previously a junior lecturer at the Johns Hopkins University, Baltimore. Judith's stop-motion animation short *A Letter of Love to You* (UK, 2016) premiered at the London Feminist Film Festival 2016 and was subsequently screened in the run-up to the Leeds Queer Film Festival, and at FiLia 2016. Judith's experimental short, *Care/ss* (UK, 2017), commissioned by Luce Irigaray, premiered at the ICA in 2017. Judith's newest work, the audio-visual essay *A caressing dialogical encounter* (2019), premieres in Oslo in 2020..

Isabelle Starkier is a former Student of the École Normale Supérieure, 'agrégée' of modern letters, associate professor directing doctoral research in theatrical studies at the University of Evry. She is also a director, actress and company director in theatre. She works on the link between theory and practice, bringing together her plays (about forty), her work as a company-in-residence and her research on otherness as well as theatre in the heart of the city. Latest plays include: *Le Bal de Kafka, L'homme dans le plafond de Timothy Daly, Le bourgeois Gentilhomme, Un gros grand gras Gargantua* and *Le tango des étoiles errantes*.

Mischa Twitchin is a lecturer in the Theatre and Performance Department at Goldsmiths, University of London. His book, *The Theatre of Death – the Uncanny in Mimesis: Tadeusz Kantor, Aby Warburg and an Iconology of the Actor* is published by Palgrave Macmillan in their Performance Philosophy series; and examples of his performance- and essay-films can be seen on Vimeo: http://vimeo.com/user13124826/videos

Rachel Velody worked for many years at the London College of Fashion as course leader on the part-time Fashion Media degree programme. Her areas of expertise concern the textual analysis of screen identities, with the fashioning of the gendered, raced body within British and North American television drama being areas of particular interest. Awarded in 2018, a three-year doctoral stipend by the University of Bristol, Rachel is, at present, exploring the fashioning of the female detective in contemporary British television crime drama.

Alexis Weedon holds the UNESCO chair in New Media Forms of the Book at the University of Bedfordshire where she is a research professor in publishing. After a spell at Hobson's Publishing in the 1980s and working with the University of Luton Press in the 1990s, she became fascinated by the potential of digital convergence for the book and in 1995 co-founded *Convergence: The international journal of research into new media technologies* with Julia Knight. She is an authority on historical bibliometrics and published *Victorian Publishing* (2003). More recently she co-authored a study of the popular romantic author *Elinor Glyn* with Vincent L. Barnett (2014). She currently leads a research group exploring digital forms of storytelling and the book.

Kiki Tianqi Yu works on two strands: documentary image and non-fiction film, especially on the social, ethical and aesthetic aspects of first person expression, the essayistic non-fiction in non-Western cinemas, amateur cinema, the political economy of international co-productions. The other strand is cinema and artists moving image in China and East Asia, especially in relation to eastern philosophies and aesthetics, on women's cinema, 'image-writing' practice, and independent cinema culture. Kiki's first monograph *'My' Self on Camera: First Person Documentary Practice in an Individualising China* (Edinburgh University Press, 2019) argues that the Confucian concept of the relational self still largely underpins how individuals understand the self, and analyses how filmmakers make socially and culturally rooted ethical and aesthetic choices. She also co-edited *China's iGeneration: Cinema and Moving Image Culture for 21st Century* (2014) and 'Women's First Person Documentary in East Asia', a special issue of *Studies in Documentary Film* (with Alisa Lebow, 2020). As a filmmaker, her first feature documentary *China's van Goghs* (co-directed with Haibo Yu, 2016) involves art history, labour politics, and globalisation, asking: could the act of copying be a path towards originality?

ACKNOWLEDGEMENTS

Any ambitious project of this nature requires a lot of support from very many people. However, in recent times a slightly curious custom has developed of saying 'thank you' to practically everybody we know, in some way devaluing those whose contribution was vital. These thanks therefore will be brief.

I am grateful to the Research Institute of Media and Performance Research at the University of Bedfordshire without whose support the initial conference would not have taken place and the book's idea would not have been born. My co-organiser Pryianka Verma deserves heartfelt thanks here. The institutional support of the Director of the Institute Professor Alexis Weedon and my Head of School Dr Jane Carr were crucial. The Dean, Professor Jan Domin, gave us permission to experiment with the format and the agenda of the conference, trusting we might arrive at something generative – and we did.

I am grateful to our publisher at Edinburgh University Press, Gillian Leslie, whose faith in the project made us push forward through dark times.

I need to recognise the help and friendship of Dr Warren Buckland, whose editorial support has been invaluable. This is a work of complexity and without his clarity and wisdom, and his experienced input on many levels, this volume would have faltered. All mistakes are of course my own.

Without my writers, without their strength and endless support and humour, without their desire to see this work published, I would have given up on the way, going off to make another film or a video essay instead. Thank you dear friends.

Last but not least, I need to acknowledge Professor Thomas Elsaesser's input into the conference and the book. Without his unswerving belief in the project, in my own work and in the concept of creating this alternative research space as a way of resisting political and institutional control through creative activity, the project would have been hard to get off the ground. He did more than encourage it; he insisted it was an important thing to do. Further, I appreciate greatly Professor Thomas Elsaesser's serene attitude to the controversies his film and his keynote evoked. Not only did he decide to stick with this volume despite having his film work and some of his ideas critiqued and even criticised, but instead he was excited that his work engendered so much discussion. It was humbling to see his generous acceptance of more junior colleagues' arguments, including my own. It is a lesson in an incredible openness and scholarly confidence. In the end, Thomas Elsaesser's ideas, as always, have opened a space for a real conversation about creative practice and knowledge, about difficult times and our response to those. Now that he is no more, we need to hold onto his example of this exceptional intellectual curiosity and courage.

This volume is dedicated to Thomas Elsaesser's memory.

Agnieszka Piotrowska

PREFACE:
LIFE IN THE POST PANDEMIC AGE

The production process of any book takes a long time. During the final stages of the work on this volume the global pandemic began to rage around the world changing our lives in ways that seemed utterly unexpected, tragic and surreal. As I am writing these words, we are still right in the middle of it, without any knowledge of what might be the final outcome of this crisis. What we do know is that at least hundreds of thousands of people globally will die as a result of it; we know that we are all traumatised by the events linked to it and we don't quite know what the future holds. Still, some reflections are already clear. First, it appears, whatever the real reason for the outbreak of the deadly virus, that it was connected to the mankind's disrespect for our environment in its broad sense. As the conspiracy theories are flying on social media, the real reason remains the same: our species' attitudes to other forms of life and this planet are problematic. We will need to change the way we are and the way we think. Second, it is also clear that some of the countries appear to have been better prepared for this crisis than others. The lack of preparedness of the UK and the USA has been linked to the extreme neoliberal policies over the years, which, to put it bluntly, prioritised profit over care. Now that we know what the result of such attitudes is we must fight even more resolutely for the different policies to ensue.

This book has always aimed to offer some ideas as how to resist neoliberalism. Now this need is more urgent. Will we embrace kindness and generosity over dominance and our unconscious individual desire for power, which psychoanalysis more than a 100 years ago identified as catastrophic for humanity?

Will we be able to offer through our creativity an alternative to the thinking that only activities that bring about immediate and measurable results are significant? Can we hold on to our rage to help bring about a different future?

Pandemics have, historically, produced a rupture and a change – not always for the better. We can begin working towards a more positive future through a re-definition of what success is and what must be valued in any society and culture. Whatever our utopian dreams are today, we do know that as species we are very flawed if very talented. We must be constantly vigilant, not just towards the governments and politicians, but also towards our own private responses, our public work and actions as however small they might appear, they do matter.

Agnieszka Piotrowska, April 2020

'In times of affective capitalism, information overkill and the neo-liberal university *Creative Practice Research in the Age of Neoliberal Hopelessness*, in exquisite and challenging ways, makes visible to which extent artistic research as system-critical craft and politics can help us to produce deep knowledge and resist the growing co-option and institutionalisation of creativity itself.'

Brenda Hollweg, University of Leeds

'The book's focus is on film and video practice as research and the ways such creative work may both produce new knowledge and create new ways in which actuality is represented as knowable and as knowledge. Many of the authors are themselves documentary filmmakers and they explore in their essay both their practice itself and their thinking about the films they have made in highly original ways. The essays offer illuminating insights and new theoretical perspectives, making the book a very important contribution to film studies and practice within the academy.'

Professor Emeritus Elizabeth Cowie, University of Kent

'This trailblazing book finally brings together two areas often and unfairly seen as discrete: practice and research. Passionately arguing for film as conveyor of scholarly knowledge and, more daringly, for the author's subjective inscription in creative work, editor Agnieszka Piotrowska launches a generative forum, where notable creators-cum-theorists engage in self-revealing, sometimes dissonant, but always inspiring dialogue. A feat to be celebrated.'

Lúcia Nagib, Professor of Film, University of Reading

'*Creative Practice Research in the Age of Neoliberal Hopelessness* offers a unique investigation of the different ways in which creative filmmaking offers its own distinctive forms of research and relates to theoretical insights. The emphasis on auto-ethnographic work, personal reflections on creative practice and the subjective dimensions of knowledge give surprising and candid cutting edge insights that are uncommon in academic texts. With variegated contributions from all corners of the world, this book provide a wealth of perspectives and practices to teach and think about in the growing field of creative audio-visual practice, research and theory.'

Patricia Pisters, University of Amsterdam

1. INTRODUCTION: COMPLEXITIES, COMPROMISES AND COMPLICITIES

Agnieszka Piotrowska

I am delighted to present you with this unruly collection, featuring essays by practitioners and theorists who have reflected on how practice research can offer different ways of producing knowledge or 'knowledges'– or perhaps just different ways of producing work which has artistic ambitions as well as academic ones.

The book is a collection of essays inspired by, but in no way limited to, the Symposium on Creative Practice Research I organised at the University of Bedfordshire in May 2018 supported by my inimitable PhD student Priyanka Verma. The event was an enormous success coming as it did in the midst of discussions about the position of practice research in the British university system and its preparations for the Research Excellence Framework of 2021. I venture that its taking place at a 'new' (meaning not Russell Group) university contributed to the sense of us doing something dangerous and on the peripheries of the restrictive academic environment. There were international participants too and we were keen to compare the different approaches globally. We were very keen to have a record of our discussions and proceedings and the book in some way is just that, although a number of people who were very important voices during the conference, including my students, for a number of reasons are not part of this collection. The reasons are many, but one has to say clearly, and perhaps brutally, that not all creative film or theatre practitioners enjoy writing, and academic writing in particular. Therein lies one of the REF problems, although of course the REF managers would dispute it.

This book is proud to include voices from different cultural and ethnic

Figure 1.1 The team organising the conference. Left to right: Pryianka Verma, the co-organiser; Dr Agnieszka Piotrowska; Charmaine Dambuza, another PhD student who offered some support during the organisation of the event.

backgrounds and some of the writers address issues of post-colonialism head on. This is my fourth edited collection (including two co-edited with Ben Tyrer) since I completed my doctoral work a few years ago, after a career in the television industry. My edited collections are 'unruly' because these volumes attempt to create a space which is not readily regimented. That is not to say that there is not one overarching ambition in this particular collection. The idea guiding this book is the notion of reclaiming the subjective, and at times the deeply personal, as the legitimate site of knowledge, particularly in creative practice research in which a personal undertaking, reflection and commitment to work carried out defines the knowledge it produces.

The collection is therefore a bold attempt to argue against mainstream academic thinking, proposing instead that knowledge produced by creative practice research is as valuable, if not more, than the work setting out to be 'objective'. It is important to note here that the patriarchal notion of knowledge having to be 'objective' can be seen as spilling itself into the discussions of methodologies in creative practice research. The recent articles and special editions of journals try to apply the tested scientific methods of gathering data and commenting on it to be applied to artistic research[1] – this attempt no doubt has value but it is not an attempt which this book advances: our task is to be rigorous but also unashamedly personal and through this personal lens we want to be engaged and politically committed.

The notion of dissecting our experience of making work and calling it knowledge is a centuries-honoured tradition and yet, in the neo-liberal academy it is often questioned and doubted, despite the statements and meetings to the contrary: the shadow of the men of science insisting that only that which is 'objective' has any epistemological value throws a long shadow over the proceedings still. There can be many reasons for this but one certainly is the difficulty of 'measuring' the subjective. In this book, authors speak in the first person, attempt to be reflective, fail at times, but they insist on positioning themselves at the centre of the conversation. They are the research.

There are two exceptions to this rule in the book – two theoretical essays written by academics who are not artists. These are the chapters by Warren Buckland and Alexis Weedon, who offer different ways of thinking about practice and as such are extremely valuable. Buckland examines the practitioner's type of knowledge (*technê*) as embedded in film form and as stated explicitly in filmmaking manuals, and Weedon, speaking from her unique position of being an actual 'REF' manager at the same time as a transdisciplinary storytelling scholar, reflects on the craft and the politics of storytelling and storytellers – as knowledge. The third more 'objective' essay is that of the notable video-essayist Catherine Grant, although it has personal elements in it.

In the other chapters, including my own, the writers give account of their own experience and how it relates both to the theories they have used in their research and their practice, and the knowledge that this reflection has produced. This alone in the current climate amounts, still (or perhaps more now than before), to a radical political gesture: we are doing something personal which, we insist, can, and does, produce knowledge. This of course immediately evokes a whole plethora of questions and I list here but a few. Can this knowledge be somehow measured, recognised and valued? This is a separate question and one that in some way speaks to the notion of 'hopelessness' in the title of this book. Can one measure identity and emotion as a contribution to knowledge if it comes through as a tangible piece of work – or is it but a fantasy of those of us who dream of a more respectful world? The added complication of the current position is that creative practice research and its embodied relationship to knowledge is by necessity individualistic – and yet, almost all contributors in this book would see themselves as radical thinkers, probably left of centre, advocating solidarity with others, and mostly those less privileged and fortunate than us, not through patronising sympathy but through real actions of inclusivity and subversion of the vertical power structures. Nonetheless, art with all its radical ambitions is indeed individualistic and one has to recognise this too.

During the conference, we discussed the difference between our creative desires and inspirations, and the reality of having to produce work which has artistic ambitions but in some way is also a contribution to knowledge that can be measured easily against governmental standards, rules and regulations. There is no problem with this notion in principle, and yet we felt that our work – which we often see as 'art' and therefore touching our very identities – is sullied through somehow becoming products that can be packaged and sold. For me, coming from the industry before doing my theoretical PhD, the tension between one's creativity and the needs of the capitalist client, in my experience as a broadcaster, were palpable for years before I decided to move to the academy. In my experience the neoliberal university, with all its issues, is still a less brutal place than broadcast television despite recent efforts to make it more like a service industry and less a haven for general liberal education and creativity. Within this tough framework, we still try to do work that we find interesting and would attempt to do in any circumstances.

This book therefore hopes to address the very notion of what creative practice research is, and challenges the portrayal of creative practitioners as either artists *manqué* or as academics bored with rigorous scholarship. We discuss our experiences and our contribution to knowledge, and examine our attempts at holding on to our creativity and our integrity during times of relentless political and economic battles in higher education, which amount to an ability to measure and quantify everything, including creative work. Do creative practitioners compromise their creativity by working within the higher education system, trading in a possible poverty of an uncompromising but potentially unemployed artist and an uncertain status of a freelance for an academic title complete with regular salaries? In other words, is the role of the academic creative practitioner a gesture of 'tactical compliance' – a phrase coined by one of our keynote speakers at the conference to which I will come back later in this introduction. If we all simply have to engage with 'tactical compliance', does it actually matter? I think it does matter and therefore the next question is obvious: How far do we acquiesce to be a part of the neoliberal project and how can we offer any resistance at all?

The title of this collection is therefore ironic but it also captures a moment in time and that moment appears to have become tougher and more problematic as time has gone on. In addition, there is no homogeneity whatever within the 'practice research' community. The book offers a space for reflection for a group of practitioners and theorists. I hope that for the readers it presents a much-needed intervention, which will certainly be of interest to all academics engaged with creative practice as research, but also, hopefully, to funding bodies and research councils involved in funding the arts.

'Practice theory', 'practice-led research' or 'practice-based theory': these terms name a field that has become one of the most hotly debated topics in university education in recent years. In the humanities generally, but especially in the arts and creative industries, such an apparent synthesis of theory and practice recognises creative work as a legitimate form of research; but, at the same time, it marks a trend to make higher education more vocational and more directly relevant to society, which can often simply mean a way to generate profit within the neoliberal university.

Can creative practice research – the term chosen for the present collection – be both empowering and perfectly fit into neoliberal flexibilisation and the bio-political labour precariat? How do these alternatives change – become exacerbated or dissolved – in light of the fact that many artists as well as academics see their work as political: activist, engaged, and promoting a socially progressive agenda?

The chapters in this book privilege the experiences of film practitioners and researchers, although it also sets out to give voice to sister disciplines, such as writing and performing. It includes reflective essays that explore the 'bold', the 'artistic' and the 'epistemological', written by notable academics who have become practitioners for a particular reason, or who see their scholarly writing and critical thinking also as a creative practice, legitimated by a willingness to take risks, and an openness to practices and experiments that challenge the boundaries of educational wisdom.

The chapters address and explore the following questions and issues: What is the relationship between traditional academic knowledge and artistic research/professional practice? Can a practitioner generate theoretical knowledge? Can practice research move beyond a narrow discussion of filmmaking practices into discussions of philosophy, ethics and gender? To what extent can creative practice research tap into areas of experience unavailable to traditional scholarship? For example, do first-person narratives contain theoretical knowledge even though they are deeply subjective? Is creative practice a tool of political resistance and, if so, how is it achieved? Can creative practice be subjected to theoretical analysis? (What is involved in the theoretical understanding of film practice?) Why do academics decide to include practice in their work? And: What is the relationship between 'high' theory and collaborative or workshop practice?

Scholarly, 'Objective', Personal?

The feminist philosopher and thinker Donna Haraway has been attempting to re-formulate the concept of knowledge for decades. She acknowledges the privileged position of patriarchal knowledge in contemporary culture and has instead been working at presenting the notion of 'situated knowledges' (1988: 581), meaning embodied knowledge originating from a particular scientist or scholar. Haraway recalls the centuries-long demand of the men of science to be as invisible as possible when reporting their findings – in order for it to be more 'objective' (Haraway 1997: 25–30). This she deems a fundamentally ill-conceived notion. Throughout the academy, including the humanities and the arts, the notion of arriving at the objective knowledge expressed in an objective language still appears to be a project that prevails and any attempt to make that knowledge something one can question, discuss and take issue with speaking in the first person, appears still to be a contested area. This is very relevant to creative practice research in which 'knowledges' produced through it have to be subjective, personal, embodied and therefore in some way feminine. I would suggest therein lies the problem of treating creative practice research seriously, for REF (Research Excellence Framework) as well as other areas. In this book, many writers describe their experiences connected to documentary, which, in particular, is also a problematic area.

Most of the contributions to this book deal with the creation of some kind of documentary by those who write about it. This itself is not uncomplicated. The documentary film project was arguably the tool of science to begin with; the expectation regarding a documentary has been similar, harking back to the famous dictum by Nichols (1991) that documentary film is a 'discourse of sobriety' similar to science. He himself has since disputed this, but it has been so influential in film studies, precisely because it links to the general idea of what knowledge might be. The essays in this volume are often deeply personal, auto-ethnographic and even autobiographical. As a documentary filmmaker who worked in the industry for almost twenty years, I have always struggled with the notion that the documentary film ought to be seen as somehow 'objective' and I have written about it extensively elsewhere (2012, 2014, 2017, 2019).

In the history of documentary film studies, the tragic misunderstanding of the nature of a documentary account has led to such classic and dramatic misrecognitions in the history of documentary film as identifying Flaherty's fictional film *Nanook of the North* (1922) as a scientific/anthropological text – which we now know that it was not.

Clearly ethnography/anthropology's difficulties with its own 'identity' have spilled over to the continuing uncertainties regarding expectations of the documentary genre too, probably until Geertz's forceful positioning of anthropologists as 'authors'.[2] It was also Geertz who said famously and controversially that he would prefer to position anthropology on 'the side of literary rather than scientific discourses' (Geertz 1988: 6). In other words, he was emphatically against an attempt to hide the author/researcher of the text as 'the author' (the researcher, filmmaker, scholar) will affect the result – 'the result' such as it is depends on the 'the author'. Instead of the insistence on 'the objective', Geertz advocated transparency in the proceedings married with a respectful stance vis-à-vis the participants of any ethnographic study.

The 'invisibility' of the author vis-à-vis the notion that he or she ought to be acknowledged and recognised is a debate which continues, both in the academy and certainly in documentary film. In my own theoretical work (2014, 2015, 2017, 2019), I have questioned over and over again the stance of expecting the documentary to be somehow 'objective': it is always a subjective text and it always carries the traces of a relationship between the filmmaker and her subject, the person about whom she (or he of course) makes a film. This book creates another contribution to this debate and privileges the first-person relationship to the work. Contemporary documentary film studies scholarship issues of subjectivity, objectivity and ethics have been discussed extensively and it is beyond the scope of this introduction to give it justice here. Pratap Rughani (2013) in his chapter on ethics and the question of whether a documentary filmmaker is an artist (and has the right to be) gives the notorious but very clear example of the German female filmmaker Leni Riefenstahl who is undoubtedly a brilliant artist but whose work remains deeply unethical for its allegiance to Hitler.

One of the most important documentary film scholars, Michael Renov, introduced the idea that non-fiction contains a number of 'fictive' elements, that is 'moments at which a presumably objective representation of the world encounters the necessity of creative intervention' (Renov 1993: 2). Elizabeth Cowie, known for her work on gender and psychoanalysis in cinema, introduced a crack into film studies scholarship, suggesting both that the 'desire' in documentary is a complex notion and the notion of 'transference' (Cowie 2011: 100) which I developed further in my work – and here too in the chapter on *Married to the Eiffel Tower*. It is quite extraordinary that such a long time after these statements we are still engaged in the problematic nature of the 'I' in scholarship. 'Autoethnography' and 'reflexivity' are but labels, then, attempting to make something fundamentally fluid, deeply subjective and even emotional at times, more 'scientific', 'objective' or at least 'scholarly'. Tessa Muncey in the preface to her book *Creating Autoethnographies* (2010) states boldly the aim of using autoethnography alongside other more established and more obviously scholarly research method which is 'to contribute to or *subvert the dominant discourses* that underpin much of our research, strategies and techniques need to be found for portraying experiences that don't rely on the affinity of shared assumptions' (Muncey 2010: xi, my emphasis). It is here that creative practice research has a major contribution to make. Muncey's descriptions go beyond 'documentaries', also insisting indeed that creative and fictional work can contribute to 'knowledge' – the knowledge about the world and not merely about how to put a film together, for example. She goes on to identify the reader for her book: 'there may be those who want to include a personal story in their study or paper and want to find a theoretical justification to do so' (ibid.: xii). A little further into her book, she defines it:

> Autoethnography is a research approach that privileges the individual. It is an artistically constructed piece of prose, poetry, music or piece of art work that attempts to portray an individual experience in a way that evokes the imagination of the reader, viewer or listener. (ibid.: 2)

For Muncey, and others who will be evoked henceforth, 'autoethnography' is any account, which uses the first-person narrative of the author, relying on the latter's memory, photographs, letters and, importantly, feelings. She argues for using 'the highly personal' alongside 'the highly scholarly' – in the interests of furthering 'knowledge' and indeed scholarship itself. It is of course very telling that she mentions creative and artistic outputs as examples of just an autoethnography.

An American-Korean Professor of anthropological education, Heewon Chang, describes autoethnography as a 'research method that utilizes the researchers' autobiographical data to analyze and interpret their cultural assumptions' (Chang 2008: 9). Chang lists a number of scholars who have already attempted to combine more traditional methods with a desire to deploy one's life's experience in a scholarly discourse. These include anthropologists, social scientists and humanities' scholars, such as Anderson (2006), the hugely influential writers Ellis and Bochner (2000), Nash (2004) or Reed-Danahay (1997). Chang is careful to observe the innovative and controversial nature of the personal in the academy:

> They have already plowed through the wilderness to make a path, and many have followed them. Yet, I still smell fresh-cut grass along the trail and have felt an urge to show my students and interested others one more way of utilizing personal stories for scholarly purposes. (Chang 2008: 10)

The above sentence alone marks the necessary shift of register in terms of the language employed in moving from a 'straight' academic discourse to autoethnography. It is interesting that Chang's style evokes risk-taking and almost danger, with her using the metaphor of 'plowing through the wilderness' and an awareness that there will be pitfalls on the way. Why would it be worth it then? Because including one's personal experience in a highly scholarly discourse is sometimes the only way in which to include the vital 'missing story' in the otherwise more traditional academic presentation (Muncey 2010: 6). At the heart of autoethnography lies a conviction that every individual's personal experience has something unique to contribute.

Chang describes this therefore as a tug of war, 'objectivity vs. subjectivity' (Chang 2008: 45) in particular. Muncey (2010: 98), too, focuses on the 'objective/subjective divide', which in her view can also be defined as the divide between the sciences and arts. Muncey strongly advocates crossing boundaries

INTRODUCTION

Figure 1.2 Thomas Elsaesser giving his talk during the conference. The organiser Agnieszka Piotrowska in the background. Photo credit: Babar Dogar Hussein.

and 'mixing art and science, illusions and reality' and states that that desire goes back to the Renaissance, but claims that John Locke, the English philosopher of Enlightenment, put a lasting halt to it – a move which she regrets (Muncey 2010: 99).

A number of other scholars, too, in their defence of autoethnography have refuted the accusation of self-indulgence, pointing to the difficulties of exposing one's vulnerabilities in disclosures which might come at a personal cost to the author – and which are necessary if the work is to be of value to others (see, for example, Mykhalovskiy 1996: 131).

For autoethnography to really work as a source of an epistemological resource it has to be truly revelationary and analytical, or at least attempt to be. The demand for disclosures, analyses, interpretations and self-interpretations is very hard, arguably harder than the traditional scholarship. It is the issue, as Haraway would put it, of taking off a mask and becoming the subject of one's research, which can be quite scary.

In this volume there are a few such attempts whilst others perhaps still stay on the safe side of the boundary, and that, I would venture, includes the contribution, both written and the actual film, of our very esteemed keynote, Thomas Elsaesser, to which I will return.

Knowledge is Gendered – Female and Feminine Autobiography as a Gesture of Subversion

The philosopher Jacques Derrida suggested that to be able to be self-analytical one has to become feminine.[3] This unexpected assertion connects his recognition of the same century-old problem of the expectation of all knowledge to be produced by white men in white coats in a laboratory as 'objective' as possible. Derrida believed passionately that one's personal experience constitutes knowledge. There is arguably a certain lack of academic training in how to be self-analytical. In my work I often draw from psychoanalysis but also from women writers. It is quite extraordinary how in supervising my PhD students I still have to fight for them to be allowed to use the first person and to establish the position from which they speak, and are allowed to speak. The psychoanalyst, writer and philosopher Shoshana Felman in her now classic book about women and literature, *What Does a Woman Want?* (1993), refers to the difficulty of a feminine desire wanting to combine autobiographical experience with scholarly theory amidst fears and hesitations regarding a certain (patriarchal) expectation of the mode of discourse. She gives a few examples of the dilemma including the famous poet Adrienne Rich when she ponders the nature of her disclosure: 'I have hesitated to do what I am going to do now, which is to use myself as an illustration' (Rich in Felman 1993: 134). Felman gives further examples of Virginia Woolf and Simone de Beauvoir, as well as herself and she points out: 'In the case of Rich, theory (the theory of "Writing as Re-Vision") hesitates to become autobiography (the personal example). In the case of de Beauvoir, autobiography (her own female destiny) hesitates to become theory (*The Second Sex*)' (Felman 1993: 134). Felman then quotes from Rich's New Introduction to her book *Of Woman Born: Motherhood as Experience and Institution* (1986): '*Of Woman Born* was both praised and attacked for what was sometimes seen as an odd-fangled approach: *personal testimony mingled with research, and theory which derived from both ...* What still seems odd is the absentee author, the writer who lays down speculation, theories, facts and fantasies without any personal grounding' (Rich in Felman 1993: 135).

Nancy K. Miller (2002) both insists on the importance of the autobiographical voice in scholarship and states a difficulty that it brings as it invites the criticism of being too egotistic on the part of the writer. She reflects on needing to be like the Reader but also different enough so that the account is of interest:

> I write, Reader, because I'm just like you; I write Reader, because there's no one like me ... On the border between the ego and the other is the potential for identification or repudiation, sympathy or revulsion, love or violence. (Miller 2002: 112)

INTRODUCTION

In more recent scholarship Mary Harrod (2018), building on the work of the importance of female autobiography, details how the acknowledgement of the female embodied encounter with the world can translate itself into a particular creativity (in her essay, this is about Lena Dunham but clearly it is relevant to female creativity as a whole). I am always fond of quoting Kaja Silverman (1988) who suggested more than thirty years ago that the issues of male and female subjectivity in cinema and elsewhere are deeply linked to the voice with which they speak – figuratively and literally. She notes that 'male subjectivity is most fully realized ... when it is least visible ... – female subjectivity is most fully achieved ... when it is visible' (Silverman 1988: 164). She also adds: 'the crucial project with respect to the female voice is to find a place from which it can speak and be heard, not to strip it of discursive rights' (ibid.: 192).

It is of course telling that even in this introduction I feel the need to refer to established, not to say famous, scholarly voices in order to give our undertaking and our writing an academic credence. This volume takes risks and invites the reader to take the risks with it and to think about creative practice, and indeed any knowledge, as an invitation to be challenged and to be challenging.

Adopting a feminine way of discussing the work might be difficult for some male scholars despite our stated desire for fluidity. I will offer below only the briefest of introductions to the essays, simply hoping that these will whet your appetites to read the whole volume. In this volume both Will Brown and Nariman Massoumi give incredible examples of how the true autoethnographic and therefore feminine mode is not only the domain of biological women. Brown introduces us to his teaching of guerrilla filmmaking conceived as a gesture of resistance. Massoumi's essay, about autoethnographic documentary work involving his family, is one of the most moving in this collection. It is interesting to me that five female contributors have chosen to work collectively and produced two very different but very important essays using the first-person autoethnographic mode alongside highly original theoretical discussions. These are the conversations between Jill Daniels, Rachel Velody and Eylem Atakav about their experiences of being creative researchers and filmmakers. There is an extraordinary and radical 'two voices' chapter on Rosa Fong's documentary film *Deconstructing Zoe*, about a transgender Asian performer, with theoretical and personal reflections from both writers: Rosa Fong, the maker, who positions her own difference vis-à-vis that of the subject of her documentary; and her colleague Jenny Barrett, who both embraces and questions the notions of postcolonial state of mind and theories.

Roberta Mock's profound and funny account of her work on the performance of the legendary Jewish comic Pearl Williams is both a thrilling narrative of her comedic prowess and researcher talents. It is also a telling testimony to the pain of resurrecting something so rooted in a particular historical time. Roberta's piece is particularly significant as it also touches upon issues of her personal history and how it relates to the history of Jewish storytelling and performance. How do you become a subversive Jewish performer when at the same time you are an important professor and manager at a British University? How do you relate to your vulnerability and how do you turn it into knowledge? Roberta Mock's piece is an example of a creative writing attempt and I hope the reader will be inspired by its courage and breadth of vision. Isabelle Starkier's piece is a different take on being a theatre practitioner and her voice brings a different tone to the conversation as she is French and works in Paris and the regions. Catherine Grant's essay is not autoethnographic but its courage lies in Grant's now historical boldness in putting the video-essayistic interrogation as a legitimate way of examining cinema. This essay, both the actual essay and the written account of it, examines Ingmar Bergman's notable film *Wild Strawberries* (1957). It is an exemplary text of using 'high' theory, namely (on this occasion) psychoanalysis, with more contemporary thinkers and writers, as well as analysing her decisions regarding the practicalities of creating the video essay. Kiki Yu reflects on documentary practices in China and her own practice as a part of it. Her article is thought-provoking and informative without losing anything of its autoethnographic strength. Tony Clancy analyses his photography and documentary filmmaking vis-à-vis some theoretical models. Tunde Alabi-Hundeyin in his fascinating essay shares his photographic practice and experiences and examines some of the ethical issues which are always in place when working with real people in a photography or documentary mode, here particularly painful as the work related to Boko Haram. Bruce Eadie offers a fascinating essay on reflectivity and psychoanalysis in documentary film, and Mischa Twitchin offers a bold chapter on his own film essay and how he combines practice and 'high' theory and in particular Adorno's ethics and philosophy. Judith Rifeser reflects on her experience of producing highly personal and rigorous work which combines the tactical and the notion of Irigaray's 'caress' in artistic practice, in particular using her own moving image practice as an example. My own chapters are about *Married to the Eiffel Tower* (2008) and my memories of that production. I also reflect on my more recent work in Zimbabwe, focusing on the film *Repented* (2019) created in a collaboration with the award-winning writer Stanley Makuwe. I interrogate the notion of translation in collaborative work across cultures.

Tactical Compliance?

The final section of this Introduction turns to the key concept of the conference and an important theme in this book, namely the notion of 'tactical compliance' proposed at the conference by Professor Thomas Elsaesser, the notable film historian and theorist, who was also a first-time filmmaker at the age of 75. This project was important and reminiscent of Roland Barthes's notion of the importance of 'late work' (2011 [1980]). In a discussion of his own desire to do something new late in life, he talked about 'a Complete Break' (2011: 214), a phrase that refers to an older accomplished thinker (or writer or artist) trying something totally new, 'a Beginning, a Vita Nova: a rebirth'. Barthes explains that such a project relates to one's desire: 'to be immortal is to be completely reborn; the work to be written is the mediator of this second kind of immortality' (ibid.: 214–15). That is to say, an immortality in which in your work will develop and change with the creator, continuously learning and creating something that will be different, innovative and generally fabulous.[4] Barthes gives examples of such moves by some writers (Mallarmé, Michelet, Proust) and of course his own planned novel was to be such a Complete Break. I wondered if Thomas Elsaesser's film project might have been designed to be that too.

It is in this context that I wanted to hear about Elsaesser's long-fulfilled ambition and what knowledge he might have felt he produced during its making. We discussed the project at length and were excited at the new challenge. It is hard to critique a work of such a notable scholar, and even more so now that he is gone, but his essay, fascinating though it is, focuses less on the knowledge or knowledges but more about what creativity might mean in general and about the practicalities of the making of his first film. Here there was the necessity of a particular moment in time (involving a German Bank taking over a building his grandfather designed), his grandfather's legacy and an uneasy relationship with his German producer. Elsaesser's essay describes his decision to proceed to work with the professional producer and editor in order to get his film made despite having profound professional and personal issues with them. Despite a multitude of reservations, he decides to work with these professionals in the spirit of 'tactical compliance'. Here the phrase simply means an opportunistic but necessary decision to use those who had professional experience of putting things together, despite conceptual and professional difficulties. At the time of the conference, his keynote phrase was a basis for heated discussion, some of which is reproduced in this volume. Here I am interested in broader issues which present themselves henceforth.

The film is based on Elsaesser's family's home movies, shot by his father before the Second World War and during it. Home movies from any historical period have a certain charm about them and this is no exception. The core of the film is the story featuring his grandfather a notable architect Martin Elsaesser and his wife Liesel, Thomas Elsaesser's grandmother. In the documentary we discover that his grandmother had a stormy and passionate love affair with her husband's colleague, a garden designer called Leberecht Migge. It was Migge's dream to create a self-sustaining paradise of a garden which would offer both nourishment and beauty. He and Elsaesser's grandmother did set up such a paradise island outside Berlin which they called The Sun Island and which is also the title of the film.

Will Brown in his thoughtful essay in this volume 'Tactical Compliance and the Persistence of Elsaesser' critiques the film and Thomas Elsaesser's stance in both the movie and his chapter. Brown juxtaposes Elsaesser's exemplary scholarly work as an academic with his film, which Brown sees as a promotional piece for Thomas's grandfather and also, therefore, for Elsaesser himself. In essence, Brown expects more from Elsaesser as a human being and a famous film scholar. My objections are both similar and, at the same time, very different.

In the spirit of the autoethnographic introspection, I need to disclose a further aspect to this. I was first aware of the film when it was at an assembly stage in May 2016. I met Thomas Elsaesser for the first time at the SCMS conference in Montreal in 2015. He became a mentor to me, as he was to so many other junior colleagues. He was very interested in my work and in particular in the whole project of combining the theoretical and the creative practice. He encouraged me to develop that strand of my work further. Kindly and generously, he introduced my experimental documentary *Lovers in Time* at an essay film event in Reading in 2015, and many others, and has written a complimentary review of it. In due course we co-authored a chapter about an essay film (2019). In May 2016 Thomas asked me, in my guise as an experienced documentary filmmaker who has made many films for broadcast television, to look at his first edit of *The Sun Island* and suggest changes/improvements. At that time Thomas Elsaesser was already infuriated by his producer Reihart's ideas regarding a possible inclusion of some general archival footage from the Second World War in the film – as a visual and contextual juxtaposition to the home movies Elsaesser presented. I saw a three-hour long assembly in Amsterdam. It was a very difficult session and I wrote long emails to Elsaesser after the event which I will not be reproducing here. Suffice to say, I suggested dramatic cuts, writing a strong narrative and working closely with the television professionals as the film needed a firm and experienced hand. Given that there were already people involved, I felt it would not have been right for me to be involved beyond that advice as that might have confused matters further. I despaired over the difficulties but suggested it might have been to the film's benefit to stay with the producers. Maybe I was in part the engineer of his 'tactical compliance' as regards the producers.

In my emails there was something else though, something far more important, and this line I will quote here: 'I can understand Reihart trying to create something against the background of the actual historical events – it is not idiotic, it's an attempt to make it all clearer. This was not but a love story. The war was raging in Europe'. For me then, and now, the bracketing of the atrocities of the Second World War is a conceptual and ethical flaw in the film, and possibly has made it into a questionable ethical gesture. There is a disquiet about focusing only on the idyllic life on the island and the romantic affairs of its inhabitants without any engagement whatever with the storms of the war of Europe at the very same time and his family's involvement in it – including the male relatives being in the German army at the time, and wearing Nazi swastikas, a fact that is mentioned in passing. On the other hand, his mother was in fact Jewish, and hiding at the time and then continuing to hide, in peace times in Germany, a very common trait and also one that I am familiar with in my own family.

Regarding Thomas Elsaesser's piece of work, I am indeed amongst many people who get 'special thanks' at the end of the film. I am certainly in good company there as Michael Renov gets a credit too and indeed many others. Some of my suggestions of writing a strong narrative and cutting the film dramatically were implemented – but not the crucial one. The film as is disavows the simple fact that in some way Elsaesser's family, as so many others in Germany at the time, was indeed complicit with the Nazi regime. The words 'compliant' and 'complicit' have the same etymological root and in some way mean a similar thing: to be acquiescent with a certain course of action. The failure to acknowledge more clearly at least in visual terms, never mind in some kind of deeper reflection, the atrocities of the Nazi regime which the Elsaesser family were in some way involved in, can be viewed as ethically problematic. Perhaps it is indeed the difficulty at getting at the feminine autoethnographic statement here but perhaps also there is a desire to hide from the demands of a painful recognition of one's own historical legacy, which in Thomas Elsaesser's case is in fact twofold: Nazi and Jewish.

In the now classic work on post-war trauma, *The Inability to Mourn* (1967), the German psychologists Alexander and Margarete Mitscherlich make a point that the Germans quickly identified with new post-war regimes without dealing with their long commitment to Hitler, creating systems of denial and forgetting. It was as if the Germans chose not to deal with the past. As a result, the authors claimed more than fifty years ago, the German psyche may have never freed itself from Hitler because it did not go through the rituals that true mourning demanded. What is quite extraordinary here is that Thomas Elsaesser used the work above in his own work quite extensively, in his own discussion of New German Cinema in his volume of 1989. Discussing Mitscherlich, Elsaesser confirms: 'Instead of discussing this past, Germans prefer to bury it' (1989: 242) and yet, somehow, when it came to making his own film these concerns are put aside.

Elsaesser's silence is palpable not only in the film but also in his keynote and in the chapter in this book. In some ways, therefore, it misses an opportunity for a more profound production of knowledge relating to his personal legacy of the Second World War that the making of such a deeply subjective film may have offered. As friends and colleagues, Thomas and I discussed the matter at length after the conference and after many screenings of his film, including some in Poland and in Amsterdam which I introduced. We discussed the matter last time in later November 2019 and agreed that the book should go to print the way it is and that there might be a time for 'a further deeper reflection' in due course. Unfortunately, and shockingly, Thomas died unexpectedly in China on 4 December 2019 at the beginning of his lecture tour. As it happens, he showed his film to Chinese students at Peking University and this is what he wrote to me in an email of 3 December at midnight his time, clearly one of his last: 'So far have found very appreciative but also very smart and critically astute audiences. Tonight's screening of my film was a special event, with Chinese subtitles and very good discussion after. Peking University is the top in the country and the quality of the students shows it. Am very lucky.' It appears that he died a few hours later.

We were scheduled to discuss the illustrations for his chapter the following day but this was not to be. What remains is a trace of our discussions and 'the deeper reflection' that Elsaesser was preparing to write will now not happen. *The Sun Island* is a very special and moving film but it is also an example of how very hard it is to produce knowledge out of autoethnographic material and how potentially ethically problematic such a project might be when the subject of the interrogation is our own life or that of our family.

The 'tactical compliance' can quite easily and imperceptibly become instead *a tactical complicity* or worse, a tactical omission and silence which gets close to the unethical. In his reflection on the process of creation (and writing in particular), Barthes sets out 'three trials' (2011: 173): the first one is to decide to embark upon 'the Work' at all, choosing 'the object', the second one is the 'step-by-step management of' the work and the third one is 'the moral trial' including a decision of how the work 'fits in with the social (historical social)' (ibid.: 173). Elsewhere in the book he talks about the ethical always trumping the aesthetic and that it is a hard call. Barthes calls one's commitment to the Work potentially 'heroic' – 'an uncompromising attachment to a Practice' (ibid.: 281), which clearly is in direct opposition to any form of tactical compliance. One has to say that Roland Barthes did of course write many very influential works – but *not* the very final one he wanted to write. Many reasons could have been behind that but undoubtedly any 'uncompromising Practice' is excruciatingly hard, a lot harder than many people realise. Whatever anybody's views on Thomas Elsaesser's film might be, it is very clear that his whole life and work is a testimony to his heroic and indeed uncompromising attachment to his practice, which of course foremost includes his academic work. He took risks and never stopped exploring and expanding his intellectual horizons. He was also prepared for younger generations to be discussing and critiquing his work, teaching us all how to open spaces for generative intellectual engagement. There is no doubt at all that his work and his spirit will continue to be a guiding light for us all.

As creative practice researchers, we need to keep questioning the rules, the law, the attitudes, the systems. We need to cross boundaries in order to stay faithful to our internal campus and question that too. Whilst aware of the pressures coming from institutional demands and goals, notably those that define research as any pursuit which is 'a process of investigation leading to new insights, effectively shared', the book therefore aims to open a space for a generative dialogue about the importance of creative practices as a site of critique and resistance through a profound personal reflection vis-à-vis the work one creates.

Notes

1. For example, *Alphaville*, Issue 17: Researching Creative Practice, published July 2018, edited by Ciara Chambers https://doi.org/10.33178/alpha.17.00>. *Media Practice and Education* has published a number of articles on methodology, including 'Using film as both embodied research and explication in a creative practice PhD' by Catherine Gough-Brady (published online: 10 October 2019): <https://doi.org/10.1080/25741136.2019.1675407>.
2. Geertz cracks a joke referring to Barthes (without naming him) that the author might be dead in other disciplines but not in anthropology (Geertz 1988: 6). Incidentally, Barthes in his last work takes back that assertion (i.e. the author is not dead).
3. 'I asked my questioner: "Are you asking me an autobiographical question? Well, yes, I would like to write, which is not to say that I will write, but that I would like to write in a woman's hand"' (Derrida 1988: 79).
4. One could argue that one of Barthes's attempted 'Complete Breaks' was the acknowledgement of the return of the author which he, too, was so involved in demolishing in his previous work.

References

Anderson (2006), 'Analytic Autoethnograpy' in *Journal of Contemporary Ethnography*, 3594: 373–95.
Barthes, Roland (2011 [1980]), *The Preparation of the Novel*, trans. Kate Briggs, New York: Columbia University Press.
Bochner, A. P. and Ellis, C. (2000), *Ethnographically Speaking: Autoethnography, Literature, and Aesthetics*, Walnut Creek, CA: AltaMira Press.
Chang, Heewon C. (2008), *Autoethnography as Method*, Walnut Creek, CA: Left Coast Press.
Cowie, Elizabeth (2011), *Recording Reality, Desiring the Real*, London and Minneapolis: University of Minnesota Press.
Derrida, Jacques (1988 [1985]), *The Ear of the Other: Otobiography, Transference, Translation*, ed. C. McDonald, trans. P. Kamul, Lincoln: University of Nebraska Press.
Elsaesser, Thomas (1989), *New German Cinema: A History*, London: Macmillan.
Elsaesser, Thomas and Piotrowska, Agnieszka (2019), 'Lovers in Time: An Essay Film of Contested Memories', in B. Hollweg and I. Kristic (eds), *World Cinema and the Essay Film*, Edinburgh: Edinburgh University Press

Felman, Shoshana (1993), *What Does a Woman Want? Reading and Sexual Difference*, London and New York: Routledge.
Geertz, C. (1988), *Works and Lives: The Anthropologist as Author*, Stanford: Stanford University Press.
Haraway, Donna (2008 [1985]), 'A Manifesto for Cyborgs: Science, Technology and Socialist Feminism in the 1980s', in N. Badmington and J. Thomas (eds), *Critical and Cultural Theory Reader*, Abingdon and London: Routledge.
Haraway, Donna (1988), 'Situated Knowledges: The Science Question in Feminism and the Privilege of Partial Perspective', in *Feminist Studies*, 14:3 (Autumn), 575–99.
Haraway, Donna (1997), *Modest_Witness@Second_Millenium*, New York: Routledge.
Haraway, Donna (2004), *The Haraway Reader*, London and New York: Routledge.
Haraway, Donna (2004), *Second Millennium. Feminism and Technoscience*, London and New York: Routledge.
Haraway, Donna and Schneider, J. (2005), 'Conversations with Donna Haraway', in J. Schneider and D. Haraway (eds), *Live Theory*, London and New York: Continuum.
Harrod, Mary (2018), *Women Do Genre in Film and Television*, London and New York: Routledge.
Miller, Nancy (2002 [1991]), *But Enough About Me – Why We Read Other People's Lives*, New York: Columbia University Press.
Muncey, Tessa (2010), *Creating Autoethnographies*, Portland: Sage Publications.
Mykhalovskiy, Edward (1996), 'Reconsidering table talk: Critical thoughts on the relationship between sociology, autobiography and self-indulgence', in *Qualitative Sociology*, 19: 131–51.
Nash, R. J. (2004), *Liberating Scholarly Writing: The Power of Personal Narrative*, New York: Teachers College.
Nichols, B. (1991), *Representing Reality: Issues and Concepts in Documentary*, Bloomington: Indiana University Press.
Piotrowska, Agnieszka (2012), 'The Conman and I: A case study of transference in documentary', in *Studies in Documentary Film*, 6: 15–28.
Piotrowska, Agnieszka (2014), *Psychoanalysis and Ethics in Documentary Film*, London: Routledge.
Piotrowska, Agnieszka (2015), *Embodied Encounters: New Approaches to Psychoanalysis and Cinema*, London: Routledge.
Piotrowska, Agnieszka (2017), *Black and White: Cinema, politics and the arts in Zimbabwe*, London: Routledge.
Piotrowska, Agnieszka (2019), *The Nasty Woman and the Neo Femme Fatale in Contemporary Cinema*, London: Routledge.
Reed-Danahay, D. E. (ed.) (1997), *Auto/Ethnography: Rewriting the Self and the Social*, Oxford and New York: New York University Press.
Renov, M. (1993), *Theorizing Documentary*, Minneapolis: University of Minnesota Press.
Renov, M. (2004), *The Subject of Documentary*, Minneapolis: University of Minnesota Press.
Rich, Adrienne (1986), *Of Woman Born. Motherhood as Experience and Institution*, London: Virago.
Rich, Adrienne (1979), *On Lies, Secrets and Silence; Selected prose, 1966–1978*, London: Norton.
Rughani, Pratap (2013), 'The Dance of Documentary Ethics', in Brian Winston (ed.), *The Documentary Film Book*, London: BFI/Palgrave Macmillan.
Silverman, Kaja (1988), *The Acoustic Mirror: The Female Voice in Psychoanalysis and Cinema*, Bloomington: Indiana University Press.

2. AGAINST THE GRAIN: WOMEN FILM PRACTITIONERS AND THEORISTS TALK CREATIVE PRACTICE AND THEORY

Jill Daniels, Rachel Velody and Eylem Atakav

INTRODUCTION

Three noted independent women film practitioners and theorists working in Britain debate the contrast and overlap in their approaches, all produced from within the academy. Eylem Atakav, a theorist, turned to practice for her film on child brides, *Growing Up Married* (2016); Jill Daniels takes a first-person approach in the production of essay films in order to comment on the social world; Rachel Velody produces 'theory-as practice'. The debate focuses on how the context of transnational moving-image production and distribution industries, areas that are seemingly tainted with neoliberal address, restrictive diversity and isolationist discourse may be challenged. We ask whether our own disparate creative practice and theory produced from within the academy enables us to challenge these dominant forms of film address and whether, and in what ways, these may effect change. We do not aim for a singular binary resolution but to explore our practice as exemplars of responses to issues that are facing us both inside and outside the academy and to outline the possibilities of a response through our future practice and dialogue with other creative practitioners and theorists.

ARRIVAL

Jill: On leaving film school in the late 1970s I had no connection to academia. I operated as an independent filmmaker. The starting point for my practice was experimental fiction. I made my first fiction film, *I'm In Heaven* (1989) about a Jewish woman estranged from her family living in a tower block. It was produced through a form of crowd funding and a small funding grant from South East Arts. The film went to film festivals and won an award. I thought that was the start of my filmmaking career. But it was the end of my fiction filmmaking career. I turned to documentary because funding was easier. My interest was in mediating contested identities, taking my secular Jewish identity as a starting point. I was politically engaged in the socialist women's movement. But I had a fine art background and I felt that conventional documentary filmmaking was very restrictive, and I couldn't see a way to bring together my political activity, my interest in the representation of human subjects and my interest in film language. I came into academia in 2003 to teach film and saw the idea of practice as research. That was how I evolved. They said I had to do a PhD if I wanted to be permanent. I had to push for practice to be taken seriously as research. I believe that people should accept that images are as important as language in research, not just writing but, and it is a bit of a contradiction, as practitioners we are also theorising and discussing our practice using spoken and written language. So how do we bridge that gap between wanting our films to speak for themselves, but at the same time expecting a level of sophistication in our spectators? To be able to understand what it is that we're doing. My practice explores memory, place and subjectivities and experiments with filmic language; my films are still documentaries but they are essay films. No solutions to problems are raised, they are reflective. Where I am now is that, because of our political era, the disintegration of neoliberal capitalism, we don't know yet whether it's disintegrating towards socialism or revolution, or to use that old-fashioned word, barbarism. I'm interested in the rise of nationalism and how one can engage against it. Without going backwards and throwing out all those ideas around aesthetics and subjectivities. Political activity? But I'm a filmmaker. My film *Breathing Still* (2018) is a letter addressed to Rosa Luxemburg and my ideas are to blur the boundaries between film practice, research, human subjects, and to break down the conventions of the mainstream film industry in documentary making.

Eylem: What Jill has been saying resonates with me. I come from a theoretical background with no experience in filmmaking. In 2010/11 I came up with the UK's first module, Islam, Women & Media. It aimed at critiquing texts from Middle Eastern media as well as UK/US/western media. Mainly looking at honour killings; FGM; forced marriage, things that are associated with Islam as well as looking at films, non-Western representations in Hollywood films. At the heart of everything I do is the concept of voice and my passion for feminist film theory. In 2011 we decided to do a press release and it got attention from *The Guardian*, *Huffington Post*, *Al Jazeera*, even *Marie Claire*. That media presence put me and my students in touch with organisations like the Norfolk constabulary who decided to come to the classroom and said they would like to talk about how they deal with the media and honour-based abuse. The BBC Asian Network came into the classroom to interview students. Suddenly students were so inspired by this exposure to non-academic interest in the module that they made a short documentary which is on YouTube called *Ostitto/Existence*,[1] about women, Islam and media, reflecting on their ideas about the module, but also some of the things we discussed. The response from the public about the module, for example comments on *The Guardian*, were thought-provoking – accusing me of being 'an alien terrorist who promotes Islamist ideologies and I was brainwashing our kids at our universities'.[2] The House of Lords were doing a report at the time on religion and belief in British public life and they invited me to write my thoughts on women, Islam and media for that report, which I did, but together with my students.[3]

In 2015 I'm sitting in my office at University of East Anglia (UEA), writing an article on honour killings and their representation with the focus on Turkey and suddenly I realised something was missing from the work I was doing. I hadn't talked to women in Turkey and I was putting them all in one box as if they were a single entity, which they are not. We have a Media Suite at UEA and amazing students looking for volunteering opportunities. I thought, I can get a camera and go to Turkey and make a film. The result was *Growing Up Married* (2016). The biggest question I've asked since working on the film is what happens if feminist film theorists start doing our own media from a feminist perspective to start changing those discourses. Not to stop critiquing media, but to do both.

Rachel: My journey has been very fractured. I moved between HE doing film practice, I got an assistantship and had to teach super 8 film production to students and had never done it, I had to teach myself and fell in love with that mode and the viscerality of film. I came back from the States and couldn't get a job in that area, so I went into TV studies and cultural studies. I did that for a long time and went to a University where I became course leader in fashion studies. During that period I lost my own voice. Two defining memories I have, was one listening to a colleague, when I asked him, 'Why are we getting these young women from modelling agencies who are incredibly thin?' He turned to me and said, 'The clothes hang better.' I've never forgotten that. The other event I remember was the beginning of staking a claim in terms of the personal. I had come across a great uncle, Mike, who had been present at one of the openings of the concentration camps and also made film. My nana had talked about him a lot but we didn't know a thing about him. I found a photo of him. I listened to an interview and I found it was him. He was talking about shooting footage outside the camps as they were opened and the impact it had on him as a secular Jew and also the impact you had after you weren't supposed to talk about it. It was a stigma and it was a sign of failure. I went to see *Night Will Fall* (2014) and saw Mike's face and saw him talking about it. Saw the footage of him shooting footage. It was shocking and brought home to me the importance of the personal is political.

In 2011 I was diagnosed with cancer and I parted company with my workplace. In recovery I started to think how do I move forward? There was a group at Westminster University doing a conference called *Different Bodies*. My recovery was attending that conference, but the real thing was saying I'm going to do it the way I want to do it. I did it as a performance not standing behind a lectern. It was terrifying but part of the process of saying what do I want the rest of my life to be in terms of patterns of communication. That started a process for me. The development of that process is how I think about primary text. I wrote the text and a very interesting issue for us as researchers, is what happens with editors. It's not the way you would normally do it in academic texts. I know in the book it will be unique. More like a comedy performance. Sardonic stand up performance. Some of it emotional, some of it moving. I was taking risks. It's been a long journey to go back to remembering who I was.

Eylem: Why are we doing what we're doing? That's really important. We need to take academic work out of journal articles and books. As much as it's important to have more traditional publications but visual media can travel much faster and be seen by many more people is more important and powerful than sitting in our 'ivory towers'.

Jill: What you both said resonates with me. The question of risk-taking and going back to remembering who I was. I may appear fully formed and I could repeat what I've done before, but I feel the world we're living in is constantly changing and we are constantly changing and our reactions to the world constantly change. Just repeating what I already know seems pointless. That's why I choose to experiment, because for me each project is a complete challenge. Sometimes you have to go back to who you are which may be helpful in finding yourself. There's a sense of being vulnerable and open.

Authorship, Subjectivity and Practice

Eylem: At the heart of *Growing Up Married* is women's voice and the significance of visibility of women through film. When women are talking about their experiences of having been in forced marriage or having been a child bride or suffering domestic sexual abuse they're politicising their experiences. Feminist literature and theory frequently talks about women interviewing women and the power relations inherent within that interview process. I gained access to four women: two were my parents' neighbours, but the other two I didn't know. I had access through my cousin who ran the women's support centre in Izmir. The most powerless I have ever felt in doing academic work was when

I was listening to the women I interviewed. Their stories were so powerful I was shocked to hear them. I was asking in my head: how are you even alive having gone through this kind of violence, physical abuse? I felt powerless as an academic, the only power I had was to act on it, and film them and get their voices and images out there.

Jill: I was thinking about the role of film in providing individual stories. Inequalities or issues like the one you were talking about, we all know about theoretically, we know statistics, what kind of political structures there are, but what we don't necessarily know is what it is like to be them and to have that experience. I'm wondering, first, about the question of empathy and the viewer. What do we want from the viewer? And how is the individual story, however powerful, taken forward towards the collective? In my films I'm dealing with people's personal experiences. In my Private Life films I'm looking at my own experience in relation to growing up in a family where my father was gay; he grew up at a time in Jewish society, where his mother was religious, and it was completely impossible for him to admit to being gay and he found his own ways to deal with it, but he couldn't be honest with his family. That story, being told from my point of view, not confronting him because of my perception of the father–daughter relationship, is that a useful methodology? Some people find the films frustrating because they want me to ask my father about how he felt. One person even thought my father *wanted* to tell me. Your situation Eylem is a little different because you're an outsider but also part of their culture.

Eylem: That comes up in the Q&As. Is this everyone's experience, all women's experience in Turkey? Obviously not. I can't see women as a single entity and there's obviously a huge risk in 'universalising' women's experiences, they're all different from each other. But the impact narrative of the film and how those four women's stories have influenced policies, for example the police work, showed how as a collective voice of four women, speaks to other cultures as well and it's to do with the power of film that made it accessible by other cultures, not just Turkey. In the film I tried very carefully, apart from the language itself, Turkish with English subtitles, there's nothing that screams 'Turkish'. It can be anywhere and everywhere. There are some nuances, the fabric of Turkey that you can identify if you know the culture. But taking the individual experiences help with how we deal with forced marriage, domestic violence, child brides, and honour-based abuse.

Rachel: In the performances I did, particularly on breast cancer, doing it as a performance in a place of academia was a risk, which I found quite scary. Anything that is anti-narrative and experimental shifts the boundaries of what is permissible to talk about. But it was essential I realised to moving forward. I wanted to say that disability is a place where you are made invisible and stigmatised. I wanted to do a very direct, unmediated performance that said we don't have to hide behind footnotes or references. Any methodology that does that is powerful and also aesthetically very beautiful.

Jill: I've been trying in my teaching to bring out the notion of subjectivity. But introducing the idea that they can bring in the personal, I find the students are quite resistant. It's seen as not professional, amateur, something that's autobiographical and personal and some of them think to be personal you have a bunch of home movies. And that will be a film. It's hard for people to understand that it is a means to look at the political, the social world through the individual and the individual can be you as the subject of the film as well as the maker of the film.

Eylem: My students on the MA are a very diverse and international body of students. But they find it really puzzling to answer research questions *with* audiovisual artefacts. Having had some experience of training from professionals who work in the film industry very recently, I realised that what we are doing in academia is almost a genre on its own, one of creative practice. How creative can we possibly be, how 'wild' can we go, if we are confined to answering research questions with our practice work? The problem that Rachel highlighted about endnotes, footnotes, and references, the very structural things that pigeonhole academic work in a particular form, how much can we challenge those in practice work if we are doing it within academic boundaries? Students find that quite confusing. It ends up being not necessarily personal, because no matter how much we highlight that the personal is political, they might see themselves making personal films as making themselves vulnerable. It would be fascinating though, given the number of students who have mental health issues, had they told their stories on digital platforms where other people can learn from them.

Rachel: Doing my doctorate I had to go to the disability office. I now learn I have dyspraxia. It's acceptable to have a physical illness, if it's something you can see. Mental health is not accepted. And, of course, there are so few mental health facilities for people.

Eylem: Whenever I screen *Growing Up Married* there are disclosures from the audience. No matter where I screened the film – Japan, US, UK, Turkey – there's always someone who comes forward during or after the Q&A who says 'my grandma had this, my mum had this' – they're asking for support sometimes. That's crucial. Film in particular has the power of creating sympathy if not empathy. It travels far faster and is more powerful, particularly in engaging with the public, compared to an academic publication. If we publish it might get read by 10 or 15 people, say 100 but in the last couple of years over 4,000 people have seen *Growing Up Married*.

Rachel: Students in their journey in HE seem to be feeling they don't have the right to speak, their life stories are not valuable. Is there a relationship between that and the fact that they are so equipped and erudite with film,

TV and social media? You would think that with social media that would be a place where you would express yourself. I'm not convinced. I'm doing a paper on #MeToo at the moment and it very much exists as a binary, you're either with us or against us. I find it disturbing. I'm not sure how advantageous that is to young people who want to make films about personal testimony, biography or just personal. They have access to film and television, swathes of this, but they're on the receiving end of that. What's lost is building in making.

Jill: Students who go to our kind of institutions, which aren't film schools, most of them have no idea what they want to do when they leave. If you ask what films do you go and watch it's usually on YouTube because it's free and they don't have money. They all have jobs. They don't necessarily want to make films in the end. We are encouraging them to be creative, but what kind of creativity do we think? You can do this, this and this. And it's legitimate. You don't have to be the one in charge. And that's why we do group work. I imagine you do as well. They have to learn how to collaborate. We always identify as being in the film industry, but collaboration, it may be technical, it may be creativity, but it might just be people who want to come along for the ride. How do we get our students to be open to looking at the world outside and their place in it? I'm not keen on this employability stuff, which is trying to put people into little boxes. They need to go out and say I'm an individual, I'm in the world, being open to that idea. It's scary for students to put themselves on the line. Just getting them to speak in front of their peers.

Rachel: It should be about identity in the world. To engage and create themselves with perspectives and political positions that they are going to test, rather than employability which seems to be the driving force and date stamped on the certificate when the students leave. The concept of education should be where people find themselves gradually and see their life as an experiment. There's no finite point.

Eylem: Moving from doing theory to practice means doing feminism in a different form to me. Teaching is sharing our passion for knowledge. We have such powerful tools to get students, to see how impactful our creative work can be. It's different to talk about or show students one's own film and explaining the story behind it. They see that passion and it becomes a little more contagious that way. In 2018, I ran a digital storytelling contest for Walsh University Ohio, 1st year freshers. This was magic. A cohort of over 300 students, working together in groups of three to four, telling their first week of university. Quite a challenge, but the energy was great with great work produced for a student film festival. We need to shift the paradigm – from consuming media to making one's own media. That's when pedagogy becomes way more innovative. Something we need to urgently integrate into our curriculum in Higher Education.

Rachel: When did you begin to think of your work as practice? Or do you draw distinctions between writing, talk and the creation of a film?

Eylem: There is value in both. The challenge and the aspect of it I love most is to link theory and practice together, so you take your teaching and research out of the classroom and outside the campus, to national and international level. You take your work with you much more easily than writing academic articles – *Growing Up Married* being screened at different parts of the world is a case in point. I must confess for about a year and a half after making the film I struggled with writing theory. I didn't lose hope or faith in writing theory, but I have been way more mesmerised by the fact that I got to talk to real people and the engagement with the public, the media while making highly significant issues visible.

Jill: I only came across the word practice when I started my PhD. I never thought of my work as anything other as filmmaking. I made films from very short to very long. Each film is a new journey. So, OK I have to embrace the terms for my PhD and I've become used to talking about it in that way. I find it quite useful to talk about the theoretical framework I've used in my work and which informs my work. I'm constantly thinking I've come to the end of the road with writing, but I never think that about filmmaking.

Eylem: Academia has changed quite a lot in the last decade, I think. When I started my first full-time job the discourse around the work we produce was very much publication-focused and now with the impact narrative, the emphasis on engagement with the public or policy makers or the media, has helped me find my own voice, to find the meaning in my work and appreciate why I am an academic. I've always been inspired by taking academic work outside academia. The impact narrative happens to help. We may be working against the grain, but it's about embracing our own identities, not just as individuals with our personal lives, but also as academics.

Politics, Aesthetics, Agitprop, Disruption

Rachel: I was thinking of the issue of doing the ugly. Anger, mourning, grieving, and whether that could be poetic. Anger is one of the things that pushes me forward in terms of producing work. My presentation on Ivanka Trump as a body of Aryan dynamics, used a Ch4 News split screen piece they did in 2018, on the day when Palestinians were being murdered on the West Bank and Gaza as Ivanka Trump was opening the American embassy in Jerusalem. I found that I worked from the outside in. I do think that it's important that journalists produce this kind of work and they don't have to be objective. Sometimes you have to tell it like it is. Just like we know that killing people is wrong, you cannot dispute the fact of what was going on that day and to show it in a very visceral juxtaposition of a split screen where Palestinians are being shot in the back and Ivanka Trump dressed in white and speaking like a nine-year-old is opening the American embassy. It politicised me more because I began to think, what is the position of the women in the Trump administration and how is an Aryan aesthetics produced? Then I began to think about how those women are constituted in a very similar commodified body. Exchange of femininity where they are all of a particular body weight. So for me it was working through primary text and saying what can it tell us about American politics at the moment. I could probably do the same thing if I looked at Teresa May and Amber Rudd and spoke about, as it's politely called, Windrush. There's a similarity there about how these women are being depicted and how they're given permission and legitimated to do what is xenophobic, racist and illegal.

I took this piece to a forum called Critical Costume. I was quite nervous about it because it's highly critical of Zionism. I fundamentally believe that Zionism is wrong. I'm a partially secular Jew, although I've been told I'm not Jewish enough, or told I'm a self-hating Jew. So for me it was twofold; it was going, making statements about myself as a person, my shock and horror at the development of what I see as Aryan aesthetics, where I see whiteness is legitimated as a controlling force, and in particular bodies that are worked, bodies that are regimented and exercised and this white colonialist discourse is being reproduced in the States then taken to Jerusalem, which is a place where many survivors of pogroms and Second World War now live. Journalists do not get the support they deserve and are at so much risk and we should be grateful for the work they're doing. Which is often a huge personal risk to their safety. That was that particular piece. I think there's a lot of anger and rage and also grieving and mourning because I know that in my own extended family there are relatives who died in those camps and I don't know anything about them. And it's my way of paying testimony to those people by saying I don't want to be part of anything that does it again.

Jill: I think it's important to be making those statements. I've been reading a Croatian writer, Daša Drndić. One of the things I was struck by is how she gives roll-calls of names of murdered people to give them back their lost identities. In *Belladonna* she talks about how in a children's playground in the Hague there are climbing frames and on each rung there is the name of a child who was deported in the Holocaust. Their names, their age; a lot were only six months old. She gives the entire list of the names in the book. It was important to me when I came across the stumbling blocks in pavements in Berlin pointing out who lived and was murdered in a concentration camp, in front of a particular house. I wanted to give some of them, particularly women, recognition and I know these have been in other people's artworks and films, but it's not a question that you can only do it once, you have to be continually saying and thinking that this was a person, this name was a person who actually lived an ordinary life and was murdered. Thinking about film theory, the way society works is political, but you can't necessarily theorise it to understand it. It can be made into a film and there can be a discourse in the film and in the use of voice, the nature of voice, the observer, the tenses, you're talking in the past; you're talking in the present in films. Having a conversation with people in a film – who aren't necessarily seen, or they might be seen – enables you to bring together these different things.

Eylem: I had about twelve hours of footage in total and bringing it down to just under half an hour is quite an ethical challenge because you are essentially writing a new story out of women's original stories. The power of editing in that editing suite is thought-provoking. *Growing Up Married* is a text of memory because it's not women going through experiences, but women remembering what happened to them early on in their lives. It really wasn't important whether they remembered things correctly or whether there were tensions in what they said; or whether they said something that didn't make sense; but what was important is *how* they remembered it and what part of their experiences they remembered. Lots of people have said that it was like those women were talking to them in that room there and then. That was good to hear. It's important to say, as you were both saying, to be sufficiently angry, turning things into challenges to overcome, because that's what our work does and should do.

Rachel: It seems to me all our work is disruptive in the best possible way but at the same time intimate. *Different Bodies* is personal testament, I was definitely conventional in the way I narrativised it because the more I wrote it the more I thought people reading it have to make sense of something around time. It's not purely poetic. I think I'm better at humour and intimate communication, so I chose that path, it's a mixture of quite traditional literary formatting in terms of past, present, future. Heading somewhere, which is telling the story of it, but disruptive in the sense of a woman who's grieving, a woman who's mourning, a woman who's angry, a woman who's confused. And getting that down through crudities, obscenity, rhetoric and humour. Then I, to some extent, some aspects of that are reiterated with the piece of political costume. I wanted it to be dramatic. I would have much preferred not to stand behind the lectern. If I go to conferences I want to find a way to completely dispense with power points. And work through perhaps drama performance. To talk about television which I still adore, but to talk about it in a different way. I would say the disruption there is the clear anger. I wanted it to be moving. Performance for me is really important and I want to experiment with that more. When I look back at the footage I was thinking oh I pronounced that word wrong. So, you still do that kind of stuff. You still interrogate yourself, don't you? Over that kind of material and how you're presenting it. I think that's what I learnt from these two pieces.

Jill: I have been thinking about creativity in our present neoliberal era. It's come into focus in practice as research that we're not the inspired artist genius. There's a debate around that: those who are saying there's no such thing as creativity and others, like me, who think about ideas, which seem to come from nowhere. You don't know where they come from and you don't need to know. To respond to the world out there that you are part of. My film *Journey to the South* began when my friend in the south of France told me a story. He said there's a story about a murder in a village, this might be one for you. When he explained the story he was saying, there's this shepherd who was murdered twenty-five years ago in a village up the road in the mountains and it was by the hunters and it was never solved; there were three trials of hunters who were all related and all blamed each other. The gun was never found. The police were corrupt. They destroyed all the evidence. I thought, this is interesting, well let's go to the village because I'm interested in villages. They are all falling to pieces in our era. Where is the village going? It was a very difficult thing to think about making because I didn't want to make an investigative film, there had been those in France already. The people who were most keen to talk to me were the outsiders who live there. They said no villager will talk to you. And they didn't, although I got one guy who is in the film, the entire conversation is in the film, because it only lasted about three minutes.

To come back to Eylem's point about editing, the film was made in the editing. At the time I was reading about what it means to be human. What does it mean to take somebody's life? That's what the film's about. It was about what it does to you. I was thinking about perpetrators who aren't able to say anything because they'll go to prison. So what did it mean to live with this terrible secret? Is it dehumanising? I constructed the film in a very oblique way. My voice, my presence through this journey of discovery, not as a creative genius artist but as somebody struggling to make a film, fictionalising my character, but it was my journey, this is how the film came into being and so its aesthetics are very much not pre-planned. If you plan it all you may come out with something quite weak.

Rachel: But beautifully judged; thinking about the shots in that film.

Jill: I think you have a sense of what you're looking for and it's instinctive and it's your body as well. It's the response to the light if you're filming landscapes, which I was; it's framing. And when you are working on your own you make an awful lot of misjudgments, accidents happen, that's spoiling what you've got. The power of the image doesn't mean it has to look professional, glossy high production values at all.

Eylem: I completely agree. Lots of people ask me if I took a film crew there? I say, 'what crew?' No lighting, cameraman, no nothing. Sometimes even the existence of the camera in the room was a bit of a problem. But in the two interviews I had to have my mum in the room because I was behind the camera, but the two women in the film were talking to my mum, their friend. Just like they would over a cup of coffee because they were neighbours.

Jill: I had that with my friend in France. He had to be a character in the film because they were all talking to him because he's French.

Eylem: Academia, higher education, universities, funding bodies, they all, quite rightly perhaps, are asking us to be very structured within forms. If you're applying for funding from any funding body you need to fill out impact narratives and how much you need to spend on what. They need to know exactly what you're doing, whereas for this project, all I did was I'll get a camera, go to Turkey, film some people, see what happens. To see if I could do a film and if I could do a trailer that I could pitch to different places and it turned out that there was enough footage to turn it into a film. Universities have the facilities and we have the intellect and why don't we put that into practice? If there's any disruption that would be it.

Rachel: How do you imagine your audience? When I was writing the piece on cancer I did imagine an audience but I just sat and laughed my head off. I was my own.

Jill: Do you think of fifty people in a cinema or a theatre or a conference or are you thinking of a person that you're talking to? That's how I do it.

Rachel: The latter.

Jill: I don't call that person an audience.

Rachel: I would think of a group of people. That could be because I did theatre at undergraduate degree and as a teenager. That idea of having an audience in your head that is meaningful to you has stayed with me.

Jill: How about you Eylem?

Eylem: With this work there was one key question in my mind: how do you represent the, at times, unrepresentable? I didn't want to be accused of representing Turkish women or Turkey in a negative light because there is a lot of that. We see that discourse a lot. How do you avoid repeating that or avoiding a problematic discourse and come up with something that encourages people to think more critically about these issues. I can't say I didn't think about how audiences would respond to the film, but doing the filming I was the spectator behind the camera, because I had my cousin there and I integrated questions once in a while and my mum. I would, therefore, regard myself as the audience in the making of the film.

Jill: Have you had a comment about the numbers?

Eylem: They find it quite chilling.

Jill: Do they know that's what it is when they're watching it?

Eylem: No. Only at the end when we reveal what it is, but because the numbers beat in a tick we're not familiar with, it's something like 1.7 seconds per tick, it becomes disturbing because we're not used to that sound. I know it's a trope that lots of filmmakers use in documentary filmmaking.

Jill: It does give the film a certain formalism. Because each section begins with ticking and then it moves up into the corner, and it enables the knowledge after a while that when it does that you're going to get another section, or person, you get a change. I think it's effective.

Rachel: *Breathing Still* is very beautiful as is *Growing Up Married*. Particularly through the intimacy. Could you talk more about the use of photography. You used stills Jill. You use this personal device to say what is basically poetry. It has this gorgeous intimate, but very beautifully judged performativity. Performance pieces. Can you talk about the aesthetics of sound and photographs, why you go for photography over moving images and you use found footage as well. And interestingly, I can remember doing my first session in film studies, oh we don't do found footage that's so passé.

Jill: I do see my films as hybrid pieces. In the digital age you can transform things into something else, your own ideas, discourse, vision, aesthetics. Two reasons for stills in that particular film. I was in Berlin and I came across posters of politicians and they were all static so there didn't seem to be a reason to have a moving image camera. I didn't need to have people walking by or a car going by and I was interested in Berlin, in walls, obviously that's a metaphor, there are so many different walls in Berlin, and they convey an enormous amount of implied information but they are closed, impenetrable. You always feel the whole city is a secret. There are these tiny plaques, memorials, they are really small, maybe 2 inches by inches, a memorial to a person. I edit static images to convey both stasis and movement and I worked hard in the editing to convey that; somebody who saw the film said they forgot they were stills, they seemed to be moving. I want to convey form that is very much about the frame and reflexivity and I'm very influenced by the Japanese aesthetic. That is an appreciation not a theoretical or intellectual reason, it's my reaction to cinema, it is a frame. If film had been invented as a circle what would we have done then? You would relate to it in a different way if it was a circle. And of course shaped paintings exist, if you think of Mondrian. The election in Berlin happened after I'd gone home. And the YouTube footage enabled me to see somebody else's point of view. Not necessarily how I would have filmed it. One has to take what you can find and that is the concept of bricolage which comes back to the idea of the handy woman, the Lévi-Strauss idea, what you find around you. You recreate it, not as this artist genius but as a transformer of found footage. I want my films to have a poetic discourse because I want them to be not something you may read in a newspaper. I want it to suggest another way of looking at things, elliptical or evocative and with implication, as against direct. To encourage thinking. And feeling.

Eylem: I agree. It would upset me if it was a circle though.

Jill: Why not? People are doing installations. All sorts of shapes and sizes. But we still come back to the idea of the frame.

Closing Thoughts

Eylem: As academics, our teaching and research, any kind of engagement activity, any activity to do with impact, becomes more meaningful when we take it out of our offices, our classrooms, our campus to make a difference at local, national and international level with the work we do. It's really important to critique the media or films from a feminist perspective; in addition to that, it is equally important to do feminism with creative practice work. Because that gives us more access to different people and our research and teaching gets more exposure to different communities and areas. There are communities, policy makers, organisations and individuals as well that really *need* our research, so that we don't just stay in 'ivory towers'. So, I would personally encourage all feminist film scholars to use creative practice more in their scholarly work, because that's when we move from trying to make a change and difference in challenging stereotypes, visual stereotypes, or existing representations which are problematic, to making a difference by engaging with media and making our own media in a different way.

Rachel: To add to that, when we talk about creative practice, that we include film, photography and editing. I was intrigued by your comment, Jill, that editing is such a huge part of the creative process, which is why we know that, for example, in journalism it's such a big issue for us. We're old enough to know what happened at Orgreave when the footage was reversed in terms of police versus marchers and the accusations that the marchers had been violent, when in fact it was to do with the editing of that particular piece. I have finally got to the stage where I really want to promote the personal as political, the political as personal and validating that, finding my voice. So looking at primary material like video in particular, and using them as sources to talk about and share and perform work, is creative practice. It's just ensuring that we take risks and don't necessarily stand behind a lectern. So it's such a release to work with editors who were very generous and allowed me to express in a way that is not deemed academic.

Jill: With teaching there's something about the curriculum isn't there? We're wanting it to be more open.

Eylem: Inclusive. Diverse.

Rachel: Honest, authentic.

Eylem: De-westernised.

Jill: De-colonialised. And to get to where students have courage, feel it's OK?

Eylem: Yes, if we share our own creative practice with students they will ultimately feel more inspired by having access to the maker of that product. It's about working *with* students rather than lecturing at them. That's much more fruitful, particularly in an environment where employability or transferable skills are key. If we really organically integrate those skills by engaging or working with students then they will achieve better and learn better perhaps. It provides different innovative pedagogies for them to take on board, to learn more easily and to apply outside. Creative practice work allows us, as lecturers, teachers and/or facilitators, to be able to offer it to your students and they take away whatever they can.

Rachel: We're all round this table, political and politically invested and I would finish with this, it's almost like a real challenge. Higher Education is very concerned to homogenise the political. It does a double speak. On the one hand it talks about diversity and inclusiveness and multiplicity, all the things that are the right things to say, but on the other hand, you're not allowed to have your trade union posters up. This kind of double speak you get from higher management, is problematic for us, because we're told two things: on the one hand, do a meaningful course, but don't talk too much. Don't step out of line and keep your politics to yourself. I also think if we don't invest personally it's really dishonest with the students. We need to be saying to them we want you to leave here having questioned identity and thought about what your identity is going to be. We don't want you to just think about what you're going to do in the workplace. We want to think about you as practitioners, whatever form that means and that means thinking about your personal sense of identity and memory and stories.

Notes

1. Arshia Aziz and Barclay Martin, Ostitto/Existence, 2012, <https://www.youtube.com/watch?v=Y2mnhD40teM>(last accessed 3 March 2019).
2. David Shariatmadari, 'UK's first course on Women, Islam and Media launched', <https://www.theguardian.com/world/2012/jan/19/uk-first-degree-women-islam-media> 29 January 2012 (last accessed 3 March 2019).
3. Report of the Commission on Religion and Belief in British Public Life, 'Living with Difference: Community, Diversity and the Common Good', December 2015, <https://www.woolf.cam.ac.uk/assets/file-downloads/Living-with-Difference.pdf> (last accessed 3 March 2019).

3. *MARRIED TO THE EIFFEL TOWER*: NOTES ON LOVE, LOSS AND KNOWLEDGE

Agnieszka Piotrowska

Married to the Eiffel Tower (2008) is the piece of work for which I am probably best known as a filmmaker. I don't particularly like this fact, given that I have done much interesting work since, but this appears still to be the case. Maybe it is the reason why I have never written about the film, at least until I was invited to contribute to a book on *Replacement* (2018) edited by Naomi Segal and Jean Owen. This piece is a longer version of that chapter and the reason I think it is worth rewriting it here is that in part it is an experiment in language. This time I state it clearly: the practice research here is concerned with the writing, the actual craft of writing and my long-standing desire – and indeed practice – to combine the theoretical and the creative in one article. In terms of the production of knowledge, which appears to be an important factor in the neoliberal university, I am less sure what I arrive at here. Perhaps the simple move to asking questions about how personal narratives affect creative paths can be generative, for it can reveal some caveats and flaws in one's own theorisations. I deploy the autoethnographic mode here, which has featured extensively in this volume, because practice research almost assumes a first-person narrative voice. Perhaps an attempt to explain my own silence has some value as, clearly, the level of complicated emotions and personal narratives exposed in this short essay is not a unique situation.

Married to the Eiffel Tower continues to be screened internationally more than ten years after its first outing on Channel Five in the United Kingdom. I think it is a good piece of work, or very good, but I don't like writing about it. My monograph *Psychoanalysis and Ethics in Documentary Film* (2014) (based on my doctorate) mentions it in passing, while it has a whole chapter devoted to another film of mine entitled *The Conman with 14 Wives* (2007) – a relatively obscure piece of work. The reasons for this situation will become clear, I hope, in the course of this essay.

It is worth saying a few words at the outset about my journey. After a long time in the industry, making documentary films which could be defined as intimate portraits of at times strange people, my doctorate and the book *Psychoanalysis and Ethics* interrogated the relationship between the filmmaker and the subject of her or his films. In it I named the strong attachment which can develop in that relationship – an attachment which I have called, following psychoanalytic clinical practice, transference. Transference is a feeling similar to love and as such it is a mechanism that must accompany any successful clinical relationship – for the work in the clinic to go on at all. The notion of transference, once taken out of the clinical context, is controversial and in my book I discuss it at length (Piotrowska 2014), following the work of Freud himself as well as Lacan and other psychoanalysts and thinkers (Freud 1915; Lacan 1998; Gueguen 1995). The notion of transference in the documentary encounter is still new and controversial, although anybody making a documentary film needs to develop a kind of friendship with the contributor to the film. Without it you may have no film as people need to trust you in order to say anything at all, particularly about painful events in their lives.

Since that book I have written extensively about my practice research in Zimbabwe (for example, Piotrowska 2014, 2016) and referenced my other film work such as *The Best Job in the World* (Piotrowska 2013). Before I discuss *Married to the Eiffel Tower*, I want to turn to a theoretical reflection – which I did mention elsewhere (Piotrowska 2014) but which does need evoking here.

Documentary: Journey to the Land of the Head Shrinkers

In 1999, Jean-Louis Comolli published an important article with the above title in *October* – a journal of art and critical theory rather than just film

Figure 3.1   Screenshot *Married to the Eiffel Tower* (2008), dir. Agnieszka Piotrowska.

35

Figure 3.2 Screenshot *Married to the Eiffel Tower* (2008), dir. Agnieszka Piotrowska.

studies. It is intriguing that this significant article by one of the engineers of contemporary (post-'68) film theory is not better known and not cited in any of the large collections I have surveyed. What Comolli puts forward is quite controversial and was perhaps slightly against the rising tide of declared concern for the potential subjects of film. The article is written in a specific moment in time when the French Government was about to introduce tighter controls regarding the use of images by filmmakers and broadcasters, including the consent of the subject of a documentary film and his or her right to decide how one's image is used. In essence, Comolli is violently against such a notion as he feels that it would encroach on the delicate process in which the filmmakers and the filmed are united, as he puts it, in a 'community of desire' (Comolli 1999: 47).

The article was published some twenty years after the heyday of *Cahiers du cinéma* in which documentary featured only marginally. At that time, Comolli practically disregarded it. This time, instead, he focuses on documentary and is adamant that its significance is quite extraordinary:

> Vague and variable as it may seem, the category called 'documentary' is central to cinema's history and experience, from the Lumière brothers and Vertov through Buñuel, Rossellini, Antonioni, Resnais, or Kiarostami, by way of Flaherty, Franju, and Wiseman, to name only a few. The cinema began as documentary and the documentary as cinema. (Comolli 1999: 36)

Comolli begins by suggesting that every film is a documentary ('*Contempt* is a documentary of Brigitte Bardot's body' (ibid.: 36)) and that any film has the key documentary component that is the relationship between 'given time (that of recording) and a place (the scene), a body (the actor) and a machine (responsible for recording)' (ibid.: 36). It is the filmed encounter of body and machine, he says, that will be recorded and viewed again, by at least one spectator. For Comolli 'this reproducibility of the encounter' is the warrant of its reality (ibid.: 36). It attests its existence – it is documentary.

He also makes a potentially important point, from a psychoanalytical perspective, that this recorded encounter is offered to the viewer as 'the scene in repetition' (ibid.: 37) because the viewer knows that there is a possibility of seeing it again, somehow, somewhere. There is a sense of sharing space and time – the viewer shares it with the creators of the encounters, with the technology and those who are in it. Comolli is fascinated by technology: 'Life goes on, and the machine remains' (ibid.: 37). There is little point in challenging his statements (the machines might break down, the film might get spoilt, even digital images can disappear, etc.). Clearly, *the recording* of the moment offers something special to all involved. In addition, and rather obviously, any contributor to a documentary knows too that such an encounter offers a chance of a 'repetition' in due course, of re-living the moment and having the moment re-experienced by somebody else, as they watch it. That knowledge, conscious or otherwise, makes the encounter special. A long time before I or anybody thought of relocating transference out of a clinic in a documentary encounter, Comolli talks about the relationship between the filmmaker and the subject of the film and the relationship between the spectator and the documentary text as a special bond and a *replacement* of a kind – of other relationships, present and past, which everybody involved may have experienced, denied or at least disavowed, and which the documentary experience, both the actual one of the production process, as well as that evoked in its reproduction and subsequent viewing, makes more possible to re-imagine and therefore to control, to tame. Making a film with somebody is a deeply special experience for everybody involved – for many reasons, but certainly the key one is the sense of forming intense bonds with those with whom one shares the experience.

Comolli acknowledges that special experience and further makes a point that in a film the work of the cinematic scene is actually the prefiguration of the moment of absence, 'intensifying through it this moment of presence, so as to intensify, finally, the presence of bodies through the promise of their coming absence. The image of the actor's body, absent but represented, finds a response, and possibly a hidden correspondence, in the real body of the spectator – a presence, certainly, but as if absent from itself in projection toward a screen' (ibid.: 37).

Comolli sees, therefore, the whole notion of the rights of potential subjects of the films as part of an attempt to commodify that special experience and to put a price on everything in a capitalist system. He thinks there is something fragile and precious in the relationships that have to occur in order for a documentary film to take place at all. Any attempt to regulate these encounters threatens the whole genre in his view. He talks about 'the gradual infiltration of commercial rights (those of the law) as the norm of interpersonal relations' – he sees the 'right to the image' as part of the problem (ibid.: 44).

Far from empowering the subject of documentary, Comolli controversially pronounces such a claim 'senseless' and dangerous: (ibid.: 44). I am mentioning it here for a reason and will return to it in due course. It is important to state clearly before I proceed (and this is important in the post #MeToo era) that Comolli assumes the consent from those who tell their stories had already been obtained and built on. It is not the notion of the consent but rather a right to retrospectively change one's mind about that consent. That would be unlawful in an actual physical encounter and he maintains there is no place for such a contract in the documentary encounter. He writes about 'desire' and uses language that wouldn't have been out of place in a discussion of a love encounter – and he feels (as indeed I do) that a certain kind of documentary is a love encounter of sorts.

Comolli sees the matter as the issue of the freedom of images (ibid.: 44) and freedom in general and goes on to say that the relationships 'inside' the film should be outside governmental regulations. What follows is his crucial statement in which he emphasises the special nature of the relationship of the filmmaker and his or her subjects:

> It's fairly clear that the link between documentary filmmakers and those who agree to be in their films is essentially undefined and undefinable. A 'two of us' is created, an ensemble that's not stated as such. If we come to use the term 'contract', it is understood as a 'moral contract' that should and does remain implicit, tacit, unspoken … You can, if you like, call it 'confidence,' but I prefer to locate it under the aegis of desire. Desire of one for the other, desire of the other in each. (ibid.: 45)

He then goes on to define this relationship indeed in terms of love: 'as a community of desire; those who are filmed, whether from Africa, Paris, or Quebec, clearly *share* the film with the one who shoots it. *Sharing* means that they're wholly present, without reserve, that they are giving what they have and also what they don't have: what they know they have and what they don't have as much as that which they don't know they have and have not' (ibid.: 45, my emphasis).

For Comolli, though the process of filming is a fragile and precious gift for all involved, the filmmakers end up with a film but the filmed ones are also gifted because the process of filming 'involves a break, the ordinary becoming extraordinary' (ibid.: 47). Comolli evokes the famous Lacanian: 'To give what one has not, that is love' (ibid.: 45) without referencing him. 'To give one's self to the image that I'm making with the other means really giving something I don't have, something that's neither my property nor my possession, not even an attribute. Can I want to sell what doesn't belong to me but to the in-betweenness of a relation, to the fertile encounter?' (ibid.: 47). Comolli stops short of actually spelling this out but he seems to be clear enough: the documentary encounter is not just a discourse of desire; it may well be a discourse of love. I have cited this extensively in my monograph (2014) supporting my argument about transference love. Here I need to disclose something that is against Comolli and indeed against myself: there are circumstances where the argument does not work.

Transference or Negative Transference?

If my whole notion of transference in documentary being like love confirms Comolli's writings about the importance of shared experience with the people one works with on a documentary, then my experience of *Married to the Eiffel Tower* denies it. The women in the film were heavily traumatised – one way or another – and my work with them aimed at presenting them well, as human beings who have found another way of being 'normal' – not as a pathological stance in the world, not even as a psychological defence but rather as a conscious choice. I also wanted to present the film as a political gesture, too, against heteronormative ideas about what relationships ought to be like, the neoliberal values being put on any emotions. I respected the women I worked with on the *Married to the Eiffel Tower* project and I respected their desire to tell their stories. In the film, one of them says very clearly: 'this is the first time that I am given the voice to talk to the human race – I want to be listened to. I want people to listen to me, to really listen to me and see what I have to say'. And so I think they did – the film is continuously commented on as one of the important documentaries which redefined the presentation of identities in television documentaries[1] and, as I mentioned, it has been screened all over the world. Its semi-illegal Vimeo site has had hundreds of thousands of views and it was re-screened on Netflix in 2016. Whatever my intentions might have been, people watch the film because of their curiosity about how these women take care of their sexual and emotional needs. I stand by my film – the piece of work is well-made, and it is satisfying to have made a film which has had so many lives and which so many people are still moved by and made reflective over.

However, inside the production process, the relationships were not easy – the women we featured really didn't like people (which is why they preferred objects) and myself and my associate producer Vari Innes, who has since gone on to become a reality TV producer/director, were not completely exempted from these reservations. The women, almost all of them, had been traumatised, in one way or another, by their difficult or impossible relationships with those who should have been the guardians of their health and well-being – their parents and more specifically their fathers. The large objects the women fell in love with, did replace the security and safety of those who let them down – in their childhood but also more recently – in their daily encounters with the world out there. The 'replacement' part of it was very clear and very painful – even without any theoretical frameworks, Oedipal traumas and other causal effects – the objects did offer a safe haven for our characters – the objects were controlled and controllable, they were fantasies which were nourishing, they offered something the world simply failed to deliver for these women. My associate producer and myself found ourselves struggling – this was a professional job and we were paid well to make the film on time and on budget for a tough British broadcaster, Channel Five. We were paid to deliver an amusing film and to endure setbacks and difficulties in the course of making it. We struggled but were each other's support and safeguards. We felt sad for the women and questioned why we should be putting them on television. The project certainly offered something important in their lives – a sense of belonging, a sense of recognition, a sense of being a part of something bigger – like a family indeed – which fitted perfectly in Comolli's schemes as described above. But the fact of the matter was that to achieve that result, we had to put ourselves on the line in very many ways – feeling, as we did, that our contributors did not like us at all, that Comolli's 'community of desire' did not quite kick in here, that they were often jealous about our ability to be able to form relationships with other people, however imperfect and however difficult our own lives might have been. They did not like the fact that we were different from them and we struggled to hold on to our integrities with tenacity and good humour.

A year before I embarked on my PhD on film and psychoanalysis, I sensed dimly the reasons for our difficulties without being able to name them: my Associate Producer Vari and myself were managing but, if truth be told, only just – we had feelings of frustration and anger, we had to field the rage of the contributors which we were never allowed to disclose or share or do anything about at all. We did not have any therapeutic support whatever and our nice executive producer Justine Kershaw was too busy to offer herself as a counsellor and in fact stepped in very late, to hold onto the film – 'the show' as she would say. In the course of the production, the only constant on the team was Vari and myself. I picked up crews around the world, too, as the film technically was 'a mixed medium project', meaning I shot some of it and used bigger crews to achieve the more glossy beautiful images. These moments with the crews were helpful to us as they offered some kind of normality. We, too, of course, through complex psychoanalytical mechanism were beginning to enter the strange world of the objectum sexuality. Their defence of replacing human relationships with those with objects began to appear fairly attractive to us too. We began discussing the attractiveness of the fences and the bridges – who could always do what we have imagined them to be able to do. No disappointments there, no missed dates or texts, no missing words as all the words in the world could simply be written by the recipient. The world of objectum sexuals can be seen as a world of writers, creating concrete relationships out of fantasies. In addition, these women struggled with their attachments to their fathers. This piece of information only became obvious as the project was unfolding. In the original research that aspect did not turn up and yet that was a very important element in these women's worldview. Vari and I were laughing at ourselves but both of us had difficult relationships with our fathers too – as it happened – like the characters of our film. Did I somehow choose the topic unconsciously wanting to examine my own emotions and memories? I did not know then why I have kept making the same film about love and betrayal and I know even less now, years after being in psychoanalysis and studying it theoretically. Ironically, in due course I chose the work of psychoanalyst Jacques Lacan as my main theoretical paradigm, and he identified the father – and not the mother – as the key holder of a person's identity and sanity.

And so Vari and I spent a lot of time discussing our own relationships with our fathers. Was the whole process of making the documentary a replacement for a proper therapy or analysis? Perhaps. But then we were lucky, we had friends, and relatives, I was married and had a son. We were fine and this was but a job – a tough job but just a job nonetheless. We had difficulties with the women, about whom we were making the documentary, but that was also part of the challenge, which we cherished.

And then, in the middle of the production schedule, when I was in San Francisco filming the main character of the documentary Erica La Tour Eiffel, aka Naisho, declaring her strong feelings for the Golden Gate Bridge (in addition to her marriage to the Eiffel Tower), my father had a stroke and was in a coma. I had a text from a close relative in Poland saying 'if I were you, I would get on the plane and come home. Now'. I was furious and it was deeply inconvenient – and I could not believe it as I spoke to my father only the day before. 'Are you sure?' I said to the relative. 'Are you absolutely sure that he is not just going to wake up tomorrow?' 'He is not waking up. You need to get on the plane and come to Poland, to the hospital. Now', replied the relative. I called Justine and told her I had completed the Golden Gate Bridge section of the filming and now had to go to Poland on a family emergency. 'Absolutely', said Justine. 'We will wait. It is your project.' I hardly remember anything of the journey. I remember the rest of the team being sympathetic and hopeful, but my heart was heavy. My relative's words were ringing in my ears – 'he is not waking up'. I arrived in Poland on a Wednesday morning, my husband and son arrived two days later, my father never woke up, and he died the following Monday.

My father was old. Every father is old but mine was really old. He had a whole life before he met my mother and had to change everything – for her and me. I should have known he was going to die. But I thought he wouldn't. I felt angry and betrayed and abandoned. 'This cannot be', I kept saying to myself. In the night I kept waking up in a horrendous and real pain. I had always known I loved him deeply and the thought of never being able to hear him play the piano again or discuss politics, or read aloud his notes about life, or argue with me, was unbearable. 'This cannot be' was the only thing I could repeat to myself, as I lay listening to my breathing and wondering how it was that I was alive and he was not. My life as I knew it was over.

The funeral happened the following Friday. My father had wanted to lie in state. He was a vain man. 'Make sure I look handsome', he said in his will. 'I can do this', I thought, 'no problem'. On the morning of the funeral I went to the funeral parlour and saw him – in a coffin, wearing an old suit, and white shirt and a navy blue chequered tie. He looked awful – they lost his dentures in the hospital. His sunken face made him look unlike the father I knew and loved. 'You cannot be serious', I said to the two men who showed his body to me. 'We must fix this – bring some toilet tissue and we will stick it into his mouth to make him look better.' They looked stunned and brought it to me and I tried to open his mouth and couldn't, and so I cried, and then with rage I started rummaging in my handbag, looking for make-up, foundation and a blusher to put on his face, tears streaming on my face. The two attendants stopped me then, looking horrified: 'Lady, please leave this now and wait in the car – we will call you when we have prepared him better'. And so they did. At the funeral, on 17 March, there was a military band playing military salutes as he was a war hero. I was obliged to give a speech because I was his only child, and my two cousins who were my father's nephews and sort of adopted sons, who were supposed to speak, couldn't and were sobbing uncontrollably. 'Oh for goodness sake', I said, and gave the speech. I vomited straight afterwards.

On Monday I called my executive producer Justine Kershaw and said I was flying back to resume the production. 'Are you sure about this?' 'I am perfectly sure', I said confidently. Replacing mourning with a production seemed an excellent plan. 'Don't even begin to talk to me about this', I said to my husband. 'This is what I shall do. This is what my father would want me to do'. My son went off to Russia on a school trip and was placed with a very old man. This was a few years before WhatsApp, so he sent an email telling me how strange it all was. 'Life is strange', I said brusquely, and told him to enjoy St Petersburg.

Meanwhile, Vari and myself met in Sweden to work with Frau Berliner Mauer – who talked a lot about her father, the model maker, who passed on to her his love for objects. Frau Berliner Mauer was married to the Berlin Wall, in case you wondered. I remember standing on the bridge in Sweden, crying, and I remember Vari being horrified and saying 'you shouldn't be here, you must go back'. But I stayed. This was my film and one way or another I had to complete it. The production schedule was tight and we had a transmission date. I was going to make this film, come what may. Yes, clearly I refused to mourn and I refused to believe my father was really gone. It is much easier to put things out of your mind, as the English say, when one is busy. And I was very busy – I had a film to make. Also, if I am to be completely honest here, I knew that the neoliberal system, or just the professional broadcasting system, would just bulldoze over my personal pain and get somebody else to finish the work. We had a transmission date and I feared they would proceed at full speed without me. Maybe it was only my fear and they would have waited. I will never know what would have happened if I had just stopped because I refused to stop, I refused to give in, and just kept going.

We went to Paris and Berlin – and our relationships with the subjects of our documentary film were deteriorating – they were annoyed at my sadness, which perhaps reminded them of their own. Naisho was keen to get intimate with the Eiffel Tower and asked for the crew to form a kind of wall around a particular section of it – a section she sat on and talked about how good it felt to feel the coldness of the steel against her body. This scene formed a beautiful sequence and the ending of the film, which is, if I may be so bold, a great ending, moving, and life affirming.

My father loved Paris. The very last conversation I had with him was on the phone – from New York – we discussed it. I said 'let's go to New York together in the spring' and he said 'No, New York is too far but perhaps we could go to Paris together'. We had travelled together before and we travelled well together. My mother never understood our passion for seeing new places and experiencing the thrill of discovery of another world, another culture. So yes, I was excited to take my old father to Paris and argue about surrealists. But that was not to be. He fell asleep and didn't wake up, and instead I was in Paris with Vari, and Naisho, and a film crew.

Naisho was happy with the film. The 'community of desire' as described by Comolli seemed to have worked after all. And then she changed her mind. 'Remove the ending', she said in an email, 'I don't want my intimacy with Eiffel Tower to be seen in this film'. I felt rising panic – this would have destroyed the whole film – the great finale was what made it. 'Oh no, no, no', I said to myself pretty selfishly, I know: 'my pain is all over this film, I am not giving up on this now'. I was in despair, far greater despair than the episode merited I am sure. The system on this occasion was on my side though, I knew it. I was right in it. The transmission date was looming. The contracts had been signed, money had changed hands, there was no way I was editing anything out. I shared the problem with Justine, knowing as I did that she would take care of it and she did. She said to me, 'We are not removing anything, her permission is clear and in fact it was her idea. Let me deal with this.'

The film went out unchanged to great reviews. I had ambivalent feelings about it but was proud too. Naisho became vitriolic for a time but then made a whole career of her objectum sexuality, giving speeches at conferences and talk shows. Amy, who was so vociferous about the voice being given to her, left the objectum sexuality chat rooms as there were some internal difficulties. She loved the film but was angry too that we just made the film and moved on. The film stayed and she loved it but in the end it could never replace the sense of profound loneliness and a sense of being misunderstood by the world at large.

I collapsed after the film was broadcast on television. The huge hole my father's passing left threatened to engulf me. The exhaustion was also linked to the whole bizarre production process and the unfortunate fall out with Naisho. I felt used, curiously, used to facilitate her intimate encounter with the structure, and then made into the unsympathetic villain. I felt guilty too and unsure about the decision I made and my executive made. But the film needed that ending to say what it did say: that love comes from within and is a conscious choice, at times against the world and its expectations. I knew my father would have found the documentary intriguing. I knew he would have asked many perceptive ethical questions in a way only he could. At times I felt I could almost feel his presence and his piano playing. But he really was gone.

I cried for a month – and in a way haven't stopped crying since, which of course is not quite true, as life has a way of replacing even the most painful memories with better ones. I feel his presence differently now, as a memory and as the never-ending encouragement to be courageous.

My father, who was an academic, left some money for me in his will too – 'do what you want with it of course, but you do have a good brain and are quite tenacious – for a woman. I always wanted you to do a doctorate – would you consider it?'

Note

1 For example: <https://filmow.com/listas/indiewire-s-stranger-than-fiction-16-documentaries-that-will-blow-your-mind-l53668/>

References

Comolli, J.-L. (1999), 'Documentary Journey to the Land of the Head Shrinkers', trans. A. Michelson in *October,* 90: 36–49.
Green, A. and Kohon, G. (2005), *Love and its Vicissitudes*, London: Routledge.
Gross, L., Katz, J. and Ruby, J. (1988), *Image Ethics: The Moral Subjects in Film, Photographs and Television*, Oxford: Oxford University Press.
Gueguen, P. G. (1995), 'Transference as Deception', in R. Feldstein, B. Fink and M. Jaanus (eds), *Reading Seminar XI*, New York: State University of New York Press, pp. 77–91.
Freud, S. (1915), 'Observations on Transference-Love (Further Recommendations on the Technique of Psycho-Analysis III)', in *Standard Edition of the Complete Psychological Works of Sigmund Freud. Volume XII*, trans. J. Strachey, London: Hogarth Press/Institute of Psychoanalysis, pp. 157–67.
Lacan, J. (1998 [1981]), *Seminar XI. The Four Fundamental Concepts of Psychoanalysis*, ed. J.-A. Miller, trans. A. Sheridan, London and New York: Norton.
Lacan, J. (2001 [1960–1]), *Le séminaire VIII: Le Transfert*, Paris: Seuil.
Lévinas, E. (1981), *Otherwise than Being*, trans. A. Lingis, The Hague: Martinus Nijhoff Publishers.
Piotrowska, A. (2013), 'The Horror of a Doppelganger', in *New Review of Film and Television Studies*, pp. 302–13 <http://dx.doi.org/10.1080/17400309.2013.807208>
Piotrowska, A. (2014), *Psychoanalysis and Ethics in Documentary Film*, London: Routledge.
Piotrowska, A. (2016), *Black and White: Cinema, arts and the politics in Zimbabwe*, London: Routledge.

4. CREATIVITY AND NEOLIBERALISM: BETWEEN AUTONOMY, RESISTANCE AND TACTICAL COMPLIANCE

Thomas Elsaesser

My several years researching, writing and directing the documentary essay film *The Sun Island*[1] have led me to reflect on the connection between my theoretical interests and my practical experience. Involving many moments of doubt, but also of sudden elation and creative energy, the creative process was challenging and, as it turned out, philosophically unsettling.[2] I was therefore delighted when asked by Agnieszka Piotrowska to show my film, and was honoured to be one of the keynote speakers at the conference 'Creative Practice Research in the Age of Neoliberal Hopelessness' organised by her at the University of Bedfordshire in May 2018. I was also daunted by the task, not least because Agnieszka – in her call for papers – introduced me with a raft of questions she wanted me to address: 'Elsaesser, after a lifetime of books and papers, has turned his hand to the making of a personal documentary featuring his family's archive. Why did he decide to include practice in his work? What has he learnt that he can share? Can a theorist analyse practice and how?'

In order to respond to at least some of these questions, I decided to divide this account into several parts. First, a few remarks about the external circumstances that brought me to making this film; then some ideas on the topic of creative practice research under neoliberalism, paying due care to the tension that creativity finds itself today not (only) between hope and hopelessness, but also between *autonomy* (that is, creative independence and authorship) and *automation* (academic bureaucratic systems on one side, algorithms and search engines automating research on the other). These reflections will bring me back to my practical experience during the years of researching and putting together

The Sun Island, which will lead to some concluding remarks that address the question: 'what has he learnt that he can share?'

External Circumstances as Impediments or Incentives?

First, then, the external circumstances that led me to make *The Sun Island*: perhaps the most banal, but in this academic context not unimportant, circumstance is that my retirement from the University of Amsterdam was mandatory when I turned sixty-five in 2008. As a significant turning point in anyone's life, it proved a useful moment to reflect on both my professional career and my personal life. But it also gave me the time – and the urgency to fill this time – with something hitherto untested and untried. In other words, as I was pushed, I decided to jump. The adventure I leaped into, however, was not to make a film about my family, but the decision to start a lawsuit against the European Central Bank, for fatally interfering with the integrity of a listed building that they had acquired from the City of Frankfurt and which happened to have been designed by my grandfather. Here, too, I was pushed but then decided to put myself up for it, and this push-pull turned out to be typical of how I backed into a range of tasks and obligations, such as creating and chairing a foundation in the name of my grandfather.[3] I had to make myself familiar with the rudiments of modern architecture, and build up an archive of his works and writings, all of which I then tried to turn around, so as to make it more my own initiative, by actively assuming what fate and circumstances had put my way. It led to the idea of making a film, and from then on, I proceeded on a kind of parallel track: I wrote a twenty-four-page treatment, on the strength of which I tried to find a producer and finance.

I also started writing a series of articles that dealt with memory and cultural topography, with trauma and time travel, with films made about The New Frankfurt, and with the fate of family sagas – typical of nineteenth-century fiction – in the age of home movies. These articles usually began as invited lectures – at conferences in Cambridge, Glasgow, New York, Tel Aviv, Ferrara, Kassel, Berlin, Frankfurt – so that I was both biding my time, as the practical film project moved at a glacial pace, *and* revising, refining and rethinking the movie in my head, but always shaped by and tailored to the business of academia: themed conferences, symposia, keynote lectures and publishable articles (see Elsaesser 2009; 2010). And since these lectures usually came with a PowerPoint presentation, I sort of turned my imagined film into a kind of photo-novel or comic strip narrative. Audiences seemed to be quite taken by it: over the years – and we are talking years – not only did the imaginary film become quite real in my mind and on the page, the response encouraged me into thinking that perhaps I did have what it takes to make an actual film.

Emboldened by the feedback I received, I sought out and eventually signed a contract with a Frankfurt producer – the third I had approached – who in turn managed to procure funding from the Hesse Film Foundation. His company, *strandfilm* also signed a broadcast deal with the German semi-commercial television channel 3Sat, co-owned by ZDF, one of Germany's public broadcasters. When I met with the commissioning editor – a man in his early thirties – he said: 'you realise, we're taking a big risk, backing a 70-year-old first-time filmmaker. But when I did my degree in German and Film Studies we had to read your books, so let's give it a try. But it would definitely help, if in your film you actually appear as yourself and mention that you're a film historian.' It was the first time that theory and practice were tied together, and it came as something of a shock.

Dieter Reifarth, my producer, then arranged for five days of location shooting in Berlin and Frankfurt with a full crew, which gobbled up a fair chunk of the budget. Since the film in my head did not require location work, I was at a loss what to film, and even though I was the writer, director and co-producer, I found myself – for the first time, but not the last – sidelined, out of my depth and considerably confused. A discussion with the producer revealed that he also had the film in his head, but it was clearly not the same as mine. I then hired a young editor and started putting together an initial version based on my treatment and lecture material: an essay film about memory and forgetting, about home movies as not only unreliable evidence, but actually as often unreadable evidence, unless supplemented with historical forensics and delicate hermeneutics. However, instead of providing this historical background with stock footage about the Nazi regime, about the war, about the deportation and mass murder of German Jews, I wanted to counter the incidental casualness of my father's home movies – the core material of *The Sun Island* – with *more* rather than less casualness and contingency (Figure 4.1).

I added the subjectivity of other personal documents and sources, such as letters, interviews, recordings and photographs – materials made on different occasions and for reasons long lost to either personal memory or even to family history. It was an intricate, self-reflexive, auto-referential two-and-a-half-hour rough cut that had a framing story within a framing story within a framing story: a sort of mirror maze of false leads and surprise twists, structured recursively around revelations of family secrets and long-hidden traumas. Without me fully realising it at the time, there was considerable evidence in the rough cut of Elsaesser, the author of books on Weimar Cinema and Expressionist films, and Elsaesser, the writer about Hollywood mind-game films, time travel and other cinematic thought experiments: in short, it was more *Shutter Island* than *Sun Island*.

Needless to say, the producer was horrified. He gave me an ultimatum: either we start from scratch, this time with an editor from *strandfilm*, or he

AUTONOMY, RESISTANCE AND TACTICAL COMPLIANCE

Figure 4.1 The incidental casualness of the Elsaesser family and friends on the Sun Island.

would withdraw from the project and enforce the small print of the contract: that is, invoice me for his own services and overheads, plus make me pay back the loan from the Hesse Film Fund. Since I had no intention of becoming a persecuted and penniless independent filmmaker, but was making the film on behalf of the Martin-Elsaesser Foundation, whose purpose it was to bring this architect's artistic legacy back to public attention, the only non-negotiable part of the project for me was to make sure the film would eventually be broadcast on television. And so began a six-month, three-way struggle between the producer, the new editor, and myself, to make a German television documentary: full well knowing that the broadcaster was mainly interested in filling ninety minutes of broadcast time as cheaply as possible; that the producer had no intent or incentive to secure festival exposure or theatrical distribution; and that 3Sat would be showing the *Sun Island* on a Monday evening at 10.30pm, to a motley viewership of late-night TV documentary buffs and insomniacs. It looked as if the external constraints were functioning as impediments to my creative vision.

The Creativity Dispositif

Which brings me to my second part: the state and nature of creativity under neoliberalism. As part of a broader cultural debate around 'hard' (i.e. useful) *knowledge* and 'soft' *skills*[4] but, above all, as a key economic factor in the formation of neoliberal society, 'creativity' has taken on a range of unsuspected and contradictory meanings. These first became an object of study in the last decades of the twentieth century, under the heading of 'creative industries': itself a kind of rebranding of the Frankfurt School term 'culture industries', but now with either neutrally descriptive or increasingly positive connotations.[5] The positive connotations derived from two sets of circumstances: first, the relevance of 'creativity' for the economic prosperity of advanced capitalist societies, when based on information technology and knowledge production; and, secondly, the emergence of a new social formation, the so-called 'creative class' (see Richard Florida 2002). It comprised persons with university education and/or engaged in scientific research, industrial design, the arts and humanities or high-tech innovation, sited in urban centres – metropolises, or mid-size cities or towns – which reinvented themselves (after their traditional industries collapsed or moved to Asia) around shopping, tourism, leisure, culture – with pedestrian inner cities, museums, galleries, music festivals and film festivals, as well as with technical and training colleges turning themselves into universities, flanked by science parks and start-up companies (see, for instance, Bas van Heur 2010).

While the conference was aimed at celebrating creativity and creative practice as knowledge production, understood as 'a generative dialogue about the importance of creative practices as a site of progress and resistance', on the assumption that, for instance, 'first person narratives [can] unveil profound knowledge even though they are deeply subjective', and that 'we learn through creative practice research [what] we cannot get at through ordinary routes', creative industries would seem to point in the opposite direction. What is usually meant by 'creative industries' is the redefinition of creativity and culture as key economic factors within an industrial and technological environment, run along the principles we generally identify with neoliberalism: financial deregulation, free markets for goods and capital, for-profit social services, and the privatisation of state-owned (i.e. public, common) assets. Engines of both the reorganisation of knowledge production and the structural transformation of consumption, the creative industries are often subsidised by the state, by local and regional governments – and in Europe by the European Union. What has emerged is the so-called the 'creativity dispositif' (Reckwitz 2017) – understood in Michel Foucault's sense as a complex of heterogeneous and even antagonistic forces operating on a single but complexly articulated discursive field of habitus and practice. To quote Andreas Reckwitz:

> Creativity [should be] taken not as a given but, rather, as an enigma, as sexuality was for Foucault. How did creativity come to be accepted as a desirable norm? ... The scope of the creativity dispositif extends beyond that of the economy. It also takes in the internal dynamics of media technologies and the human sciences, above all psychology, with its techniques of the self. Since the 1980s, the dispositif has also been propped up by state control in the form of cultural governmentality. (Reckwitz 2017: vii)

Rather than seeing the creativity dispositif merely as yet another system of control and domination, Reckwitz takes the longer view. The dilemma started with (German) romanticism, whose artists and writers experienced, for the first time, the tension between an 'anti-institutional desire for creativity' and the 'institutionalized demand for creativity': a tension that has come to a head under neoliberalism. Highlighting the 'affective dimension' of the creativity dispositif, and the existence of what he terms 'aesthetic sociality', Reckwitz sees creativity today fully implicated in the so-called experience economy that directs an audience's 'sensuous, affective attention' (Reckwitz 2017: viii) to the work of art, but also to the commodity-as-experience.

Reckwitz identifies four historical phases for the 'creativity dispositif'. Phase one and two are European Romanticism and the early twentieth-century avant-gardes, while the third phase was the 1960s and 1970s counter-culture and protest movement: relatively unified, politically left-wing, but hedonistic in its combination of sex, drugs and rock-n-roll. It embraced and celebrated as 'liberation' what turned out to be a tremendous boost to consumer capitalism. In this reading, the 1968 flower power generation significantly contributed to softening up the ground for neoliberalism's appropriation of creativity. The last phase reaps the benefits of all the previous ones, while shedding any 'anti-institutional' pretence: 'In the form it has been assuming since the 1980s, the creativity dispositif ... draws on such diverse phenomena as aesthetic and popular subcultures, post-industrial labour, fashion and experience-oriented consumption, philosophical vitalism, developments in media technology, "cultural regeneration" in urban planning, and political measures for fostering creative potential' (Reckwitz 2017: 30).

However, Reckwitz tries to recover a critical dimension, for which he coins the term 'aesthetic normalization'. This deliberately paradoxical expression focuses on the institutional constraints and their counter-intuitive or unintended consequences, which ensures that the creativity dispositif is more contradictory than merely affirmative:

> The creativity dispositif brings about a paradoxical kind of aestheticization. It effectuates an aesthetic normalization ... The disparate practices and discourses of the creativity dispositif are aimed not at the creation of calculable, standardized behaviour – at least not on the first level – but rather at the production and reception of novelty for its own sake. Now, in order to arouse attention, novelty must always diverge from the past and the habitual, and it must involve an element of surprise and unpredictability. This can be put in terms of information theory: *communication* rests essentially on redundancy, whereas *information* presupposes a minimum of novelty. This applies even more to aesthetic information. The creativity dispositif ... demands surprise and unpredictability and ... aesthetic normalization is therefore based on the paradoxical attitude of expecting the unexpected. (Reckwitz 2017: 27)

In order to retain some of the connotations of creativity as 'a site of progress and resistance' (as the conference call puts it), Reckwitz makes an important distinction between 'aesthetic practices' and 'aesthetic apparatuses'. While individual aesthetic practices can be self-referential, detached and thereby function as subversive, once they aim to present themselves in the public sphere,

> these practices tend to gravitate to the centre of more capacious aesthetic apparatuses, larger institutional complexes aimed at the production and reception of aesthetic events, such as the film industry, football, museums and galleries, the fashion industry, tourism or experimental gastronomy. As institutional complexes focused on results, they always involve non-aesthetic, purposive and normative practices (administration, advertising, craft, technology, service, etc.). (Reckwitz 2017: 28)

In the end, it is these apparatuses rather than the individual aesthetic practices that provide the precondition for the permanent production of novelty and innovation, which may or may not constitute 'knowledge'.

What Reckwitz, a disciple of Niklas Luhmann and systems theory,[6] calls 'aesthetic practices [that] gravitate to the centre of more capacious aesthetic apparatuses', I call the push-pull, 'jump-before-you're-shoved' logic that bedevils our discussion around creativity, where we feel – no, where we *know* – that our desires and creative urges, our best emotional energies and most daring ideas are already pre-programmed into the system as its lubricant and fuel, are already discounted as politically ineffectual and of no practical consequence. They are actively harvested and mined for what Reckwitz calls the 'cultural imaginary promising durable affective stimulation'. In other words, creativity can be the drug that we ourselves administer, unaware of how we have become addicted, either not knowing who our dealers are, or actually pleading with our dealers to give us more. What this does to young people can be seen in Elisa Giardina Papa's mash-up of YouTube clips, called *need ideas!?!PLZ!!*[7]

Neoliberalism, Creativity and Agnotology

The neoliberal demand for creativity, flexibility and innovation easily lends itself to self-exploitation in the name of self-improvement, self-maximisation in the name of self-reflexivity, while giving a positive spin to hire-and-fire precariousness, to the gig economy and various other forms of disposability and marginalisation. Since women, as unpaid domestic and affective labour force, and as relative latecomers to the job market also in the academy, tend to be at the sharp end of these developments, it is feminist thinkers – Judith Butler, Wendy Brown, Lauren Berlant, to name just three – who have been particularly vociferous and rigorous in analysing the nefarious effects of neoliberal double-speak, when it comes to creativity and flexibility (see Brown 2015; Butler 2004; Berlant 2011).

Yet there is a further reason why the relation between neoliberalism, creativity, knowledge generation and emancipatory thinking has become problematic. This has to do with the very values and tactics we once thought were progressive, either aesthetically or politically, such as – in realm of artistic practice – the virtues of ambiguity, non-linearity and open-endedness; in the realm of academia, the crossing of disciplinary boundaries, and – in the realm of politics – the tactic of being disruptive and subversive. Now that interdisciplinarity and transferable skills are on every university administrator's agenda, and now that every tech sector start-up dreams of bringing to market a disruptive technology in a particular industry or social practice, and now that subversive is a word that only advertisers use, and a ploy that only alt-right groups seem to wield with any degree of success, it's time to also rethink what progressive politics or progressive teaching might entail. Even in philosophy, the very inventor of social constructivism, Bruno Latour, has had second thoughts:

> While we spent years trying to detect the real prejudices hidden behind the appearance of objective statements, do we now have to reveal the real objective and incontrovertible facts hidden behind the illusion of prejudices? Entire Ph.D. programs are still running to make sure that good American kids are learning the hard way that facts are made up,

that there is no such thing as natural, unmediated, unbiased access to truth, that we are always prisoners of language, that we always speak from a particular standpoint, and so on, while dangerous extremists are using the very same argument of social construction to destroy hard-won evidence that could save our lives. Was I wrong to participate in the invention of this field known as science studies? Is it enough to say that we did not really mean what we said? Why does it burn my tongue to say that global warming is a fact whether you like it or not? Why can't I simply say that the argument is closed for good? (Latour 2004: 227)

In a similar vein Michael J. Blouin, in his book *Magical Thinking, Fantastic Film, and the Illusions of Neoliberalism* (2016), argues that neoliberalism's real achievement in the sphere of culture is not the appropriation of creativity, nor the corruption of a once progressive political vocabulary, but the *aestheticisation* of terms like 'destabilizing' and 'disorienting', which instead of threatening the symbolic order, as Derrida and deconstruction once might have claimed, merely give cover to deliberate strategies of confusion and obfuscation, creating the climate where fake news flourishes and where we are systematically being stunned into silence and elaborately made stupid. There is even a word for this strategy of systematic obfuscation: agnotology – the science of making ignorant (Proctor and Schiebinger 2008). Blouin writes:

> Neoliberalism celebrates the idea of absolute freedom (individuals pursuing their private desires) and, in the same breath, sustains an illusion of egalitarianism. It re-appropriates the rhetoric of both liberalism and democracy to distract citizen from the reality that neither ideal has come closer to fruition under its reign. In fact, quite the opposite: Unwieldy cries for enhanced self-interest contradict the veneer of democratic fraternity. Neoliberalism functions parasitically. It eats away at any whiff of collective action, in favor of the illusion of personal freedom. Meanwhile, a gluttonous cadre sustains the (impossible) notion that ever-enhanced freedom for the individual will simultaneously strengthen communal coalitions. Through agnotology, for example, neoliberal think tanks ... might promulgate claims that climate change is a Left-wing fiction, thus manufacturing doubt where doubt has no reasonable place. Agnotology exploits a legacy of confusion born at the crossing of the Freiburg School (i.e. Heidegger and deconstruction) and the Frankfurt School (i.e. Adorno and Horkheimer). (Blouin 2016: 205)

But we need not invoke these patriarchs of philosophy and high theory. If agnotology is defined as 'the study of culturally induced ignorance or doubt, particularly the publication of inaccurate or misleading scientific data',[8] then what we need is a critical media agnotology that studies the (ab)use of media for the purpose of not-knowing, for sowing confusion and for stoking controversy over issues and facts that are not in doubt. Any talk show host, CNN presenter or Sky News anchor person is a master at agnotology, parading several outrageously partisan pundits on every conceivable issue, whether it is healthcare or taxes, the drug wars or incarceration, Brexit or Global Warming. You watch and listen – whether for thirty minutes or two hours – and you're no wiser, while your concern over the issues have in the meantime soured into apathy and your activism has wilted to cynical indifference.

So what is to be done? How can artistic research and creative practice get us out of this treacly morass of half-truths and hyperbole, of ambiguity and disinformation, of scepticism and cynicism: in short, out of neoliberal hopelessness? Let's first look at what we understand by 'artistic research', or rather what a friend of mine says on the topic:

> Artistic research is treated as one of the multiple practices which are defined by indefinition, constantly in flux, lacking coherence and identity. In ... current debates around artistic research, [it seems that] one of the most important concerns is the transformation of artistic research into an academic discipline. There are discussions about curriculum, degrees, method, practical application, pedagogy. On the other hand, there is also substantial criticism of this approach. It argues that the institutionalization of artistic research is complicit with the new modes of production within cognitive capitalism: commodified education, creative and affective industries, administrative aesthetics, and so on. Both perspectives agree on one point: artistic research is at present being constituted as a more or less normative, academic discipline. (Steyerl 2013)

Hito Steyerl, whom I am quoting here, is one of the most successful and renowned filmmakers and installation artists of the new century (see Bradley 2017). She is also a prolific author, and a full professor at the University of the Arts in Berlin.[9] We can therefore assume that she knows what she is talking about. She, too, not unlike Reckwitz, sees a more hopeful underside to the institutionalisation of creativity and artistic research:

> A discipline may be oppressive, but this is also precisely why it points to the issue it keeps under control. It indexes a suppressed, an avoided or potential conflict. A discipline hints at a conflict immobilized. It is a practice to channel and exploit its energies and to incorporate them into the powers that be. Why would one need a discipline if it wasn't to discipline somebody or something? Any discipline can thus also be seen from the point of view of conflict. (Steyerl 2013)

'Seen from the point of view of conflict' a discipline creates the space for action and for friction, while providing a framework that can act as a creative constraint. Taken at face value, she argues, artistic research as it is conceived, debated and practised in the academy today, is indeed hopelessly compromised in its overt and covert collusion with neoliberalism, quite apart from being a very privileged Western preoccupation that lords it over the rest of the world, thanks to a global art scene of Biennales, documentas, Art Fairs together with an ever growing number of Museums of Contemporary Art: all fully integrated into the creativity dispositif, if not actually the flagships of this dispositif.

Yet if we flip it over, according to Steyerl, and look at artistic research from the perspective of social struggles, while also taking a more historically informed view, then 'a map of practices emerges that spans most of the 20th century and also most of the globe. It becomes obvious that the current debates do not fully acknowledge the legacy of the long, varied and truly international history of artistic research, which has been understood in terms of an *aesthetics of resistance*' (Steyerl 2013). Referring herself to the title of a famous book by Peter Weiss, she argues that

> since the 1920s, extremely sophisticated debates about artistic epistemologies were waged around terms like 'fact, reality, objectivity, research' within the circles of Soviet factographers, cinematographers and artists. For factographers, a fact is an outcome of a process of production. Fact comes from facere, to make or to do. So in this sense the fact is made or even made up. This should not come as a surprise to us in the age of poststructuralist, metaphysical skepticism. But the range of aesthetic approaches which were developed as research tools almost 100 years ago is stupefying. Author-artists like Vertov, Stepanova, Tretjakov, Popova and Rodchenko invent complex procedures of investigation, such as the kino-eye, the cine-truth, the 'biography of the object' or (interventionist techniques like) photomontage ... We could also mention the efforts of the artists employed by the FSA (Farm Security Administration) of creating essayistic photojournalistic inquiries during the Great Depression in the US. In all these cases, the artistic research is ambivalently co-opted into state policies – although to a different extent and with completely different consequences. Around the same time as Tretyakov was assassinated during the Stalinist terror, Walker Evans had a solo show at the MoMA. (Steyerl 2013)

Steyerl acknowledged that the problem of co-option and appropriation has been with us for a very long time, and also that not all artistic research has served emancipatory ends, given that some of it we would now consider 'propaganda'. But Steyerl goes on to make an important supplementary point: 'It is no coincidence', she writes,

> that many of the practices mentioned here have been dealing with classical problems of documentary representation from very different perspectives: documentary's function as power/knowledge, its epistemological problems, its relation to reality and the challenge of creating a new reality. Documentary styles and forms have forever grappled with the uneven mix of rationality and creativity, between subjectivity and objectivity, between the power of creation and the power of conservation. (Steyerl 2013)

Steyerl's rousing plea in favour of documentary methods and essayistic forms is the right cue for me to return to my own film practice, which – without comparing myself to any of the names she mentions – nonetheless fits into her genealogies. As it happens, I also co-taught with Noam Elcott a course at Columbia University on 'The Documentary Impulse in the Arts' during the Spring Semester 2018, where we did indeed discuss Vertov and Tretyakov, Esfir Shub and Walter Ruttmann, Erwin Piscator and Bert Brecht, Walker

Figure 4.2   The Sun Island as seen from the lake in 1940

Evans and Joris Ivens – all the way to Harun Farocki and Hito Steyerl, Trevor Paglen and Eyal Weizman.[10]

In this respect, my academic research retroactively benefited from my filmic practice, because *The Sun Island* certainly understands itself as propelled by a documentary impulse. In my attempt to bring back to life something that was not only forgotten, but was never remembered, having been bound up with so many personal and historical traumas, *The Sun Island* documents the very process of *making facts* and not simply *presenting* them, and it is clearly situated between what Steyerl calls 'the power of creation and the power of conservation'.

Before I do return to my film practice, however, I want to raise another issue, in part because – given the situation we find ourselves in, and in light of neoliberalism's many strategies of co-option – I differ from Steyerl's 'aesthetics of resistance'. As she herself points out, almost all the historical methods of artistic research she mentions were either 'tied to social or revolutionary movements, to moments of crisis and reform', or were produced as resistance to repressive dictatorships and oppressive colonial regimes. Neither of these conditions apply today in our part of the world, however much the Revolutionary Left might secretly hope to be reinvigorated by the rise of the alt-right, in its populist, nativist or nationalist forms. What I want to propose, or rather what I found myself as practising – often much against my initial theoretical beliefs and political positions – was not an aesthetics of resistance, but, on the contrary, an 'aesthetics of tactical compliance'.

CREATIVITY BETWEEN AUTONOMY AND AUTOMATION: GREENBERG, ADORNO AND BAZON BROCK

How did I come to this at first glance rather defeatist-seeming stance? The theoretical reflections that followed on from my sometimes painful self-observation during and after making my film, brought me back to my origins as a cinephile, even before I became a film scholar – namely the belief in 'auteurism', the unshakeable conviction that not only anyone who is the writer, director and producer is the author of a film, but also the director even when he or she 'fights the system' and is neither the writer nor the producer. The auteur theory either can be dismissed as a naïve – and retrograde – belief in the romantic conception of the artist as finding in the uniqueness of subjectivity and self-expression his or her originality, imagination and creativity. Or it can be seen as indeed an 'aesthetics of resistance', where the author draws strength, persistence and inspiration from the very constraints that the system – in this case, the Hollywood studio system – imposes on him or her. There are evidently many other versions of the auteur theory: for instance, the auteur as an effect of the text (Wollen 1972), or the auteur as the transferential fiction of the critic as the would-be author of meaning and intentionality (see Elsaesser 1981: 8; 2016). But what I want to hold on to in our context is the problematic concept of *autonomy*.

Autonomy in relation to art and creative practice is a concept that has been debated throughout the twentieth century, ever since it became one of the key tenets of aesthetic modernism. In its Greenbergian version of self-reference and medium specificity, dominant in the post–Second-World-War era of abstract expressionism and beyond, autonomy has mutated – since the 1960s – into the bad object of postmodernism and contemporary art, mainly because of its perceived elitism and apolitical stance.[11] Its other proponent, T. W. Adorno, hardly fared much better, but this rested on an even greater misunderstanding, because for Adorno, the autonomy of art and of the artist was a profoundly dialectical concept. Here is a handy paraphrase of Adorno's position:

> Every artwork is autonomous insofar as it asserts itself as an end-in-itself and pursues the logic of its own inner or formal development, without regard to the dominant logic of society; but every work is also a 'social fact' in that it belongs to, manifests and confirms the reality of society, understood as the total nexus of social relations and processes. The autonomy of art is furthermore both a memory and a promise, in that it preserves the possibility of a non-alienated humanity as described luminously by the young Karl Marx. As such, the artwork always contains a force of resistance to the powers that be, albeit a fragile one. (Ray 2009: 80–1; see also Adorno 1997: 5)

Another way of thinking of autonomy as having this dual function of resisting the appropriation inherent in autonomy as independence ('independence' now being the very name of the artistic and academic precariat), while nonetheless maintaining a proactive (as distinct from 'progressive') relation to society and the social order, is the stance advocated by Bazon Brock, a German artist-writer-activist coming out of the Fluxus Movement and the Situationists.[12] He sees creative practice as a high-wire act without a safety net, so that radical autonomy is absolutely essential for focus and concentration. Creative practice is the balance pole with which the tightrope walker perpetually preserves his equilibrium, using opposing forces to keep his poise and posture, in order not to fall off. Artists – and maybe non-tenured philosophers! – are the only ones who not only know, but actually thrive from knowing that there is no ground under our feet: that when we look down, there is only the void; that there is neither justification nor legitimation for art, no pre-defined sense or purpose – what Brock calls 'no claim to either external truth or an effective form of agency' (kein Wahrheits- oder Wirkungsanspruch).[13] In short, there is nothing that can provide the artist either with a set of definitions of what is art, or with a practice that protects her from failure and abject isolation. And yet, in the wider scheme of things, the artist is for her time and place, for her culture or society, the proverbial canary in the coal mine: the early warning system and the vanguard, who every day puts at risk life, limb and sanity.

At first glance, Brock's figure of autonomy as high-wire act seems merely to be a radicalisation of the romantic myth of the genius starving in his garret, maligned by the critics and misunderstood by the masses. But Brock has another purpose in mind, and for this I need to make a further brief detour. One element that my discussion of the creativity dispositif alludes to, but does not quite spell out, is the degree to which neoliberalism not only stands for free markets, speculative indeterminacy and entrepreneurial risk-taking as the epitome of individualism and personal freedom: economic neoliberalism is itself in the process of being appropriated by cognitive and affective capitalism, where even the skewed values of neoliberal individualism, such as initiative, flexibility and creative self-fashioning are being mimetically emulated by machines – no longer the bureaucratic machines of Foucault's biopolitics, but the insinuatingly intuitive, and seductively personalised machines of social media, ever more perfectly 'mirroring' the creative self, caught in the illusion of exercising its autonomous agency, while floating in the selfie-culture and echo-chamber of the online information filter bubble.

Autonomy is therefore no longer the counter to 'the system' – however we view it – but finds itself at once solicited by it and superseded by *automation*. Automation is here understood as the deployment of technologies which can enact practices or emulate skills as mere special effects which were once the result of manual labour, human ingenuity, craftsman's skill or artistic inspiration: photographs that emulate paintings, digitally produced photo-realism, a word-processor emulating a typewriter, or a computer disguising itself as a telephone. But automation evidently also includes algorithms that *model* human behaviour and *format* subjectivity, as well as search engines that automate research, generating bibliographies and footnotes, supply illustrations and images on any topic whatsoever, or make connections, generating combinations that are only possible when having random access to large data sets, having digitised archives accumulated over centuries and swimming in vast oceans of information.

My Own Practice: Between Coherence and Contingency

It is due to creativity now oscillating between autonomy and automation that the 'aesthetics of resistance' will have to be rethought. At one and the same time *supported* and *usurped* by whatever name we will eventually give to the forces which now instrumentalise – and bend to its ends – both neoliberalism and classical liberal democracy, creative autonomy has become a dangerously self-delusional mirage. My practical experience of making my film has in this respect served to suggest another strategy, which I am calling 'aesthetics of tactical compliance' as my substitute or supplement to the 'aesthetics of resistance'.

At the beginning of my account, I looked at the external circumstances that brought me to making *The Sun Island*, which ended with me realising how little effective control and autonomy I had as writer-director-producer, once television was one of my masters. The commissioner was always all smiles and affability, but when my producer didn't like one of my ideas, he would simply say: 'it'll never pass the TV bosses', or 'the technicians controlling the broadcasting standards won't accept it' – and that was the end of the discussion. But these external circumstances can also be an incentive: I soon came to appreciate that my film owes its existence to a set of apparently incompatible agendas and structurally adversarial relationships: my producer instrumentalised my scenario, because the film is partly set in Frankfurt and deals with the ECB's controversial new headquarters, a topic for which he knew he could get funds from the Hesse Film Foundation. The producer at ZDF/3Sat instrumentalised me, because he could fill ninety minutes of schedule time, at a bargain basement price. And I instrumentalised the broadcaster, because I needed a medium and platform, fully established in the public sphere, in order to advertise the existence of the Martin Elsaesser Foundation, and to promote my grandfather's architectural legacy. Now everybody seems happy, and 3Sat told me the film had 130,000 viewers: 'not bad for our Monday slot'. But those six weeks of editing were a perpetual battleground, with endless fights, harsh words and compromises that gave me sleepless nights: in short, for much of the time, I practised an aesthetics of – useless and frustrating – resistance.

Were I to do it again, I would adjust tactics. Besides the tightrope walker, one of the other images that Bazon Brock likes to invoke when he talks about artistic practice is that of the Etruscan Smile. Nobody knows exactly what it means – apparently it's the smile on Greek or Etruscan sculptures that wants to say: it is what it is, 'que sera sera' – the smile of active acceptance rather than resignation.[14] But for Brock it is more: it is a positive agreement with the forces that seem to determine one's fate, because these forces invariably reveal themselves as either inherently antagonistic, and therefore full of interstitial spaces of freedom and agency – much the same point that Hito Steyerl made regarding creative practice as an academic discipline – or they are so chaotic and contingent that *riding them, rather than resisting them*, generates new energies and open paths that lead to surprising discoveries. On the one hand, this is reminiscent of Joseph Conrad's famous dictum from *Lord Jim*, 'in the destructive element immerse yourself', which has served writers as different as Philip Roth and Fred Jameson as their motto, when either 'letting the unpalatable in' or when making a plea for a dialectical view of history.[15] Jameson invokes the phrase in connection with Hans Jürgen Syberberg, applauding him for his *Hitler A film from Germany*. Syberberg's thesis is that Germany, in the first half of the twentieth century, devastated not only Europe and destroyed the Jews, but it also destroyed itself and its 250 years of cultural Enlightenment and creativity in the arts. Jameson's case (1981) is that by acknowledging this destructive element and facing it, Germany managed to reinvent itself, not least thanks to its filmmakers.

On the other hand, riding the tiger of neoliberalism and even spurring it on, is also the tactical move of the Deleuze-Guattari-inspired philosophical current that goes by the name of accelerationism. Accelerationism is the idea that capitalism, in its present psycho-techno-economic development needs to be expanded and accelerated in order to generate radical social change (see Mackay 2014; and Srnicek and Williams, 2015). The starting point is

Figure 4.3 Hans Peter Elsaesser, the author of the home movies appropriated by *The Sun Island* (2017).

Figure 4.4   Hans Peter Elsaesser, the author of the home movies appropriated by *The Sun Island* (2017).

Deleuze-Guattari's notion of deterritorialisation, meant to overcome the countervailing tendencies of social democracy and the welfare state, which aims merely to *contain* the excesses and *mitigate* the socially reprehensible consequences of neoliberalism. But it can be argued that accelerationism also goes back to Karl Marx himself, when in 1848 he said: '[while] the free trade system is destructive, it does break up old national boundaries, and pushes the antagonism of the proletariat and the bourgeoisie to the extreme point. In a word, the free trade system hastens the social revolution. It is in this revolutionary sense, gentlemen, that I vote in favor of free trade.'[16]

My own strategy was confused and contradictory. On the one hand, I wanted my film to have the stamp and coherence of a personal work, and to put it on the screen as it existed in my head. On the other hand, the whole process of how I came to make the film should have prepared me for the

Figure 4.5 Hans Peter Elsaesser, the author of the home movies appropriated by *The Sun Island* (2017).

presence of centrifugal forces right from the start. First, there were the many external circumstances that pushed me into making a film rather than just writing an article or two; then, there were the coincidences, chance encounters, discoveries and unexpected convergences – for instance, how certain sequences of my father's home movies suddenly were echoed ('corroborated', if you will) in a letter that I found only after my mother's death; how I stumbled across the Leberecht Migge story, merely because someone came up to me after a lecture I gave in Berlin on *Metropolis* and *Kuhle Wampe* – all this should have alerted me that it was not a matter of containing, mitigating or translating these disparate forces and serendipitous discoveries into one complex, convoluted storyline, as I had devised it in my head. Rather, it was my duty to let the home movies, the letters, the mementos and photographs first speak back to me, and not only that: I also had to let my producer and editor speak back to me more freely and more openly, and so prevent an atmosphere from arising, where each of us already hedged and self-censored what they wanted to say, in anticipation of it being criticised or rejected. Elementary, my dear Elsaesser, you might say, but when you are preoccupied with being the author, intent on realising your vision, or when you feel you have been outfoxed or outmanoeuvred, it is very hard to keep the Etruscan smile.

Conclusion

So what have I learnt? I have learnt much about my family, about family dynamics in general, and especially about father–son relationships (of which there are several in the film) and about mother–daughter relationships (where the elective daughters fare better than the blood-and-kin daughters). The personal lessons are ongoing, and I will have to absorb some painful insights in the years to come: they may even result in another work of creative practice. So what can I therefore claim for this aesthetics of tactical compliance that I promised myself to follow next time round?

First of all, the whole process was a reminder of the uses of creative constraints. If the brutal ultimatum from the producer was one of the more severe creative constraints, the other one was that the partial loss of control over the film actually made me more open in a different direction: the ability to invite or tolerate the interference of coincidence, of accident and chance, and letting these factors, both external and internal – what in my book on German cinema I call a film's 'parapractic' moments, that is, the Freudian slips of history and creative thinking especially when trauma, memory, guilt and loss are at issue – letting the parapraxes of the creative process impinge more on my work in the final stages of the film.[17]

Second, while some of these fortuitous findings came about through personal encounters and the proverbial skeletons in the family closet, the vast majority were the results of online searches, with Google now playing the role of the Wheel of Fortuna and the roll of the dice. Whether it is the political importance of an item in the background of a single photo (the *Volksempfänger*), the historical significance of the car that my grandfather proudly poses with (the *Standard Superior* as the precursor and originator of the *Volkswagen*), the life-story of an island visitor that leads me to the Freud translators and Bloomsbury figures James and Alix Strachey (*Josephine Dellisch*), or the writer killed by Italian snipers (*H. G. Rexroth*), whose novel, published after his death but never distributed, I am re-editing with a professor of German, while the writer's long-suffering wife (*Irmgard Kern*) brought me into contact with the blog of a retired librarian in Pasadena. Or the lesbian couple, who were friends with Siegfried Kracauer, and whose performance of a suite for violin and piano, T. W. Adorno had reviewed in the Frankfurt papers – all these lives and their connections with the island, with the lost world of the Weimar Republic, as well as with today's world, would never have been rediscovered had it not been for the computational power, the machine memory and the global reach of Google's servers.

Third, the aesthetics of tactical compliance has also influenced my practice of screening the film, now that it is completed: I am fortunate in being able to show *The Sun Island* to a live audience, sometimes one that does in fact know me as a film scholar and theorist, but at other times, to people who only attend because they are interested in the topic, or because they are loyal to their local film club. There it helps that my producer has no interest in distribution (his profit and overheads were written into the budget), and it even helps that our contract with television prevents us from offering the film commercially on DVD or for streaming. And because of the live audience, I try to pay close attention to what viewers have to say in the Q&A: to understand how they talk back to me, to listen to the questions behind the questions, and to let them – insofar as they are willing – make their own film out of mine. There it helps that I was not able to make the film in my head, that I do not feel defensive, that I neither need to justify it as the television documentary that it also is, nor blame the producer for all that went wrong, as an 'auteur' might be tempted to. Some viewers respond to the *Sun Island* as a film: does it qualify as an essay film, how obtrusive is the voice over, how much of the story that I am telling is fictional licence, why did I include the sprocket parts (the open gate) of the frame in the home movie footage? Others are confused, baffled or made uncomfortable by the story: they want more historical context, they do not think the reality of the war, and what we know about the Nazis, gets enough attention, or, on the contrary, they are intrigued to see Germans – during the war and among the horrific Berlin bombing raids – lead such banal and normal lives. And finally, there are those for whom the film triggers personal memories: about their grandparents, an uncle or another relative who made home movies, where they saw their parents or relatives when they were much younger or when still alive. After a screening in Frankfurt, for instance, I had a woman in tears, because she remembered how, as a late arrival in the family, she saw her siblings (whom she only knew as grown-ups) in her father's home movies, but how the siblings had hated these home movies, because of a tyrannical father herding them in front of his camera, while for her, they were a precious window on a world from which her late birth had excluded her.

Creative practice in the era of neoliberal hopelessness, in short, has to be a creativity *after* neoliberalism, but also – this is the more contentious thesis – *after* resistance and *after* authorial autonomy: it has to include distributed authorship and retroactive or looped learning processes, it has to devise practices open to contingency and chance, and it may have to treat external constraints as an invitation for tactical compliance with – as well as tacit attentiveness to – the mysterious forces that are regenerative in the universe out there, and creative not only in one's head, but in the minds of others.

Notes

1. *The Sun Island* (Germany, 2017). For more information, see <www.sunislandfilm.com> and <https://www.imdb.com/title/tt8452430/>.
2. A reflection on some of the issues arising from the use of found footage in the creation of public memory can be found in Elsaesser (2019).
3. The foundation resulting from the lawsuit with the European Central Bank is the *Martin Elsaesser Stiftung* (<http://www.martin-elsaesser-stiftung.de/stiftung.html>), set up in March 2009.
4. Soft skills are usually defined as 'a combination of people skills, social skills, communication skills, character or personality traits, attitudes, social intelligence and emotional intelligence … that enable people to navigate their environment, work well with others, perform well; [they] do not depend on acquired knowledge: they include common sense, the ability to deal with people, and a positive flexible attitude.' See Wikipedia entry <https://en.wikipedia.org/wiki/Soft_skills>.
5. Important texts for defining 'creative industries' were Richard E. Caves (2000) and David Hesmondhalgh (2002).
6. See Niklas Luhmann (2013). Systems theory is an interdisciplinary field for the study of the nature of complex systems in nature, society, and science. More specifically, it is a framework by which one can analyze and/or describe any group of objects that work in concert to produce a certain state of affairs or specific result. It offers different models of causality and determination.
7. Elis Giardina Papa, 'need ideass!?!PLZ!!', <https://vimeo.com/27488845> (last accessed 3 January 2019).
8. 'Agnotology', Wikipedia (<https://en.wikipedia.org/wiki/Agnotology>) (last accessed 3 January 2019).
9. <https://en.wikipedia.org/wiki/Hito_Steyerl> (last accessed 7 April 2019).
10. 'The Documentary Impulse in the Arts': <http://www.columbia.edu/cu/arthistory/courses/spring-2018/graduate-courses.html>
11. Clement Greenberg first formulated his views in 'Avant-garde and Kitsch' (1939). A fuller statement of his Modernist views can be found in Clement Greenberg, *Art and Culture* (1961). For a critical assessment of his legacy, see Alice Goldfarb Marquis (2006), 7–9, 12–13.
12. Bazon Brock (*1936) <https://en.wikipedia.org/wiki/Bazon_Brock> (last accessed 7 April 2019).
13. See Bazon Brock, 'Kunst Machen? Selbstverwirklichung ist das Ideal von Vollidioten' (<https://bazonbrock.de/werke/detail/?id=250&sectid=727>) (last accessed 3 January 2019).
14. Brock's 'Etruscan Smile' is also known as the 'Archaic Smile': see Wikipedia (<https://en.wikipedia.org/wiki/Archaic_smile>) (last accessed 3 January 2019).
15. Philip Roth, 'In the Destructive Element Immerse …' <https://www.webofstories.com/play/philip.roth/126> (last accessed 7 April 2019).
16. Karl Marx, 'On the Question of Free Trade', speech delivered before the Democratic Association of Brussels on 9 January 1848. <https://en.wikisource.org/wiki/On_the_Question_of_Free_Trade> (last accessed 3 January 2019).
17. See Thomas Elsaesser (2015), especially Chapter 3 'The Politics and Poetics of Parapraxis: On Some Problems of Representation', pp. 94–114.

References

Adorno, Theodor W. (1997), *Aesthetic Theory*, trans. Robert Hullot-Kentor, Minneapolis: University of Minnesota Press.
Berlant, Lauren (2011), *Cruel Optimism*, Durham, NC: Duke University Press.
Blouin, Michael J. (2016), *Magical Thinking, Fantastic Film, and the Illusions of Neoliberalism*, New York: Palgrave Macmillan.
Bradley, Kimberley (2017), 'Hito Steyerl is an Artist with Power. She Uses it for Change', *New York Times*, December 15: <https://www.nytimes.com/2017/12/15/arts/design/hito-steyerl.html> (last accessed 7 April 2019).
Brock, Bazon (2002), *Der Barbar als Kulturheld*, Cologne: Dumont Literatur/Kunst Verlag.
Brown, Wendy (2015), *Undoing the Demos: Neoliberalism's Stealth Revolution*, New York: Zone Books.
Butler, Judith (2004), *Precarious Life: The Powers of Mourning and Violence*, London: Verso.
Caves, Richard E. (2000), *Creative Industries: Contracts between Art and Commerce* (Cambridge, MA: Harvard University Press).
Elsaesser, Thomas (1981), 'Vincente Minnelli', in Rick Altman (ed.), *Genre: The Musical*, London: Routledge/Kegan Paul, pp. 8–27.
Elsaesser, Thomas (2009), '*Sonnen-Insulaner*: On a Berlin Island of Memory', in Uta Staiger, Henriette Steiner and Andrew Webber (eds), *Memory Culture and the Contemporary City*, Basingstoke: Palgrave Macmillan, pp. 32–51.
Elsaesser, Thomas (2010), 'Berlin Isle de Memoire: Mediale Spuren einer Geschichte', in Simone Costagli and Matteo Galli (eds), *Deutsche Familienromane*, Munich: Wilhelm Fink, pp. 233–50.
Elsaesser, Thomas (2015), *German Cinema: Terror and Trauma*, New York: Routledge.
Elsaesser, Thomas (2016), 'The Global Author: Control Creative Constraints and Performative Self-Contradiction', in Seung-hoon Jeong and Jeremi Szaniawski (eds), *The Global Auteur: The Politics of Authorship in 21st Century Cinema*, London: Bloomsbury, pp. 21–42.
Elsaesser, Thomas (2019), 'The Home Movie as Essay Film: Making Memory Posthumously', in Julia Vassilieva and Deane Williams (eds), *Beyond the Essay Film*, Amsterdam: Amsterdam University Press.
Florida, Richard (2002), *The Rise of the Creative Class, and How It's Transforming Work, Leisure and Everyday Life*, New York: Basic Books.
Greenberg, Clement (1939), 'Avant-garde and Kitsch', *Partisan Review*, 6:5, 34–49.
Greenberg, Clement (1961), *Art and Culture*, Boston: Beacon Press.
Hesmondhalgh, David (2002), *The Cultural Industries*, London: Sage.
Heur, Bas van (2010), *Creative Networks and the City: Towards a Cultural Political Economy of Aesthetic Production*, Bielefeld: Transcript.
Jameson, Fredric (1981), '"In the Destructive Element Immerse": Hans-Jürgen Syberberg and Cultural Revolution', *October*, 17 (Summer), 99–118.
Latour, Bruno (2004), 'Why Has Critique Run out of Steam? From Matters of Fact to Matters of Concern', *Critical Inquiry*, 30:2 (Winter), 225–48.
Luhmann, Niklas (2013), *Introduction to Systems Theory*, London: Polity.
Mackay, Robin (ed.) (2014), *#ACCELERATE: The Accelerationist Reader*, London: Urbanomic.
Marquis, Alice Goldfarb (2006), *Art Czar: The Rise and Fall of Clement Greenberg*, Boston: MFA Publications.
Proctor, Robert N. and Londa Schiebinger (eds) (2008), *Agnotology: The Making and Unmaking of Ignorance*, Stanford: Stanford University Press.

Ray, Gene (2009), 'Towards A Critical Art Theory', in Gerald Raunig and Gene Ray (eds), *Art and Contemporary Critical Practice*, London: Mayfly Books.

Reckwitz, Andreas (2017), *The Invention of Creativity: Modern Society and the Culture of the New*, Hoboken, NJ: Wiley-Blackwell.

Srnicek, Nick and Alex Williams (2015), *Inventing the Future. Postcapitalism and a World without Work*, London: Verso Books.

Steyerl, Hito (2013), 'Aesthetics of Resistance? Artistic Research as Discipline and Conflict', Athens Biennale Agora (<http://athensbiennale.org/event-as-process/aesthetics-of-resistance-artistic-research-as-discipline-and-conflict/?from=ab4>)

Wollen, Peter (1972), 'The Auteur Theory', in *Signs and Meaning in the Cinema*, Bloomington: Indiana University Press, pp. 74–115.

5. TACTICAL COMPLIANCE AND THE PERSISTENCE OF ELSAESSER

William Brown

This essay considers Thomas Elsaesser's debut film, *Die Sonneninsel/The Sun Island* (Germany, 2017), in particular in light of the concept of 'tactical compliance', which Elsaesser himself developed during his keynote paper, reproduced herein, at the Creative Practice Research in the Age of Neoliberal Hopelessness Conference at the University of Bedfordshire on 11 May 2018.[1] The aim is to work through what tactical compliance might mean in the age of neoliberal hopelessness – and in some senses to take issue with the concept. I shall do this by situating *The Sun Island* within the context of Elsaesser's own theoretical work, in particular his understanding of the so-called *Persistence of Hollywood* (2012), which itself springs perhaps from his contribution to Vivian Sobchack's edited collection on *The Persistence of History* (1997). The aim is not to produce an *ad hominem* 'attack' on Elsaesser and his work, but to understand tactical compliance as a means towards persistence, while also relating persistence to systems of power. In other words, the ideas of Elsaesser will be linked to Elsaesser-as-idea (as author, as filmmaker), with no real concern for Elsaesser-as-man (if that is how he would define himself and/or if that is what Elsaesser is).

What follows will nonetheless seem to conflate the personal with the political because *The Sun Island* is in some senses a deeply personal film. The film is primarily about the rehabilitation of the reputation of the filmmaker's grandfather, Martin Elsaesser, an architect who played a significant role in the design of Frankfurt between 1925 and 1932, and whose most famous work, the city's Großmarkthalle, or Central Market, was to be destroyed to make way for the new headquarters of the European Central Bank in the first part of the twenty-first century. However, the film also is a consideration of the Elsaessers's family history – including perhaps most significantly the relationship between the filmmaker's grandmother, Liesel, and landscape designer Leberecht Migge. Migge, whom Elsaesser has referred to elsewhere as 'something like the Grandfather of the German Green movement' (Elsaesser 2009a: 47) is the person mainly responsible for the titular Sun Island, which started out in 1932 as a kind of project for sustainable living, where inhabitants would be able to survive without the interference of the modern world. In this sense, the island could even be read as a sort of utopian escape from the political turmoil that Germany was undergoing from the 1930s onwards, and during which time the bulk of the film's story takes place.

Indeed, Martin Elsaesser finds himself losing favour under National Socialism, while Migge also is something of an outsider as a result of the radical nature of his ideas of conservation, including the *Siedlung* or growing house that exists on the island. Migge then dies in 1935 while in Liesel's company, despite having a wife and eight children who live in Worpswede. When the war starts, Liesel is almost overwhelmed by the amount of work that is required to maintain Migge's project, but she gets help from Trudel, a young woman who eventually becomes the wife of Hans Peter Elsaesser, Martin and Liesel's son, and the filmmaker's father.

Not only is Hans Peter the filmmaker's father. In some senses, he is himself also the filmmaker since *The Sun Island* is comprised in large part of home movie footage shot by Hans Peter of life on the Sun Island and elsewhere. Thomas Elsaesser thus arranges the material, which also includes photographs, contemporary film footage and more, while giving to the film a voice-over that allows him to reflect semi-theoretically and semi-personally on events from the 1920s through the 1940s and up until the present day, where finally Martin Elsaesser's legacy is recognised, and a testament to the architect is created in the ECB building that stands on and incorporates some aspects of the earlier Central Market.

In a relatively simple fashion, *The Sun Island* is a campaign film that seeks to save Martin Elsaesser from oblivion and to restore to him a place in German history. More than this, the film is an exploration of the home movie archive, while also demonstrating how the Elsaesser family was connected via Migge to the incipient green movement. An essay-film and a documentary, the film equally explores Germany's history during the war, since while various members of the Elsaesser family served in the German military during the war (with two of Migge's sons joining the Nazi party before being killed on the Eastern Front in 1944), Trudel was also a half-Jewess (not devout), meaning that the film in some senses is also (or could lay claim to being) about the saving of Jews during the war. Finally, the film is very clearly a treatment of family and the role that images can play in creating a sense of family, lending to the film a tinge of melodrama that at no point is forced upon the viewer.

In fact, the film seeks at all points in time to force as little on the viewer as possible, with the filmmaker's position often seeming absent, in spite of the seemingly personal nature of the film, and in spite of the filmmaker's own voice being that which we hear most on the soundtrack, with the filmmaker also occasionally appearing on the image track, for example to wander around the Sun Island today, placing his hands on a dilapidated building in order to feel the history of this *lieu de mémoire*. Indeed, the film seems to want to be deliberately ambiguous, with Elsaesser during his keynote claiming that he wants audiences, insofar as they are willing, to 'make their own film out of mine' (see this volume p. 66). And yet, *The Sun Island* also takes care to maintain within it claims to dealing with all of the major issues of German history and the global present in a politically correct fashion: ecology, architecture, war, Holocaust, history, family and more. In some senses this makes the film fascinating. But in other senses, it seems that the film wants to be the sort of documentary equivalent of the access-for-all blockbuster that Elsaesser feels is characteristic of contemporary Hollywood: deliberately ambiguous, it can be understood and taken in many different ways in a bid to reach as wide an audience as possible. Or, put in terms that are less compliant, it says everything, but ultimately it means nothing. This ability to have no properly identifiable position on anything, and yet to be able to make reference to it all, is what Elsaesser (2012) characterises as one of the key aspects of *the persistence of Hollywood*.

The Sun Island is clearly not a Hollywood blockbuster, but we shall return later to what it is – and how this relates to tactical compliance as we are yet to develop it.[2] For the time being, though, we might read the film against another piece of Elsaesser's work that is framed not by the persistence of Hollywood, but by the persistence of history in cinema, namely his essay in Vivian Sobchack's edited collection of the same name. In that (typically wide-ranging) essay, Elsaesser (1997) explores the treatment of the Second World War by post-war European filmmakers, taking in a range of ideas that might help us to understand *The Sun Island*. First, the film is in some sense an example of what Elsaesser refers to as *Alltagsgeschichte*, or the 'history of everyday life', in that the film records and reports the lives of relatively common folk (the Elsaesser family is *bourgeois*) over an extended period of time (Elsaesser 1997: 159). Here, 'Nazism ... [is] a daily reality', as opposed to a subject that has to be treated with any sense of hysteria or melodrama (Elsaesser 1997: 160). Quoting Martin Broszat, Elsaesser says that the genre functions as a means for Germans 'to be able to talk about the "Third Reich" as "the German people's own history" and thus for individuals to take responsibility for what had occurred' (Elsaesser 1997: 160). In this way, the genre is considered in relation to the war to be 'apologetic in tendency if not intent' (Elsaesser 1997: 160). That is, the *Alltagsgeschichte* normalises Nazism, offering an apology for it in the sense of a defence or an excuse rather than in the sense of saying sorry for taking part in it (Nazism was everyday reality and so of course everyday people got caught up in it). Given that the Elsaesser family connections with Nazism are glossed over without much investigation or comment, there is a loose sense in which *The Sun Island* might also contain elements of this genre.

Earlier in the essay, Elsaesser invokes Jean Baudrillard to suggest that the German 'retro-cinema' of the 1970s and 1980s that looked back at the war can be explained as follows: '[t]he attraction of a return to history as story and image was the illusion it could give of a personal or national destiny: a need fascism had tried to gratify on a collective scale' (Elsaesser 1997: 155). In other words, the desire to mine one's own history involves an attempt to give meaning to one's life (to give it a destiny), a tendency for desiring meaning that fascism itself has so skilfully explored. Indeed, the perceived 'affinity between fascism and show business' (Elsaesser 1997: 151) functions as an ongoing thread throughout Elsaesser's essay, which soon turns its attention to Steven Spielberg's *Schindler's List* (USA, 1993), which was critiqued by Claude Lanzmann, among others, for offering a sentimentalised, middle-of-the-road and typically American perspective on the Holocaust. Why should the middle-of-the-road nature of the film be surprising, though, Elsaesser asks, before going on to suggest that Spielberg chooses 'for the cinema and its history: whether this makes him a postmodernist, and whether a postmodern stance makes him necessarily either morally or historically irresponsible towards the Holocaust, is a point worth pondering' (Elsaesser 1997: 163). But either way, Spielberg has a 'typically postmodern hubris, namely the faith that the cinema can redeem the past, rescue the real, and even rescue that which was never real' (Elsaesser 1997: 166) – a perspective wholly different to that of Lanzmann, who has signally more modernist tendencies.

Perhaps one can see where I am going with this. Hans Peter and Thomas Elsaesser alike document their family in a bid to redeem the past, to rescue the real and perhaps even to rescue that which was never real, namely an island of sun during times of darkness. Perhaps this is because instead of telling a story, 'an activity closer to therapeutic practice has taken over, with acts of re-telling, re-membering, and repeating all pointing in the direction of obsession fantasy, trauma' (Elsaesser 1997: 146). But what is the trauma (or the obsession fantasy) that the Elsaesser family has suffered? Might it be the trauma of having been, like Martin Elsaesser, left out of history? But what is that history? That under a different regime, the genius of Martin Elsaesser would have been recognised? But this is history as a counter-factual, the rescue of a past that was never real. For what really happened is that, in however banal a fashion, Martin Elsaesser donned the uniform of the German army and played his part in the war. As a result, 'Germany appears a nation of victims' (Elsaesser 1997: 171), with the attempt to rescue Martin Elsaesser from the dustbin of history leading to the realisation that, in a kind of strange inversion of what happens when Elsaesser watches *Mr. Klein* (Joseph Losey, France/Italy, 1976), one wants to rescue all Germans from the inescapable past: 'we are shattered by the knowledge of our total impotence; but which is also the knowledge of our own collusion and complicity' (Elsaesser 1997: 175).

Surely to elicit such a complex set of reactions makes of Elsaesser's film an astonishing piece of work. Nonetheless, there is more for us to consider, including in particular how the filmmaker achieves this. Also, in the persistence of history essay, Elsaesser speaks of 'the 'political unconsciousness' of a popular text that by definition exceeds the control of the maker and which becomes a cultural or historical fact precisely because of this excess' (Elsaesser 1997: 168). In its deliberate ambiguity – in its access-for-all nature – does the film exceed the control of the maker, or is the excess of control performed (the ambiguity is deliberate), and yet which performance masks another excess, which is the understated presence of a fascism with which the Elsaesser family was at least tactically compliant, if not outright collusive/complicit?

Thomas Elsaesser himself evoked in the Bedfordshire discussion of *The Sun Island* how he felt he was tactically compliant with those who commissioned and who worked with him on its making. That is, while Elsaesser had his own ideas about the film that he wanted to make, he could not make the film in exactly the way that he wanted – and that his film was stronger as a result of this. That is, for Elsaesser tactical compliance with the powers that be led to a film that got to be screened on German television, played at various festivals around the world, and which continues to get played at campuses in many places (perhaps as a result of Elsaesser's formidable reputation as a film scholar). In other words, while a documentary, it was by adopting the relatively mainstream aesthetics of the access-for-all work that the film was, or has been, validated. Success in the attention economy, then, is the criterion according to which Elsaesser defines success as a filmmaker. Compliance with (relatively) mainstream aesthetics (not least through the use of an authoritative, masculine voice-over) leads to mainstream results. A middle-of-the-road and accessible aesthetic is necessary to convince viewers that cinema can redeem history, including a history that never was. It is this that allows history to persist. It is this that allows Hollywood to persist. And it is this that allows Elsaesser to persist – since Hollywood is history and history is Hollywood, and if Elsaesser can make himself Hollywood, then he writes himself and his grandfather (back) into history, and only tactical compliance can achieve this.

When discussing the film at a screening at the University of Southern California in April 2018, interviewer Michael Renov pointed out how Elsaesser is almost a Zelig-like figure due to his and his family's capacity to be at the centre of history (the family past on the Sun Island, with the filmmaker also being in Paris during 1968, the west coast of the USA during the counterculture of the 1970s and more). Indeed, Elsaesser has himself addressed how he happens almost accidentally to have persisted as part of the history of film studies when he says that 'you can do quite well, it seems, by repeating your mistakes, provided you persist with them long enough' (Elsaesser 2009b: 123). The desire to inscribe oneself in history, even if it means floating Zelig-like on its waves, never quite having a proper identity for oneself, an absence of self that perhaps also is an originary trauma that compels one to make cinema and to write history ... perhaps signals history as precisely a history of blank, Zelig-like men who celebrate themselves while around them others live and die in their efforts genuinely to achieve a position, or as a result of having a position and an identity imposed upon them (the sense of envy that at least Jews have the Holocaust to help define them), the primary narcissism when someone else gains attention and not oneself, the desire to have said everything, to create and to become the walking equivalent of an access-for-all cinema; in Elsaesser's own words, recognition 'soothes the worry that what one has done doesn't really amount to much; it soothes the worry that what one is personally most proud of has gone unnoticed or unrecognized; and ... is a wonderful plaster on the narcissistic wound and a palliative for any soul not immune to self-doubt' (Elsaesser 2009b: 121); furthermore, Elsaesser – of course! – has also anticipated and thus in some senses already made his own counter-argument when he implores scholars not to 'put us on a pedestal; try occasionally also to push us off the pedestal' (Elsaesser 2009b: 127).[3]

To be clear: the above paragraph is not a psychoanalysis of a human being whom I do not know well, with whom I have had some arguments, but who on the whole I find generous, intellectually curious, and good-humoured (by which I mean that he has had the good taste to laugh at at least a couple of the jokes that I have made in his presence, while also offering generous feedback on and engagement with a proof version of this very piece of writing). But let us run with the metaphor of Zelig as read through tactical compliance. And then let us think about what this does or can mean in the contemporary context of neoliberal hopelessness.

Elsaesser proposes that tactical compliance is a proposed way out of neoliberal hopelessness, since, in reference to the filmmaker as *auteur*, he or she 'draws strength, persistence and inspiration from the very constraints that the system – in this case, the Hollywood studio system – imposes on him or her' (see this volume p. 58). It is, he continues, akin to wearing what art critic Bazon Brock terms an *Etruscan smile*: 'it is a positive agreement with the forces that seem to determine one's fate, because these forces invariably reveal themselves as either inherently antagonistic, and therefore full of interstitial spaces of freedom and agency, or they are so chaotic and contingent that riding them

– rather than resisting them – generates new energies and open paths that lead to surprising discoveries' (see this volume p. 61). However, if for Elsaesser-as-filmmaker, tactical compliance, after initial resistance to commercial and other pressures, means 'letting the parapraxes of the creative process impinge more on my work', he is not here talking specifically about allowing his film to include the kind of 'beautiful accidents' that Orson Welles describes as being central to cinema in *Filming Othello* (West Germany, 1978) (for more on this, see Brown 2018: 147–8). And when Elsaesser describes 'external constraints as an invitation for tactical compliance' (see this volume pp. 66–7), he is not just talking about the way in which Lars von Trier sets creative and technical challenges for Jørgen Leth to work around in *De fem benspænd/The Five Obstructions* (Denmark/Switzerland/Belgium/France, 2003). For, he is also suggesting that one complies not with contingency, but with capital, and that one complies not with chance, but with systems of control. The Etruscan may smile at the perversity of fate; but if the control society makes her smile while eating shit, then what sort of Etruscan smile is that really?

Indeed, to smile while eating shit (to be tactically compliant with the neoliberalisation, with its attendant phenomena of fear, precarity, overwork, and a general reduction of enjoyment for the purposes of work) is not particularly palatable – even if the image evokes Pier Paolo Pasolini's *Salò o le 120 giornate di Sodoma/Salò, or the 120 Days of Sodom* (Italy/France, 1975), a film that fits into Elsaesser's schema of a Baudrillardian cinema that uses the fascism of cinema against itself. Using the fascism of cinema against itself may be precisely what Elsaesser means by tactical compliance. But in writing this essay, I do not feel that I am undertaking tactical compliance with those who want to make me eat shit. I am, rather, directly confronting them with the violence of my language and imagery, trying *à la* Pasolini and not so much *à la* Elsaesser and middle-of-the-road/access-for-all film aesthetics to make my shitty message palatable – precisely because it should not be, and shit should be called out as shit, not polished and dressed up as *haute cuisine*. What is more, it does not seem that tactical compliance with neoliberal capital will redeem me in any way; it takes my blood, sweat and tears, my life force, and has no interest in giving back to me. On the contrary, it seeks to make me not feel safe or protected, but precarious and in danger – for the purposes of making me work ever-harder in a fearful fashion, aspects of contemporary life to which Elsaesser himself made reference in his keynote address. Tactical compliance might work if it were precisely that: com-pliant. Which is to say that it might work if it involved capital adapting to me as much as it involves me adapting to capital. But rarely if at all does capital seem to accommodate me (this is not about money; I am made persistently to feel shit about myself regardless of my relatively comfortable material existence, while also being told to feel lucky that I have a job); if I do not accommodate it, it will simply discard me and that is that. I will lead a bare life on the outside, abjected and forgotten (my relatively comfortable material existence could be taken away at any instant).

But perhaps this is precisely the point of my interest in an aesthetics of so-called non-cinema, in which abjection and the obscure are not brought into the light as is Martin Elsaesser, but instead remain precisely in the darkness, both because the darkness is a more powerful force than the light (the light suffers from the illusion that it does not need the darkness, but it does) and so as not to destroy the very darkness that constitutes its being. Rather than become light by becoming cinema, I wish to explore how my desire to become light is a shameful denial of the darkness that I know lies within me. This, to me, seems a more honest way of living: it is to recognise my propensity for and attraction towards fascism in a bid to rise above it and not to indulge it, rather than flatly to deny it in the self-promotional cacophony of the contemporary world.[4] But to admit to failings and to failure (to admit to the potential for fascism within oneself), even if in a *de facto* performative fashion (but what else is there other than performance?), is to resist rather than to be compliant with neoliberal capital.

I wrote once that Steven Spielberg might possibly be understood against himself as a kind of Lorenzaccio figure. In Alfred de Musset's 1834 play of the same name, Lorenzino de Medici becomes complicit with the ruling tyrant, his cousin Alessandro, so as to get close enough to him to kill him. Lorenzo understands that in doing so, no one will believe that he really is a rebel deep inside (see Brown 2009). But this is a sacrifice that he is willing to make in order to topple Alessandro. Similarly, then, Spielberg might be some sort of accelerationist filmmaker who is speeding up the train of capital in order to derail it, a trope drawn not from Spielberg but rather from the film *Speed* (Jan de Bont, USA, 1994). I am not sure that I buy this possible case of tactical compliance, not least after seeing the shimmering shit that was *Ready Player One* (USA, 2018), in which we do not see acceleration used to derail the train, but rather in which the reverse gear is used in order to keep the train running – even if the film gestures at some anti-corporate rhetoric based on the fandom of highly mainstream items that have long since been marketed as 'cult' for the purposes of interpellating those fans into endless nostalgia reboots.

What is more, I have also spent a whole monograph arguing that one can get philosophically progressive ideas out of mainstream Hollywood blockbusters (see Brown 2013). But giving mainstream cinema its due (or at least to recognise its potential for resistance, as opposed to its persistence) was only ever (or so I say) then to flip our considerations of cinema in the digital era and to argue that so-called 'non-cinema' is not only the equal to cinema, but perhaps also its superior (see Brown 2018). For, to invoke another couple of films mentioned in Elsaesser's history essay, I am well aware that if one spends too long among the mainstreamers, then one can like Marcello Clerici (Jean-Louis Trintignant) and

Lucien Lacombe (Pierre Blaise), respectively the anti-heroes of *Il Conformista/ The Conformist* (Bernardo Bertolucci, Italy/France/West Germany, 1970) and *Lacombe, Lucien* (Louis Malle, France/Italy/West Germany, 1974), simply become seduced by fascism. Give to me that outrageous and liberatingly offensive film work of Christoph Schlingensief.

I am stupid. I read slowly. I get things wrong the whole time. I am terrible at relationships. I am self-absorbed. I crave attention. I am lazy. I am exploitative. And more. It may be that I need the Holocaust. Indeed, to confess tactical compliance, or to be Zelig-like, is perhaps simply an act of honesty. I know that I do not in my heart of hearts do enough to help my fellow humans to free them from the yoke of capitalism, while also living off many of the comforts that the capitalist world affords (including, for example, being able to travel from London to Los Angeles and by extension to attend a screening of *The Sun Island* at USC – the carbon footprint of which journey alone makes it questionable). What is more, I know full well that I suffer from a deep narcissism that wants attention and for myself to be inscribed into history, and which drives me to work in a Stakhanovite fashion since this quasi-accelerationist (and thus compliant – as Elsaesser also suggests!) policy is my personal way of resisting (I'll give you more productivity than you can or will want). So on one level, we must recognise the already-existing nature of tactical compliance if we are to progress.

Nonetheless, I say such personal things because to the best of my stupid understanding, the resistance has to start with the self, within the self, perhaps even against the concept of the self – as Elsaesser perhaps implies when he talks of 'the perpetual plea bargaining between me and myself' (Elsaesser 2009b: 121). One has to divide oneself, to find the many selves that lie within the otherwise supposedly unified subject. I have then to put my selves to work – to bring all of my selves into what it is that I do. I have to make personal my life, to have my selves resound through my whole existence in order to be a per-son (so-called because of the sound/*son* that comes through/*per* the mask). Not to be a person only some of the time – that is when not at work (which in this day and age is when?). To be a person all of the time (perhaps especially when at work).

Elsaesser has made a personal film that in some ways is very beautiful. But through tactical compliance, it also becomes an oddly impersonal film about a very personal topic. As Agnieszka Piotrowska asked at the conference, what does the filmmaker himself feel about any or all of this? Clearly something because he is making the film. And clearly something because he is making the film to rehabilitate the reputation of his grandfather. There is a kind of love here – and it is certainly not my place to demand that love only take on a form that I can recognise. But at the same time, the film hides more than it reveals.

In our performatively confessional culture, to reveal oneself might well be perceived as a means to attract attention, to become light and to put oneself forward for surveillance, and thus to play into the hands of neoliberal capital's attention economy. Nonetheless, many such performances are insincere, disingenuous and done for the purposes of garnering and maintaining attention. They seek to live forever. But to disavow the pull of immortality is surely also to be insincere. Is the trick not as consciously as one can to confess not one's sins, but one's attraction towards confession? Is to achieve atheism not to address one's need for god? And is to know god not to confess to her that one does not believe in her?

'[T]he crimes named by Nazism and the Holocaust cannot possibly be "our" history, just as it need not only be "our" testimony or mourning work. Therein lies a hope, but also an obligation' (Elsaesser 1997: 179). Perhaps Elsaesser bravely does not claim as 'his' one history that is not 'his' to claim – although since the film is about the rehabilitation of Martin Elsaesser, this suggestion seems hard to uphold. Indeed, perhaps the filmmaker also denies a history that we might hope is his obligation to address. In the age of neoliberal hopelessness, perhaps it is our obligation to essay towards making the conditions for new hope – even if one is quixotically on a course towards failure. Perhaps we must see giants where there are windmills and tilt madly towards them. Perhaps it is only a kind of *amour fou* – madness as love – that will allow us to hope for a better, different world. Tactically to be compliant with it (not least if compliance really results not in mutual bending, but in implication) is to play its own game, aesthetically and politically. Perhaps now is the time to be mad and to go mad. To fail and to fall outside, or to be abjected from the inhuman world in order to find a more personal engagement with the world in a minor fashion that will be neglected, will die, will not be commemorated, but which will humbly feed back into the humus that feeds all life. Not to become light, but to become dirt. Not to slide along with neoliberal capital in a tactically compliant fashion, but strategically to experience the erotics of erosion as one resists and grinds oneself down against it (to be more like Liesel Elsaesser than like Martin, whom Thomas Elsaesser can claim is thus embodying such an attitude in his access-for-all film, even as she is not front-and-centre and as Martin is the main focus of the film's narrative?). To lead such a life may not be cinema or cinematic, but it is to give to one's life a project, or to create a life's work, to make of oneself dust that will breed yet more life. To be a human rather than to be an image – at a time when our students are calling out for human connections even as they are interpellated into the attention economy of the image society. Perhaps resistance is not to seek to live forever or to be commemorated in (phallic) light (to be placed on a pedestal), but rather to accept death, to absent oneself from life. To ex-ist rather than to per-sist. Perhaps to exist is the new hope that can be found in this otherwise persistent age of neoliberal hopelessness.

Notes

1. This essay is a partial reproduction of a report on Creative Practice Research in the Age of Neoliberal Hopelessness published in *Cinema: Journal of Philosophy and the Moving Image* (see Brown 2019). Many thanks to Sérgio Dias Branco and Susana Viegas, the editors of *Cinema*, for allowing us to reproduce the essay here. Thanks also should be reiterated towards Thomas Elsaesser and Agnieszka Piotrowska for their help and support.
2. Elsaesser describes how 'without me fully realizing it at the time, there was considerable evidence of Elsaesser, the author of books on Weimar Cinema and Expressionist films, and Elsaesser, the writer about Hollywood mind-game films, time travel and other cinematic thought experiments [in an early version of the film]: in short, it was more *Shutter Island* [Martin Scorsese, USA, 2010] than *Sun Island*' (see this volume p. 48). Perhaps the final version went more in the direction of *Avatar* (James Cameron, USA, 2009) than *Shutter Island*!
3. There is an ambiguity here between Elsaesser having simply been the beneficiary of what he terms the 'parapraxes' of history and the 'narcissism' to which he also makes reference. Note that he only asks scholars to *try* to knock him and his fellows from their SCMS-created pedestal (Elsaesser places himself alongside Laura Mulvey, Robin Wood, Noël Burch, Stuart Hall and Richard Dyer). Either he does not really want it to happen, or he believes that it is not really possible ...
4. It is perhaps telling that in 2000 I made a short film called *The Hitler*, which is about a young WW2 obsessive who wakes up one morning to discover that the war never took place and that Hitler was instead a celebrated artist; unable to cope with this alternative reality, the main character becomes Hitler so as to bring this alternate reality in line with the history that he has only otherwise known.

References

Brown, William (2009), 'It's a shark-eat-shark world: the ambiguous politics of Steven Spielberg', *New Review of Film and Television Studies*, 7:1, 13–22.

Brown, William (2013), *Supercinema: Film-Philosophy for the Digital Age*, Oxford: Berghahn.

Brown, William (2018), *Non-Cinema: Global Digital Filmmaking and the Multitude*, London: Bloomsbury.

Brown, William (2019), 'Notes on Creative Practice Research in the Age of Neoliberal Hopelessness, University of Bedfordshire, UK, 10–12 May 2018', *Cinema: Journal of Philosophy and the Moving Image*, 10, pp. 199–218.

Elsaesser, Thomas (1997), 'Subject Positions, Speaking Positions: From *Holocaust*, *Our Hitler* and *Heimat* to *Shoah* and *Schindler's List*', in Vivan Sobchack (ed.), *The Persistence of History: Cinema, Television, and the Modern Event*, London: Routledge, pp. 145–84.

Elsaesser, Thomas (2009a), '*Sonnen-Insulaner*: On a Berlin Island of Memory,' in Uta Staiger, Henriette Steiner and Andrew Webber (eds), *Memory Culture and the Contemporary City*, Basingstoke: Palgrave Macmillan, pp. 32–51.

Elsaesser, Thomas (2009b), 'Stepping Sideways: SCMS Lifetime Membership Address, March 6, 2008, Philadelphia, PA', *Cinema Journal*, 49:1, 121–7.

Elsaesser, Thomas (2012), *The Persistence of Hollywood: From Cinephile Moments to Blockbuster Memories*, London: Routledge.

6. STORYTELLING AND GAME PLAYING

Alexis Weedon[1]

I am thinking there is an opportunity for a new game. It is the TEF wars. It runs like this: pick a character, a bouncy Mario-style avatar of a university of your choice. At level 1 your goal is to pick up as many NSS points as you can. However, you cannot hold them all in your backpack if you have too many REF stars. Even so you need REF stars to get you through the QAA hoops, because only they can give you that extra jump height and agility. Other avatars seek to steal your REF stars and shorten the life of your NSS points. But you can win or steal armour from the competing avatars too. If you have many REF stars you can join in a tribe. Joining a tribe gives you access to gold and dark matter which can increase your resilience and you are less likely to die. At all times you are seeking to protect, train and grow your Tneduts, Tneduts give you life, nutrition and NSS stars. You must give them tools, spells and increase their magic powers. You and your Tneduts lives are linked. If you thrive they do too. When they are trained as wizards they go out into Krow, and you get a life boost. When they are happy in Krow, they gain star dust for themselves and for you.

Once you have achieved level 1, you need to change your game strategy for level 2. You need to collect Measures, these come in different forms, but regularly mutate. Some contain hexes, so be careful, they can freeze you and lay you open to attack. If you are lucky you will have enough to NSS points to convert to TEF stars. If you are in the same tribe TEF and REF stars combine in a shield wall that is unbreakable except by Hegemony. If you spend too much time obtaining Measures, you will drop your REF stars and lose TEF points.

Once you have gained enough star dust, spells and the right Measures – not the hexes – you progress to level 3.

Your task at level 3 is to change Hegemony. This is risky as Hegemony holds all the Measures. So you need to capture some hexes without them damaging you. You will need to power up your TEF and REF stars to ignite the transforming cauldron. Once caught and cast into the cauldron, hexes' negative power is reversed and they become Measures of your choosing. You may choose to become Hegemony, and play the game for longer battling the other tribes or you may ChangeTheGame. If you CTG your Tneduts in Krow will send you stardust and you will win.

Introduction

As Game Studies was finding its feet in the early millennium, we offered a forum through the series of 'Under the Mask: Perspectives on the Gamer' conferences (2007–12). The intervention was to shift the focus of research from studying the artefact onto the player. The conferences caught the intellectual need of the moment and a great deal of good research emerged. I and my colleagues benefited: I as co-editor of the journal *Convergence: The International Journal of Research into New Media Technologies* on the look-out for rich veins of new research in the cultural changes brought about by the revolution in technologies of communication we are living through; my colleagues Dr Gavin Stewart, Dr Steve Conway who were the conveners of the conference in finding a community of researchers, developing new ideas resulting in publications and curriculum innovation and ultimately benefiting in their subsequent careers. While the debate over whether games should be studied as narratives or whether they required a different approach which recognised the player's active participation (Ludology vs Narratology) has largely been resolved with the recognition of the attraction of storytelling in many games, game studies as it developed has come to provide us with profound insights into how play fits us for the complexities of everyday life.

As an event and an intervention it has much in common with the Creative Practice Research in the Age of Neoliberal Hopelessness conference (May 2018). In both cases there was a challenge to orthodoxy which brought together researchers who shared a common concern that here was an area of knowledge production which was not recognised. The conference convened by Agnieszka Piotrowska hit the moment and united a diversity of academics who were troubled by the role of creative practice in the time of research audit. Whether or not delegates knew it, it too was part of a longer debate, traceable back to the move in 1992 to redress the hegemony of the University sector and consider the research qualifications of other institutions delivering tertiary education. At the time such institutions made the case and won the argument:

they became universities, passing a rigorous standard of research output and infrastructure for support. Art colleges, conservatoires, polytechnics hitherto outside the University sector were now embraced. Was this a result of a fundamental change in the way we viewed the production of knowledge? Was the output of the personal, creative, inspirational artist new knowledge in the way teams of geneticists isolated and identified segments of the human genome? Ostensibly yes, but subsequent forms of research auditing from the Research Assessment Exercise to the Research Excellence Framework have perpetuated the division.

Auditing ascribes a value to research, and that, if viewed through Marxist economics, may be an exchange value, price or utility. Simplistically we may see the move to assess research impact as a correlation to utility, exchange value to the relative position of one University and Unit of Assessment to another, and price to the funding council's linked decisions financial allocations. Thus research is objectified, commodified and this audit becomes a measure of competency. Yet the auditing function, painful or downright wrong as you may see it, assigns a value to the quality of research outputs not only the quantity and we as academics assess that quality. If not you and I, then those we ask to serve for us on the Panels and Subpanels. It is a tool for the division of research funding from the government and for the evaluation of British University's reputation at home and abroad. I believe some periodic reassessment is necessary, as it is our only mechanism for reflecting the evolving ecologies of Universities and voicing and listening to those narratives of change. It is important to remember that it is a system we as a body of academics have endorsed and it runs only because we want to tell our stories and play the game.

The gamification of the research evaluation exercise caused concerns in the REF2014 because of the trade in academics and their commodities just before the REF deadline. But gamification has not been decreased by the implementation of the Stern report, it has simply made the game more complex through codes of practice for inclusion or exclusion of staff, through redrawing UoA boundaries, and through increasing the significance of impact. Wherever there is measurement there can be gamification, whether it is the REF, TEF or KEF. In 2015 I proposed the game outline printed above to display the effect of the newly announced TEF impact on the REF (and also because humour was my way of recognising and dealing with the new burden of assessment). My original version had the character dying, but feedback was strongly against that. There had to be a way to win. The game scenario has a story. It recognises certain values as in the lecturer-players' commitment to educating and developing students, and it exposes the competition between the attainment of teaching excellence and research excellence. More serious and deeper stories are now being written about our research for the REF templates: stories of impact and environment in which we portray ourselves and our colleagues in a *mis en scène*. Undoubtedly there is something unifying in the way we tell theses stories of common themes, nurturing our students and ECRs and how this reflects our institutional values. Reading the REF2014 templates it is easy to see the commonalities, but the distinctions are important and we need to listen to these stories of transformation and change in the research ecologies of Universities.

Yet both game playing and storytelling have negative connotations: playing a game is fake reality; storytelling is making-it-up and it is a commonplace belief that it is something we do in childhood and grow out of. In this chapter I want to move away from the immediate discussion of the REF to a wider consideration of the importance of storytelling as a cultural means of the transmission of knowledge. Storytelling is not confined to print culture, indeed it has earlier roots in oral ones. Humanities research tells us that storytelling is ubiquitous across all human cultures and times. Even today as researchers, colleagues, neighbours, parents, we tell stories to communicate our knowledge insights and shape the forms of thought in others. Such stories have power beyond the mere statement of fact.

Storyteller and Storytelling

Our innate desire for stories and the psychological and social benefits of fiction have been the subject of scientific inquiry and experiment (László 2008; Oatley 2011; Hsu 2008; and many others). In childhood stories form the brain and neural paths; they are a way of making sense of and connecting disparate events. Our brain grows to recognise story patterns like facial recognition. Importantly each generation learns *how* its society tells stories and storytelling changes as a cultural practice as the needs of our culture and society change. The greatest impact of story is in imagining and experiencing life outside our everyday physicality.

Storytelling is a folk art, driven by popular participation which surfaces particular concerns of the time, while also renewing the perennial of bonds of society. Stories, and particularly fables, myths and folk tales have been studied by leading structuralists for insights into their function within societies. The question of what knowledge they contain and how they transmit it exercised the leading minds of Vladimir Propp, the folklorist, who identified and enumerated generic components of Russian folk tales and Claude Lévi-Strauss, the French anthropologist and ethnologist who analysed myths for their underlying and recurrent patterns of thought, for example. Such stories codify expectations of societal behaviours such as family and tribal allegiances, as well as depicting life journeys and through their performivity in rites of passage ensure psychological well-being. Such scholarship sought to discover the enduring structures of story whatever the medium. But how the communication of knowledge through storytelling has changed and in what medium matters too. When oral traditions documented by scribes gave way to authorship of the written text, the dissemination of knowledge became by way of print (Roberts 2010; Gadd 2010). As media scholars have noted, the printing press was the dominant means of distribution until the electronic age (Innis 1950; Williams 1965; McLuhan 1965). Nevertheless, vestiges of orality remained in habits of reading aloud, private and public performance and in the electronic age, on radio, film and thence to online media. Print culture which was so dominant has shifted to accommodate these new modes of storytelling. Information and knowledge has been accumulated, organised, verified, commodified and communicated by all these media.

It is only quite recently that the terms storytelling and storyteller have diverged (Weedon 2018). Significantly *telling* trailed the *teller* until 1982–3 when *telling* became the more commonly used term in the Google text Corpus. The trajectory of divergence becomes significant from 1992 when storytelling becomes much more widely used. While storytelling has a longer history than I have presented here, we can trace the origins of many of the commercial and cultural practices recognisable today to the early twentieth century. Self-designated storytellers of this period, that is authors, playwrights, scriptwriters, etc. who used the term about themselves, consciously made the distinction between storytelling as an activity and the medium. The story may hold the information, but it takes a storyteller to communicate knowledge (the information rendered useful by learning and experience). At this time we also see the rise of brands and trademarking begun by the adverting company James Walter Thompson Ltd. In the 1930s, Napoleon Hill's study of Andrew Carnegie extended this to the notion of personal branding (Hill 1937). Some authors such as Elinor Glyn embraced this new commercialism, endorsing beauty products as a means to keep their name and image in the media as well as an extra source of income (Barnett and Weedon 2014). Thus there is a coincidence of timing between this observed rise in the frequency of the word *story* and the rise of brands. Today, of course, brand storytelling is recognised as a powerful technique in advertising to promote loyalty and forge a relationship with customers beyond the mere use-value of the product or service.

Storytelling in the 1920s extended from domestic or theatrical performance of oral recitation onto the new media of radio.[2] The record of the change is captured in the new radio listings column within the newspapers. Mass Observation and Reading Experience Database have evidence that the practice of reading aloud did not die out with silent reading but was continued as a separate social practice and etiquette manuals show that developing a good voice and delivery which held your audience in rapt concentration was a social skill to be perfected (Post 1922; Glyn 1916). With the advent of radio the intimacy of reading aloud in the family circle or the pub became something which could be accessed by strangers at greater distance. For Benedict Anderson this is part of the 'imagined community' arising from print capitalism, giving rise to national identities, though in my reading, the community, even at this stage, is more like a social network as individuals seek those with similar tastes (Anderson 1983). Detractors of radio pointed to changes in behaviour perceived to be dangerous and of digests of information delivered on air (Goodman 2010). For us these criticisms of 'fast' information or communication with your remote social network while present in another gathering seem familiar.

In the new millennium the term retains its oral-folk origins but has mutated into different publishing sectors: in business storytelling shapes brands and is a tool for organisational change; in education and experiential learning it engages and transforms students; in law it analyses evidence and proof; in psychology it is the narration of our identity. Yet it is predominantly applied to the creativity of digital media: in radio, filmmaking, journalism, animation, visual media and creative and non-fiction writing, titles abound in describing the techniques of storytelling. In fiction it has been extended into the new media through IF (interactive fiction), book apps and game-books of various sorts. Vertical integration of media companies and digital convergence has enlarged the potential for storytelling. Now the use of the term has been extended into 'digital storytelling practice' and today the term is applied to transmedial and cross-medial storymaking linked to the globalisation of brands and the growth of franchises. For such brands the importance of story*telling* has overtaken the importance of the story*teller*. Like journalists threatened by the rise of citizen journalism, some designers have sought to reflect on what the professional designer can offer over and above the storygathering technology now makes easy (Lugmayr et al. 2017). In film, as Kathryn Millard pointed out in 2014, 'studios increasingly purchase ... intellectual property in the form of television series, comics, books, games, blogs, graphic novels and toys. They buy up these for exploitation across a variety of platforms' (p. 4). Nevertheless, the author retains the important role of maintaining coherence. Millard (2014: 179) adds: 'In this environment, a single high-profile author is seen as a guarantee of quality across the various elements of a transmedia project.'

Today society in the West has problematised the authenticity of the self on television and social media platforms and problematised our own provenance in the traces and trails of our digital identity. The multimodal social roles we have leads to the fragmentation of forms of address. Our media storytelling, particularly those offering a choice of protagonist, or alternative storylines reflect these realities and has changed as a cultural practice. In 1995 Nicholas Negroponte told us that by *Being Digital* we could embrace communication across distance, time and through multiple channels and with infinite ability to recombine, remix and preserve the original. He wasn't entirely right – there is degradation even when duplicating a digital original – but the potential for the editing of diced digital information has led to questions about the relevance of our notions of intellectual property, copyright and the curation of information. As we move into an age where the algorithms of AI take over the functions of selection and combination, preservation and maintenance, we find that writing, editing, publishing is far more than curation. It requires the ability to listen to stories in society and react to them. Algorithms can do this, but eventually they produce stale goods, so we value the revitalising human qualities of prehension, risk-taking and trust.

Storytelling, Play and Games

Walter Ong reminds us that storytellers do not have to be readers (Ong 1982). Orality has its own characteristics of aggregation, homostatis, redundancy. It is agonistic and concrete rather than abstract. Many of these qualities in stories have been lost through the dominance of print culture but new media forms of storytelling have invoked 'the large number of related existing literacies that can be identified in the digital age, such as news literacy, television literacy, film literacy, computer literacy, Internet literacy and digital literacy, as well as other emerging concepts like social media literacy' (Grizzle et al. 2013). For UNESCO a new literacy strategy is needed which harmonises and encapsulates all these. Print is only one of the dominant symbol systems of a culture and if there are to be new directions in print culture these need to reach into the complexity of the encoding systems within film, media, graphic and performing arts. Digital book adaptations such as 80 Days (2014), Sorcery (2013), SENS (2016) are exploring the crossover into these systems – often taking the lead from games.

Arguably the best stories are those that you are 'lost' in. A deeply affecting story rolls round your mind, inhabits your waking hours until you can immerse yourself in it again. This is not to say you are uncritical, but you are emotionally engaged in the story. It is something like childhood sleep: heavy, deeply refreshing, purging, restorative, formative. This desire for immersion in the storyworld pervades discussions of the potential of a new technology from the early days of radio to 3D cinema and VR. With VR technology you can 'make someone feel like they have been teleported to a destination', according to Patrick Milling Smith of production company Vrse.works (Temperton 2015). Despite the hyperbole of the statement, I have to agree.[3] You are immersed, whether you are following the arrows in the line art VR storyworld of 'SENS', or riding the friendly beast in 'The Turning Forest' (2016), or in Liberia in the middle of the lived experience of a village's recovery from an Ebola outbreak as in 'Waves of Grace' (2015). Deep immersion or hyperfocus has been dubbed psychologically dangerous, as well as liberating and fulfilling, and VR does have this potential (Wilson and Soranzo 2015). However, immersion in storytelling, although similar to Csíkszentmihályi's 'flow' (1990) in games in that it focuses concentration intently on the present moment and distorts the subjective experience of time, does not give the reader a sense of control over the event, nor require participation involving reflex physical action. Significantly, immersion in storytelling does not preclude an awareness of a medium's deictics. In fact, a nuanced awareness of the distance between the reader and the characters through the grammar of the medium is essential to the appreciation of the story.

Arcadia, Iain Pears's 2015 multilinear fiction on a book app and published in hard back is a reflection on story, and on the traditions of orality. There are ten character storylines which you can follow: one is an author Prof. Lytton who is drawn into the world he imagined and finds it had 'Taken a few pencilled jottings and extrapolated outwards, adding the details he had never bothered with' and 'had developed some huge crisis out of it all' (Pears 2015, Lytton listens). In the book the Storytellers have ossified the story, retelling it as truth, giving rise to accretions of rhetorical embellishment, citation and precedence, with fantastic achievements of memory and learning – but not inquiry. Lytton rebuffs them: 'I wish you to question not obey. Doubt, not trust. That is the purpose of the Story' (Pears 2015, Preliminary remarks).

In his review in *The Guardian*, Stephen Poole says: 'We live in an age in which storytelling is considered the highest possible literary virtue.' Yet according to Poole: 'The valuing of storytelling above all else does risk the promotion of an infantalized literary taste' (Poole 2015). And he places *Arcadia* in the young-adult crossover market with Cornelia Funke's German trilogy *Inkheart*, *Inkspell* and *Inkdeath* (2003–8) and its 2008 movie adaptation directed by Iain Softley. In David Lindsay-Abaire's screenplay, the fable and its story characters take on a 'real' life through the power of the reader. As with Choose Your Own Adventure stories, interactive fictions and book-games, choice, role play and play itself are somehow considered lesser; and playing a role to gain the attributes of the character – such as the hero, princess, superhero or lover – is something we grow out of. It is often argued that this is because they only offer escapism as in a similar way adaptations of classics have been accused of a cheap emotionalism (Giddings and Sheen, 2000).

The issue for these psychologists is whether the emotion extends our compassion and understanding. Gottschall (2012) would argue that when playing, the child-protagonist is at the centre of the experience – as, Bruner and Lucariello caution, we are in our own renarrations of ourselves – and that this does not promote empathy (Bruner and Lucariello in László 2008). This would define 'infantalized literary taste' not in aesthetic terms but in psychological. In such fictional worlds or game-play it is argued there is no assimilation of alternative roles, no empathy, and the world is built with artificial rules where in the real world there may not be any, or they may be unknown. Therefore 'play' is deemed an inauthentic story enacted from external pressures and conformity and, if without empathy, is unable to enlighten or improve emotional intelligence (Oatley 2011).

Nevertheless, we are attracted to the emotions in stories as they offer the self-emancipation and fulfilment (see James 1917; Damasio 2005). In his 1967 essay 'Cybernetics and Ghosts', Italo Calvino imagines a poetic-electronic machine along the lines of Turing's computer which can 'perform all the permutations possible on a given material' and play the 'combinatorial game' of the storyteller in his tales of figures and actions. Calvino imagined a machine that churns out stories applying Chomskian grammatical rules and recombining figures and actions from the Proppian analysis of folk tales and Jungian archetypes. But, he argues, the meaning of the story does not come from this machine. The 'poetic result will be the particular effect ... The shock that occurs only if the writing machine is surrounded by the hidden ghosts of the individual and of his society' or, as he phrases it, an explosion into myth (p. 20). With this, Calvino locates the *affect* of Story within society.

Ong says homeostasis is a characteristic of oral storytelling, I suggest story blossoms in periods when new technologies of storytelling combine with social and cultural transformation. MacDonald points to the 1920s as a time when scriptwriting emerged as a distinct skill of visual storytelling separate from the writing of plays or novels (2008). This followed the 'chasm' of the First World War which Clemence Dane said only young writers were able to bridge. Dane meant that only they were able to reject the past and seek to make sense of the shakeup of roles between men and women, older and younger generations, and redraw a national heritage (Dane 1929). Their new or renewed stories imbued with emotion sought to find meaning in the vicissitudes of individual and social lives. Over time, stories that no longer connected to a psychological or social need because that need had been fulfilled or had gone, became stale or lost.

What is common in both periods is a rise of visual storytelling. The technology which facilitated this mediated the experience, making the act of storytelling distinct from the storyteller. This separation appears to go beyond a cultural shift from literacy to orality, or the fade out of the writerly and fade in to readerly texts. Storytelling has always been a folk art in its origins, and it is again as we all can tell stories on Instagram, Snapchat and Facebook and through the multitude of apps for the mobile which allow the user to combine photos, audio, music and video (Aciman 2015). In storybots for children, these stories can be populated by cartoon characters and can have pre-set story arcs. Too easily dismissed as superficial, digital storytelling can lead to a profound response. At a recent event at the British Library called Off the Page Chapter 2, Stella Wisdom drew together poets, researchers, game makers and authors of adaptation, pointing the spotlight on the depth of emotional experience in, for example, short vignette games or Mata Haggis-Burridge's full length 'Fragments of Him' about loss. Between storytelling and gaming lies the playful questioning of the rules that we choose to govern (or 'rule') us, and as such digital gaming is irreverent, questioning, wry and analytical: many of the qualities which make a good researcher. Humour and play are also necessary techniques of mental distantiation from the subject. The modern player, like the modern researcher, is a co-creator and likely to be conscious of playing the game. Many players enjoy providing a meta-commentary by coding cheats, recording play-throughs, or replaying the game for alternative endings. Designers expect this and hacking and offer rewards for meta-engagement in the form of concealed extensions, extra play or hidden 'eggs'. In these stories the rules themselves have become the objects of interrogation and witty re-creation. Some are made for performance or role-play allowing the participant to play with a multimodal postmodern identity (Gizmet Game Poems 2010–13; Norwegian Style 2015–19). Players demonstrate Elsaesser's tacit compliance with the rules of the game in the knowledge that they are constructed and fallible.

Storytelling is an essential skill for the researcher who needs to convey the relevance and utility of information as it is a means of communicating knowledge. But, of course, not all information adds to knowledge nor is all knowledge new. In certain disciplines and practices stories are the subject of research or the means of locating knowledge. But research is distinct. It is not social or political action, or the production of an artwork (whether a piece of poetry or a book), although it can provide the basis for any of these. It has to rigorously and objectively assess the evidence and offer an interpretation which gives new insights. Good research advances on solid foundations of previous research and should stand the test of time. It is not repetitive, it is not commentary: it provides new methods, new ideas, new data. The distinction between research and argument, evidence and interpretation, fact and activism needs to be maintained. However, for research to have impact and change behaviour it must have *affect*, and it can do that through the power of storytelling.

Drawing a historical comparison between the two periods' adoption of new media, illustrates how deeply storytelling can affect and repair our society.[4] In essence, it remains the emotional connection that we feel to a story which gives it its ability to change and transform us. When we lose ourselves in a story in a book, through listening or in a cinema, and through the empathetic connection with the storyworld, we find we have a different apprehension of the world on our return. Of course, this may or may not last, but this is why it is used in change management, politics, social science and other fields. Print culture has been successful in capturing and telling a compelling story at the right moment. Now, however, it needs to consider both the moment and the medium.

Notes

1. University of Bedfordshire. This chapter is a development of a paper presented at the conference and 'Story, Storyteller and Storytelling' in the special issue on 'New Directions in Print Culture' of *Logos: Journal of the World Publishing Community*, edited by Caroline Davis and Vincent Trott, 29:2–3, 46–53.
2. The Mass Observation Archive and the Reading Experience Database have evidence that the practice of reading aloud did not die out with silent reading but was continued as a separate social practice.
3. The Network Effect aggregates from the net and google images, videos and word frequency, is situationalist anchoring audio video clips in the real world and demonstrates redundancy. It is, however, non-fiction: <http://networkeffect.io/>
4. Employing Ian Hutchby's term, the 'affordance' of the material object or technology lies in its material constraints and use which is relational: radio is a technology without pictures. It relates to orality.

Fiction and Games Cited

80 Days (2014), Inkle, iOS 6.0, Android 2.3, Game
Funke, Cornelia (2003–8), *Inkheart, Inkspell, Inkdeath*, translated from German to English by Anthea Bell for Chicken House Publishing.
Pears, Iain (2015), *Arcadia*, Faber and Faber & Touch Press, available from the Apple App store.
Sorcery (2013), Inkle, iOS 7.0 Android 2.3, Role playing
SENS (2016), Arte Experience, iOS 6.0 Android 5.1, VR narrative
The Network Effect (2015), Jonathan Harris and Greg Hochmuth, <http://networkeffect.io/> (accessed 1 April 2020).
The Turning Forest (2016), BBC, Android 7, VR fairy tale
Waves of Grace (2015), UN Vrse, Within, VR storytelling, <https://with.in/watch/waves-of-grace/> (accessed 17 January 2018)

References

Aciman, Alexander (2015), 'These 6 Apps Will Help You Tell Amazing Stories With Just Your iPhone', *Time*, 6 January, <http://time.com/3649722/iphone-photo-video-apps/> (accessed 23 January 2018).
Anderson, Benedict (1983), *Imagined Communities: Reflections on the Origin and Spread of Nationalism*, London: Verso.
Barnett, Vincent L. and Alexis Weedon (2014), *Elinor Glyn as Novelist, Moviemaker, Glamour Icon and Businesswoman*, Aldershot: Ashgate.
Calvino, Italo (1967), 'Cybernetics and Ghosts', in *The Uses of Literature*, San Diego/New York/London: Harcourt Brace & Company, pp. 3–27.
Csikszentmihalyi, Mihaly (1990), *Flow: The Psychology of Optimal Experience*, New York: Harper and Row.
Damasio, Antonio (2005), *Descartes' Error: Emotion, Reason, and the Human Brain*, Harmondsworth: Penguin Books.
Dane, Clemence (1929), *Tradition and Hugh Walpole*, New York: Doubleday & Co.
Gadd, Ian (2010), *History of the Book in the West: 1455–1700*, London: Routledge.
Giddings, Robert and Erica Sheen (2000), *From Page To Screen: Adaptations of the Classic Novel*, Manchester: Manchester University Press.

Gizmet Game Poems (2010–13), <http://gamepoems.gizmet.com/> (accessed 14 April 2019).

Glyn, Elinor (1916), *The Career of Katherine Bush*, New York: Grosset & Dunlap.

Goodman, David (2010), 'Distracted Listening: On not making sound choices in the 1930s', in David Suisman and Susan Stresser (eds), *Sound in the Era of Mechanical Reproduction*, Philadelphia: Philadelphia University Press.

Gottschall, Jonathan (2012), *The Storytelling Animal: How Stories Make Us Human*, New York: Houghton Mifflin Harcourt.

Grizzle, Alton, Penny Moore, Michael Dezuanni, Sanjay Asthana, Carolyn Wilson, Fackson Banda and Chido Onumah (2013), *Media and Information Literacy: Policy and strategy guidelines*, Paris: UNESCO.

Hill, Napoleon (1937), *Think and Grow Rich*, The Ralston Society.

Hsu, Jeremy (2008), 'The Secrets of Storytelling: Why We Love a Good Yarn', *Scientific American Mind*, 18 September.

Innis, Harold A. (1950), *Empire and Communications*, Oxford: Clarendon Press.

James, William (1917), *The Varieties of Religious Experience*, London: Longmans/Green and Co.

László, János (2008), *The Science of Stories: An Introduction to Narrative Psychology*, London: Routledge.

Lugmayr, A., E. Sutinen, J. Suhonen et al. (2017), 'Serious storytelling – a first definition and review', *Multimedia Tools Applications*, 76: 15707.

MacDonald, Ian W. (2008), '"Mr Gilfil's Love Story": The Well-made Screenplay in 1920', *The Journal of British Cinema and Television*, 5:2, 223–41.

McLuhan, Marshal (1965), 'The Future of Man in the Electronic Age', in McLuhan speaks special collections at <http://www.marshallmcluhanspeaks.com/interview/1965-the-future-of-man-in-the-electric-age/> (accessed 12 January 2017).

Millard, Kathryn (2014), *Screenwriting in a Digital Era*, London: Palgrave Macmillan.

Negroponte, Nicholas (1995), *Being Digital*, New York: Knopf Doubleday Publishing Group.

Gizmet Game Poems (2010–13), <http://gamepoems.gizmet.com/> (accessed 14 April 2019).

Norwegian Style (2015–19), Norwegian roleplaying games in English, <https://norwegianstyle.wordpress.com/> (accessed 14 April 2019).

Oatley, Keith (2011), 'In the Minds of Others', *Scientific American Mind* (Nov./Dec.) 22:5.

Ong, Walter (1982), *Orality and Literacy: The Technologizing of the Word*, Hove.

Poole, Stephen (2015), 'Arcadia by Iain Pears review – a fantastical extravaganza', *The Guardian*, 11 September, <https://www.theguardian.com/books/2015/sep/11/arcadia-iain-pears-review> (accessed 18 January 2008).

Post, Emily (1922), *Etiquette in Society, in Business, in Politics and at Home*, New York and London: Funk & Wagnalls Co.

Pullman, Philip (2017), *Daemon Voices: Essays on Storytelling*, Oxford: David Fickling Books.

Roberts, Jane and Pamela Robinson (2010), *History of the Book in the West 400AD–1455*, London: Routledge.

Rose, Jonathan (2001), *The Intellectual Life of the British Working Classes*, New Haven, pp. 243–4, <http://www.open.ac.uk/Arts/reading/UK/record_details.php?id=4245> (accessed 15 January 2018).

Temperton, James (2015), 'Experience the horror of Ebola in this new VR film', *Wired*, 1 September, <http://www.wired.co.uk/article/waves-of-grace-ebola-virtual-reality-film>

Weedon, Alexis (2007), '"Behind the Screen" and "The Scoop": A cross-media experiment in publishing and broadcasting crime fiction in the early 1930s', *Media History*, 13:1, 43–60.

Weedon, Alexis (2018) 'Story, Storyteller and Storytelling', *Logos: Journal of the World Publishing Community*, special issue by Caroline Davis and Vincent Trott on New Directions in Print Culture, vol. 29, nos 2–3: 46–53

Williams, Raymond (1965), *The Long Revolution*, Harmondsworth: Pelican Books.

Wilson, Christopher J. and Alessandro Soranzo (2015), Review article, 'The Use of Virtual Reality in Psychology: A Case Study in Visual Perception', *Computational and Mathematical Methods in Medicine*, vol. 2015, Article ID 151702.

7. AUTONOMY AND THE OTHER WOMAN: QUEER ACTIVE AGENCY AND POSTCOLONIAL EXPECTATIONS

Jenny Barrett and Rosa Fong

Deconstructing Zoe is a British documentary film about transgender actor Zoe/Chowee Leow (2016), directed by Chinese British filmmaker, Rosa Fong. Written together with British film scholar Jenny Barrett, the following chapter is presented as a self-conscious reflection upon the practices of documentary filmmaking and the critical analysis of the film's subject from our different perspectives. It draws attention to a particular dilemma that arises in the enabling of a 'voice' to Zoe, a form of ethnographic statement in which she declares her transgender status and her racialised performance, and in the mediation of both the documentary format and the academic essay. The chapter is divided into two sections which indicate the author and help to create a negotiation of reflective practice and criticism. In the process, taking the lead from scholars Mohan J. Dutta and Ambar Basu in their autoethnographic study of subalternity and neoliberalism (2018), we explore and interrogate our own positions of privilege and autonomy in a neoliberal environment.

From a theoretical approach, Rosa seeks to articulate Zoe's 'unfixing' of her identity, creating what Homi Bhabha (1994) refers to as a 'double consciousness' of the colonised mind, not simply in Zoe's identity as a woman, but in her performed identity as a Chinese woman, the 'Other' woman, in her stage performances, in the documentary and in everyday life. First, by observing Dorinne K. Kondo's 1990 analysis of David Henry Hwang's play, *M. Butterfly* (1988), we can recognise Zoe's dissolving of the boundaries of both gender and race in an elected identity that can be understood as self-authored.

Then, by comparison with the Chilean artist, Pedro Lemebel, Jenny presents Zoe as the author of a marginalised identity that, in this case, evokes a pro-colonial discourse and yet is unmistakably subversive. The documentary allows Zoe's 'voice', as subaltern, to be heard, within which she theorises her own identity, and in this we hear the voice of both Self and Other, an endeavour that a postcolonial worldview would have good cause to celebrate. However, whilst Zoe's Orientalist performance destabilises Eurocentric authority and essentialism, and is thus a postcolonial activity, her racialised identity is pro-colonial, and so resists a postcolonial worldview. Ironically, if Zoe is understood as subaltern, postcolonial thought would celebrate her autonomy and self-authorship, and so would defend her right to author her own ethnography. Zoe's deviation from the 'norm' of postcolonial thought, then, itself a dominant ideology in the neoliberal environments of British independent filmmaking and of Western-based academia, can be seen as a creative practice that resists hegemony.

Rosa

In 'Deconstructing Zoe: Performing Race' (2018), I explore the means and implications of embodying a gendered and racialised identity in my documentary, *Deconstructing Zoe*. I argue that Zoe's self-aware performance as a Malaysian Chinese trans-woman in Britain is evidence of a queer active agency. The documentary presents interviews and performances by Zoe in which her racialised, feminised identity is expressed, both to articulate her own selfhood and, she makes clear, to express her sexual identity. I have considered, then, how Zoe, whilst playing to an Orientalist stereotype that she calls 'the Orchid', is able to create agency and ownership of her identity. She is able to do this because she understands that the Western Orientalist tropes assigned to East Asian women are somehow considered innate, saying 'The Orchid represents my gender, my race and how I'm seen in the West as this delicate little flower' (*Deconstructing Zoe*, 2016). Yet when it comes to her own identity, Zoe embraces the notion that it is not fixed, but is forever shifting and cannot be shackled by convention. This understanding of her own identity draws to mind Edward Said's seminal work, *Orientalism* (1978), which offers insights into the binary opposition of the central Self and decentralised Other. But Zoe resolutely refuses to be one or the other; she is knowingly both, simultaneously. A deconstructionist postcolonial approach, offering a more nuanced perspective, acknowledges a 'double consciousness' (Bhabha, 1994: 256) whereby the coloniser and the colonised cannot be clearly identified in a binary opposition. This is because there are multiple perspectives available to the subaltern subject creating manifold identities of contestation. I have said elsewhere (2020) that Zoe grew up in the former British colony of Malaysia and has experience first-hand of the colonial rhetoric, potentially furnishing her with this 'double consciousness' of the colonised mind in the process of colonial mimicry. Bhabha utilises a Lacanian notion of mimicry as camouflage, which produces ambivalence or hybridity. Indeed, Zoe demonstrates how she plays with this ambivalence when she says, 'I think the Orchid is a metaphor for a race or culture which is foreign to someone and I feel as Zoe there is this exotification of myself.' Zoe uses this knowledge to play 'the submissive butterfly' but sees this act of submission as a 'powerful tool' (*Deconstructing Zoe*, 2016). In her analysis of the Tony Award-winning theatre production *M. Butterfly*, a rendering of the early-twentieth-century Giacomo Puccini opera, *Madama Butterfly*, Dorinne K. Kondo explains how the act of submission, which Zoe also utilises, can result in power. The play adapts the opera's tragic love story by changing the American male from naval officer to French civil servant ('Pinkerton' becomes 'Gallimard') and his Chinese partner from a woman to a male performer whose on-stage role is female ('Butterfly' becomes 'Song Liling'), although Gallimard does not realise that Song is physically male. Kondo describes how Gallimard demands to see Song naked, which would expose Song as a man. Kondo explains how Song, 'in a brilliant stroke realizes that Gallimard simply desires her to submit' (1990: 18). Song kowtows to Gallimard and he yields, ultimately making Song the victor in a contest for power. Kondo asserts, 'Indeed, it is at the moment of his greatest submission/ humiliation as a woman that Song consolidates his power as a man' (1990: 18).

Zoe's own gendered and sexual politics use a similar ambivalence to great effect, declaring that,

> When I'm Zoe I sometimes project the idea of a delicate Oriental butterfly. Because that, in itself, is quite a powerful tool. I think it's only powerful because I'm playing it from an Asian male's perspective. Because an Asian male is seen as something lesser, I guess. (*Deconstructing Zoe*, 2016)

Zoe's understanding of postcolonial power relations enables her to negotiate the hegemonic structures of power and meaning. In particular, there is a recognition of her gendered identity in the geographical locus of power in the West, specifically Britain where she lives. Asian men are seen as less desirable, or, in Zoe's words, 'lesser' in the West: Zoe's 'submission' to the pro-colonial trope of an Orientalised woman, gives her power as an East Asian man.

Kondo uses her analysis of *M. Butterfly* to articulate how 'in anthropological theories of the self or the person ... gender and race are mutually implicated in the construction of identity and the pervasive insidiousness of gender and racial stereotypes' (1990: 6). Her analysis evokes Gramsci's theory of hegemony, whereby power is re-established by coercion and consent rather than force. Here, this is through the iteration of stereotypes. Kondo's approach lends itself to a deeper understanding of the tactics employed by Zoe to author her own selfhood. She outlines the different frameworks of self from anthropology and philosophy, which define persons, selves and selfhood and are reliant on characterisations of 'the concept of self' (1990: 14), which reify an abstract notion of an essential selfhood. She proposes that in *Madama Butterfly*, the opera, identity is fixed and essentialised. However, in *M. Butterfly*, 'selves in the plural are constructed variously in various situations' (ibid.). These 'selves' are multiple and ambiguous, and they both shape and are shaped by 'relations of power' (ibid.). Zoe, similarly, constructs a self that is multiple, performing both gendered and racialised stereotypes as a means of claiming power.

Kondo also draws our attention to how gender power relations are mapped onto geography in the binary of West/East and male/female, again found and explored in *M. Butterfly*. That the East submits to the West is one of the enduring narrative conventions of Orientalism. Indeed, Said (1978) illustrated how the gendering of the East as 'female' operates via Western imperial hegemony. Alessia Belli and Anna Lorentori explain that this demonstrates that 'the East is not only a cultural construct but also a sexual one' (2017:485). This is an important distinction that allows us to unpick the interconnected power relationship between geography, race and gender, which Kondo asserts is explored in *M. Butterfly* (1990:7). Zoe's complex renegotiation of her identity which allows her to create agency is perhaps illustrated by Kondo's analysis of the scene in *M. Butterfly* where Song is almost unmasked as a man but submits by kneeling to Gallimard, as discussed earlier.

Similarly, Zoe's apparent submission to Western essentialist notions of the Oriental 'Other woman' allows her to 'dissolve the boundaries' of gender and race, history, culture and narrative conventions (1990:15) to create agency. What is important to establish, is that Zoe chooses to both perform and identify as, and so is, this Oriental Other woman. Belli and Loretoni explain that 'in modernity, the configuration of identity should have an elective character', that is, a recognition of our ability to be the authors of our own identity (2017: 483). A similar approach could be employed to create a critical framework to help unpick Zoe's performative strategies. Belli and Lorentoni cite the work of Judith Butler who theorises identity 'as an affect that is produced or generated' (2017: 494). Understanding identity in this way allows a person 'greater access to agency' (ibid.). Using these conceptions of active agency in the authoring of identity, we can argue that Zoe creates agency whilst/despite using Western essentialist stereotypes. The authors also highlight the limits of 'liberal patriarchalism' (2017: 484), which often disavows the heterogeneous nature of minority cultures. They point towards the 'ethnically charged paternalism towards other cultures, judged to be incapable of internal dynamism' (ibid.). To demonstrate the vibrant nature that minority cultures often employ in self-representation, Belli and Loretoni utilise the concept of 'fluid identity' (2017: 493) to describe the shifting nodes of identity formation. Indeed Zoe actively makes use of such an approach to her own identity as she describes how gender is a spectrum and her gender identity fluctuates within that continuum depending on how she feels on any given day (*Deconstructing Zoe*, 2016). Zoe's proactive use of fluid identity formation allows her to create self-authorship in order to surmount pro-colonial inscriptions of race and gender.

In making *Deconstructing Zoe* (2016) I have taken a subjective approach to the filmmaking process, which brings a personal dimension to my research. My methodology utilises personal experience as a tool to understanding cultural experiences and is known as autoethnography (Ellis et al. 2011). An important tenet of autoethnography is the recognition that personal experience influences the research process and that the selection of research literature to analyse experience is also subjective. My own research analysis draws on postcolonial debates and notions of hybridity and queer politics. These theoretical precepts have enabled me to articulate my experience as an East Asian woman living in Britain. When talking to Zoe about how people respond to her as a woman, I started to recall the original impetus for my research. Seeing Zoe in the early years of her 'coming out' and making the transition from a stage persona to a lived identity as a transgender woman, I was often struck by the attention she would get from men. In those early years, Zoe's performance as a Chinese woman seemed larger than life and hyper-orientalised. Zoe's version of a Chinese woman seemed to play up to the stereotype of oriental exoticness. It was at odds with how I wanted to be perceived as an East Asian woman. Experience had taught me that when men say that they wished I was 'more Chinese', I knew this was another way of saying that they wished I was more like the submissive fantasy some Western men have of East Asian women. When reflecting on this it became apparent that the attraction for these men was not gender per se, but an imagined geography of race (Fong, 2020). These reflective musings were the starting point for my research question, which was to explore how race can be performative. I have described elsewhere (Fong, 2017) how I drew on Judith Butler's theory of gender performativity (1999) and Katrin Seig's study of ethnic drag (2009) to analyse racial performativity. I discuss the filmic strategies I used to draw out the nuances in Zoe's racial and gender performance and I described how I captured and responded to the performative act in front of the camera and in the editing process (ibid.). This approach to my creative practice opens up the possibility of developing a dynamic response to knowledge formation, through the interplay between critical research and the process of filmmaking. With this in mind I'm reminded of Nicola Mai's discussion on the limitations of academic writing, whereby he felt he was not able to 'convey the embodied, sensuous, affective, performative and intersubjective dimensions of knowledge production' through writing alone (Mai, 2016: 9). Mai turned to a form of filmmaking called ethno-fiction, which he says 'tries to represent the way knowledge happens during ethnography and qualitative interviewing' (Mai 2016: 10). Much in the same way, as a visual thinker the medium of film/video allows me to reflect and respond to the subject in front of the camera in a way that writing does not. In addition to that, the sensorial nature of film creates an embodied representation creating an emotional and intellectual moment of understanding for the viewer. For instance, in my documentary we are able to witness Zoe's performative strategy when using the idea of the East as a bankable commodity – that is the intellectual proposition of orientalism as a commodification of a race. As we watch her performance both on and off stage this creates an insight into how this racialised gendered performance operates.

Ellis et al. describe how writers of autoethnography use the storytelling characteristics of autobiography and scientific approach of the ethnographic study of people and cultures (2011). Autoethnographic filmmaking embraces the characteristics of both and it creates an embodied as well as a cognitive moment of knowledge formation. In my article 'Deconstructing Zoe: Performing Race' (2017), I describe my autoethnographic approach to research for the documentary. I outline the very personal, subjective stance I took in making the film and how the creative process is underpinned with theoretical analysis. What makes autoethnographic filmmaking valid as research is that it interrogates experience analytically (Mitch Allen, quoted in Ellis et al. 2011). Autoethnographic filmmaking can also be transformative and perhaps allows 'rhetorical agency', which is a person's ability to act on evaluations of the self and to be the author of their own narrative. In a recent discussion with Zoe about her experience making *Deconstructing Zoe*, she described how it helped change her outlook. She said the process of making the film helped her 'distil' her identity. It made her more conscious of who she was and how she presented herself to the world. She questioned, how do people perceive me? She considered how she might 'create' the person she'd like to present to the world. Zoe now does not make the distinction between her female and male persona. She now uses her birth name Chowee, whether she dresses as female or male. The binary distinction no longer exists as she embraces her gender fluidity. When reflecting on Chowee's epiphany from the process of making the film, I am reminded of the closing statement in my previous article: '*Deconstructing Zoe* [thus] reveals racial and gender discourse, and by revealing, empowers' (Fong, 2017).

Jenny

Watching *Deconstructing Zoe* for the first time, I was faced with a problem. Whilst I was able to acknowledge the significance of Zoe's opportunity to present herself as her chosen identity, I was also struck by the particular characteristics of her performance. As a scholar and lecturer, the expectations of postcolonial theory are indelibly fixed in my mind from my own scholarship and numerous lectures on ethnicity and representation, providing a 'lens' if you will through which I automatically assess (judge) moving image texts. My automatic response on regarding a racialised performance such as Zoe's is to recoil, to resist its apparent embracing of a colonial discourse, to reject it as valid in the twenty-first century. However, through several months of conversation with Rosa about her film, my perspective has taken a new shape. This is not, I would claim, a softening of my attitude towards colonial discourses, nor a consequence of getting to know the filmmaker herself and so adopting a positive attitude to her creative output. Instead, through a reconsideration of Zoe's racialised performance as a form of self-aware resistance, I am able to see it as a form of empowerment made possible through the film's mediation of her voice. Our participation in the dissemination and analysis of that voice, however, presents an additional problem in terms of Zoe's commodification, which I will explore below.

Above I referred to regarding Zoe through the lens of postcolonial theory. In fact, as we meet her in the documentary, she can be regarded through a range of lenses, one of which is recognising her as author of her own performed and lived identity, albeit one that is controversial. She is not alone in this: there are many artists whose public, performed persona, gender expression or sexuality has created controversy. Alejandro Urrutia's perspective on the 'credible authorship' of the Chilean *crónica* writer, novelist and performer, Pedro Lemebel, is helpful in this respect, particularly because of Lemebel's reputation as a gay creative artist whose practice and public appearances were often as shocking as they were political. Urrutia explores ways of regarding Lemebel as an author through an analysis of the writer's published works and recorded performances, most of which are still untranslated from their original Spanish. Lemebel (1952–2014) wrote and performed his 'chronicles' as a means to challenge both the right-wing, military dictatorship of Pinochet's Chile and homophobic left-wing political groups with which he at times associated himself. His identity as an author and artist is typically referred to by commentators and scholars as 'he', whereas his identity in his tales and memoirs as 'la Loca', a 'Queen' persona often characterised as a feminine gay male, is often referred to as 'she'. In fact, Melissa M. González uses both pronouns in her article on Lemebel and subversion in the neoliberal marketplace (2018). Thus, Lemebel had (and has) an ambiguous, flexible, gendered identity that was designed to disrupt fixed social categories not only on his own behalf, but also as a means of speaking the 'voices' of the marginalised in his country. Like Zoe, Lemebel features as a character in his own art, meaning that he 'interferes' with a reading of that creative work (Urrutia 2017: 139). Lemebel's one published novel, *Tengo miedo torero* (*My Tender Matador*, 2001), for example, features his persona as the 'Queen' as an intervention within the *guerrilla* genre, wherein the protagonist is typically an 'ideologically conscious and consistent militant in a Marxist organization and preferably male and heterosexual' (p. 144). The story tells a fictionalised account of an assassination attempt on Pinochet and displays similarities with what Urrutia calls a 'Lemebelian discourse': 'challenging class, sexual normativity, and social injustice, and advocating the struggle for social rights and the positing of alternative identities' (p. 144). Lemebel can be clearly identified as a character in his own novel (as the 'Queen'), and his politics also feature prominently, both in terms of gendered and sexual politics and the nation's political heritage.

Zoe also, in Rosa's film, features as a character in her own artwork (the performance as the 'Orchid') and the interviews create a space for her to more fully describe her politics which advocate the right to identify as a Chinese woman challenging not only sexual or gendered normativity, but also ethnic boundaries. Both Lemebel's Queen and Zoe's Orchid personas are situated in quasi-fictional spaces where a conventionally marginalised identity can be authored/spoken. In both cases, the author has a presence both inside and outside the fiction through, in Lemebel's case, written fiction, recordings, public appearances and interviews, and, in Zoe's case, in the interview and performative sequences of *Deconstructing Zoe*. This helps to further establish the performer/writer as 'author'.

Although Lemebel has typically been explored within the discipline of Latin American studies, his work and life are also interpreted and discussed within queer studies and subaltern studies frameworks, which are equally appropriate for the analysis of Zoe as author and performer. Certainly, Lemebel's political and cultural context is vastly different from Zoe's, practising in a country and time of overt state suppression of specific practices, lifestyles and politics. His practice, however, gives us a means to regard Zoe's self-authored identity and performance (on and off-stage, on and off-camera) as both non-conformist *and* conformist in the alleged 'freedom' of the neoliberal environment. Melissa M. González (2018) works from each of the disciplines mentioned, along with a recognition of the neoliberal context, to expose the irony of Lemebel's creative practice and public recognition: that he was fully aware of 'the delicate dance between subversion and co-optation that she performs in the context of neoliberal capitalism' (2018: 138, *change of pronoun deliberate*). This 'dance between subversion and co-optation' refers to a status where marginalised voices gain value through cultural or academic acceptance, and consequently the marketplace vigorously assimilates then promotes their message (or the speakers of the message) for profit. Whilst Lemebel remained steadfast in his exposure of social inequalities, he knowingly accepted the benefits of his public success, retaining his subversiveness and yet conforming to the rubric of neoliberalism whereby his own exoticised difference was used as capital. Gonzalez argues that he 'is fully aware of the exoticism that inspires at least one segment of her audience to consume her cultural production, and that she is unapologetic about the financial exchange involved' (2018: 145). Lemebel was equally unapologetic about the offence he caused when invited to television interviews and university events, including antisocial behaviour when invited to speak at Harvard University in 2004:

> Throughout the talk, Lemebel consumed copious amounts of whiskey, spoke through the time reserved for audience questions, joked that fellow Chileans assumed she was going to Harvard just to do the academics' hair, and famously stated that she never had to come out of the closet because poor people have wardrobes, not closets. (pp. 140–1)

Lemebel is both knowing and unapologetic, and these traits, whilst found in a different cultural context, can be found in Zoe's work and everyday performance. As the quotation from the documentary reveals, cited earlier, the Orchid persona represents not only her gender, but her chosen race also (Chinese, not Malaysian). She demonstrates the same knowingness as Lemebel in her performance of Otherness, with the distinction that she is fully aware of the colonialist discourse with which she exoticises herself, one that exaggerates an identity as 'subaltern'. However, as indicated above in relation to Lemebel, academia places a value upon the marginalised voice, assimilating it into a scholarly 'marketplace' which profits the scholar.

Postcolonial communication scholars Mohan J. Dutta and Ambar Basu present an interruption in the conventional academic discourse on subalternity and postcolonialism in their autoethnographic article of 2018, 'Subalternity, Neoliberal Seductions and Freedom: Decolonizing the Global Market of Social Change'. They discuss their own complicity, as part of a self-confessed educated elite of South Asian origin, in a political and academic reinforcement of Indian communities as subaltern in a neoliberal age (p. 84). Guilty of commodifying 'exhibits' within the academy, along with other scholars, specialists and members of NGOs, they expose a neocolonial practice, whereby their work serves a postcolonial worldview, yet excludes the voices and opinions of the very communities they work in/for. They refer to this as a form of 'erasure' or a recognition of their efforts as the establishment of 'colonial sites', making them complicit, as they put it, in 'reproducing the margins' (p. 84). Dutta and Basu have provided us, then, with a means of both exploring Zoe's autonomy and our own participation in the telling of/interrogation of her story. By situating Zoe's life and practice in a neoliberal environment, her 'freedom' to identify racially as Chinese and female in terms of gender can be acknowledged, her authorship of herself can be witnessed. However, this same neoliberal environment presents Rosa and I with a situation whereby this academic output commodifies her for our benefit as scholars. Given this tension, we need to consider Zoe's own role in self-authorship and commodification, as well as our role in mediation and interrogation.

Dutta and Basu, amongst other things, draw attention to the potential given by neoliberalism for neocolonialisms to emerge, whereby the voice of the subaltern remains unheard. In their summary of 'neoliberalism' they describe it as: 'a political, economic and cultural logic that is based on the idea that the market brings about solutions to problems of access, citizenship, and development' (p. 92). Whilst this predominantly concerns late capitalist enterprise, western health models and more, it also includes academic discourses, particularly postcolonialist scholarship written from a place of privilege, which concentrates, for example, on the former British colonies of India and Singapore. They argue:

> Postcolonial work as high theory rewrites and reworks the colonial enterprise, reiterating the tools of the colonial master in its celebrations of theory as removed from the everyday struggles of/in subaltern communities and detached from the messiness of everyday life. (p. 89)

They conclude that the way forward is to move away from 'theorizing on' these communities and towards 'theorizing with' them (p. 89), thus defending their particular scholarly approach which involves gathering and mediating stories from and with the communities themselves.

Dutta and Basu's confrontation with their own identities forces us to do the same: I am a British white scholar who explores racialised identities in popular culture; Rosa is both a scholar and a practitioner, and is a British Chinese woman. Through her mediation of Zoe's story in the documentary, and through our participation in this chapter we are, one could argue, both providing Zoe with a space to have her voice heard *and* presenting Zoe as a 'specimen', something that Dutta and Basu might regard as the scholarship of 'exotica'. Rosa's own ethnic identity suggests that she employed the documentary form in order to 'theorize with' Zoe as an active subject, whilst this chapter considers Zoe's racialised performance, and is therefore a means to 'theorize on' her as a passive object. All over again, Zoe becomes both Self and Other simultaneously. This presents a problem which is exacerbated by a conventional postcolonial response to Zoe's particular racialised performance.

As we have established, if we were to regard the representation of the Chinese woman as Other, 'butterfly' or 'Orchid', the submissive, exotic female stereotype established through centuries of institutional and cultural racism, as part of a colonial discourse, then Zoe's racialised performance is pro-colonial. Her racialised identity, as claimed and performed, perpetuates a sign of colonial privilege, particularly as her interviews make it clear that this is part of her sexual independence. It goes beyond the mimicry that Rosa indicates, from Bhabha, in her discussion of the double consciousness of the colonised mind. Surely, then, Zoe's autonomy becomes an instrument of erasure, a means of silencing postcolonial resistance to conceptions of the 'Orient'. Does she not subjugate herself to a colonial discourse? Has she re-colonised herself? The answer, given Dutta and Basu's call to 'theorize with' instead of 'theorize on', is 'yes' and 'no'. As a person from an immigrant background, someone who might be labelled 'subaltern', the typical postcolonial approach would be to argue for her voice to be heard, for her to author her own identity. This is certainly the impulse behind Rosa's film. But when we look at the choices that Zoe makes, the postcolonial mindset is confused. The relative freedoms both of British filmmaking and academia mean that Zoe's voice can be heard, despite it presenting a controversial message. The documentary is her ethnographic statement as much as it is her expression of herself as a woman. Through it she theorises herself. The uncomfortable irony is that the apparent freedoms of the two outputs (the film and this chapter being produced and available in a public forum) mean that Zoe's voice is both heard *and* commodified.

What is important to highlight, however, is Zoe's deviation from the norm. The postcolonial expectation is that the Orchid persona is unacceptable, it belongs to and should remain in another time. Socio-political, cultural and academic activities work to exclude such stereotyping and prejudice from our world with very good reason. However, creative and cultural expression, often known for its nonconformity, may be found to play with dominant expectations of identity and behaviour and thus draw attention to their hegemonic nature, as we have seen in the case of Pedro Lemebel. Lemebel's knowingness of his own participation in a neoliberal world as an artistic commodity sat alongside his controversial creativity. Zoe, similarly, knowingly expresses her right to nonconformity not only as a trans-woman, as a performer and in the everyday, but also as a colonial type. Zoe's racialised identity, following a pattern rejected by postcolonialism, is thus a controversial act of resistance which forces us to acknowledge that a racialised performance may be as valid as any other aspect of our identity. Specifically, Zoe's agency can be said to have a deconstructing function towards essentialist, postcolonial expectations of Chinese Malay identity in Britain.

Rosa and Jenny

In 2010 the UK government made the decision that undergraduate degrees in the arts, humanities and social sciences would not be funded by public money as they are not considered to be priority areas for public investment. It was a decision described by journalist Andy Worthington as the 'disturbing sub-text' to the Browne Report (Worthington 2010). This is especially unsettling at this time, when the neoliberal phase of political economics leaves little to no room for art which is deemed to have no commercial value, as is often the case with works that deal with minority cultures and topics. Furthermore, a critical art practice which uses a personal experience in order to question cultural experience might be seen to have no immediate intrinsic value. It is only after a period of gestation that the impact of that research might be felt. This all entrenches a perception that higher education is a commodity to be bought and which first and foremost prepares undergraduates for work. It implies that the value of a critical education in the arts and humanities is only for the preserve of an elite (McGuigan 2016:109) or, even worse, is not necessary at all.

What this draws attention to is the vital role that research through critical arts practice in the academy has in creating knowledge formation, not to provide answers but to raise questions. Curricula are increasingly designed with employment as the priority, above the consideration and study of issues in our world that have no clear 'black and white' explanation. The desire to have the answers, to provide incontestable solutions to ethical questions in our research, practice and writing, needs to be met in some cases with resistance. It is, instead, the processes of thinking and debating matters that must be kept at the heart of the humanities. Henry A. Giroux's perspective on the contemporary US academy sees scholars subject to 'new regimes of neoliberal governance' which focus more on grants, budgets and career progression than on meaningful enquiry (Giroux 2014: 17). He writes, 'many academics have disappeared into a disciplinary apparatus that views the university not as a place to think but as a place to prepare students to be competitive in the global marketplace' (ibid.). He cites the novelist Toni Morrison from her own scholarship who emphasises the vital role of universities, which is, in part, 'as interrogator of more and more complex ethical problems' (2014: 19). The dilemma that Zoe presents to us, in the authoring of a flexible identity that challenges our perceived 'correct' worldviews, could be understood as such a complex ethical problem. She refuses to fit and this forces us to think. Equally, our role as academics and filmmakers in a privileged part of the world, working on attempting to understand Zoe's identity whilst giving her the platform to voice it, draws attention to Zoe as object case study. The dilemma thus extends to our motivation in this written reflection: do we present and theorise Zoe's lived identity as a means of 'chasing theory for its own sake' as Giroux (2014: 17) puts it? Can we argue that our intention is to raise issues that have no definitive resolution? Whether or not we can answer these questions is not the point. What matters is the mandate of critical arts practice to raise those complex ethical questions in the first place.

REFERENCES

Belli, A. and A. Lorentoni (2017), 'Gender, Identity and Belonging: New Citizenships beyond Orientalism', *Journal of Balkan and Near Eastern Studies*, 19:5, 483–98.
Bhabha, Homi K. (1994), *The Location of Culture*, New York: Routledge.
Butler, J. (1999), *Gender Trouble*, London and New York: Routledge.
Dutta, M. J. and A. Basu (2018), 'Subalternity, Neoliberal Seductions and Freedom: Decolonizing the Global Market of Social Change', *Cultural Studies – Critical Methodologies*, 18:1, 80–93.
Ellis, C., T. E. Adams and A. P. Bochner (2011), *Autoethnography: An Overview*, Forum: Qualitative Social Research/Socialforschung, vol. 1 (1) Art 10 January 2011, <http://www.qualitativeresearch.net/index.php/fqs/article/view/1589/3095> (accessed 1 May 2019).
Fong, R. (2017), 'Deconstructing Zoe: Performing Race', *Zapruder World International Journal for the History of Social Conflict*, vol. 4, <http://zapruderworld.org/journal/archive/volume-4/deconstructing-zoe-performing-race/> (accessed 20 February 2019).
Fong, R. (2020), 'Chinoiserie Drag: Masquerading as the Oriental Other', in S. Farrier and M. Edward (eds), *Contemporary Drag Practices and Performers: Drag in a Changing Scene Volume 1*, London and New York: Bloomsbury.
Giroux, H. A. (2014), *Neoliberalism's War on Higher Education*, Toronto: BTL Books.
González, M. M. (2018), '"It's Like Biting Your Own Tail": Pedro Lemebel's Queer Response to the Challenge of Subversion in Neoliberal Times', *Journal of Latin American Studies*, 27:2, 135–55.
Hwang, D. H. (1989), *M. Butterfly*, London and New York: Plume.
Kondo, D. K. (1990), '"M.Butterfly": Orientalism, Gender and a Critique of Essentialist Identity', *Cultural Critique*, 16, 5–29.
Mai, N. (2016), 'Assembling Samira: Understanding Sexual Humanitarianism through Experimental Filmmaking', *AntiAtlas Journal*, 1 [Online], 13 April, <http://www.antiatlas-journal.net/01-assembling-samira-understanding-sexual-humanitarianism-through-experimental-filmmaking> (accessed 4 May 2019).
McGuigan, J. (2016), *Neoliberal Culture*, New York: Palgrave Macmillian.
Said, E. (1985 [1978]), *Orientalism*, Harmondsworth: Penguin.
Sieg, K. (2009), *Ethnic Drag: Performing Race, Nation, Sexuality in West Germany*, Michigan: The University of Michigan Press.
Urrutia, A. (2017), 'The Credible Voice in Pedro Lemebel's Oeuvre: Identity, Gender and Censorship', *Interlitteraria*, 22:1, 139–53.
Worthington, A. (2010), 'Did you miss this? 100 Percent Funding Cuts to Arts, Humanities and Social Sciences Courses at UK Universities', <www.andyworthington.co.uk>, 22 November (accessed 25 June 2019).

FILMOGRAPHY

Deconstructing Zoe, film, directed by Rosa Fong. UK, 2016.

8. FROM NEOLITHIC TO NEOLIBERAL

Tony Clancy

1.

The *Creativity in the Age of Neoliberal Despair* conference offered compelling articulations of what it is to be a creative practitioner in the current academic world. It was a timely reminder to reconsider what it means to practise and to teach an arts subject (as well as a very welcome opportunity to listen and join in an important and fascinating conversation). My background is in still photography. In this essay I will discuss my recent short videos and think about why time-based pieces have become the main focus of my practice, and how they relate to and incorporate the still image. I will talk about some of the particular characteristics of the photograph (especially as delineated by Christian Metz) and why I currently make time-based work, but why the still image keeps its importance to me. I will look at the work of photographers whose images relate to the conference themes and my work. I will then reflect on two short films that I have made: *The Plate Spinner* is a scripted comedic piece with non-naturalistic narrative that has some direct echoes of the conference themes; the other is a more loosely structured piece, *Stone Ghosts*, that uses an assemblage of visual and sound devices to contemplate nature, myth and prehistory.

2.

Berthold Brecht had reservations about the value of the single photograph: he thought its naturalism was too simple to say anything useful about social relations (though he saw photomontage as a useful tool). Christian Metz took a psychoanalytic approach to distinguishing between how film and the single still image signify. In his essay 'Photography and Fetish' he says:

> While the social reception of film is oriented mainly toward a show-business-like or imaginary referent, the real referent is felt to be dominant in photography ... a film is only a series of photographs. But it is more precisely a series with supplementary components as well, so that the unfolding as such tends to become more important than the link of each image with its referent. This property is very often exploited by the narrative, the initially indexical power of the cinema turning frequently into a realist guarantee for the unreal. Photography, on the other hand, remains closer to the pure index, stubbornly pointing to what was, but no longer is. (1990: 156)

Metz goes on to further differentiate between photography and moving image by discussing how the photograph is silent, and how its frame permanently excludes what is outside it (in contrast to film which can pan and use off-frame sound). It is a frozen fragment of time giving the photograph a hallucinatory quality:

> ... film is able to call up our belief for long and complex dispositions of actions and characters (in narrative cinema) and images and sounds (in experimental cinema). [With photography] its poverty constitutes its force – I speak of a poverty of means, not of significance. The photographic effect is produced not from diversity, from itinerancy or inner migrations, from multiple juxtapositions or arrangements. It is the effect, rather, of a laser or lightning, a sudden and violent illumination ... Where film lets us believe in more things, photography lets us believe more in one thing. (1990: 162–3)

Metz's essay was published in 1985, just before digital photography became widely available and to some extent undermined its strong link with the indexical referent that he speaks of. The photograph's sense of truth is far more malleable in the age of photoshop and the ocean of social media images that threatens our sensibilities. (Erik Kessel's' installation *24 Hours in Photos* (2011) give a powerful physical realisation of this – he printed out the 1 million images that had been uploaded to Flikr by its users in a day and piled these up in a gallery, giving a physical presence to the vast number of images – mainly from smartphones – that appear on social media platforms.)

The signification of a body of still images is fragmentary, and has to be pieced together in the mind of the viewer. Despite this, many photographers maintain their stance as uncompromised witnesses. The particular power of photography's link to the referent (where this is still seen to hold) may give it a degree of authority against the erosion of belief in the neoliberal era. This sense of authority may be illusory, but can stand against disinformation. Michael Wolf's *Tokyo Compression* series shows images of commuters crammed into trains, an indelible vision of anonymous city dwellers, tired and exploited. Faces are framed and partially obscured through misted windows, some literally asleep on their feet, still conveying deep anxiety. A few awake eyes catch the camera's stare; one man is alive enough to give the photographer (and us) the finger, another puts his hand up to retain his privacy, others just glare blankly at the intrusive lens. These fleeting glimpses would be absorbed into the flow of existence if seen in everyday life. Grouped together and suspended in the silence of the photograph they become potent icons of the effects of the city on humanity. If the city was a place of exhilaration in early-twentieth-century experimental film, it is a place of exhaustion in Wolf's images. Exhaustion is a theme in another work of Wolf's, the installation '*The Real Toy Story*' where walls covered in the plastic debris of discarded toys surrounds photographs of the factory workers who make them. One image shows two members of the production line in deep sleep on the floor on cardboard boxes under their workbench, surrounded by disembodied dolls' limbs. Looking at these images it is hard for us to disavow what happens at the sharp end of mechanical reproduction in a consumer-driven world. This is the world of the automated, where workers are as alienated from their lives as consumers are from the workers who make their goods.

Other examples where photography can stand as witness to the corrosive effects of neoliberalism on societies and the world include: Alec Soth's images of individuals on the edges of society in *Broken Manual*; Gideon Mendel's images and displays of items retrieved from refugee camps in *Dzhangal*; Susan Meiselas's images of Kurdish communities; Shahidul Alam's courageous images of violent repression in *Crossfire*.

These photographers show that the still image retains potency. Paradoxically, the photograph's accelerating hyper reproducibility in the internet age has been matched by a fetishisation of the printed image in the art market, undermining the still image's role as a teller of truths. Documentary images are not always points of resistance, immutable in meaning and honest in intent; their truth can be reframed. I remember seeing large prints from Boris Mikhailov's *Case History*, exhibited in the Saatchi gallery in London. This work consists of people posing in degrading poses in post Glasnost Russia, a freak show photographed with voyeuristic flash, poverty commodified as art. If the images themselves are problematic, Mikhailov's comments make them even more dubious:

> I have taken pictures of them and I have enjoyed it, and maybe the whole world has a better understanding of the post-communist dramas through these sequences taken directly after nature. (Saatchi Gallery)

Showing us shocking images of life in post-Soviet Russia may have good intentions, but displaying these at the Saatchi Gallery is bleakly ironic. One of the Saatchi advertising company's main clients was the UK Conservative party, who it helped to power in 1979 where it initiated neoliberal reforms leading to a collapse of many industrial communities in the United Kingdom. Shock in these images is co-opted as exotic novelty by billionaires of the neoliberal era.

3.

Roland Barthes's essay on the tableau, 'Diderot, Eisenstein, Brecht' (Barthes, 1977), began to open up for me ideas about how still images convey narrative and how they relate to moving images. Some time ago I produced a series of Eisenstein-influenced narrative tableaux still photographs, aiming to make work that would, in Diderot's words, 'Touch me, astonish me, tear me to pieces' (1995 [1765]: 222). I succeeded, I think, mainly in perplexing my viewers. Still images are embedded in a fixed viewpoint (literally and figuratively). One aim of my recent work has been to decentre the viewer, to strive to find ways of experiencing the world from other perspectives. Moving image has been a more effective medium for this, its dimensions of movement and sound making for a more immersive experience and bringing a broader palette of possibilities to experiment with.

The Plate Spinner (2016)

> A mad race of shadows on the screen, not even a promise of something better to come, you're just sitting there, getting dumber by the minute; where are you going to get to by going faster? (Tolstoy, quoted in Tsivian 2010: 21)

My short video *The Plate Spinner* could be seen as a parable for an everyman figure living in neoliberalism, a comic take on the world that Michael Wolf shows us. When making this piece, I had in mind Buster Keaton, and his use of mobile camera work to portray a precarious modern world in films such as

FROM NEOLITHIC TO NEOLIBERAL

Figure 8.1 From *The Plate Spinner* (2016), Tony Clancy.

Sherlock Jnr (1924). Another influence was the plays of Eugene Ionesco where characters living banal lives become, for no apparent reason, overwhelmed by surrealist proliferations that engulf their reality. *The Plate Spinner* begins with a man setting up his act in an empty room. He begins his performance and once the plates are spinning, he runs out of the room. The camera follows him running up staircases and along corridors till he comes to a space where there is another set of plates waiting for him. Once these are in motion he runs back to the first room, noticing along the way that one corridor has another set up for him to attend to. Eventually there are three lots of plates in motion, and we see him dashing between them in a continuous loop edited at increasing speed. In between the frantic rushing we see the plates when the performer is out of the room, spinning calmly in their own universe, graceful and indifferent objects in motion.

The nameless character is tied to his compulsive need to keep the plates aloft; as demands multiply, his equilibrium is threatened (as is that of the plates). He is depicted first as objectively observed, then we begin to see his performance from his own point of view and are drawn into his world as it accelerates in pace, building up to an unsustainable frenzy. The film emulates the exuberant energy of Eisenstein and Vertov. Narrative time and space are compressed to an absurd degree. The effect is almost believable as having been made in real time, though of course this would have been impossible; the viewer is pulled between believing the action and knowing it is film fiction. This is an old-fashioned variety act that should be light entertainment, but there is the sense of a half-awake nightmare, an obsessive repetition and a feeling that it will not stop, or if it does it will end catastrophically. The act of plate spinning (strange in itself if we stop to think about it) becomes stranger and taps into deep anxieties about control, a control over our lives that we might feel we have already lost, echoing Benjamin's dark view of the machine age:

> Benjamin and Brecht shared the intellectual project of disrupting frozen patterns of perception in order to forge a new, more critical attitude toward social reality ... While Brecht embraced shock with absolute conviction, for Benjamin it entails great dangers: the likely emergence of a mass of 'traumatized automatons; the vanishing of private space; the coming of an era where experience, devoid of tradition, is incapable of finding meaning'. (Polgovsky Ezcurra 2012: section 5, para 3)

Plate spinning is a common enough metaphor for the pressures of work, here multiplied to absurdity. The performer seems trapped in an unending cycle of demands, perhaps a metonym for the neoliberal condition, the state of a stupefying chasing of nothing. The shots of the plates continuing their delicate balancing act are moments of calm unseen by the spinner – beautiful but highly precarious, liable to fall at any second. This instability again might be taken as a metaphor for a more general sense of a present overshadowed by the anxiety of impending collapse. It is this that spurred the making of this film – a feeling of being overwhelmed by the demands of work, and at the same time experiencing a strange compulsion to further add to it, a need to keep the plates spinning even if at times I cannot remember why (a compulsion I see amongst many friends and colleagues).

The character in the film is, then, akin to the commuters in Wolf's images. Wolf witnesses people caught in the cycles of work in the real world; we see them voyeuristically objectified, as markers of the harsh reality of working life. In *The Plate Spinner* the character is a fictionalised everyman figure, but through him we re-experience the mania of compulsion that ties us to our routines.

Stone Ghosts (2018)

> And we lost our feeling for matter, began to give cement the form of stone, iron the form of wood. (Shklovsky, quoted in Robinson 2008: 83)

Stone Ghosts is a very different piece and comes from a more Romantic world view, exploring, among other things, the acoustics of rocks and myths of transmogrification. The film is not about Neolithic society, but takes as one starting point a people (not far distant from our own in geological time or evolution, but, in the popular mind, a primitive other) where metal and all its contingent technologies (from the wheel to the internet) were not possible without the knowledge and skills which came shortly after. Rock was important for its use in making tools and weapons, and also for its symbolism. As there was no writing, this world remains enigmatically hidden behind a veil with a few (very tangible) traces left to us. There appears to have been an organised society where spectacle played a prominent role, evidenced by the stone circles, avenues and burial chambers that they left behind. Visiting these monuments now, especially the better-known ones, is often a disappointing experience. We know that there is a deep history associated with the objects we see before us, but their material is commonplace and seems unremarkable. Looking for their 'aura' can lead to a feeling of literally stony blankness. This may be in part because of stone's inscrutability; it may also be because, in the nineteenth and twentieth centuries, many sites, which had fallen prey to the vagaries of five thousand years of passing time and humans, were moved and reset (Stonehenge is a notorious example of this). These places which were once sacred, we assume, became commodified tourist simulacra of themselves, stage sets disconnected from their own history and mystery.

Stone Ghosts is an experiment in progress that had its origins in some pieces I made for a project on biosemiotics (a discipline where researchers try to understand the world not as 'our world' but as a world we are not central to). Talking about the relationship between humans and rocks, Jeremy Jerome Cohen says:

> ... something potentially propulsive unfolds within both frames at the moment of contact between mortal flesh and lithic substantiality: the advent of a disorienting realisation, no matter how dimly perceived, that stone's time is not ours, that the world is not for us, even as material continuity becomes palpable. (2015: 83)

Stone Ghosts is an attempt to find ways to decentre the human view of the world, to try to find a way to see and to listen to rock that undoes our over-familiar relationship and evokes something of the sense of awe and enormity of what we see. Even a casual knowledge of geology should make us marvel, but to experience it as more than cerebral is difficult, it seldom enters our affective world. Myths such as Sysiphus, Medusa, Pygmalion help us to connect more fully to the lithic by dramatising an imagined relationship between rocks and humans. There is an anxiety in these narratives where stone is seen as related to human suffering and death. (As with Metz's description of the photograph, rocks and statues are generally seen as frozen, silent and death-like; Pygmalion, more benignly, is a stone statue that becomes human.)

I look then to make rock strange again, to renew our sense of it and to try to reconnect in some small way with the sheer weirdness of rock to which we become inured. In the opening sequence of *Stone Ghosts,* a cave is gradually revealed, lit up piece by piece, at the same time accompanied by musical sounds from an (at that point) unidentified instrument. Camera shots then move over rock formations lit up in the cave. The walls of the cave are in vibrant greens and reds, at times almost flesh like. In a later section a large, obviously false, prop megalith is carried across the landscape by a man dressed in modern clothing, intercut with shots of the odd but melodic soundtrack music being performed on rocks. There is a deliberate clash of narrative modes here, a reframing of the film's continuity. This is intentionally part comic; the megalith is ironically weightless, a nod to the achievements of our Neolithic ancestors in moving large stones over long distances with no modern machinery or wheels. A rapid sequence of still images then takes the viewer on an ecstatic joy ride around stone circles. Each rock is photographed with flash (evoking Christian Metz's description of the photograph as hallucinatory, and giving the sequence a look – I am told – similar to a drug experience). This section again links to sequences in Russian films from the 1920s that intoxicate the viewer with a deluge of images. Here, the use of rapid succession of stills that imply movement, sits between film and still photography, not quite part of either medium. Together with the insistent rhythm of the soundtrack the effect is to take the viewer out of a rational relationship with the flow of the film and to suggest something more primal where everyday logic no longer applies. When the sequence ends, the figure carrying the rock, now asleep in front of it, is turned to stone (by the power of low-grade special effects) as the music continues. By the end of the piece, the viewer has experienced rocks represented in different

Figure 8.2   From *Stone Ghosts* (2018), Tony Clancy.

ways – sonically, theatrically, and through moving image and an animated stills sequence.

Sound is the element that underpins and structures the film. The music that forms the soundtrack is played on rocks from the Preselli Hills in West Wales, which was the source for the bluestones that made up the early stone circle of Stonehenge. How the rocks arrived in the middle of England remains a much-pondered mystery and there is no final consensus on this, though most archaeologists believe that they were taken there by humans rather than glaciers – if true, a remarkable feat. A long-standing question is, why were the fifty or so stones brought so far? Weighing an estimated two tons each, this was a vast undertaking. Recent work by Jon Wozencroft and Paul Deverieux has conjectured that the rocks were valued for their sonic qualities (Wozencroft and Deverieux 2014). On a trip to Wales to see one of the sites where some of the stones are known to come from, I found for myself that indeed the rocks from this area do have a musical ring, and a random set that I picked up played a scale. That they can make music was a wonderful surprise to me when I found them, a connection – almost magical – to the sound world of our distant ancestors. These were the rocks used to perform in the film by musician Mike Adcock and they integrate the materiality that the film contemplates into the soundtrack.

> [Berthold Brecht's desire was] ... for the *Verfremdungseffekt* to reveal the workings of the theatre in order to empower the spectator to question rather than to have a pleasant experience ... Brecht wanted the artifice of the theatre to be stripped down so that the spectator, rather than suspending her disbelief, could instead become a co-author of the performance. (Piotrowska 2014: 67)

Similarly, in this film, the viewer cannot settle into an easy relationship with the material, but is made aware of the different and sometimes clashing registers of representation. The somewhat menacing feeling of the footage of actual stones and caves is undercut by the musician's hands shown playing the soundtrack, the fake prop rock, the use of sequences of stills, the retro-TV sci-fi-style special effects.

Without overstating the case, rock is analogous to the '*pure, stubborn index*' that Metz speaks of in photography,[1] the most stable of referents (though also polysemous and indeterminate) that brings the transience of human existence into relief. Metz talks about the photograph as a fetish, a disavowal of change, ageing, death. Rock also has an otherworldly permanence that defies time (at least in our ability to perceive it). Rocks can be both spectacle and a metaphor for all that is inert; in Stone Ghosts they are animated through sequences of stills that suggest movement and luminosity, and by the music that rocks can make.

4.

My two films are very different, each an experiment in using moving image to bring about an experience for the audience where the world is made strange. Looking over my work, I find myself poised, or lost, between opposing impulses: on the one hand, the wish to see and depict the world afresh in all its excitement, lit up with the energy that distinguished the art of the Russian revolution, sweeping away ossified views and celebrating the freedoms that new technologies bring; on the other hand, wanting to connect the viewer to a yearned for permanence, a sense of calmness that is closer to an elusive 'real'. This is offered to some degree by traditional photography, and is also connoted by the obdurate permanence of stone; both mark time and lives that have been, and stand against the erasure of loss. They are a counterpoint to the precarious act of plate spinning. They also connote reality rendered immobile, trapped in a past tense.

Neolithic monuments are a meditation on time; they stand as a very tangible trace of peoples whose investment of labour may appear primitive, but which have survived for thousands of years. In our age, our short-term addiction to progress and the disposable new finds itself condemned in Pieter Hugo's still images in *Permanent Error*: workers in Ghana stand amidst the debris of the affluent world's discarded electronic technology, where they pick it over to sell the materials for recycling. Their lives are shortened and blighted by the toxic chemicals released; they pay the cost for our constant movement into the future through accelerated technological innovation. This is the end point for the smartphones, tablets and computers that are made in atrocious conditions in factories elsewhere in the world, a reality we constantly disavow. Our dependence on social media helps to drive the consumption of these goods and add to this cycle. We are all snared in this web – the computer I write this on, the cameras I make my videos on, etc. etc. will probably one day end up on the dumping grounds that Hugo shows us. Whilst I do not for one minute think we can or should return to stone age living, to meditate on rocks gives a counterpoint to the virtual absurdities of an age where reality is so eroded.

A touchstone for me has been Viktor Shklovsky's ideas and legacy. In thinking about how culture and creativity can be acts of resistance to the sweep of neoliberalism that we are all subject to, the ideas that he wrote about and the work that these helped to foster in the early part of the twentieth century still stand as inspiring examples of political art. Despite later criticisms of their effectiveness and legacy, their energy and verve are still compelling and they still hold deep sway over our culture. His writings do not leave a manifesto. Rather I see them as a reminder to aspire to make work that challenges and does not fall into predictability, to keep finding ways to connect to the real and not fall into automated responses to it. I find in them an appealing spirit that gives me a place to see beyond the weight of conformity that chains us to our habits, steers us to our pension plans and blinds us to the world we live in. I did not set out to consciously explore or to illustrate the idea of *ostranenie*, but Shklovsky's words are very apposite to what I set out to achieve in my work.

> this thing we call art exists in order to restore the sensation of life, in order to make us feel things, in order to make a stone stony. The goal of art is to create the sensation of seeing, and not merely recognizing, things. (Shklovsky [1917])

Thomas Elsaesser in his keynote speech at the conference spoke about Foucault's idea that the mechanisms of society absorb the challenges of the avant-gardes and indeed use them to compound a sense of discontinuity and disbelief in stable values, making us less able to act collectively and so more vulnerable to the machinations of the neoliberal elite. He also spoke about how making art could be an act of resistance in itself. My films, I hope, are small acts of resistance against the institutional steamroller of bureaucracy that threatens to overwhelm and to automate us.

NOTE

1. Metz himself, writing when personal photography was still mainly consumed as prints, describes the surface of a photograph as '*petrified*'.

REFERENCES

Barthes, R. (1977), 'Diderot, Eisenstein, Brecht', in *Image, Music Text*, trans. Stephen Heath, London: Jonathan Cape, pp. 69–78.
Cohen, J. J. (2015), *Stone: An Ecology of the Inhuman*, Minneapolis: University of Minnesota Press.
Diderot, D. (1995 [1765]), *Diderot on Art*, trans. John Goodman, New Haven: Yale University Press.
Metz, C. (1990), *Photography and Fetish*, in C. Squiers (ed.), *The Critical Image*, London: Lawrence and Wishart, pp. 165–74.
Mikhailov, B., https://www.saatchigallery.com/artists/boris_mikhailov.htm (accessed 31 March 2019).
Piotrowska, A. (2014), *Psychoanalysis and Ethics in Documentary Film*, London: Routledge.
Polgovsky Ezcurra, M. (2012), *On 'Shock': The Artistic Imagination of Benjamin and Brecht*, Contemporary Aesthetics, vol.10.
Robinson, D. (2008), *Estrangement and the Somatics of Literature*, Baltimore: The Johns Hopkins University Press.
Shklovsky, V. (1917), *Art, as Device*, trans. A. Berlina. <https://warwick.ac.uk/fac/arts/english/currentstudents/undergraduate/modules/fulllist/first/en122/lec-turelist-2015-16-2/shklovsky.pdf> (accessed 23 September 2019).
Tsivian, Y. (2010), 'The Gesture of Revolution, or Misquoting as Device', in Annie

van den Oever (ed.), Ostranenie: *'Strangeness' and the Moving Image. The History, Reception, and Relevance of a Concept*, Amsterdam: Amsterdam University Press, pp. 21–32.

Wozencroft, J. and P. Deverieux (2014), 'Stone Age Eyes and Ears: A Visual and Acoustic Pilot Study of Carn Menyn and Environs, Preseli, Wales', *Time and Mind: The Journal of Archaeology, Consciousness and Culture*, 7:1.

ARTIST WEBSITES

Alam, S., *Crossfire*, <http://shahidulnews.com/CROSSFIRE/> (accessed 23 September 2019).

Hugo, P., *Permanent Error*, <http://www.photographermagazine.net/pieter-hugo/> (accessed 23 September 2019).

Kessel, E., *24 Hours in Photos*, <http://www.kesselskramer.com/project/24-hrs-in-photos/> (accessed 23 September 2019).

Meiselas, S., *Kurdistan*, <http://www.susanmeiselas.com/archive-projects/kurdistan/#id=mass%20graves> (accessed 23 September 2019).

Mendel, G., *Dzhangal*, <http://gideonmendel.com/dzhangal/> (accessed 23 September 2019).

Soth, A., *Broken Manual*, <https://alecsoth.com/photography/projects/broken-manual> (accessed 23 September 2019).

Wolf, M., *Tokyo Compression*, <http://photomichaelwolf.com/#tokyo-compression/> (accessed 23 September 2019).

VIDEOS

The Plate Spinner (2016), T. Clancy, <https://vimeo.com/281529326>
Stone Ghosts (2018), T. Clancy, <https://vimeo.com/245643565>

9. FIRST-PERSON EXPRESSION ON 'NON-WESTERN' SCREENS: CHINA AS A CASE STUDY

Kiki Tianqi Yu

This chapter was originally my keynote speech at NECS 2018 (European Network for Cinema and Media Studies) in Amsterdam. I feel tremendously grateful for the generous invitation from Professor Patricia Pisters and all committee members of the conference. As a filmmaker and a scholar working in cinema, I spend a large amount of time researching and practising camera-mediated self-expression. As a vital force that shapes art and cultural practices, self-expression is also shown in diverse dispositions and forms. In different historical periods and geopolitical entities, individuals and collectives have been searching for methods of articulation and assertion. The individual *self*, situated in the complexity of social, cultural and cosmic relations, is not only shaped by its past, but is also constantly shaping the future self.

My last feature documentary *China's van Goghs* (2016) received its world premiere at International Documentary Film Festival Amsterdam, and consequently was theatrically released in the Netherlands, Italy, Japan, Hong Kong, etc.; it received many awards including Best Feature Documentary at the Beijing International Film Festival 2017 and at the Los Angeles Chinese Film Festival 2018, Netpac Award at the Moscow International Film Festival 2018, and the BAFTSS Practice Award in 2019. The film is an interdisciplinary work that interrogates art history and cultural sociology, asking if copying can be a path towards originality; it also reflects the dynamics of documentary production itself. An intimate portrait of peasant-turned-oil-painters transitioning from making copies of canonical masterpieces to creating their own original work of art, the film investigates self-expression on two levels. On the one hand, the making of this film allowed us to construct the first-person expression and desire of copy painters in Dafen Shenzhen, whose encounter with Van Gogh through the hundreds of hand-made copies not only provide them with financial means, but also inspire them to see the original and to create their own original work. On the other hand, the film reflects our own self-expression as the filmmakers, whose practices, just like the painters, are also shaped by transnational creative, economic and labour forces. Both self-expressions in painting and in filmmaking are linked by globalisation and internationalism, and involve constant negotiation with artistic, cultural and financial factors.

The understanding of multiple agents involved in shaping the production of painting in *China's van Goghs* probes me to rethink the possibilities of auteurism, which Astruc idealises in his concept of *caméra-stylo* (2002 [1948]). The limitations placed on Dafen painters are by no means exceptions, but exist in a wider production context, including filmmaking. Thus, this chapter explores when we take cameras, just like painters using brush and paints, to explore ourselves in first person, how we use the special media of film and video that could also capture and even modify the change of time, to present our self-becoming on the canvas of screen, while negotiating with different forces.

Growing as a popular strategy, especially in the current context of digital and social media, first-person documentary has been practised by filmmakers, artists and amateurs around the world. This chapter specially focuses on this practice in contemporary China. In the contexts of an increasingly individualising Chinese society, diversified technologies of media platforms and intensifying political constraints, first-person filmmaking practice embodies multiple meanings and problematises the Western enlightenment notions of individualism and individuality.[1] In the following sections, I discuss how individual filmmakers deal with ethical dilemmas and make aesthetic choices that are socially and culturally rooted. I choose to illustrate this through a self-reflexive analysis on the position and perspective I take in developing grounded theory for understanding the local specifics of this film practice. By doing so, I hope to be able to demonstrate how these films share similarities with first-person films made elsewhere, and how they contribute new knowledge to this global practice.

Positioning: From Transnational Practice to Localised Research

I started practising first-person film when I was eager to understand my own cultural identity in a transnational context, especially when working on a BBC documentary in London which investigated China after the economic reform. My ethnographic instinct compelled me to observe how this British professional film crew represented the China in which I grew up. I was drawn into different historiographies of China in the 1980s, especially, of course, the 1989

Tian'anmen incident, and China's consequent focus on economic development in the 1990s. Knowing little about this before, I was fascinated by different historical narratives and started to question my own understanding, the one based on my education back home. But I was also aware of what the ideologies of a modern democratic system promote, and the specific historical trajectory of China. With a small DV camera in my hand, I began to shoot my daily negotiations with the crew. When the crew did not get visas to go to China to film, as the only Chinese person in the crew I was jokingly called a Chinese spy, with typically British sarcasm; but the 'joke' had a strong psychological impact on me. I began to ask myself, 'Which side should I belong to?' Overwhelmed by the clash of values, I also made intensive personal video diaries. This reflexive ethnographic footage was edited into a first-person film called *London Diaries* (2009). Watching it with a selected audience gave me a chance to see the complex process of my own self-becoming. During that period, I also made another short essay film *Memory of Home* (2009), which explores, in a more abstract manner, the psychological difficulty of positioning myself: a Chinese outside China, in the West, learning about China's rapid transformations and urbanisation from afar.

My transnational position made me wonder if there are similar documentaries made by Chinese filmmakers within China, and what new knowledge they present to us on being Chinese today. That is how I started my theorisation of first-person films. Being a filmmaker, I was naturally drawn to look beyond the film texts as aesthetic and cultural objects, to examine the filmmaking

Figure 9.1   Expressing the difficulties of locating home in *Memory of Home* (2009), directed by Kiki Tianqi Yu

practice as social intervention which itself is set within various limitations. During the process of this research, it was pleasing to see film studies moving more boldly beyond textual analysis to considering films as social practices and cultural productions. In addition to early writings on film cultures (Harbord 2002), new film history methodologies (Chapman et al. 2007) and the political economy of film as production (Spicer et al. 2014) have also gained more attention. These developments in film studies helped me further my argument that the filmmaker as a social agent should not only be positioned in the field of film industry, but also as a citizen with certain social roles in the larger world.

I notice that the practice of self-expression on film often serves as a method of reconnecting with *laojia*, the old home. In China's dramatic urbanisation, *laojia* as a disappearing geo space and a set of traditional family relations creates psychological tensions that affect almost everyone. The disappearing *laojia* adds a sense of urgency to the action of nostalgic reconnection, and the self-expression coming out of it. These films also demonstrate how filmmakers probe broken family relations, and negotiate new patterns of communication, which inevitably challenge traditional social ethics based on Confucianism. There are also filmmakers who use cameras to engage with their surroundings, sometimes to deliberately enrage the public, so as to provoke a more politicalised public space, as in *Criticising China* (2008), for example. Through various aesthetic strategies of self-inscription on screen – such as self-revelation in video diaries, provocative and performative action documentary, interactive online streaming (*zhibo*) and essayistic image writing (*yingxiang xiezuo*) – these filmmakers present us with the most pressing concerns of individuals in contemporary China.

From making first-person films, to theorising this practice, my position changed from being a transnational filmmaker seeking to understand China from the outside, to a researcher trying to understand this practice and its cultural and social contexts through an insider's perspective. Seeing from the outside, I take China as a specific geopolitical entity, with its unique historical and cultural path. Observing from the inside, I saw the desires of individuals, their eagerness to find and define themselves, in relation, largely, to their past, the traditional social ethics, and to their local environment, social and political, if not all globalised. These are very specific contexts, against which, individual selves construct their subjectivities.[2]

Interrogating West versus Non-West Binary Division

Such a transnational position examining the body of my research both as an outsider and an insider inspires me to think more deeply about knowledge production in the so-called West and non-West. Admittedly, the majority of existing studies on first-person documentary practice and personal cinema (Renov

1996, 2004, 2008; Lebow 2008, 2012, 2013; Rascaroli 2009, 2014, 2017) have provided me with great inspiration, but they are primarily on Western cultural expression, where the individual is understood as an enlightenment subject. Such expressions are often centred around identity politics, memory and post memory, and the frustrations and struggles of understanding oneself in the postmodern Western world, including influential works by Jonas Mekas, Chantal Akerman, Marlon Rigg, Carol Morley, Alan Berliner, etc. Scholars on non-Western culture and societies in general are alert to using theories developed in western socio-political and historic conditions to understand social formation in non-Western societies. In film studies, Chinese cinemas studies particularly, scholars have been discussing whether the postmodern conditions exist in China, and what is specific to post-socialist China (Lu 2002; Berry 2004, 2007). While I am seeking useful concepts, frameworks and paradigms grounded in specific culture and art tradition, I also ask whether the Western and non-Western division is a useful tool, and consider the problematics of this binary devision in developing new knowledge of cinema and film practices.

De-westernising knowledge production has long been advocated by scholars and educators (Dissanayake 1988; Curran and Park 2000; Chen 2006; Kim 2002; Ba and Higbee 2012). Over the past decade, it has gained popularity in film studies, especially in the subfield of world cinema, partly due to the increasing global influence of non-Western countries, such as China and India. One would argue that this division could be helpful for us in paying attention to cinema and media in cultures and geo-entities outside the familiar American and European cinemas. The West versus non-Western binary division is a result and response to Western centrism. However, it still takes the West as a simplified, unifying concept and entity against which to measure the non-West.

If we approach cinema through the perspective of multiple modernities (Eisenstadt 2002; Fourie 2012), we see how different cultural, social and historical contexts shape film productions and receptions, and how cinema as a modern art form and cultural practice arises in different modern conditions and has different histories. It is perhaps more useful to recognise the diversity within the so-called West, while valuing cultural differences in what we usually group as the non-West, such as the Middle East, Asia, Africa, South America, Eastern Europe, etc., and all of which consist of varying modern nation-states with local cultures.

In addition, it is important to acknowledge the ongoing dynamic cross-cultural contamination in cinema aesthetics and film practices across the globe, making it difficult to separate what is non-Western from what we know as Western, and vice visa. For instance, the influence of the French New Wave, Italian neo-realism and German expressionism on East Asian cinemas, and Eastern philosophers and artists on certain 'Western' directors.[3] That said, one should not neglect the fact that new thoughts and art forms from abroad, in the process of reterritorialisation, are often interpreted through local understandings and life experiences, with layers of imagination, such as what *Le Moulin* presents, the rise of local surrealist literature in Taiwan through the influence of surrealist art in France received via Japanese translation.

This leads to my next point: if this binary division enables and is in favour of a Western and non-Western comparison, one should not ignore the vigorous influences from one's neighbouring cultures. Such cultural exchanges are often made possible through past political alliance, that is China with Russia, and East Europe in the form of socialist realism; as a result of commercial trades and human migration, such as East and Southeast Asia on the popularisation of regional melodrama, and the dissemination of Bollywood cinema in Middle East and East Africa; or simply because of geographic proximities, the regions of South America, East Asia, Northern Europe, and North America. This approach helps to mitigate the post-colonial perspective by enabling further possible comparisons and contrast.

For example, 'Asia as a method', developed by Japanese writer Takeuchi Yoshimi,[4] has received much scholarly attention recently, among historians, Asian studies scholars, political scientists in and on East and Southeast Asia. Yoshimi sees Asia could form subjectivity that is uniquely built on its cultural past and history, rather than simply through Western imperialism (Wang 2019). Revisiting this concept, Kuan-hsing Chen advocates what he calls 'de-imperialization' so to better understand Asia (2010). Yoshimi also advocates an inter-Asian comparison, given that neighbouring culture and societies could be a more effective point of reference for developing valuable understanding on Asia (Wang 2019). 'Asia as a method' inspires me to consider how to approach art practices in Asia, in response to cultural and knowledge imperialism.

I ask: outside the dominating theories and criticisms in English and French language of cinema studies, what thoughts, philosophies and approaches developed in Asia could provide us with new understandings of cinema? How do we understand first-person film practice, which follows its own paths of self-expression within China and receives influences from other Asian countries?

First-person Expression on Screen in Contemporary China

In the research on first-person film practice, I started with the philosophical notion of the self and its transformation from ancient to modern China. To unpack the motivations and ethical tensions around first-person filmmaking practice, I also conducted an in-depth exploration of the historical and anthropological debates on the notion of self. One key finding is that Confucian notions of self, which played a dominant role in ancient China, still underpin understanding of the self in China today. Historians and political theorists understand Chinese society as 'familistic' (Parsons, quoted by King 1985: 58), and ethical-relations centred (Liang Shuming 1990: 79–95), following what Dong Chongshu, an ancient Confucian follower, observes: 'Three cardinal guides, and Five constant virtues'.[5] In this understanding, the self is situated within familial and quasi-familial relationships in social contexts, and conforms to the larger whole. Recent studies demonstrate how this is still in evidence in everyday life and how individuals try to break through such family-centred social relations. It is also shown through the films I observe. Of course, I am also aware of the influence of Daoist and Buddhist philosophies on an individual's daily practices, but the social relations that govern the individuals, especially on how one relates to others, are primarily based on Confucian ethics. At the turn of the twentieth century and during the May Fourth Movement, the relationship between the modern individual and the state conceived by the intellectuals at the time was still largely in line with the traditional vision of a relational individual conforming to the larger whole. Though the notion of autonomy was discussed and translated as '*zizhi*' by an early modern intellectual Liang Qichao, Liang's notion of *zizhi*, when translated back to English, means 'self-discipline' or self-legislation, which correlates with the Confucian value of self-cultivation to achieve moral autonomy (Svarverud 2010: 207). The traditional social ethics was seriously attacked during Mao's Cultural Revolution and only restored after the 1980s, when the whole society was facing a serious cultural, social and economic transformation.

In contemporary China, through his long-term fieldwork, anthropologist Yan Yunxiang observes some key features of individuals which are instrumental to understanding how individuals are situated in post-socialist China. This includes the disembodiment of the individual from former encompassing social categories, such as work unit and production team; increasing mobility of individuals enabled by the party-state, made possible through economic reform and urbanisation; the emergence of identity politics, especially in urban areas; and the rise of new types of social intercourse in public spaces – which promote rights assertion movements but are still lacking social trust, leading to increasing moral challenges (Yan 2009, 2010).

To understand the aesthetic traditions, I observed first-person expression in art and literature historically, and in China and East Asia at large. This includes Chinese traditional essay, autobiographical writing, self-portraits, performing art, Japanese I novel, I photography, and I film. It is not surprising to discover that Japanese 'I Film' has a strong influence on how Chinese filmmakers understand first-person films as 'private image' (*si yingxiang*), just like the Japanese modern literature of 'I novel' inspired the rise of personal writing in 1920s and 1930s China. Such a tradition of first-person expression in ancient and modern China demonstrates the rhetorics, styles and approaches of expressing oneself through various art and literary forms.

These philosophical, historical, anthropological and aesthetic explorations help to build a theoretical framework unique to approaching the specific films and film practices in contemporary China. I also conducted ethnographical fieldwork and interviews with filmmakers, in addition to examining the film texts. With the relational sense of self under Confucian ethics as an underlining theme, the films and film practices I studied could be put into four groups: first, the familial self, negotiating gendered expectations and nostalgic for *old-home*; secondly, the problematic public self in action, activism and dealing with ethical dilemmas; thirdly, instant and interactive self-construction on social media, most prominently on *Zhibo*, live streaming broadcast; and, finally, the 'image writing', a response to recent political tightening up, which is also influenced by the growing popular form of 'essay film' on international festival circuits and traditional Chinese literature essay writing.

The 'familial self'

With regard to the 'familial self', I first explore the relational self under gendered expectations, especially in women's first-person film practices, such as Wang Fen's *They Are Not the Only Unhappy Couple* (2000), Yang Lina's *Home Video* (2001) and Tang Danhong's *Nightingale, Not the Only Voice* (2000), as well as films by Wen Hui, Song Fang, Liu Jiayin, Zou Xueping and Zhang Mengqi. Arising from a subversive impulse, their films are socially and also aesthetically pioneering: not only do they depart from earlier male filmmakers' independent documentaries in the 1990s, which tended to highlight marginalised others, but they also challenge the traditional role of women constrained by patriarchal expectations. Employing various aesthetic strategies, including performative staging, participant observation, interviews and confession, these women's films are a form of 'communicative practice', quiet yet powerful, confrontational yet not didactic. They negotiate filial duties by paying attention to their parents, or strengthening female kinships that are rarely discussed in either personal family histories or grand official histories. These films, however, have not been widely screened even in former independent film festivals, and received much hostility on the rare occasions when they were shown. This indicates that society still does not fully accept women who openly challenge parental and patriarchal power, even in the supposedly progressive milieu of the independent cinema scene.

The 'familial self' is also interrogated by male filmmakers, whose first-person films often serve as a nostalgic reconnection to the disappearing '*laojia*', the old home. During the nationwide urbanisation process in post-Mao China, individuals from the countryside had been 'liberated' from the traditional familial collectivism and the former communist mode of collective production. This means the nuclearisation of traditional big families. Early amateur DV

Figure 9.2 Setting up a tombstone, a sign of remembrance, with local kids in *Children's Village* (2012), directed by Zou Xueping.

filmmaker Hu Xinyu has been making long-term domestic video ethnography on his parent's home, particularly exploring generational conflicts and the constraints of traditional family ethics on individual family members, such as in *Family Phobia* (2009). Another filmmaker Yang Pingdao revisits his village and captures the sense of decline of traditional family ritual ceremonies in *My Family Tree* (2008). In urban areas, demolition and reconstruction have caused the relocation of the family home for citizens who previously enjoyed many social welfare benefits. Shu Haolun's *Nostalgia* (2006) is a first-person critique of urban demolition and neoliberal consumerism in his home city, Shanghai. All these filmmakers take a dual role, as insiders in their own families, and outsiders whose filmmaking practices constitute a significant social act that offers valuable insights on how family relations have been affected by China's dramatic socioeconomic transition.

'The public self'

With regard to 'the public self', I focus on how filmmakers search for their social identities as public citizens and politicise the space they are in by using the camera to engage and interact with, or even enrage others. Most prominently, two younger generation filmmakers, Wu Haohao and Xue Jianqiang, put their role as 'author-performer' explicitly, and define their practice as 'first-person action documentary', similar to the practice of Japanese filmmaker Hara Kazuo. Like Hara, they are keen to reach out from their personal space, eager to communicate with their subjects, or even to provoke their subjects for a response. In my 2010 interview with Wu Haohao, he comments that 'We are so poor, but not in terms of materials – though we are not rich either. We are poor because we desperately need communication, and emotional care.'

Their films illustrate the absence of community in the individualising urban cityscape, where young individuals are constrained in their own spaces, longing for communication and emotional caring. With a personal camera as a weapon, these filmmakers challenge current social conditions, and disrupt the established social structure, even in '*minjian*', grassroots public spaces. In Wu's *Criticizing China* (2008), he takes his camera to document the local debating corner, but receives a hostile reaction from the locals who see themselves as the elder and, therefore, deserving of respect. In Xue's *I Beat the Tiger when I was Young* (2010), he criticises the older generation of independent filmmakers for 'hiding' behind the cameras. Nevertheless, these films also expose their problematic 'public self' in interpersonal communication. The way they criticise the older generation mirrors the violent autocratic manner they are critical of, as they aim to entirely demolish the old without any space for negotiation.

There are also filmmakers who use cameras to participate in political events, which I regard as 'camera activism', such as Ai Weiwei's *Disturbing the Peace* (a.k.a. *Lao Ma Ti Hua*, 2009). Ai's practice produces a shared political subjectivity through documenting activist movements, confrontational filmmaking and disseminating the films widely through social networks. Yet the film also illustrates Ai's performative public persona, an authority in his own right who is surrounded by his followers, making his activism problematic.

The community engaged 'China Villagers Documentary Project' is a fascinating example that explores the socially less empowered, subaltern selves. While this project has attracted scholarly attention (Johnson 2014; Huang 2016), the power relations between the project's 'creative instructor' Wu Wenguang and the village amateur filmmakers are largely neglected. Behind the collaboration is how the villagers unconsciously and consciously resist their 'given' social identity. Their action of rebelling against the idealised peasant image portrayed by intellectuals reflects their effort to reconstruct their own identities through filmmaking. This project affects Wu Wenguang as much as the villagers. Beyond the surface of the villagers' self-portraits is the negotiation process through which both the villagers and Wu have achieved a deeper self-understanding.

Technologically interactive self

Thirdly, the changing technological conditions in the post-cinematic era contribute to the proliferation of personal videos and live streaming of personal lives on social media, such as on *Zhibo*, live-streaming online broadcasts. As a new kind of social media, *Zhibo* allows individuals to communicate with, and perform for, an interactive audience through a personal camera on her or his smart phone or a tablet device. Though these are not, strictly speaking, structured documentary films, what *Zhibo* platforms present are non-edited camera mediated first-person expression on screen, which accentuates the actual process of presenting the self while interacting with an audience. The self is presented as situated in what Yan regards as a new kind of socialites (2009), interacting with stranger-audiences who are out of the usual 'familial' or quasi-familial relations. Among various online identities, such as sexy young women, individuals doing extravagant actions, creative migrant workers and foreigners, a typical type of presenter-performer is a young pretty girl set in a private or pretend-to-be private space, watched by anonymous and imagined stranger-audiences, manipulating and being manipulated by the audience's imagination.[6] The live interactions are displayed and constantly updated through *danmu*, live chat, messages over the streaming screen. The performative act of presenting the self through *zhibo* questions the binary opposition of staged and non-staged, performing and non-performing, real and unreal in first-person expression. Expressing the self for profit also complicates the ethics involved in the process of 'self-making'.

'Image writing'

Finally, as my research on the first-person expression continues, the recent *yingxiang xiezuo* draws my attention. Literally meaning 'image writing', *yingxiang xiezuo* is an independent non-fiction film practice of experimenting with and 'writing' through moving images, as artistic expression and social intervention. As a concept, it is similar to *caméra-stylo*, and the aesthetic form associated with it could be seen as essayistic in the Chinese context. Essay film, as an interrogation of image through creative and critical use of narration and sound is high associated with the literary and the linguistic. I argue that current criticism and theorisation around essay film is largely rooted in western film studies, and associated with the form of essay as a modern French and English literary form. Not holding an essentialist position to advocate completely different sets of aesthetics, I suggest that features of the essayistic in cultures with different art and literary traditions, linguistic structures and socio-political contexts, such as those in China, require different methods of interrogation. For this, I examine recent essayistic non-fiction films by Zhao Liang, Cons Feng, Leilei, etc., which demonstrate how specific language features and art tradition influence their practice of 'writing' with image (Yu 2019b).

Conclusion

As a filmmaker, I found first-person filmmaking practice has been a useful constructive force, taking me onto an ongoing process of negotiating cultural, social and gender conventions, while expressing my *self* on camera. Without a doubt, transnational has become my own reality and part of my self-becoming, through education, working environment and everyday life. While I continue to play the role of producer of international co-production,[7] and make film in international contexts, I also search deeper within myself: how should I respond to my transnational everyday life, while living with the rich Chinese culture and art tradition I receive from China in the past and today?

The idea of transformation in Daoism as philosophy has inspired me to examine beyond a binary view – to see lives and self-making as a process of one influencing the other. Daoist understanding of the cosmos also inspires me to position human individuals within the larger universe, whose self is not just shaped by relations with other human beings, but also how one relates to the natural environment, animals and objects. Locating cinema in relation to Eastern philosophy and within the larger field of art history, I investigate whether traditional Chinese aesthetics in Chinese poetics and landscape paintings influence contemporary cinematic practice; if so, how do filmmakers and artists in China, like myself, respond to the aesthetic and philosophical heritage? With these as the central questions of my current project, I hope to be able to share more in the future.

NOTES

1. For an extensive discussion, please see my monograph '*My' Self on Camera* (2019a).
2. I did not look at overseas Chinese, for whom the transnational has become their unique reality, and the forces of constructing the subjectivities are more complicated and mobile.
3. Such as David Lynch and Denis Villeneuve.
4. Over the last century, Asia as a cultural and historical entity has been discussed as a response to Western imperialist materialism, imperialism and colonisation. Takeuchi Yoshimi developed this concept in 1962, after observing and rethinking how China fought against Western imperialism during the May Fourth Movement as a way of forming its own subjectivity.
5. The three cardinal guides (*sangang*) include: the ruler guides the subjects, the father guides the son, and the husband guides the wife; and the five constant virtues are (*wuchang*) of benevolence, brother-hood, propriety, wisdom and loyalty.
6. The feature documentary *People's Republic of Desire* (dir. Wu Hao, 2018) offers an intimate portrait of *zhibo* presenter-performers, and the economics behind it.
7. Recently, I have completed producing another international co-production feature documentary, a seventeen-year long-term observation of a transgender migrant worker in Southern China.

REFERENCES

Astruc, Alexandre (2002), 'The Future of Cinema', *La Nef*, 48 [1948], reprinted in *Trafic*, 3 (Summer), 151–8.
Ba, Saer Many and Will Higbee (2012), *De-Westernizing Film Studies*, Routledge.
Berry, Chris (2004), *Postsocialist Cinema in Post-Mao China: The Cultural Revolution after the Cultural Revolution*, New York and London: Routledge.
Berry, Chris (2007), 'Getting Real: Chinese Documentary, Chinese Postsocialism', in Zhang Zhen (ed.), *The Urban Generation: Chinese Cinema and Society at the Turn of the Twenty-First Century*, Durham, NC and London: Duke University Press.

Chapman, James, Sue Harper and Mark Glancy (2007), 'Introduction', in *The New Film History: Sources, Methods, Approaches*, London: Palgrave Macmillan.
Chen, G. M. (2006), 'Asian communication studies: What and where to now', *Review of Communication*, 6:4, 295–311.
Chen, Kuan-hsing (2010), *Asia as Method: Toward Deimperialization*, Durham, NC: Duke University Press.
Curran, J. and M. J. Park (eds) (2000), *De-Westernizing Media Studies*, New York: Routledge.
Dissanayake, W. (1988), *Communication Theory: The Asian perspective*, Singapore: Asian Mass Communication Research and Information Centre.
Eisenstadt, Shmuel (2002), *Multiple Modernities*, Transaction Publishers.
Fourie, Elsje (2012), 'A future for the theory of multiple modernities: Insights from the new modernization theory', *Social Science Information*, 51:1, 52–69.
Harbord, Janet (2002), *Film Cultures*, London: Sage Publications.
Huang, Xuelei (2016), 'Murmuring voices of the everyday: Jia Zhitan and his village documentaries', *Journal of Chinese Cinemas*, 10:2, 166–86.
Johnson, Matthew D. (2014), Wu Wenguang and the NGO aesthetic', in M. D. Johnson, K. B. Wagner, T. Yu and L. Vulpiani (eds), *China's iGeneration: Cinema and Moving Image Culture for the Twenty-First Century*, London: Bloomsbury Academic.
Kim, M. S. (2002), *Non-Western Perspectives on Human Communication: Implications for theory and practices*, Thousand Oaks, CA: Sage.
King, Ambrose Yeo-chi (1985), 'The individual and group in Confucianism: a relational perspective', in Donald J. Munro (ed.), *Individualism and Holism: Studies in Confucian and Taoist Values*, Ann Arbor: Center for Chinese Studies Publications, University of Michigan, pp. 57–70.
Lebow, Alisa (2008), *First Person Jewish*, Minneapolis: University of Minnesota Press.
Lebow, Alisa (2012), *Cinema of Me: The Self and Subjectivity in First Person Documentary*, New York: Wallflower Press.
Lebow, Alisa (2013), 'First-person political', in Winston Brian (ed.), *Documentary Film Book*, London: BFI.
Liang, Shuming (1990), 'Zhongguo Wenhua Yaoyi (The essentials of Chinese culture)', in *Liang Shuming Quanji*, vol. 3, Jinan: Shangdong People's Press.
Lu, Sheldon H. (2002), *China, Transnational Visuality, Global Postmodernity*, Stanford: Stanford University Press.
Rascaroli, Laura (2009), *The Personal Camera – Subjective Cinema and the Essay Film*, London: Wallflower Press.
Rascaroli, Laura (2014), 'Working at home: tarnation, amateur authorship, and self-inscription in the digital age', in L. Rascaroli, G. Young and B. Monahan (eds), *Amateur Filmmaking: The Home Movie, the Archive, the Web*, London: Bloomsbury Academic, pp. 229–41.
Rascaroli (2017), *How Essay Film Thinks*, Oxford: Oxford University Press.
Renov, Michael (2004), *The Subject of Documentary*, Minneapolis: University of Minnesota Press.
Renov, Michael (2008), 'First-person films. Some theses on self-inscription', in Thomas Austin and Wilma de Jong (eds), *Rethinking Documentary: New Perspectives, New Practices*, Maidenhead: Open University Press, pp. 39–50.
Renov, Michael and Erika Suderberg (eds) (1996), *Resolutions: Contemporary Video Practice*, Minneapolis: University of Minnesota Press.
Spicer, Andrew, A. T. McKenna and Christopher Meir (eds) (2014), *Beyond the Bottom Line: The Role of Producer in Film and Television Studies*, London: Bloomsbury.
Svarverud, Rune (2010), 'Individual self-discipline and collective freedom in the minds of Chinese intellectuals', in M. Halskov Hansen and Rune Svarverud (eds), *iChina:*

The Rise of the Individual in Modern Chinese Society, Copenhagen: Nias Press, pp. 193–225.

Yan, Yunxiang (2009), *The Individualization of Chinese Society*, London: London School of Economics.

Yan, Yunxiang (2010), 'Introduction: Conflicting images of the individual and contested process of individualisation', in M. Halskov Hansen and Rune Svarverud (eds), *iChina: The Rise of the Individual in Modern Chinese Society*, Copenhagen: Nias Press, pp. 1–38.

Wang, Hui and Beichen Yang (2019), '"Asia" as a New Issue in World: Wang Hui Talks about "Asia as Method"', *Dianying Yishu (Film Art)*, issue 387, 3–11.

Yu, Kiki Tianqi (2019a), *'My' Self on Camera: First Person Documentary Practice in an Individualising China*, Edinburgh: Edinburgh University Press.

Yu, Kiki Tianqi (2019b), '"Image-writing": The Essayistic/*Sanwen* in Chinese Nonfiction Cinema and Zhao Liang's *Behemoth*', in Brenda Hollweg and Igor Krstić (eds), *World Cinema and the Essay Film*, Edinburgh: Edinburgh University Press.

10. SCHOLARLY EXPLORATION OF THE CREATIVE PROCESS: INTEGRATING FILM THEORY AND PRACTICE

Warren Buckland

The problematic relation between theory and practice has vexed Western thinking for the past two-and-a-half thousand years, and it is no surprise to discover this problem troubling film studies degree programmes and filmmaking courses. In the 1970s, Vlada Petrić (who co-founded the Harvard Film Archive in 1979 with Stanley Cavell and filmmaker Robert Gardner, and who curated the Archive until 1998) wrote a series of papers addressing pedagogical problems in the teaching of film:

> The split between theory and practice in the study of cinema results in a ludicrous situation: students in cinema studies lack the practical experience without which they are unfit to fully comprehend the specificities of the medium, and students in film production are deprived of the theoretical/historical background which is crucial to their development ... A university curriculum cannot be conceived with the intention of avoiding scholarly exploration of the creative process or the historical and theoretical analysis of an artistic achievement. (1976a: 3–4)

Petrić proclaimed the need to integrate theory and practice by developing a pedagogy that would combine film theory, film history, film analysis and film practice. The core of this integrated approach consists of the shot-by-shot analysis of film sequences in order to study what he called the filmmaker's (usually the director's) 'cinematic strategy' – their filmmaking knowledge plus practical shooting procedures and methods.

In this chapter I develop a theoretical understanding of film practice via Aristotle's concepts of *epistêmê*, *technê* and *praktikos*, although these concepts need to be reformulated and updated with recent advances in analytic philosophy, particularly Jason Stanley's rethinking of the opposition between 'knowing-that' and 'knowing-how' (2011). My aim in this chapter is therefore to develop a theory of a specific type of knowledge – of filmmaking as a problem-solving activity, which includes knowledge of the *filmic* options available to solve *filmmaking* problems. This theoretical understanding of film practice will be used to examine the way technique is conceptualised in filmmaking manuals (especially Karel Reisz's *The Technique of Film Editing* [1968]) and in Petrić's studies of cinematic strategy in his shot-by-shot analysis of film sequences (Petrić 1976b; 1982; 1987). I argue that the core competence behind cinematic strategy consists of first-person modal knowledge that guides 'decision-making' and 'problem-solving'.

THEORY, PRACTICE, POETICS

Aristotle articulated the theory/practice opposition as part of his three-way distinction between theoretical, productive and practical knowledge:[1]

- Theory: *epistêmê*, wisdom (*sophia*)
- Production: *technê*, *poiêtikê* (creating or making [*poiesis*] an artefact)
- Practice: *praktikos/phronesis/praxis* (activities and experiences).

Aristotle separated theory from practice and defined theory as self-sufficient and autonomous: it is general, abstract, necessary, predetermined invariant knowledge of first causes and principles (as spelled out in Book I of *Metaphysics*). Practice in his strict definition (*praktikos*) refers to actions, experiences and perceptions; it is particular and contingent, and is based in part on chance and conjecture. Between theory and practice lies poetics or *technê*: '*Technê* involves having the requisite rational conception of what needs to be made and the understanding of how to make it which precedes the actual production of it' (Mikhailovsky n.d.). In this definition, *technê* is a form of knowledge that has a function or purpose – the production or making of concrete artefacts (whereas theory in itself does not produce artefacts). *Technê* is not invariant knowledge, but neither does it consist of contingent and *ad hoc* actions; instead it is historical productive knowledge generated from an external cause guided by theoretical precepts that bring artefacts into existence. Possessing *technê* means that one understands (but does not need to physically carry out) how to make an artefact, which involves a practitioner (the efficient cause) shaping a physical substance (material cause) via a predetermined plan (formal cause) to realise the artefact's function or purpose (its final cause). In

Aristotle's poetics, the artefact's purpose, or function, determines its form, and the knowledge used to produce the artefact, plus the process of making it, reside in its form. We can therefore analyse this form not simply in itself, but in terms of its multiple causes (as defined by Aristotle) – its functions and the *technê* that produced it (which I define below in terms of decision-making and problem-solving). The actual process of making an artefact may be successful or unsuccessful, due to error or contingent factors: one may possess *technê*, but one's physical ability to carry it out (*praktikos*) may be imperfect; knowing how is distinct from ability.[2] Although Aristotle separated theory from practice and positioned poetics in the middle, he argued that poetics is governed primarily by theoretical knowledge. In other words, he integrated theory (*epistêmê*) and poetics (*technê*) while separating both from practice (*praktikos*). He therefore maintained a clear distinction between theory and practice, while forging close links between theory and poetics.

Aristotle also conceived poetics as a two-way process: it is the knowledge practitioners need in order to make an artefact but also the knowledge critics need in order to understand and explain an artefact – to explain its provenance, how and why it was made. *Technê* and poetics are close to theory in that they designate the knowledge (but not the physical activity) the practitioner needs to make an artefact and the critic needs to explain it. The practitioner does not contribute material to the artefact, but instead imposes on it one type of knowledge (*technê*), a particular way of thinking that shapes and forms it. The critic begins with the finished artefact and studies, not the artefact in itself, what it is, but instead the artefact as the end result of *technê* and poetics. The critic's task is to identify in an artefact's form traces of its making, and from those traces rationally reconstructs the knowledge (the *technê* and poetics) that produced it. In one of his favourite examples, house building, Aristotle argued that 'the act of building is in the thing that is being built' (*Metaphysics*, quoted in Dunne 1993: 339). The final product is not autonomous but is tied to the process of its making and to its final cause. In Aristotle's three-way distinction, practice seems to be cut off from *technê* and theoretical knowledge. However, according to Joseph Dunne, Aristotle's statement on house building does link up *technê* and *praktikos* to the extent that the physical matter of the artefact embodies the *technê* in its form. For Aristotle, all physical objects, including artefacts, combine matter and form. However, we will need to supplement Aristotle's account of poetics with recent developments in analytic philosophy to spell out in adequate detail the way theory relates to practice (and vice versa).

KNOWING-THAT AND KNOWING-HOW

In twentieth century analytic philosophy the theory/practice opposition was formulated in terms of knowing-that and knowing-how. Gilbert Ryle

(2000 [1949]) regarded know-that as systematically organised propositional knowledge: just like Aristotle's formulation of theory (*epistêmê*), know-that is explicit, deductive, contemplative and resides in an abstract realm of pure thought. In contrast, know-how is tacit: just like Aristotle's formulation of practice (*praktikos*), know-how is implicit, inductive, particular and resides in behaviour. Like Aristotle, Ryle (2000 [1949]: chapter 2) argued that know-how is distinct in kind from know-that. But, unlike Aristotle, he focused almost exclusively on know-how, defining it as a disposition – a tendency or inclination to behave in certain ways under particular conditions – rather than as propositional knowledge. Ryle's position is behaviourist because he does not refer to propositions or inner states of mind to explain behaviour; instead, he argued that knowing how to do something is simply having the ability to do it.

Recent developments in analytic philosophy challenge Ryle's position. In *Know How* (2011) Jason Stanley argues that, when talking about know-that and know-how, it is not a matter of privileging one side over the over. For Stanley, know-that is not isolated from action, and know-how is not isolated from propositional knowledge: in other words, know-how is a form of know-that and know-that is a form of know-how. Far from being isolated from each other, know-that and know-how overlap and share many properties. This position argues that intellectual activity informs actions, that knowing-how is a manifestation of knowing-that. But the reverse is also true: knowing-that, or theoretical knowledge, is not purely contemplative and abstract, but is shaped by mental acts and physical actions: 'the value of knowledge lies in its connection to action' (Stanley 2011: viii).[3]

More specifically, Stanley's position consists of several interlinked components: (i) know-how is a form of know-that; (ii) knowing how is knowing answers to the question of how to do something; (iii) knowing how is first-person knowledge (self-knowledge); (iv) knowing how is modal ((iii) and (iv) are closely linked, for knowing how to do something = knowing how *you would* or *could* do it); (v) know-how is functional; (vi) know-how is distinct from physical ability; and (vii) know-that is not inert knowledge.

Stanley critiques Ryle and supports the 'intellectualist' position, which redefines practice (Aristotle's third category) as a propositionally informed activity based on theoretical knowledge, or know-that. Stanley gives the example of learning how to swim: 'learning how to do something is learning a fact. For example, when you learned how to swim, what happened is that you learned some facts about swimming. Knowledge of these facts is what gave you knowledge of how to swim' (2011: vii). Stanley then carefully modifies and justifies this counter-intuitive statement: 'Of course, when you learned how to swim, you didn't just learn any old fact about swimming. You learned a special *kind* of fact about swimming. The fact you learned is the proposition that answers a question – the question "How could you swim?" Knowing how to do something therefore amounts to *knowing the answer to a question'* (2011: vii; emphasis in the original). To reach this conclusion, Stanley has not simply imposed the traditional definition of propositions on activity and practice. Instead, he challenges and revises the notion of what a proposition is. Traditionally, a proposition is the semantic content of a sentence that states or affirms something. It is traditionally conceived as purely intellectual, as passive and contemplative, and distinct from action. This understanding of propositional knowledge constitutes what Aristotle called theoretical knowledge, and what Ryle defined as know-that. In challenging this traditional account of propositions, recent analytic philosophers have instead proposed *functional* and *act-based* conceptions of propositional content, linking propositions to know-how. Stanley's argument that know-how is functional means that it involves a practical way of thinking about objects, to seeing objects in terms of the functional role they play (2011: 123–6). This functional perspective is also central to Aristotle's concept of *technê*, an activity based on theoretical knowledge that has a purpose. To think of a hammer in a practical way is to conceive it not as an object in itself but in terms of its function of knocking in nails. We shall see below that studying an artwork from a functional perspective, in terms of a practical way of thinking, involves conceiving it as the solution to a series of artistic problems.

Crucially, extending knowledge to practice and activity redefines propositions as modal first-person knowledge: propositions are not disembodied and impersonal but are tied to the self and to action. What this means is that one of the preconditions for performing (or intending to perform) an action, as well as knowing what to do at what time, is that an individual must know that they can perform that action. Know-how therefore consists of a series of know-that propositions that represent to an individual how to perform an action. Ryle ruled out propositional knowledge guiding action because, he argued, it leads to an infinite regress: before performing an action, we need to check our propositional knowledge, but then we need to check that we checked our propositional knowledge, and so on *ad infinitum*. The regress argument enabled Ryle to separate know-how from know-that and to develop an anti-intellectualist position by downplaying know-that. Stanley argues that there is no such infinite regress, for individuals directly know about and are guided by their propositional knowledge, which they do not need to check in advance (2011: 12–22; 25–9). By overturning the regress argument, Stanley concludes that both know-how and know-that are based on propositional knowledge, that knowing how to do something is premised on knowing that.

Although Stanley does not discuss Aristotle or poetics, his argument that propositional knowledge guides practice explains the way theoretical propositions, poetics and practice work together. When viewed through Stanley's work, practice and poetics (as defined by Aristotle) are brought closer together, for both are guided by propositional knowledge. ('Guiding' is normative, for it prescribes a certain way of performing an action and excludes other ways, an issue taken up in the section on film manuals.)

Expertise and Creativity

For Ryle, expert knowledge is acquired through inductive behaviour (observation, imitation, stimulus, response and conditioning) rather than the learning of propositions. In contrast, Stanley defines knowing how and the performance of actions in terms of propositional knowledge, which defines the expertise of practitioners. For Stanley, the transition from novice to expert involves proficiency in deploying propositional knowledge that constitutes knowing how:

> The novice must repeatedly engage in distinct actions of 'consulting' the propositional knowledge she has acquired ... Once one achieves expertise, one ... no longer needs to engage in a distinct action of *consulting* the propositional knowledge, since one is in a position to apply the propositional knowledge directly to the situation at hand. (Stanley 2011: 184; emphasis in original)

For both novice and expert, knowing how to solve a problem involves knowing *that* there are prescribed ways of problem-solving and knowing the most relevant way. But, unlike novices, experts draw upon their activated propositional knowledge to carry out their tasks (to answer a question and solve a problem) without apparent effort; what in fact happens is that expert propositional knowledge becomes the expert's first-person modal knowledge.

Stanley's intellectualist account of expertise is akin to Noam Chomsky's rationalist theory of linguistics. For Chomsky, the central factor linguists need to address is the language user's ability to produce and understand new and novel sentences based on limited exposure to language: 'a grammar mirrors the behavior of the speaker who, on the basis of a finite and accidental experience with language, can produce or understand an indefinite number of new sentences' (1957: 15). The language user's knowledge of language is not simply acquired through exposure to speech and writing, but is based on an innate cognitive ability, the language faculty, which creates and understands new sentences from the generative capacity of grammar – from the expansion of a finite and fixed number of core or kernel sentences into a potentially infinite number of sentences, which is achieved by repeatedly applying rewriting and transformational rules to the finite kernel sentences. According to this early model of transformational generative grammar, knowledge of language consists of finite kernel sentences, finite rewriting rules, and finite transformational rules, from which speakers can generate and understand a potentially infinite number of sentences.

Chomsky, in effect, developed a theory of linguistic 'production' in Aristotle's sense – the purposeful creation or making (*poiesis*) of new artefacts (sentences) based on a finite series of rules and conventions, which constitute the knowledge (*epistêmê*) of the language user. Chomsky's work therefore presents a formal model of the production or creation of artefacts.[4] But we need to distinguish three senses of creativity: *rule-following* (e.g. routine production of new artefacts guided by pre-existing rules); *rule-changing* (inventive production of novel artefacts guided by the innovative use of rules, or deliberate breaking of them); and *free unfettered invention*.[5] The first sense of creativity is traditionally aligned to craft, and the second to art. The third (Romantic and existential) sense, based on what Keats approvingly called 'negative capability', is untenable, for it ignores contextual and institutional constraints, reduces creativity to the random contingent acts of isolated individuals, and cannot be explained or taught. The first two types of creativity can be taught (and codified in manuals and textbooks).

Michael Baxandall's discussion of early (analytical) cubism offers an instructive account of rule-changing creativity in terms of problems and solutions (1985: chapter 2). His over-arching issue is to ask why analytical cubist paintings were created around 1908–12, and how an example such as Picasso's *Portrait of Kahnweiler* came to take the specific form it did (1985: 49). Baxandall conceives Picasso as addressing three problems common to painting: 1. General problem: representing three-dimensional space on a two-dimensional surface. Old solution: use perspective to create the illusion of depth, the impression that the canvas is a transparent surface opening on to a volumetric space defined in terms of converging lines. This old solution tries to deny the flat surface of the canvas. Different solutions emerged in the late nineteenth century. The Impressionists, for example, played on the tension between surface and depth. Picasso addressed this problem in his early cubist paintings. 2. Tension between form and colour. This tension is also a general problem, but received new solutions in cubist painting. These cubist solutions in part recognise the stability of form in relation to the variability of colour, which in turn frees up colour so that it does not need to fit into the painting's form. 3. Time: painting represents a moment of experience, but takes much longer to create, resulting in a tension between represented time and time of production. Picasso and other cubist painters acknowledged this tension by incorporating into their paintings the temporal dimension, by showing the subject from several perspectives (fragmenting the internal space), with the subject lit differently from each perspective.

Picasso addressed these primary problems between 1908 and 1912 and discovered rule-changing solutions. Moreover, as Picasso painted, secondary unexpected problems emerged, including figure/ground relations, illumination, scale and texture: 'There is a problem, newly heightened by the leaving open of the plane edges of the figure, of distinction between figure and ground, between man and what lies around and behind him' (1985: 64). Picasso's solution was to re-establish the distinction via tonality and hue: the figure is darker and less yellowish than the background. This modification of tone and hue acknowledges the painting's temporality by giving the impression of a change in illumination over time. This secondary unexpected problem of hue demonstrates that not all creative problems can be foreseen in advance, for some emerge only when the artwork is far advanced.

Rule-changing creativity defined in terms of problems and solutions is also evident in filmmaking. Cinematographer Bill Butler said in an interview that he conceives of cinematography as a problem-solving activity: 'the day-to-day business of making movies is a matter of problem-solving. You are constantly problem-solving from the time you arrive on the set until you quit shooting in the evening' (in Schaefer and Salvato 1984: 76). We can see his creative and innovative problem-solving at work in his cinematography on *Jaws* (1975): neither screenwriters Peter Benchley-Carl Gottlieb nor storyboard artist Tom Wright conceived of filming the action in the sea at water level. This technique was made possible by Butler's invention of the water box – a box with glass at the front, into which he lowered the camera when filming at sea. Butler did not develop the water box as a device for getting flashy camera angles just for the sake of it. Instead, he designed the water box to solve a particular problem in *Jaws*: to increase the audience's psychological engagement with the film's characters in the water, by placing the camera with them on the water's surface.

FILMMAKING MANUALS

Following explicitly stated normative rules offers filmmakers a reference point with which to define the boundaries of their work. If a filmmaker says that they are creating something completely original, outside institutional constraints and rules, what they are in fact doing is simply following rules (usually inconsistently) that they are unaware of. Knowing the rules enables filmmakers to create innovative films in a measured (rather than haphazard) way, by deliberately changing or breaking those normative rules. Such rule-changing/breaking is sometimes mistakenly identified with unfettered creativity; however, breaking rules is an unrealised but potential option rather than a completely original invention, for rule-breaking is still defined in terms of rules and conventions (is understood as deviation from the rules).

An expert practitioner's knowledge includes propositions that guide his or her decision-making process – to choose the most appropriate action within a set of prescribed norms, in which each option involves endorsing a set of implicit normative assumptions about what does and what does not follow from choosing one particular action (in chess, for example, an essential component of a grandmaster's knowledge involves seeing several moves ahead). Awareness of these implicit assumptions and norms (which are also propositions) enables the expert to choose the appropriate action and to distinguish between routine and innovative actions.

Expert actions are guided by a high level of activated propositional knowledge, whereas in unskilled actions this knowledge remains undeveloped. The expert practitioner is not simply producing artefacts, but is also producing solutions to problems (in Stanley's terms, producing answers to questions): the expert knows what the problem is, and possesses the necessary knowledge and decision-making procedures to solve it. With their knowledge, experts know of many (perhaps all the) potential ways to solve a problem (including innovative, rule-changing/breaking, and previously unrealised solutions), whereas the novice may only know a few preferences.[6] Expert action involves choosing an appropriate option from the available preferences, which is not simply a matter of personal choice, but is determined by intrinsic and extrinsic factors (internal constraints such as the nature of the film medium, the technology, and external constraints such as commitment to a worldview, tradition, genre, social norms) all of which determine what a problem is, what constitutes a solution and what preferences are available at any given time.[7]

An expert critic or practitioner can judge whether the right option was chosen (a matter of theoretically informed *technê*) and whether it was carried out effectively (a matter of *praktikos*). Karel Reisz was both critic and practitioner: he wrote the first edition of *The Technique of Film Editing* in the 1950s and made feature films from the 1960s to the 1990s (including *Saturday Night and Sunday Morning* (1960) and *The French Lieutenant's Woman* (1981)). In *The Technique of Film Editing* he criticised Hitchcock for filming the whole of *Rope* (1948) using only long takes and camera movements rather than the classical Hollywood industry norm of editing together several camera setups; in Reisz's expert opinion, Hitchcock's technical preferences decrease the film's dramatic effectiveness. In the film's denouement, Rupert (James Stewart) accuses Brandon (John Dall) and Phillip (Farley Granger) of strangling their friend David Kentley. Rupert pulls out of his pocket the piece of rope they used to strangle Kentley. The revelation and reaction are filmed in one continuous take with camera movement:

> Suddenly [Rupert] turns around to face the boys, holding the rope in front of him (2b) – giving the final proof that he knows who murdered David. While he goes on speaking, the camera slowly pans away to the right, recording in its path first the corner of the room (2c), then a neon sign visible outside the window (2d), and then finally reaching the

reaction shot of the boys (*2e*). It takes the camera 10 feet [6.5 seconds of screen time] to reach the boys and a further 5 feet [3.25 seconds] to come to rest on them. (1968: 233)

Reisz illustrates his description with frame enlargements, labelled 2a to 2e (reproduced on p. 235 of *The Technique of Film Editing*). He then mentions another option from the potential preferences available, a straight cut from the image of Rupert holding the rope (2b) to the reaction of the two murderers (2e):

> If the film had been normally edited, the editor would at this point [*2b*] have cut to the reaction shot (*2e*) so that the spectator could immediately see the effect of the previous image. The image *2b* poses, as it were, the dramatic question 'How will they react?' and *2e* answers it: the most effective continuity is therefore to cut straight from the one to the other. As it is done here, there is a considerable interval between seeing the rope and the boys' reaction. (1968: 234)

Reisz not only focuses on the film but also emphasises the role of editor and the effects of editorial decisions on spectators. He justifies his hypothetical technical option (a straight cut) by describing the images in terms of a logic of question and answer, and he defends his option as more effective, for it eliminates inessential details (the corner of the room, the neon sign) that Hitchcock's technical choices take several seconds to film. Reisz argues that his option is more effective than Hitchcock's because it is the most efficient technical solution to solving the filmmaking problem in this scene – how to create dramatic conflict between Rupert and the murderers.

Reisz also addresses the potential justification of Hitchcock's technical choices in this denouement scene – that they create suspense for they delay the murderers' reaction. But Reisz argues that the technical choices Hitchcock employed to create the delay is ineffective: 'The delay in the reaction is brought about by showing the audience something that has nothing to do with the story: the dramatic conflict is momentarily side-tracked' (1968: 236). Instead, 'If the director had not been bound to this particular formula of presentation, he could have delayed the reaction equally well by cutting' (1968: 236). In other words, delay could still be achieved by holding the shot of Rupert for three or four seconds before cutting to Brandon and Phillip. According to Reisz, this option is better because it keeps on screen only relevant story information while eliminating inessential details.

Reisz uses a negative example to demonstrate how an editor's *technê* or film-making knowledge, his or her decision-making and problem-solving abilities, controls timing and suspense. He criticises Hitchcock's *technê*, specifically his decision-making process – his technical choices (long takes and camera movement), as well as the technical presentation or actualisation of the shots (for the large studio camera moves slowly and not always smoothly).[8] By the 1940s, Hitchcock was of course a master filmmaker who possessed expert knowledge of all the filmmaking options available to him. The reasoning behind his choices can be justified as technical experimentation with untried options, a creative attempt to break the rules of scene dissection – which he had demonstrated in previous (and future) films. In the end, *Rope* is an exercise in rigorously and consistently sticking to two inflexible choices (sequence shots and camera movement) in an attempt to challenge and break industry norms, but such an exercise ended up severely limiting the film's dramatic effectiveness. Reisz presents expert knowledge by discussing a set of technical preferences and demonstrating his own expertise by choosing different options. Nonetheless, he prescribes to practitioners to follow the rules when making decisions and solving editing problems, rather than to experiment via rule-breaking.

Film Studies: Textual Analysis and Cinematic Strategy

Film studies pedagogy is dominated by textual analysis, a close (sometimes shot-by-shot) analysis of film sequences. Textual analyses can be divided into six main categories, each generating different types of knowledge and insights about film:

- Technology
- Film Form
- Film Style
- Aesthetic Evaluation
- Storytelling (Narrative and Narration)
- Interpretation.

When a textual analysis describes camerawork, editing, sound design or lighting, it focuses on the technological creation of a film. When a textual analysis studies film's formal properties, it refers to medium-specific characteristics which shape that film. When a textual analysis takes film style to be its main focus, it examines textual traces of how an author, period, place or school manipulated form in a specific and consistent way. When a textual analysis passes judgment on a film's formal properties, defining it as art or non-art, or when it focuses on the experience and effects of film form and style on spectators, it becomes an aesthetic analysis. When a textual analysis examines storytelling, it focuses on narrative structure, processes of narration, or both. And when a film is interpreted, the analysis tries to explain that film in terms of its underlying social, psychological and ideological values. Of course, many textual analyses combine categories; each textual analysis can in fact be distinguished in terms of the emphasis it places on the various categories. The manuals discussed in the previous section, for example, focus on technology and aesthetics – they jump from a technological analysis to an aesthetic evaluation. A formal analysis focuses on non-mimetic dimensions of film; more accurately, a radical formalist analysis only focuses on non-mimetic dimensions of film, whereas moderate formalism studies the interaction of form with subject matter, examining the way form configures the subject matter. Each artist or school or period of art configures the subject matter differently – each is distinguishable according to its own mode of style, technique and expression. A formal analysis identifies the intrinsic properties film possesses (in opposition to properties metaphorically attributed to film, such as 'depth', or 'sadness', or other attributes imposed upon it by the 'pathetic fallacy'). When a film's intrinsic formal properties are foregrounded, classical film theorists such as Rudolf Arnheim (1957) attribute to that film the value of 'art'. Whereas a strictly formal analysis only identifies the intrinsic properties of a film, both technological and stylistic analyses examine the filmmaking process, the knowledge imposed on the film medium. They emphasise the process of how a film was made, examining the activity itself (the movement of the camera, the actor's performance), which is different from an intrinsic description of film form, and different from an interpretation.[9]

Vlada Petrić combines several categories in his textual analyses: moderate formalism, technology and aesthetics, with an emphasis on *technê* and *praktikos*, which he calls 'cinematic strategy':

> Following Eisenstein's concept of the analytical procedure, students are encouraged to use a method which may lead them along 'the same road that the author (filmmaker) traveled in creating the image, and forming the integral unity of his work'. By discovering the 'creative road' through which the author 'travelled' in making his film, the analyst becomes capable of defining the cinematic strategy by which a film is conceived and realized. (Petrić 1976b: 453)

For Petrić, the film analyst is encouraged to travel in reverse along the same road that the filmmaker travelled in creating a film. This is not a mere description of film techniques but is a functional account of their use in a specific sequence of film; the procedure is thereby a type of reverse engineering, carried out via a textual analysis of film sequences. The analysis of film technique reveals the filmmaker's cinematic strategy – the cinematic knowledge and thinking (the cognitive capacity) behind the film, which guides the filmmaker's decision-making, problem-solving and implementation of filmmaking knowledge.

Petrić analyses a seemingly inconsequential sequence of nine shots near the beginning of *The Rules of the Game* (Renoir, 1939): a confrontation between Geneviève (Mila Parély) and her lover Robert (Marcel Dalio) in Geneviève's salon. Petrić focuses on the way Renoir's choice of filmic techniques ('the duration of the single shot, the composition of the image, the distribution of light within the frame, the size of the shot, the pace of montage, the camera position, and, above all, its mobility' (1982: 264)) transforms the filmed events into a filmic sequence. After describing the sequence shot-by-shot, Petrić is able to identify Renoir's cinematic strategy, one that succeeds in combining the virtues of both editing and camera movement. The sequence begins and ends with tracking shots, which alter the composition, camera angle, and shot scale without the need to cut. The remaining seven shots are static, organised into a shot/reverse shot pattern as Robert and Geneviève confront each other. However, the angle and shot scale change each time the sequence returns to a character, for Renoir did not film the characters from the same angle and distance but altered both of these formal parameters as the sequence progresses. Renoir's strategy was therefore to present a new view of each character as their confrontation unfolds: 'Alternating his set-ups between two characters who face each other, Renoir never repeats pictorial arrangements nor match-cuts his shots mechanically' (Petrić 1982: 275). Even though the individual shots within the shot/reverse shot sequence are static, overall they are dynamic because the composition changes in each shot, heightening the visual impact of the conflict between the two characters. Renoir therefore employs editing to imitate some of the benefits of the long take filmed with a moving camera – a constantly changing image track. Like all film sequences, this sequence embodies in its form the director's knowledge – Renoir's cinematic strategy (problems and decisions), and it is this strategy that Petrić reads from the shots. This type of analysis begins to unite filmmaking and film analysis, because these two types of film education focus on the same type of knowledge – theoretically informed *technê*, but from opposite perspectives. Film analysis becomes a study of the *technê* and final cause that produced the film, which are embedded in the film's form.

As well as attempting to bridge the theory/practice gap by studying cinematic strategy, in the 1970s Petrić also proposed bridging the gap between film theory and film history via textual analysis. He recommended a 'Visual-Analytical' approach to film history, premised on the examination of films shot-by-shot. Petrić argued that film history should primarily be taught via the shot-by-shot analysis of key film sequences because he conceived film history as a history of successful and unsuccessful solutions to filmmaking problems. From this perspective, unsuccessful films are understood as works made by novices who possess insufficient knowledge to solve filmic problems, who do not know how to use the specific properties of the medium to solve problems and, significantly, do not even understand what filmic problems need to be solved in making a film. Conversely, accomplished films are successful solutions to filmmaking problems. To make the jump to the level of the expert, the novice filmmaker needs a detailed knowledge of film technology, form, style and aesthetics, needs to learn from the history of cinema the way previous filmmakers successfully solved filmmaking problems, and needs to know how the specific properties of film can be purposively used to solve filmmaking problems – problems of representation and storytelling, of character engagement, problems of expression, and problems of style and technique (especially establishing and following a set of intrinsic stylistic norms). In addition, filmmakers need to be able to draw upon first-person modal knowledge to judge whether their problem-solving is successful or not (whether the choices they make are appropriate). Solving filmmaking problems is not simply a technical skill but is an intellectual capacity supplemented with technical skill. Although Petrić advocated this analytical approach to film history in the 1970s before copies of films were readily available for study, the problem persists today, for film history continues to be taught separately from film theory classes.

Teaching Film

> If it *is* possible to describe the artistic process as a series of problems and their controlled resolution, the ensuing generalizations may be of no small consequence to the teaching of art. (David W. Ecker 1963: 284; emphasis in original)

Claiming that know-how is propositional is to declare that it can be verbalised and therefore made explicit in various forms – in teaching, in interviews with experts, in professional manuals and in film studies textbooks. For Aristotle, an integral part of *technê* is the ability to communicate the knowledge, to give a rational account of it (cf Dunne 250: 286). Yet, many filmmaking degree programmes implicitly endorse Gilbert Ryle's privileging of know-how (defined as *praktikos*) over know-that. Unanchored from propositional knowledge and how to use it to solve problems, filmmaking becomes an activity governed by chance and contingent events. It is quite common for filmmaking programmes to emphasise practice by proclaiming that 'Students get a camera in their hands day one'. But such statements reinforce the popular belief that filmmaking is not an intellectual activity involving knowledge, but is a physical activity guided only by the filmmaker's intuition.

This statement, 'Students get a camera in their hands day one', follows the traditional, common-sense fallacy that limits knowledge to practical activity. Following Jason Stanley's re-reading of Gilbert Ryle, I argue that if a film school proclaims that they put cameras in students' hands on day one, this does not mean that the film school is teaching those students filmmaking. (Also, these days students can put a camera in their own hands, without the need to go to film school.) *What students need from film school is the knowledge behind filmmaking*, an *understanding* of the film medium and its technology and, most importantly, how to use that knowledge and understanding to solve filmmaking problems.

Teaching filmmaking therefore requires propositional input, not just practical input: the ability to teach film involves the verbal articulation of the propositional content manifest in the skilful intentional actions of filmmakers. (This verbal articulation is equally relevant to film studies students and to filmmaking students.) Simply making films during a filmmaking degree will not automatically turn one into an expert filmmaker. Students can spend those years making the same unsuccessful films, and making the same mistakes, or only making incremental advances. This type of teaching promotes a form of imitation or rote learning, one that simply reproduces clichéd ways of filmmaking.

An expert knows many potential ways to perform an action, knows when to choose one option at the right time, and knows when and how to deviate from institutional norms. A filmmaker cannot make expert choices in constructing a shot or sequence simply by holding a camera in his or her hands. Nor can they make these choices by simply possessing technical competency or by mechanically following a series of steps. Expertise requires the filmmaker to take possession of a series of propositions that articulate the knowledge of filmmaking. Those propositions do not constitute passive, contemplative knowledge, but a deep knowledge of filmmaking as a problem-solving activity, knowledge of the options available to solve problems, and the competence to make a reasoned choice from those options.

NOTES

1. My reading of Aristotle is based on chapters 8 to 10 of Joseph Dunne's book *Back to the Rough Ground* (1993), and on Richard Parry, 'Episteme and Techne' (2014).
2. For example, the cellist Jacqueline du Pré is renowned for her performance of Elgar's Cello Concerto in E Minor. From Stanley's intellectualist position, we can argue that she retained her unrivalled knowledge even when she suffered from multiple sclerosis and lacked the physical ability to perform the piece. Her knowledge was not simply in her physical performance, but in the series of propositions that constituted her know-how, propositions which she retained after contracting multiple sclerosis.
3. George Lakoff (1987) is more radical. Like Jason Stanley, he links cognition to bodily action (and the environment), but he redefines cognition in terms of schemata, rather than propositions, and he places emphasis on the body and environment in determining the abstract mental schemata. But my aim here is not to establish the exact representation of knowledge in the mind (action-oriented propositions/ schemata, etc.), but simply to point to its influence over practice.
4. This sense of production/creation is also prevalent in the earlier structuralist models

of language. Lévi-Strauss argued that creativity is an effect of the specific selection and combination of pre-existing codes and structures: '[Humans] never create absolutely: all they can do is to choose certain combinations from a repertory of ideas which it should be possible to reconstitute' (quoted in Miriam Glucksmann 1974: 89). The 'code user' (speaker, writer, filmmaker) therefore submits to the code, to its meanings and limits, but reconstitutes it (using rules of permutation and transformation) to create new meanings.
5. Following Chomsky (1964), Umberto Eco (1976: 161; 1979: chapter 2) distinguishes between 'rule-governed' and 'rule-changing' creativity, in which the latter involves the invention of new codes and new rules of combination. He analyses metaphor as a form of 'rule-changing' creativity.
6. This tension between the novice and expert filmmaker was played out in Eisenstein's seminars, as represented in *Lessons with Eisenstein*, based on the notes of one of his students, Vladimir Nizhny (1962).
7. Thomas Nickles defines a problem as 'consist[ing] of *all* the conditions or *constraints* on the solution plus the demand that the solution (an object satisfying the constraints) be found' (1981: 109). Constraints determine the problem and the range of admissible solutions; they constitute the limit conditions: 'The constraints characterize – in a sense "describe" – the sought-for solution. Specific types of problems will, of course, possess special features' (109). The constraints characterise the sought-for solution: constraints rule out inadmissible solutions, thereby narrowing down the possible range of admissible solutions.
8. The technical option to use a steadicam now exists, which can create rapid and fluid camera movements.
9. When discussing textual analyses, we also need to consider the claims the analysis is making, the evidence (and the way it is presented), the theoretical assumptions that link the evidence to the claim, comprehensiveness of the analysis, and the degree of significance attached to the represented content.

REFERENCES

Arnheim, Rudolf (1957), *Film as Art*, London: Faber & Faber.
Baxandall, Michael (1985), *Patterns of Intention: On the Historical Explanation of Pictures*, New Haven, CT: Yale University Press.
Chomsky, Noam (1957), *Syntactic Structures*, The Hague: Mouton.
Chomsky, Noam (1964), *Current Issues in Linguistic Theory*, The Hague: Mouton.
Dunne, Joseph (1993), *Back to the Rough Ground: Practical Judgment and the Lure of Technique*, Notre Dame: University of Notre Dame Press.
Ecker, David W. (1963), 'The Artistic Process as Qualitative Problem Solving', *Journal of Aesthetics and Art Criticism*, 21: 3, 283–90.
Eco, Umberto (1976), *A Theory of Semiotics*, Bloomington: Indiana University Press.
Eco, Umberto (1979), *The Role of the Reader*, Bloomington: Indiana University Press.
Glucksmann, Miriam (1974), *Structuralist Analysis in Contemporary Social Thought*, London: Routledge.
Lakoff, George (1987), *Women, Fire, and Dangerous Things: What Categories Reveal About the Mind*, Chicago: University of Chicago Press.
Mikhailovsky, Alexander (n.d.), 'Heidegger and Aristotle on techne and phusis', <http://hobbydocbox.com/Art_and_Technology/66735234-Heidegger-and-aristotle-on-techne-and-phusis.html>
Nickles, Thomas (1981), 'What Is a Problem That We May Solve It?' *Synthese*, 47:1, 85–118.

Nizhny, Vladimir (1962), *Lessons with Eisenstein*, trans. and ed. by Ivor Montagu and Jay Leyda, London: George Allen & Unwin.
Parry, Richard (2014), 'Episteme and Techne', *The Stanford Encyclopedia of Philosophy*, Edward N. Zalta (ed.), <http://plato.stanford.edu/archives/fall2014/entries/episteme-techne/>.
Petrić, Vlada (1976a), 'The Projector and the Camera: Integrating Courses in Cinema Studies and Filmmaking', *Journal of the University Film Association*, 28:2, 3–7.
Petrić, Vlada (1976b), 'For a Close Cinematic Analysis', *Quarterly Review of Film Studies*, 1:4, 453–77.
Petrić, Vlada (1982), 'From *Mise-en-Scène* to *Mise-en-Shot*: Analysis of a Sequence', *Quarterly Review of Film Studies*, 7:3, 263–91.
Petrić, Vlada (1987), *Constructivism in Film: The Man with the Movie Camera: A Cinematic Analysis*, Cambridge: Cambridge University Press.
Reisz, Karel and Gavin Millar (1968), *The Technique of Film Editing*, 2nd edn, London: Focal Press.
Ryle, Gilbert (2000 [1949]), *The Concept of Mind*, London: Penguin.
Schaefer, Dennis and Larry Salvato (1984), *Masters of Light: Conversations with Contemporary Cinematographers*, Berkeley: University of California Press.
Stanley, Jason (2011), *Know How*, Oxford: Oxford University Press.

11. TEACHING PRACTICE AS THEORY: GUERRILLA FILMMAKING

William Brown

In this essay, I shall describe the content and the delivery of a module (referred to in some institutions as a course or a unit) that I designed at my institution, called Guerrilla Filmmaking. The reasons for doing this are several. Since the module springs in some senses from my own theoretical research into and practice as a zero-budget filmmaker, Guerrilla Filmmaking exemplifies how to bridge practice and theory in the classroom, or, to put it in the language of this edited collection, how to teach practice-research. As the making of zero-budget films springs from the development of readily available digital technologies, the module also allows students themselves to bridge practice as research, in that the module involves the adoption of new media technologies in order to explore their expressive possibilities, which also means that practice (for example, making films with smartphones) involves research (working out what sorts of film a smartphone can help to produce), which in turn helps to generate a theoretical understanding of what (in this example) smartphones *mean*. As we shall see, by exploring the expressive possibilities of new media technologies, students (and teachers) on the module begin to understand that they are not 'inferior' to conventional cinematic technologies, but simply different – a shift in outlook/theoretical thinking that the module conscientiously ties to a history of 'imperfect' cinema (both as a theory and as a practice), which shift itself is linked to a 'decolonisation' or a 'liberation' of thought in relation to film and perhaps to the world more generally. In order to understand how Guerrilla Filmmaking does this, though, let us begin with an overview of the module.

The Pragmatics of Guerrilla Filmmaking

Guerrilla Filmmaking is a module in which, over the course of an eleven- or twelve-week semester, students are invited to make a portfolio of three to five short films (typically I ask them to have a duration of between one and three minutes, although some can be slightly shorter and some longer). The three highest scoring of these films are carried forward as the first of two assignments that students complete for the module. Each of the films involves a formal and a thematic 'constraint', in that students must make a film on a certain topic, or which answers a certain question (about which more below), while at the same time only using certain filmmaking techniques. As I shall explore in more detail below, the idea behind this is for each film to constitute a challenge for the student that they must overcome by thinking creatively – or which, if you will, involves the student researching the expressive possibilities of the medium.

The reason for only carrying forward three of the five grades (which typically are averaged to create a single score) is twofold. First, by giving the students two films that they can 'get wrong', the module potentially has a 'sandbox' component that encourages the students to experiment without fear of this affecting their final grade since the lowest two scores can simply be discarded – this is important as the module can potentially be intimidating at first. Secondly, and on a much more pragmatic note, since students in UK higher education are increasingly holding down near-full-time jobs in order to fund their studies, this does allow students to make only three short films rather than all five if their time is pressured.

The second assignment that students must complete is a critical reflection on the module, which can take either written or audiovisual form. Notably, this assignment is worth 50 per cent of the module's final grade, and students are directly encouraged to relate their portfolio of films to the scholarly and cinematic work that also forms part of the module's content. For, the module typically runs for four hours during each of the eleven or twelve weeks of the semester (including one independent study session). Each four-hour session is split into two blocks, the first of which involves the viewing and discussion of a film that has been made in a 'guerrilla' style, which typically means involving the use of limited funds and/or equipment, and the second of which involves continued discussion of that film as well as a lecture component that relates the film to scholarly and other texts, some of which the students are asked to read for each week. This second session also provides an opportunity for students to brainstorm their films (it invites thinking that is independent from my teaching), and, as the semester progresses, it is increasingly given over to the students to showcase and to discuss their own work, with students being invited both to present and to ask and answer questions about each other's films. I shall address later some of the pragmatic issues involved in the running of the module, but typically by the end of the semester this second session is almost exclusively given over to the consideration of student work.

Typically the module scores highly in terms of external examiner and student feedback – not least because it simultaneously satisfies many students' desire simply to produce work (traditional production modules can often seem to students to progress very slowly) and because it asks students to engage with and to think about new technologies that are readily available, most often being already in the palms of their hands – while also providing them with a portfolio of work that they can use to showcase their talents in their bid to find work in the film and other media industries after (or before) graduation.

Having given this overview of the module, let us now engage with it in more detail. In order to do this, let us first situate it within the new technological context that I evoked above, since this allows us to consider how the module responds to and draws upon strong currents of contemporary filmmaking practice.

The Digital Context

It perhaps goes without saying that digital technology has heavily changed film production, distribution, exhibition and reception. As a result of smartphones equipped with (increasingly high definition) cameras, the saying goes that anyone can make a movie, while websites like YouTube (which is central to Guerrilla Filmmaking, in that it is to this site that students upload their work) allow filmmakers to exhibit their films. Social media and other platforms (Facebook, Twitter, Instagram) allow filmmakers to spread word about their films, thereby increasing the number of 'hits' that their work receives, while the ability to obtain (via ripping and/or downloading) and to rework existing material means that we have seen a rise in the overlapping practices of the mash-up, found footage filmmaking and the video-essay. In short, we live in an age of what Axel Bruns has termed *produsage*, which neologism conveys the blurred distinction between production and usage that digital technology seems to have engendered (see Bruns 2008).

Guerrilla Filmmaking clearly invites students to engage with this technological context, not least through the formal constraints that are placed on students for each of the films that they must make as part of their portfolio. Indeed, listed below are the five challenges that were set for students during the 2017–18 iteration of the module:

1. Make a film that does not feature moving images and which responds to the question: what is home?

2. Make a film that consists only of one take and which responds to the question: why is a refugee?
3. Make an experimental, animated or found footage film that takes the form of a letter to a loved one.
4. Make a film that does not feature any synchronisation between image and sound and which is about the animals of Roehampton.
5. Make a film using a smartphone or tablet, which features total strangers who have agreed to take part, and which is about inequality.

Although only the last of these explicitly asks students to use a smartphone (or tablet), each is asking the students to think about film form, and it is not uncommon for students to make all of the films in their portfolio using only their smartphone (and digital editing software and YouTube), with image and sound quality being considered as less important in terms of grading and feedback than the student's ability to answer the question and/or to engage with the challenge at hand (although if the student wants to offer up an explanation of refugees using a voiceover, and the voiceover is inaudible, then unless the student explains clearly why they have used this technique – perhaps because the voices of refugees are themselves often inaudible in mainstream culture – then this might well diminish their score, since that technique has directly diminished their answer to that question).

From the thematic constraints that these films involve, we can perhaps glean that the module is asking students directly to engage with other political contexts in addition to the contemporary technological one. Nonetheless, the module is also asking students to engage in practice with contemporary audiovisual technologies, in effect actively to become 'produsers,' while also asking them to relate this practice/produsage to contemporary political and other realities (the animals challenge is, for example, designed to encourage students to think about ecological concerns). In this way, the module hopefully gets students to think about contemporary digital filmmaking practice and the contemporary (digital) world *from within*, with the critical reflection assignment then asking the students (still via practice if their reflection is audiovisual in nature) to give a more considered overview about what this means and/or what can be achieved politically via such practices. Put differently, the module is an example of what Judith Rifeser (notably a graduate of the Guerrilla Filmmaking module), via Barbara Bolt, refers to in this volume as a case of practice becoming theory-generating, 'rather than theory generating or explaining the practice' (see Bolt 2010: 33; Rifeser this volume). Practice has become research.

Indeed, from a personal perspective it seems clear to me that my own zero-budget digital filmmaking practice, from which this module in part springs, has also helped me to generate such theoretical concepts as 'non-cinema', which I use as a term to try to understand low-budget digital filmmaking practice from around the world, directly linking the aesthetic to the political components of that work (see Brown 2018). In other words, for practice to generate theory, or for the two to be blurred, seems, particularly in relation to film, a logical consequence of the technologies that allow 'users' to become producers (produsage), which blurring is itself best theorised through practice, that is by being a producer/produser.

That said, with regard to the history of cinema, from Sergei M. Eisenstein through Andrei Tarkovsky and Laura Mulvey to the likes of Agnieszka Piotrowska today, there is a long and rich history of filmmakers who produce theory and theorists who have also been filmmakers. It is with some of this work in mind, particularly as produced by non-Western theorists and filmmakers, that the module endeavours to introduce students to, and to get them to engage with, a history and the present of guerrilla filmmaking from around the world. It is to this history and to the scholarly content of the module that I shall now turn.

A (Partial) History of Guerrilla Filmmaking

As with most/all university modules, it is impossible to cover any given topic in total depth, not least because of the explosion of scholarship and the increased specialisation of scholars in the contemporary world. With this in mind, I personally develop modules that are designed to give students a relatively coherent but not necessarily a complete understanding of a field, and for that to function as either the spur for further study that the student undertakes for themselves (preferably outside the university context, in that the aim is to encourage the student to study for its own sake/for the sake of personal edification, and not for the purposes of a piece of paper that confers a qualification to them), or as a kind of depth-charge that encourages thinking not just during the film programme but also at later points in life as the student discovers artefacts and realities that relate to and make them revisit – at least mentally – some of the topics that we did manage to cover during the module. I say this because surely others might offer a different history of guerrilla filmmaking (starting with the role of filmmaking in the political career of Mexican revolutionary Pancho Villa, for example), or feel that the one offered here is incomplete or imperfect, which surely it is. My point is that we might consciously and productively engage with imperfection, as we shall see imminently.

The module opens with a screening of Lars von Trier and Jørgen Leth's *De fem benspænd/The Five Obstructions* (Denmark/Switzerland/Belgium/France, 2003), a film in which the former challenges the latter to remake five times his short experimental film *Det perfekte menneske/The Perfect Human* (Denmark, 1968), each time with a set of constraints/obstructions (e.g. the film must consist only of shots that last for twelve frames, with the remake being done in Cuba). The reason for starting with this film is hopefully evident: to provide students with an example of how constraints/obstructions can also be creative opportunities as the film charts how Leth at every turn overcomes the challenges that von Trier sets for him. It also allows us to discuss von Trier's work more generally, including his historical engagement with new filmmaking technologies, in particular as part of the dogme 95 movement, in order to produce aesthetically and politically challenging work.

Since dogme 95 (and much of von Trier's work in general) involves a deliberate 'impoverishment' of sound and image for the purposes of formal experimentation (think handheld camerawork, low-grade digital images, and so on), this then leads to a consideration of what Julio García Espinosa conceptualised in post-revolutionary Cuba as 'imperfect cinema'. That is, imperfect cinema embraces 'inferior' filmmaking equipment (for example, low gauge film stock) in order to create an aesthetic that gives voice to the new political reality of a Cuba independent of the global north and excluded from its dominant and 'perfectly' cinematic aesthetic (see García Espinosa 1979). We relate this to other work from Latin America, including Glauber Rocha's aesthetic of hunger (1997), and the concept of underdevelopment that Fernando Birri also puts into dialogue with filmmaking (see Birri 1997). The inclusion of Birri is also important because in his native Salta, Argentina, he used to run film classes in which students were asked to make films using only still cameras and audio recorders, since there were no film cameras available. This directly informs the first challenge that the module sets for students, namely to make a film featuring no moving images and which responds to the question 'what is home?' Remaining in the Latin American context, students view Jonás Cuarón's film *Año uña/Year of the Nail* (Mexico, 2007), since this is also a film comprised only of still images and which explores Mexican-American relationships, thereby giving to students some hopeful inspiration regarding how they will themselves respond to the challenge.

The content of the module then varies from year to year, but often we will engage with contemporary low-budget digital filmmaking movements such as Mumblecore – although I also enjoy showing to students Mike Ott and Carl Bird McLaughlin's documentary about student filmmaking, *Kid Icarus* (USA, 2008), since this funny and touching tale of disastrous organisation and over-ambition can also help students to focus on the pragmatics of filmmaking: what can they achieve with the means at their disposal, and how can they use the technologies and techniques available to them in an expressive manner, rather than simply lamenting the lack of opportunities or access before them (for more on Ott's work, see Campbell 2018)? In addition, we also look at digital activist filmmaking such as Mahdi Fleifel's *A World Not Ours* (UK/Lebanon/Denmark/UAE, 2012), about Palestinian refugees in Lebanon, and Emad Burnat and Guy Davidi's *Five Broken Cameras* (Palestine/Israel/France/Netherlands, 2011), which is about the Israeli encroachment upon the Palestinian territories. These also function as means for the students to think about the relationship between form and politics, as well as about the relationship between the personal and the political, in that both works ostensibly constitute diary films that nonetheless bespeak political realities concerning space, identity and other fundamental issues.

Typically, students would also see 'underground' digital films from places like China, Iran and the Philippines, with respective examples being works such as *Wo men hai pa/Shanghai Panic* (Andrew Y.-S. Cheng, China, 2002), *In film nist/This Is Not a Film* (Jafar Panahi and Mojtaba Mirtahmasb, Iran, 2011) and/or *Mondomanila: Kung paano ko inayos ang buhok ko matapos ang mahaba-haba ring paglalakbay/Mondomanila, or: How I Fixed My Hair After a Rather Long Journey* (Khavn de la Cruz, Philippines, 2010). These films, respectively about the Shanghai queer community, being under house arrest and banned from filmmaking in Tehran, and squatter kids in Manila, give to students the chance to understand that certain national contexts dictate the kind of film that can or cannot get made, and thus the kinds of reality that cinema makes visible and/or which it keeps invisible – and in contradistinction to which underground filmmaking functions, but once again with access only to 'low-level'/'imperfect' filmmaking equipment, shooting without permits, using non-professional actors, working on the fly, and so on. Reading considerations of digital film production by filmmakers from these contexts, for example writings by notable Sixth Generation Chinese filmmakers Jia Zhangke (2003) and Wu Wenguang (2006), also allows students to note that theory can function prominently in relation to practice, as well as helping them to understand the importance of, and to develop their own attempts at, situating their own work and establishing audience expectations, a point to which I shall return.

The module typically also takes in work that embraces new filmmaking technologies to engage with queer identities via films like Todd Haynes's unlicensed Barbie doll Carpenters biopic *Superstar: The Karen Carpenter Story* (USA, 1988), Sadie Benning's PixelVision punk classic *Girl Power* (USA, 1992), Rose Troche's low gauge New York lesbian flick *Go Fish* (USA, 1994), and Jenni Olson's essay-film travelogue *The Royal Road* (USA, 2015). These are related to theories of minor cinema (see Deleuze 2005: 207–15; White 2008). Minor cinema is also a useful conceptual framework through which to consider machinima, a form of filmmaking developed through the use of game engines and thus somewhere between cinema and animation, and which is offered along with considerations of various found footage films, as examples for the students to follow of animated, experimental or found footage films that in the 2017–18 iteration of the module were required to take the form of a letter to a loved one (for more on machinima as minor cinema, see Brown and Holtmeier 2013).

Finally, we might also look at cult 'trash' films like the work of Giuseppe Andrews, Christoph Schlingensief and/or contemporary British punk filmmaker Fabrizio Federico (who has visited students as part of the module) in order to encourage participants to feel free to contravene the so-called 'rules' of filmmaking for expressive purposes, especially when giving voice to, or making visible, realities such as the trailer park 'trash' figures that star in so many of Andrews's films, or the presence of disabled bodies in work like Schlingensief's *Freakstars 3000* (Germany, 2004). Not only can we relate this and the students' own work to conceptualisations of trash via theorists like Jeffrey Sconce (1995), but we also situate it within discourses that explore the relationship between politics and aesthetics, such as the work of Jacques Rancière (2006).

In this way, Guerrilla Filmmaking engages with a history of alternative filmmaking practices, the majority of which actively use a lack of budget, expertise and/or equipment in order to give expression to a political reality that is in fact conveyed more powerfully as a result of perceived technical and technological imperfections, rather than falsified through the conventions of mainstream cinema (high definition images, the presence of stars and/or professional performers, fast-cutting rate, spectacle and more). What is more, since the participants are more often than not young filmmakers only now making a start with their practice, the module allows them to embrace their own lack of access and/or experience, and again to use this proactively to express their reality, including the reality of the political context in which they find themselves (for example, Britain in the era of Brexit, the refugee crisis, the growing gap in wealth, the so-called sixth era of mass extinction and so on).

As hopefully can be seen, the material that we cover is also global in outlook – with the module clearly suited for further examples of low-budget filmmaking practice such as work from the video-based filmmaking industry in Nigeria (Nollywood), Uganda (Wakaliwood) and other parts of Africa. In this way, the module aims to contribute to the so-called 'decolonisation' of thought that relates to the endeavour of downplaying eurocentrism in the contemporary era of globalisation, during which we might become conscientious global citizens who are responsible for each other and for our environment. By combining practice with theory (by rendering practice as research), the module thus aims to generate new understandings not just of cinema but also of the world. As Brazilian liberation practitioner-theorists Paolo Freire and Augusto Boal put it, 'it is only as they [the students] rethink their assumptions in action that they can change' (Freire 2017: 81), and '[o]nly out of constant practice will the new theory arise' (Boal 2008: 69).[1]

LIBERATION OF THE OPPRESSED

To relate Guerrilla Filmmaking to so-called Third World liberation theory might seem an overstatement. Although from highly diverse backgrounds, students at a Western metropolitan university are in principle not 'oppressed', or at least not in the way that a rural Brazilian might have been in the second half of the twentieth century, when Boal developed his Theatre of the Oppressed and when Freire wrote his similarly themed *Pedagogy of the Oppressed*. Indeed, one might contend that to arm 'privileged' fee-paying students with such theories is to undermine the original context and intention of that work, and to give a sense of oppression to those who are not oppressed at all.

While in some senses this is a valid contention and one that must (in the spirit of Freire) undergo constant and ongoing scrutiny and discussion, the reality of even the Western world nonetheless remains, as far as cinema is concerned, that access to the medium is highly protected. Or rather that very few people gain access to high-end filmmaking equipment, which is perceived as more valid or real than low-end filmmaking, even though many more people now engage in the latter than in the former. In other words, our perceptions of validity, and I would suggest of reality itself, remain 'oppressed' by the aesthetics of perfection, which is in turn an aesthetics of capital given that it costs money (or at the very least requires very good contacts) in order to have 'perfect' lighting, a beautiful *mise-en-scène*, spectacular action, celebrity performers, and so on.

Furthermore, if a story about transsexual sex workers in Los Angeles featuring non-professional performers and shot on the streets of the city is unlikely to attract a big budget because of how its subject matter challenges mainstream sensibilities, which in turn might mean that a producer does not recoup the money of their investors, then to make visible that world by making a film about it must almost by definition be done using 'inferior' technologies such as an iPhone – as director Sean Baker so famously did with *Tangerine* (USA, 2015). In other words, the capitalist imperative of professional cinema determines what is made visible and thus what enters into the consciousness and perceived realities of the general populace. This in turn means that the reality that we perceive is structured via economic imperatives, something that does clearly limit, or, in the language of Boal and Freire, oppress us. By this rationale, we are all implicated in a system of oppression, and we are all in some senses oppressed – at the very least in our thinking – as should be clear to anyone at a contemporary British university, where the effects of neoliberalism can be felt by staff and students alike. It may not be that the typical fee-paying student is 'as oppressed' as a Brazilian rural worker, but we can all nonetheless engage with and seek ways to move beyond the system of oppression, particularly once we have seen that the Brazilian rural worker and the UK university student live on the same planet – as I hope to make clear during the module by showing Jorge Furtado's *A ilha das flores/The Island of Flowers* (Brazil, 1989), a short that precisely shows the connections between the rich and the poor in a globalised world.

If what we see is in some sense the measure of what we consider to be real (if we do not see it, how do we know that it exists?), then in a related fashion what we see (what is visible, perhaps especially via our media) determines what we can imagine. I mentioned earlier the benefit of obstructions, which paradoxically emerge, then, as ways of liberating vision. In order to demonstrate how this is so, I typically introduce students to Georges Perec's remarkable novel, *La disparition* (1969), which is a novel written without a single use of the letter e, even though e is the most common letter in the French language and even though it appears four times in the author's name. Why would Perec set himself the task of writing a novel that does not feature the letter e? As he himself explained in relation to Greek mythology, it is only by going blind that Oedipus can see; and it is thus only by setting ourselves obstructions that in some senses we can truly learn to be creative. Or as Giuseppe Andrews explains in *Giuseppe Makes a Movie* (Adam Rifkin, USA, 2014), a documentary about his trailer park filmmaking practice, 'boy, someone gave that guy like a million dollars, or half a million dollars, and that's an independent film? I make films for a thousand bucks, you know.'

What is more, we might also think of James Joyce, in whose *A Portrait of the Artist as a Young Man* (1916), the narrator Stephen Daedalus describes how

> [t]he language in which we are speaking is his [the Englishman's] before it is mine [the Irishman's]. How different are the words *home*, *Christ*, *ale*, *master*, on his lips and on mine! I cannot speak or write these words without unrest of spirit. His language, so familiar and so foreign, will always be for me an acquired speech. I have not made or accepted its words. My voice holds them at bay. My soul frets in the shadow of his language. (Joyce 1992: 146)

There is plenty to pick apart here, especially the fact that the English words that seem so unfamiliar to Joyce/Daedalus are redolent of identity (home) and the trappings of colonialism (Christ, ale, master). However, the point to make simply is that as an Irishman writing in English, Joyce is not writing in his own language, and thus in some respects cannot even think in his own language. Read this way, it is no surprise that Joyce begins to stretch, to twist and to make unfamiliar the English language such that it almost reaches breaking point in novels like *Ulysses* (1922) and *Finnegans Wake* (1939), in which words seem to last lines and sentences stretch on for pages as they morph into each other and meanings are twisted in every which direction. In doing this, Joyce is in effect trying to establish a new language within the English language, one that can adequately express what it is to be Irish, since the English language, imposed upon the Irish as a result of colonialism, is clearly insufficient for the task. What is true of English, then, can also be thought of in cinematic terms: are not all of our imaginations shaped by the domination of mainstream media, which in turn we might disrupt in order to produce new languages that are more proper to our existences? Guerrilla Filmmaking thus uses practice-research to decolonise thought, which decolonisation must involve the production of a shift in theoretical thinking/must involve the production of new theories.

It is for me important that I draw upon two novelists in order to make this point, not only to remind my students that reading is an important part of an education, even film education (not least because the printed word offers an alternative mode of expression and thus of imagination to what is offered by cinema), but also because Perec and Joyce both here do theoretical work even as they write creatively. In keeping with the mutual inclusion of theory and practice that is at the core of the module, the aim of the obstructions is, then, to help in the process of liberation through the development of what we might call artistic vision or voice. If the students become aware of and take part in the creation of 'new cinematic languages' via the embracing of imperfection, then they also in some senses learn that to fail (from the perspective of the mainstream) is not necessarily a bad thing, but perhaps even a necessary part of the learning process – thus making even more adventurous, hopefully, their ideas and how they try to realise them. Indeed, one of the consequences of Guerrilla Filmmaking so far has been that various participants have begun to present their work at international film festivals, while also continuing to practise independent filmmaking. What is more, a compilation film that I curated and which bears the title *Roehampton Guerrillas (2011–2016)* (various directors, UK, 2017) also exists as an independent entity that equally has screened at a small selection of film festivals, thus helping the participants with their careers as would-be/already filmmakers – be that independent or otherwise.[2]

Also of use with regard to the development of voice are the sessions that involve students presenting their work to their peers. For, as we repeatedly look at manifestos and other paratexts that accompany films over the course of the module, then so, too, do students begin to learn that the presentation of work is sometimes equally as important as the work itself, and that helping audiences to understand the work (providing a theoretical framework for practice) is a crucial part of building audiences for that work. We also touch upon the importance of gatekeepers (for example, the important role that Alexis Tioseco played in the making-prominent of contemporary Philippine digital filmmaking; see Tioseco 2007), and by extension the importance of developing a network of friends and supporters, whom one in turn mutually supports again in order to build audiences (sharing networks).[3]

CONCLUSION

As per the outline above, Guerrilla Filmmaking hopefully helps to develop both creative and critical thinking, in which obstacles become opportunities and in which students learn to become more confident in producing and presenting their own work (they learn not to fear failure and to embrace imperfection). This in turn hopefully will be of benefit both to students and to future employers, should the students not want to continue working in an independent fashion (professional or otherwise). It also aims to expand their thinking regarding what constitutes a film, as well as broadening horizons in terms of global cinema and philosophies of difference.

If Augusto Boal argues for the placement of the means of production in the hands of audiences (see Boal 2008: 98), then digital technology has in some senses done this in terms of film: everyone can make a movie, and many people are doing this. Indeed, if Henry Jenkins has suggested that there is 'enough work [in the new media environment] to keep us all investigating and theorizing ... for decades to come' (quoted in Dixon 1998: 9), then Guerrilla Filmmaking helps us to generate those theories through practice, while also helping students to develop that practice, which may conceivably lead to important creative work in the future.[4] As a result, Guerrilla Filmmaking constitutes an important example of how potentially to teach practice-research, which in turn helps to generate new theoretical frameworks through which to understand the contemporary world, especially as these relate to histories of non-Western and 'imperfect' cinemas, which themselves were politically informed practices aimed at trying to bring into being a more just and equitable world.[5]

NOTES

1. For a specifically Brazilian but similar take on film education that combines theory and practice, see the work of Cezar Migliorin and colleagues (Migliorin et al. 2014), as well as their film *Educação/Education* (Cezar Migliorin and Isaac Pipano, Brazil, 2016).
2. *Roehampton Guerrillas (2011–2016)* can be seen online at the following address: <https://vimeo.com/197619051>.
3. On a related note, I allow students to make joint films (in groups of up to three), since I encourage collaboration. That said, I only allow participants to work with the same group once – in a bid precisely to get them to work collaboratively with a range of people (a goal also encouraged in the challenge that demands that students work with strangers).
4. The Guerrilla Filmmaking YouTube channel can be found at the following address:

<https://www.youtube.com/channel/UCocCiKqAvEq_yK6NVuR8kaA>. There are over 600 films on the channel for the viewer to browse.
5. On a pragmatic level, Guerrilla Filmmaking runs via a YouTube channel, the password to which is updated annually, and on to which participants log in order to upload their work. If the student does not want their work to be publicly visible (e.g. for religious reasons), then the video can be set to private. While my institution does have filmmaking equipment that students can use, it is up to the students to source that equipment, and it is also up to the students independently to undergo any training that they feel is necessary in order to complete the module. In this sense, the students are given a sink-or-swim situation in which they must learn to solve problems for themselves. No student has ever failed the module except by not completing the assignments. Typically, I tend to grade generously the portfolio of films that the student produces, especially if the student is on hand to introduce and to discuss and explain their work; I feel it is important to reward their bravery in standing alone with their work in front of their peers and want to encourage that as much as possible, together with experimentation and glorious failures (i.e. work that is at least trying to do or say something unusual). I also try to give feedback on work as quickly as it is presented in class – although if a student does not come to present their work in class, but only uploads it to the YouTube channel, then I tend not to grade that work until after the deadline, because I want the students to remember that their presence and participation in class is expected, and, indeed, in this module it is rewarded.

For, while I grade the portfolio 'generously', I am more 'academically rigorous' with the critical reflection, during which I ask students to reflect upon their contribution to the module, the way in which they have tried to frame and build audiences for their work (i.e. by participating in class, but also via the use of social media and, perhaps, the creation of independent screening events and/or festival participation) and the way in which their work ties in with the films and readings that we have discussed over the course of the module. Failure to engage with the academic components of the class, as well as failure to engage with the class through absenteeism and/or an unmitigated refusal to participate, result typically in weaker grades. The basic trend is that the more you put into the module, the more you get out of it – and so while the workload is quite intense, those who embrace the module and who complete five films, as opposed to simply the requisite three, tend to do better. Notably, and perhaps as a result of the habituation to more conventional filmmaking methods on their other production modules, students with no production experience whatsoever tend to do better than those who have some. First-time filmmakers certainly seem to be at no disadvantage when compared to students with production experience. Students who read also tend to be at an advantage over students who do not.

References

Birri, Fernando (1997), 'Cinema and Underdevelopment,' in Michael Martin (ed.), *New Latin American Cinema*, Detroit: Wayne State University Press, pp. 86–94.
Boal, Augusto (2008), *Theatre of the Oppressed* (trans. Charles A. and Maria-Odilia Leal McBride and Emily Fryer), London: Pluto Press.
Bolt, Barbara (2010), 'The Magic Is in the Handling', in Estelle Barrett and Barbara Bolt (eds), *Practice as Research: Approaches to Creative Arts Enquiry*, London: I. B. Tauris, pp. 27–34.
Brown, William (2018), *Non-Cinema: Global Digital Filmmaking and the Multitude*, London: Bloomsbury.

Brown, William and Matthew Holtmeier (2013), 'Machinima: Cinema in a Minor or Multitudinous Key?' in Jenna Ng (ed.), *Understanding Machinima: Essays on Filmmaking in Virtual Worlds*, London: Bloomsbury, pp. 3–22.
Bruns, Axel (2008), *Blogs, Wikipedia, Second Life, and Beyond: From Production to Produsage*, Oxford: Peter Lang.
Campbell, Robert (2018), 'Small Form Films: The (Non-)Cinema of Mike Ott,' *Jump Cut: A Review of Contemporary Media*, 58, <http://www.ejumpcut.org/currentissue/CampbellMikeOtt/index.html> (accessed 2 January 2019).
Deleuze, Gilles (2005), *Cinema 2: The Time-Image* (trans. Hugh Tomlinson and Robert Galeta), London: Continuum.
Dixon, Wheeler Winston (1998), *The Transparency of Spectacle: Meditations on the Moving Image*, New York: State University of New York Press.
Freire, Paolo (2017), *Pedagogy of the Oppressed* (trans. Myra Bergman Ramos), London: Penguin.
García Espinosa, Julio (1979), 'Toward an Imperfect Cinema,' *Jump Cut: A Review of Contemporary Media*, 20: 24–6.
Joyce, James (1972), *A Portrait of the Artist as a Young Man*, London: Wordsworth.
Migliorin, Cezar, Isaac Pipano, Luiz Garcia, Alexandre Guerreiro, Clarissa Nanchery and Frederido Benevides (2014), *Inventar com a Diferença: cinema e direitos humanos*, Niterói: Editora da UFF.
Perec, Georges (1969), *La disparition*, Paris: Gallimard.
Rancière, Jacques (2006), *The Politics of Aesthetics: The Distribution of the Sensible* (trans. Gabriel Rockhill), London: Continuum.
Rifeser, Judith (this volume), 'Feminist "Pensive-Creative Praxis" and Irigaray: A Porous, Dialogical Encounter', in Agnieszka Piotrowska (ed.), *Creative Practice Research in the Age of Neoliberal Hopelessness*, Edinburgh: Edinburgh University Press.
Rocha, Glauber (1997), 'An Esthetic of Hunger' (trans. Randal Johnson and Burnes Hollyman), in Michael Martin (ed.), *New Latin American Cinema*, Detroit: Wayne State University Press, pp. 59–61.
Sconce, Jeffrey (1995), '"Trashing" the Academy: Taste, Excess, and an Emerging Politics of Cinematic Style', *Screen*, 36:4 (Winter), 371–93.
Tioseco, Alexis (2007), 'Shifting Agendas: The Decay of the Mainstream and the Rise of the Independents in the Context of Philippine Cinema', *Inter-Asia Cultural Studies*, 8:2 (June), 298–303.
White, Patricia (2008), 'Lesbian Minor Cinema', *Screen*, 49:4, 410–25.
Wu Wenguang (2006), 'DV: Individual Filmmaking', *Cinema Journal*, 46:1, 136–40.
Zhangke, Jia (2003), 'The Age of Amateur Cinema Will Return' (trans. Yuqian Yan), <http://dgeneratefilms.com/academia/jia-zhangke-the-age-of-amateur-cinema-will-return/> (accessed 2 January 2019).

12. BAITS OF FALSEHOOD: THE ROLE OF FICTION IN DOCUMENTARY OR FROM UNTHEORISED PRACTICE TO UNPRACTISED THEORY

Bruce Eadie

This essay has no place in this book. I am involved in neither practice-led theory nor in theory-generating practice. For much of my career I made interview-based, historical documentaries very often concerned with traumatic and violent events still within living memory. After a break of a decade I returned to documentary as a theorist writing a doctoral thesis on the role of fictions in documentary film. My current interest in theory is in part an attempt to understand my own past practice and in part an attempt to understand the increasing tendency in current documentary practice to deploy fictions within the documentary frame; a tendency profoundly at odds with my past practice. At the heart of that practice was a belief that it was the documentary maker's ethical duty not to fictionalise that 'real' world in the name of a compelling narrative.

Untheorised Practice

Looking back, my approach to documentary filmmaking in the late 1980s and 1990s was remarkably uninformed by theory. Somehow, I absorbed from the ether a way of making films which just seemed to be how one put together one-hour or feature-length documentaries at the time. Working at the 'serious' end of the commercial sector, making films for BBC2 or Channel 4 in the United Kingdom and for similarly minded broadcasters abroad, I was aware of what other filmmakers were producing and the sort of films that received plaudits at the various documentary-film festivals. These films became the untheorised model or blueprint for my own documentary-making. There was little sense of working within a genre that had a history that offered a variety of forms and radically different possible approaches to filmmaking.

It was of course very difficult in the 1980s to gain a sense of the history of the documentary genre even if one wanted to. I remember spending months trying to get hold of a VHS copy of Peter Watkins's BBC docudrama *Culloden* (1964) after it was recommended to me. If you missed one of the rare screenings of a classic documentary at the National Film Theatre it might be months or years before the opportunity arose again. Documentary study has been transformed – has been made possible – by the increasingly ready availability of documentaries on VHS and then DVD and finally online. In the 1980s, documentary was an ephemeral art. Documentary history has only very recently made the transition that art history made in the nineteenth century as printed reproductions of works of art in books made modern art-historical scholarship possible. With a few notable exceptions, there was also very little written about the history of documentary. It is easy to forget how recently documentary scholarship established itself in the academy and how publications like the *Visible Evidence* series (and its associated conferences)[1] have not so much transformed documentary scholarship as brought it into being.

With the excuse that my untheorised approach to documentary-making in 1980s was partly a product of a lack of the necessary physical and intellectual resources, I have recently (with the excuse no longer valid) tried to work out what I was up to in that distant past. Re-watching some of my own documentaries on VHS tapes that I still possess, I seem to have been working in what might loosely be described as the American *direct cinema* tradition. The camera is essentially transparent, providing a window on a reality which unfolds before the viewer. There is none of the reflexivity and self-reflexivity of direct cinema's (very much non-identical) French twin, *cinéma vérité*. Borrowing Allan Casebier's definitions (1991: 157–8), a reflexive documentary in Brechtian mode, unmasks the mechanics of the filmmaking process in documenting a subject; the camera is acknowledged as actively creating what it then records. Looking at my past documentary work there seemed to be an attempt to refuse any hint of reflexivity especially in the editing of interviews where the questions the interviewee was asked are edited out and their responses strung together as if their words were a spontaneously-generated soliloquy. And there is absolutely no hint in these films of self-reflexivity, which Casebier describes as the process of mediation involved in the reception of the documentary playing out within the documentary itself; a highly self-conscious mode of filmmaking, where the documentary (and the process of its making) becomes a subject of the documentary.[2]

What is odd when considering the form these documentaries took is that the form did not reflect my understanding of the nature of the filmmaking process at that time. I can remember being surprised by newspaper reviews that took the absence of voice-over narration as evidence of the film allowing protagonists to speak directly to the audience without authorial or editorial interference. When editing these films, I was acutely aware of cutting up synchronised interview and rearranging the bleeding chunks into an argument. The final form the films took was highly mediated and manipulated. I was also aware at that time that the direct cinema approach was as constructed as any other approach. It is a style of documentary in which protagonists are often asked to *act-out* or *enact* their ordinary lives for the camera. What the viewer is presented with are protagonists *playing* or *acting* themselves in a reconstruction of their ordinary lives. One of the great, iconic documentaries of direct cinema, the Maysles brothers' *Salesman* (1968), is in essence a dramatic reconstruction by a salesman of his own life in which the documentary director has asked him to play himself in the style of an observational documentary. Just because the audience does not see the camera, does not mean the protagonists do not see it or are not profoundly affected and influenced by it. Direct cinema is no more *direct* than any other form of documentary. It is simply a form that does not uncover its own artificiality.

I was also deeply suspicious of re-enactment despite being able to acknowledge that even a realist approach like direct cinema was, to an extent, performative and an act. Through the 1980s and 1990s more and more television documentaries, especially where the narrative looked to some past event, introduced low-rent, *am-dram* re-enactments whose only function seemed to be to provide pictures to fill the screen for want of something else. More profoundly – and here I was aware of the tradition – documentary seemed to have been born in very dubious circumstances with Robert Flaherty's much celebrated anthropological films of the 1920s, *Nanook of the North* and *Moana*. The films presented an almost entirely fictionalised account of Inuit and Samoan life. My critical attitude to Flaherty's films was not so much that he had to stage events (this was inevitable given the cumbersome nature of film equipment at the time) but in his insistence that his subjects dress, and hunt, and pretend to live lives that no Inuit or Samoan had actually lived for two or three generations – if ever. The films are less anthropological documents than romantic fantasies designed to appeal at the box office. If anything, my attitude to fiction and fictionalisation in documentary was that it should be avoided; it should be stripped out of documentary where possible as it was antithetical to the documentary project.[3]

Looking back at my films, they seem to have taken a form that was conventional for the time when they were made but which did not, even then, reflect my own thinking about the nature of documentary. In this, they now appear somewhat disingenuous and I would certainly approach a documentary project in a different way today. But what has not changed in my thinking about documentary is the belief that documentary – for all its constructedness – is able to tell us something about the 'real' world *out there* (even if to be truthful in the telling we must reveal our own complicity in co-creating and co-forming that reality[4]). In short, I have resisted and still resist the pressure from post-structuralist theory to concede the fictionality of all forms of narration (and indeed of all forms of meaning-making) including those that make referential claims like historiography and documentary. With Elizabeth Cowie, I would argue that for all its 'deformations' and 'fabrications', documentary film 'sets out a contract with its audience by its self-declaration as a documentary. Its fabrications do not thereby make it not nonfiction' (2011: 45).

Unpractised Theory

So much for the past and my own efforts as a documentary-maker. Returning to the academy in recent years, I set out on a project that took documentary film as its object and sought to theorise the relation between documentary film and the real, non-fictional world it claims to describe and represent. The project began as an attempt to justify documentary's implicit claim to its own non-fictionality. I soon became interested in a small number of recent documentary films – all concerned with traumatic histories – that have deployed fictional interludes or have adopted modes of representation *more commonly* associated with fictional film: animation, dioramas with clay models, re-enactment, the use of actors (who sometimes take the place of the principal protagonist who is also present in the diegesis), dream or hallucinatory sequences (for example, Albertina Carri's *The Blonds*, 2003; Guy Maddin's *My Winnipeg*, 2007; Ari Folman's *Waltz with Bashir*, 2008; Rithy Panh's *The Missing Picture*, 2013; Joshua Oppenheimer's *The Act of Killing*, 2013).

Of course, none of these devices or representational techniques are entirely new to documentary. The first animated documentary (McCay 1918) even pre-dates John Grierson's coining of the term 'documentary'; and the use of the term *docu-fiction*, which has come to prominence since the millennium to describe an apparently 'new' form of documentary, was in limited usage as early as 1980 (Candeloro 2000), with examples of the sub-genre extending back, in all but name, to Flaherty's films. And documentary and fiction film have a long history of borrowing and counter-borrowing of filmic styles and tones of voice (post-war Italian neorealist features had a marked influence on documentary style, and in the 1960s *cinéma vérité* profoundly influenced the look of many features, not least those of Jean-Luc Godard). What I think is new in the last twenty years or so, is a new permissiveness in the range of filmic devices (especially fictions), representational forms and tones of voice that documentary filmmakers have adopted and mixed together, not least the voice of the first-person director with its unashamedly subjective perspective which for Michael Renov '*reinvents the VERY IDEA of documentary*' (Renov 2009: 42, capitals and italics in original). If Grierson's definition of documentary as the 'creative treatment of actuality' (1966: 147) is of any value, the question becomes perhaps, how creative can you be before the creation is no longer documentary? How creative can you be before you cross an invisible taxonomic line (which is hard to define but tangible to both producers and viewers of documentary) and you cease to 'address *the* world in which we live rather than *a* world imagined by the filmmaker' (Nichols 2001: xi, emphases in original) and documentary dissolves into fiction?

Two questions arose. Are these films still documentary in the sense of telling us something about the real, non-fictional world? And, given the prevalence of fictions within documentaries that treat traumatic histories, what function might a fiction play in illuminating or explicating a very real, non-fictional traumatic past?

To answer these questions, I looked to two very different bodies of film theory: phenomenology and psychoanalysis. Just as the documentaries at the core of my study seem to be doing something new (even if there are precedents for all the devices that are deployed stretching back almost to the birth of documentary) so, likewise, these theoretical approaches have long been applied to film but in recent years they have been repurposed to look specifically at documentary film and its very particular claim to tell us something about the real lives of the protagonists we see on screen. In Vivian Sobchack's ground-breaking revival of phenomenological approaches to film in the 1990s, she makes a very clear distinction between documentary and fictional features (1992 and 1999: 241).[5] They are different sorts of intentional object; objects of which we ask very different questions and seek very different answers. Similarly, in recent years in the work of Elizabeth Cowie (1999, 2011), Michael Renov (2004), Alisa Lebow (2008) and especially Agnieszka Piotrowska (2014, 2015), psychoanalytic (predominantly Lacanian) film theory has been repurposed as a tool for exploring documentary film and these and other scholars have drawn parallels between the interpersonal encounters that take place in documentary and the encounter between analyst and analysand in clinical analysis (for example, Waldman and Walker 1999: 26, Berman 2003: 221–2, Berman quoted in Chanan 2007: 215–16, Macdonald in Cousins and Macdonald 2006: 392, Bruzzi 2015: 94). In the 1970s Christian Metz, Laura Mulvey and others used Lacanian categories to explore the relationship between the film text and the spectator. Piotrowska has taken Lacanian theory *inside* the documentary film to explore 'real', non-fictional relationships and to explore the role of fictions within the non-fictional frame of documentary.[6] My own exploration of contemporary documentary films about traumatic personal histories, takes a similar path.

I have to admit to approaching some recently produced documentary films with a high degree of scepticism. What place could fictions have within a film genre whose *raison d'être* was its non-fictionality and which had defined itself since its inception as cinema's non-fictional form? As Bill Nichols put it, '[d]ocumentary arises, with Grierson and Dziga Vertov, in response to fiction' (1994: 94). Direct cinema may not be what it claims to be and what we see on screen may be a performance of reality rather than reality itself – and so a form of fiction – but its fictionalisations remain within quite narrow bounds. Ari Folman's largely animated documentary *Waltz with Bashir* (2008) contains animated dream sequences and reproduces waking hallucinations that played in the director's head; and Joshua Oppenheimer's *The Act of Killing* (2013) has scenes in which the central protagonist (a mass murderer) plays himself in some indeterminate 'other world' being forgiven his sins and in another scene being decapitated and having his internal organs eaten by a man in drag.[7] Surely these films have crossed the invisible taxonomic line? But on watching them, I was surprised to find myself not only thinking that I was still watching documentary – something that told me about the real world – but that the fictions had opened up aspects of the real world that might otherwise have remained hidden. The films seemed to pass the test that – for all the attempts to define the documentary – remains the fallback position of many scholars with many different theoretical axes to grind: a documentary is a documentary if its producers think it is a documentary and market it as a documentary and if, even more crucially, the viewing public receive the film as a documentary.[8]

My experience of these filmic objects coincided with Vivian Sobchack's description of the non-fictional documentary object where we look both at the screen and through the screen; we are dependent upon the screen for knowledge but are 'also aware of an excess of existence not contained by it'. I had experienced the filmic object (the *film-as-intentional-object*) as non-fictional and felt as if a space had been opened up *through* or *behind* the screen giving me access to aspects of the life of the on-screen protagonist beyond the screen (Sobchack 1999: 242, 245–6). The reality that seemed to become available in watching these films was often not a historical reality that most historians would recognise. Rather the fictions seemed to give access to a psychic reality in the lives of the on-screen protagonists. As such the fictional interludes are not fictional in the sense that *anything goes*. They are 'real' in perhaps in one of three ways. They are fictions in search of a non-fictional historical 'truth' where the historical account is difficult to recover (often as a result of traumatic disruptions of memory) and can be seen as an attempt to re-imagine an historical event which is out of reach. Or secondly, they are entirely invented but may evoke powerful responses in the traumatised on-screen protagonist – even if those responses may be affective or somatic responses and evade verbal description – and so suggest that something 'real' is in play. Or thirdly they reproduce 'real' imaginings or fears or hallucinations that have played in the mind of the protagonist. Many philosophic accounts of reality would not categorise these 'events' as real even though these interludes seem to be attempting to reproduce a present or past *psychic* reality or to imagine a lost historical reality. This suggests that they are only unreal or fictional in a limited sense. Here I want to re-purpose an argument that the philosopher and psychoanalyst Cornelius Castoriadis deployed about the nature of being, both to critique the way many philosophers have approached and described reality and to critique my own past attitude to 'fiction' in documentary:

> Remember that philosophers almost always start by saying: 'I want to see what being is, what reality is. Now, here is this table. What does this table show to me as characteristic of real being?' No philosopher ever starts by saying: 'I want to see what being is, what reality is. Now, here is my memory of my dream last night'. (1997: 5)

Following Castoriadis, I would argue for the 'reality' or the 'non-fictionality' of these fictions, or at the very least describe them as *true* fictions or, better, reproductions of psychic realities. Castoriadis's argument seems to coincide with (or was perhaps even derived from) Martin Heidegger's distinction between the *factual* (the ontic or *factum brutum*) and the *factical* (or existential-ontological). The *factual* lends itself to empirical validation (or at least has that potential) whilst the *factical* has a reality in lived experience but not in the external, historical world (Heidegger 1962 [1927]).

There are two 'fictions' or fictional-films-within-the-film at the heart of Ari Folman's animated, autobiographical documentary, *Waltz with Bashir* (2008) – the second fiction being precipitated by the first – and both fall into the category that Castoriadis has sought to reposition as elements of reality: a dream and a hallucination. The film opens at night in Tel Aviv with a large pack of ferocious dogs running through the streets. It is a frightening scene and begins without any accompanying explanation or context. It emerges that the scene reproduces a recurring nightmare of Ari Folman's friend, Boaz Rein, whom Folman had known since they both served as teenagers in the Israeli Army occupying Beirut during the Lebanon War of over twenty-five years before. In the scene following the nightmare, Rein is seen meeting Folman to ask if his description of the ferocious dogs sparks any memories for Folman. Rein is convinced it is connected in some way with their experiences in the Lebanon War. Folman tells Rein that not only does the description of the nightmare not spark any memories but that he is surprised to realise he has virtually no memories at all of his time in Lebanon and Beirut. An actual meeting between Rein and Folman (which is reproduced in animation in the film) is the event that prompted Folman to make *Waltz with Bashir*. The film that emerges is an unfolding filmic record of Folman's quest to recover this 'lost' past, as

Folman visits friends, former soldiers and a psychologist in his attempt to both remember and try to understand why he cannot remember.

As the film progresses, aspects of Folman's youthful army experiences come back to him, sometimes as a result of others recalling events at which Folman was present. Folman even begins to understand that Rein's dream might be a nightmare memory of the Israeli army's practice of killing the dogs which prowled the outskirts of Lebanese villages, before a night-time attack; the dogs being killed to prevent their barks alerting enemy fighters to the Israelis' presence. Rein's night terrors were perhaps precipitated by his memory that the sound of the dogs barking would have meant discovery and the danger of being killed in the Lebanon. But Folman's abiding recovered recollection (sparked by his engagement with his friend's nightmare) is a not really a recollection at all but a kind of recurrent waking hallucination in which Folman sees himself and other young Israeli soldiers emerging naked from the sea off Beirut against a bizarrely illuminated urban backdrop. This hallucination – like Rein's nightmare – seems to defy rational description or explanation. Folman's desire to understand his hallucinatory vision takes over as the driving force of the film's narrative and does eventually lead Folman to recover a memory of his involvement as a bystander during the Christian

Figure 12.1 Folman's hallucination. Screen grab from Ari Folman's *Waltz with Bashir*, 2009 [2008] (DVD: Artificial Eye).

Phalangist massacre of Palestinian men in the Sabra and Shatila suburbs of Beirut; the bizarre illumination of the scene in the hallucination perhaps recalling the flares that were used to illuminate the sky and assist the Phalangists in finding hidden Palestinians at night. It is a deeply troubling memory for Folman, especially as the child of Holocaust survivors, as he remembers he stood by and allowed mass murder to occur.

It is the two 'fictions' – Rein's nightmare and Folman's hallucination – which open a route to understanding the traumatic past for Folman (and hence for the viewer). Both are fictions in a strict historical sense, but both are very real aspects of the present psychic reality of two veterans of the Lebanon War and fit with Castoriadis's expanded conception of reality, which includes 'Now, here is my memory of my dream last night'. These *ontic* fictions but *factical* realities are Folman's only route to recovering the past and to understanding why he had suppressed all memories of his time in Lebanon. Ironically, the quest for Folman began not as an attempt to understand a traumatic past which was troubling him; his initial amnesia seemingly acted as a very successful defence against trauma. But once prompted by his friend's nightmare, the desire to know, to understand and to produce a meaningful account of a very real past became a driving obsession.

That the use of 'fictions' in documentary has been prevalent amongst documentary-makers, like Folman, trying to explore traumatic pasts, is perhaps a product of the nature of trauma itself. The three major theoretical accounts of trauma that currently co-exist – the psychoanalytic, the post-structuralist (usually labelled 'trauma theory'[9]) and the psychiatric account of post-traumatic stress disorder – have divergent philosophical underpinnings but agree on the symptoms of trauma: the generation of disturbing thoughts, feelings, dreams or hallucinations which cause mental and physical distress; or sometimes just a debilitating feeling of blankness. All these symptoms seem to entail disruptions of memory ranging from the absence of all representational memories of the traumatic event, ranging through partial recall or recall that displaces or screens the traumatic event (in effect fictionalising the traumatic event), to vivid, flashback memories that *seem* to replay the past in the present in a heightened or terrifying form. If documentary is to approach the reality of trauma, then it would be odd not to explore these psychic or symptomatological realities. In doing so, documentary-makers have sought to stage these manifestations of trauma in dramatic performance or in animation or in imaginative reconstructions of the past, reaching for forms of representation more usually associated with fiction.

These fictional interludes (or 'fictional'-films-within-the-documentary) are not fictional in the sense of *fictitious* (untrue or a lie) but closer to *fictive*; they emerge from the imagination or perhaps the unconscious or are provocations that have the power to reconfigure understandings of what might be conventionally described as the 'real' world. Perhaps better still, we could think of them as alternative frames of experience that interact with and modify other frames of experience which appear more straightforwardly non-fictional. It is the carrying over to documentary of one of the oldest literary techniques, the *frame story* or the *story-within-the-story*, where the inner story has the power to modify the outer story or to reveal a 'truth' in the outer story that would not have emerged otherwise. It is in the dynamic encounter between the frames that insights ('truths' or meanings about a real non-fictional world) become available.

In Piotrowska's account of the place of fictions within documentary, she turns to Lacan (and to Derrida following Lacan) and the idea that the truth 'declares itself in a structure of fiction' (Derrida quoted in Piotrowska 2014: 20) as 'it is often *only* through fictional stories, which offer a distance to the unrepresentable pain, that we can express the essence of the matter'; it is the only way to 'represent something which remains largely unspeakable' (2017: 75). I find this a convincing account that does not simply *justify* the place of fictions within the ostensibly non-fictional frame of the documentary but sees these fictions as *necessary* if we are ever to approach the truth or (as I would prefer to characterise it) if the traumatised protagonist is ever going to find or create a meaningful account of a profoundly traumatic personal history.

But in my reading of a number of recent documentary films that deploy fictions in pursuit of a truthful or meaningful account of trauma, there seems to be an intermediary stage between the witnessing of the fiction and possible emergence of truth or meaning. Again and again, the response of the traumatised protagonist to witnessing a fiction within the diegesis is at first seen by the viewer to register in the protagonist in non-verbal, affective or bodily reactions.[10] These reactions to the fictional representation again take the trauma outside the sphere of representation and, for meaning or understanding to emerge, these bodily and affective responses need in turn to be reflected on within the diegesis. That said, these initial affective and bodily responses to the fictional representation seem to be a clue that we are on a path that might lead to the emergence of something truthful or meaningful. This realisation prompted me to question whether the truth lies in the structure of the fiction or whether the truth is flushed out of its hiding place through the provocation of the fiction.

To develop this argument I turned to two versions of the play-within-the-play in *Hamlet* and to Freud's appropriation of one of these in his 1937 essay *Constructions in Analysis* (Freud *Constructions in Analysis*, vol. 23: 255–69).[11] The most well-known version of the play-within-the-play in *Hamlet* is Hamlet's staging of the fictional drama *The Murder of Gonzago* in front of his Uncle Claudius, who Hamlet believes has murdered his father. Hamlet says he will watch Claudius closely ('I mine eyes will rivet to his face') as Claudius watches the play, in the hope that the fictional play will be the vehicle to 'unkennel' his uncle's 'occulted guilt' (*Hamlet*, III, ii): that is, for the truth to emerge. But Hamlet seems to know the truth will not emerge as a verbal account or confession of the circumstances of his father's death but rather it will register in his uncle's involuntary bodily or affective responses to witnessing the play. As Hamlet says, he will have his players:

> Play something like the murder of my father
> Before mine uncle; I'll observe his looks;
> I'll tent him to the quick: if he but blench,
> I know my course.
>
> (*Hamlet*, II, ii)

It is the affective or somatic response of his uncle (the 'blench') that will be the tell-tale sign that some sort of truth is in play. And this is precisely what happens: his uncle flies into a rage and storms out of the room in which the play is being performed. It is only later, in a soliloquy overheard by Hamlet, that Claudius confesses his guilt in words. It is only at this later point that Claudius's affective and somatic reactions to the provocation of the fictional play are given meaningful form.

In the second example of the play-within-the-play in *Hamlet*, the fiction of the play is much closer to what we might describe as fictitious. It is not fiction that incorporates certain elements of an apparently real event – what Hamlet calls '*something like* the murder of my father' (my italics) – but an outright invention. In *Constructions in Analysis*, Freud suggests a method of dealing with the most impenetrable manifestation of trauma, where the original traumatic event appears to be entirely forgotten (or never to have registered) and all the normal analytic tools deployed in treating neurotic conditions have failed. In these circumstances, the analyst must imaginatively produce a representation – a construction – of the missing representation and offer it to the patient. Freud is making the radical suggestion that a narrative that has no historical basis – a fictive narrative – can nevertheless produce a transformatory therapeutic result every bit as powerful as the recovery of the lost (historical) memory. Its value can only be judged by the effect it has upon the patient; it is the patient's conviction that the construction is of importance that is the key.

> Quite often we do not succeed in bringing the patient to recollect what has been repressed. Instead of that, if the analysis is carried out correctly, we produce in him an assured conviction of the truth of the construction which achieves the same therapeutic result as a recaptured memory.
>
> (Freud, *Constructions in Analysis*, vol. 23: 265–6)

Freud compares his method to that of Polonius in *Hamlet*. Polonius, keen to know what sort of life his son Laertes is leading whilst away at university in Paris, instructs his servant Reynaldo to tell lies about Laertes in the hope that the lies would prompt Laertes's friends into inadvertently revealing the truth about Laertes's way of life.[12] Freud compares his *constructions in analysis* to a 'bait of falsehood' that could take 'a carp of truth' (Freud *Constructions in Analysis*, vol. 23: 260–1) echoing Polonius's instruction to Reynaldo to perform '[w]hat forgeries you please' so that:

> Your bait of falsehood takes this carp of truth;
> And thus do we of wisdom and of reach,
> With windlasses and with assays of bias,
> By indirections find directions out.
>
> (*Hamlet*, II, i)

Here, in effect, Polonius is the writer and director of a fictitious scenario, a play, which Reynaldo is to perform (although we, as the audience of *Hamlet*, never see the performance). What Freud called a *construction in analysis* was indeed a forgery or a bait of falsehood – a fiction within the frame of the analysis – but not just any fiction would suffice. The bait of falsehood had to hook something real and his test for this was that it *touched* the patient (Freud, *Constructions in Analysis*, vol. 23: 260); that the forgery precipitated some sort of affective response in the patient, just as Reynaldo's forgeries were to be judged by the responses they provoked in Laertes's friends. By paraphrasing Polonius's line in *Constructions in Analysis*, Freud is making a very serious point about the role of fictions, of constructions, of 'plays' within the analytic frame. Where a traumatic past has left little or no registration in the mind of the analysand, the analyst must arrange the fragments that do become available into a coherent narrative; fragments to be found in the analysand's speech or affective responses, or in the gaps and absences in the analysand's account, or in the analyst's reflection on images or feelings generated in the counter-transference. This narrative, although fictional, has value if it generates something meaningful for the analysand; something that *touches* the underlying trauma. This meaningfulness becomes apparent in the framing analytic encounter as the analytic pair try to understand the *touch*.

Constructions in Analysis is a highly ambiguous text that carries certain tensions that run throughout Freud's work. Although it ostensibly seems to concern the value of a 'construction' in analysis – an *out-and-out* fiction or bait of falsehood of the sort Polonius advocates – Freud often slips back into claiming a *re*-construction of a past historical event is what is required to understand a current trauma (his long-favoured model of psychoanalysis as archaeology). It is the same tension that is never fully resolved in Freud's writing on seduction: is the traumatic seduction simply fantasy or a dimly recollected memory of a real event? But this ambiguity is valuable in thinking about documentaries that deploy fictions in the attempt to understand trauma: these fictions can resemble Hamlet's *The Murder of Gonzago* (historical reconstructions 'something like' what is thought to be the real traumatic event) *and* they can also resemble Polonius's fictitious construction (an *out-and-out* fiction). But whichever sort of fiction is deployed in documentary (Polonius's or Hamlet's), it is not *itself* the truth or even an approximation of the truth and neither is it necessarily a fiction structured like truth. Instead, the fiction is a *bait* or a *trap*[13] that is set to 'take' an involuntary bodily or affective response (a *blench* or a *touch*).[14]

A number of recent documentaries that delve into traumatic histories use fictional scenes within the documentary frame in ways that are not dissimilar to Freud's use of fictions within the analytic frame: fictions that help to reveal something about the trauma that was formerly hidden, lost or repressed. Just as in analysis, the value of these fictions is to be judged in their impact on the traumatised protagonist. It is not enough that a documentary director presents a fiction to us as the extra-diegetic audience. The traumatised protagonist has to witness the fiction playing out within the diegesis as it is only in the traumatised protagonist's response to the fiction that its capacity to take the carp of truth can be judged. Does it *touch* the protagonist? And, if so, what does the *touch* mean? But, unlike Freud's example, the author of the fiction in documentary is invariably the traumatised protagonist and not a third-person director acting as proxy analyst (that is not the director's role). The documentaries that deploy these fictions are either autobiographical (first-person documentaries) or third-person documentaries where control of the production of the fictions has been handed over to the traumatised protagonist.[15] In Joshua Oppenheimer's *The Act of Killing*, the fictional reconstructions and fantasy scenes are devised by the traumatised principal protagonist and mass murderer Anwar Congo rather than by the director. But it is in Congo watching back his own filmic fantasies and fictions on a monitor after they have been edited, or in reflecting on his own affective and somatic responses whilst playing a part in one of his own fictions, that the impact can be seen. Congo's own fictions bring him close to physical collapse, and later as he reflects on his bodily responses to his fictions his psychic distress seems to deepen as he is forced to confront his own guilt (which for years he had tried to avoid).[16]

The way the fictions function in *The Act of Killing* and in other recent documentaries that explore traumatic histories, requires a complex structure. In order to witness the fictions, the traumatised protagonist must become a member of an intra-diegetic audience watching and reacting to their own fictions. We as extra-diegetic audience members watching the documentary watch the intra-diegetic audience watching the fiction. It requires a self-reflexive form of documentary where, to quote Casebier again, 'the process of mediation involved in the reception of the documentary [plays] out within the documentary itself ... where the documentary itself becomes a subject of the documentary'. It is a structure that seems to mirror aspects of the analytic encounter where fictions (dreams, memories, hallucinations, *factical* psychic realities, constructions) are presented, reflected on, and returned to over time. The self-reflexive structure of *The Act of Killing* – the protagonist and Oppenheimer watching back on a monitor scenes that have already been shot – mirrors the analytic encounter where stories told in earlier sessions are picked up, reflected on, and reformulated in the light of evolving understandings. The fictions play themselves out within the self-reflexive structure of the documentary or the analysis. The hope is that some carp of truth – some truth about the real non-fictional world – can be taken. But, of course, in a documentary with a third-person director, a sceptical viewer might ask to what extent the fictions are the protagonist's creation (or the co-creation of protagonist and director) and to what extent they are the creation of a director who has full creative and editorial control, who stages the scenes, who positions the material within the film structure and who may even incite the protagonist to perform in ways that conform to the director's 'vision' and not the protagonist's.

Notwithstanding these pitfalls, in the deployment of fictions in an attempt to understand a traumatic history, the documentary filmmaking process can come to mirror the analytic process[17] (or at least the analytic process conducted as a self-analysis). In several recent autobiographical documentaries that deploy fictions to pursue a traumatic personal history, the director/protagonist embarks on the filmmaking process in the hope that in understanding the past through a filmed fiction within a documentary there will be a therapeutic effect: that the psychic pain of the trauma will be ameliorated.[18] It is the same epistemophilic urge that I take to be the driving force behind the analytic encounter.[19] Guy Maddin's autobiographical *My Winnipeg* (2007) opens with Maddin telling us he feels trapped and depressed in Winnipeg: 'I need to get out of here. Out of here! What if ... I film my way out of here?'. He decides to explore traumatic episodes in his childhood that he feels lie at the root of his depression. He does this through a fiction: a filmed reconstruction of traumatic moments in his childhood. He rents his old childhood home as a set, casts Anne Savage as his controlling mother and hopes that 'perhaps once this isolation through filmed re-enactment is complete, I can free myself from the heinous power of family and city and escape once and for all.' How successful Maddin is in filming his way out of his depression is unclear by the end of the film but Maddin certainly embarked on the film project as a form of therapy that deployed fictions to bring understanding of his traumatic past, with the hope that understanding would relieve the symptoms of trauma.

PRACTICE AND THEORY COMBINED

Where does this leave me in terms of practice and theory; in trying to put together my untheorised practice of the 1980s and 1990s and my recent unpractised theorising? I would certainly approach a film project very differently now if working with a protagonist with a traumatic personal history. I would now concede that there is a place for certain forms of fiction within documentary but that these fictions need to be bound into a self-conscious and self-reflexive structure. Following Freud and following *Hamlet*, these fictions do not tell us about the 'real', non-fictional world in and of themselves but they can serve as a 'bait of falsehood' – a catalyst – that may reveal some 'truth' (something meaningful as I would prefer to call it) about the nature of traumatic experience. It is in the response to the fiction of the protagonist within the diegesis that meaning might emerge. But if I was ever to try to make such a film, I would understand that any fictional components must be the creation of traumatised protagonist.

NOTES

1. *Visible Evidence* began as a conference at Duke University in 1993. There have now been twenty-five annual conferences and more than twenty-five volumes of essays on documentary have been published by the University of Minnesota Press.
2. By the late 1980s and early 1990s, British television documentary did have a more reflexive and self-reflexive model of filmmaking available in the work of Nick Broomfield but I remember finding the self-reflexivity of Broomfield's films irritatingly solipsistic, telling us more about Broomfield than the world beyond.
3. I was not aware at the time of Jean Rouch's use of fiction in *Moi, un noir* (1958) or *La pyramide humaine* (1959) which *might* have changed my attitude although I suspect that in the 1990s I might have been hostile to Rouch's fictions as not appropriate to documentary.
4. As Agnieszka Piotrowska has said, 'not editing yourself (the director) out of a documentary film is in itself an ethical gesture' (2019: 71–2).
5. Allan Casebier (1991) was also central to this revival but his work is less useful to me in thinking about fictions within documentary.
6. Piotrowska offers a succinct overview of the evolving application of psychoanalytic and Lacanian categories to film and ultimately to documentary (Piotrowska 2014: 29–37).
7. The difference between first-person (autobiographical) documentaries like Folman's and third-person documentaries like Oppenheimer's (where director and protagonist are separate) will be considered below (where I argue that as Congo creates the fictions we see on screen, we can view *The Act of Killing* as a third-person documentary with a first-person film within it).
8. This rule of thumb definition can be found in many scholarly texts (for example: Eitzen 1995: 81).
9. 'Trauma theory' emerged from the Department of Comparative Literature at Yale University and is best known from the work of Cathy Caruth in the 1990s (for example: Caruth 1996). It combines elements of Paul de Man's deconstructive

literary theory, the neurophysiology of Bessel van der Kolk and a version of psychoanalysis.
10. For example, Anwar Congo is scarcely able to complete a reconstruction of his past killing methods in *The Act of Killing* (Oppenheimer 2013) as he is overcome by bodily convulsions, or, in *The Blonds* (Carri 2003), when Albertina Carri represents the bodies of her tortured and murdered parents through a fictional (metaphorical) equation of their bodies with the bodies of tortured cattle on a farm, both audio and picture start to disintegrate (filmic effects which we take for Carri's attempt to represent her own affective and bodily responses to witnessing her 'fiction').
11. William Shakespeare's play of c.1599–1602 *The Tragedy of Hamlet, Prince of Denmark,* is cited hereafter as *Hamlet* followed by the relevant act and scene number. Freud's essay *Constructions in Analysis* is cited hereafter as Freud *Constructions in Analysis* followed by the volume and page number in the Standard Edition of Freud's work.
12. Feature film and documentary director Abbas Kiarostami – who frequently used fictions in his documentaries – seemed to echo Freud and Polonius when, in a 1995 interview, he said: 'We can never get close to the truth except through lying' (Zaatari 1995).
13. Polonius describes his fictions as bait ('a bait of falsehood') whilst Hamlet prefers the term trap as he reveals when he tells Claudius that the play is called *The Mousetrap* rather than *The Murder of Gonzago* (*Hamlet*, III, ii).
14. In trying to understand these affective and bodily responses to the provocation of documentary's filmic fictions, I have looked to psychoanalytic accounts that emphasise the affective, the bodily and the performative elements (non-linguistic elements) of the analytic encounter including role reversal and 'acting out'. So rather than looking to Lacan as several scholars have done, I have looked to the work of Wilfred Bion, André Green, Howard Levine, Joyce McDougall, the practice of psychodrama and to Donald Winnicott (to help think about the fictional interludes as a play space – a potential space – within documentary).
15. Just as Jean Rouch allowed his protagonists to construct their own fictions in *Moi un noir* (1958) – although of course here the 'truth' that was sought was a social or psychosocial truth rather than a psychic truth about trauma.
16. Guilt (which like Claudius's guilt in *Hamlet*) is *unkenneled* as involuntary affect in his encounter with a fictional play-within.
17. Several scholars have made the link between the documentary process and the analytic process (again, see Piotrowska 2014: 29–37).
18. Piotrowska, in thinking about third-person documentaries, writes, 'whatever else a documentary process might be, its aim is not the cure of its subject' (2014: 33): the director is not a proxy analyst. But the opposite seems to hold for a number of first-person documentaries where the director/protagonist embarks on the documentary-making process in the hope of lessening the psychic pain of trauma. I take this process to be a form of self-analysis through film in search of a cure. Ari Folman, for example, described the process of making *Waltz with Bashir* as 'four years of therapy' (Schäuble 2011: 210).
19. Freud wrote of the 'drive to know' (the *Wissentrieb*) and of an 'epistemophilic instinct' (see Freud, *Standard Edition*, vol. 7: 194–7; vol. 10: 245; vol. 12: 324; vol. 15: 327–8), as did Melanie Klein. And at the heart of Wilfred Bion's work is the notion that human beings are meaning-seeking, driven by an epistemophilic urge to make sense of the world. In conditions of psychic distress, this urge ('K') breaks down and becomes *minus-K* ('-K') as the sufferer fails to link up ideas and impressions and so fails to create meaning (Bion 1994). And even if the driving

force behind Lacanian analysis is desire (the desire of the Other), this carries an epistemophilic component in that the objective of analysis is: '[t]o restore to the symptoms their meaning, [and] to provide a place to the desires they mask' (Lacan quoted in Patsalides and Patsalides 2001: 207).

REFERENCES

Berman, Emanuel, Timna Rosenheimer and Michal Aviad (2003), 'Documentary Directors and Their Protagonists: A Transferential/Countertransferential Relationship?' in Andrea Sabbadini (ed.), *The Couch and the Silver Screen: Psychoanalytic Reflections on European Cinema*, Philadelphia: Taylor and Francis, pp. 212–32.
Bion, Wilfred (1994 [1962]), *Learning from Experience*, Lanham, Boulder, New York, Toronto and Oxford: Rowman & Littlefield.
Bruzzi, Stella (2015), 'Re-Enacting Trauma in Film and Television: Restaging History, Revisiting Pain', in Claudia Wassmann (ed.), *Therapy and Emotions in Film and Television: The Pulse of Our Times*, Basingstoke: Palgrave Macmillan, pp. 89–98.
Candeloro, Jean-Pierre (2000), *Docu-Fiction: Convergence and Contamination between Documentary Representation and Fictional Simulation*, PhD thesis, Lugano: USI Università della Svizzera Italiana, <https://web.archive.org/web/20110911104733/http://www.bul.unisi.ch/cerca/bul/memorie/com/pdf/9900Candeloro.pdf> (accessed 24 April 2019).
Caruth, Cathy (1996), *Unclaimed Experience: Trauma, Narrative, and History*, Baltimore: Johns Hopkins University Press.
Casebier, Allan (1991), *Film and Phenomenology: Toward a Realist Theory of Cinematic Representation*, reprinted 2009, Cambridge: Cambridge University Press.
Castoriadis, Cornelius (1997), *World in Fragments: Writings on Politics, Society, Psychoanalysis, and the Imagination*, ed. and trans. David Ames Curtis, Stanford: Stanford University Press.
Chanan, Michael (2007), *The Politics of Documentary*, London: BFI.
Cousins, Mark and Kevin Macdonald (eds) (2006), *Imagining Reality: The Faber Book of Documentary*, revised edn, London: Faber & Faber.
Cowie, Elizabeth (1999), 'The Spectacle of Actuality', in Jane Gaines and Michael Renov (eds), *Collecting Visible Evidence*, Minneapolis: University of Minnesota Press, pp. 19–45.
Cowie, Elizabeth (2011), *Recording Reality, Desiring the Real*, Visible Evidence, vol. 24, Minneapolis: University of Minnesota Press.
Eitzen, Dirk (1995), 'When Is a Documentary?: Documentary as a Mode of Reception', in *Cinema Journal*, 35:1, 81–102.
Freud, Sigmund (1953–74 [1886–1939]), *The Standard Edition of the Complete Psychological Works of Sigmund Freud*, ed. and trans. James Strachey, 24 vols, London: The Hogarth Press and The Institute of Psycho-Analysis.
Grierson, John (1966), *Grierson on Documentary*, ed. Forsyth Hardy, revised edn, London: Faber & Faber.
Heidegger, Martin (1962 [1927]), *Being and Time*, trans. Edward S. Robinson and John Macquarrie, San Francisco: Harper and Row.
Lebow, Alisa S. (2008), *First Person Jewish*, Minneapolis: University of Minnesota Press.
Nichols, Bill (1994), *Blurred Boundaries: Questions of Meaning in Contemporary Culture*, Bloomington: Indiana University Press.

Nichols, Bill (2001), *Introduction to Documentary*, Bloomington: Indiana University Press.
Patsalides, Beatrice and André Patsalides (2001), '"Butterflies Caught in the Network of Signifiers": The Goals of Psychoanalysis According to Jacques Lacan', in *Psychoanalytic Quarterly*, 70:1, 201–30.
Piotrowska, Agnieszka (2014), *Psychoanalysis and Ethics in Documentary Film*, London and New York: Routledge.
Piotrowska, Agnieszka (ed.) (2015), *Embodied Encounters: New Approaches to Psychoanalysis and Cinema*, London and New York: Routledge.
Piotrowska, Agnieszka (2017), 'On Touching and Speaking in (post) (de) Colonial Discourse', in Agnieszka Piotrowska and Ben Tyrer (eds), *Psychoanalysis and the Unrepresentable: From Culture to the Clinic*, London and New York: Routledge, pp. 74–93.
Piotrowska, Agnieszka (2019), *The Nasty Woman and the Neo Femme Fatale in Contemporary Cinema*, London and New York: Routledge.
Renov, Michael (2004), *The Subject of Documentary*, Minneapolis: University of Minnesota Press.
Renov, Michael (2009), 'First-Person Films: Some Theses on Self-Inscription', in Thomas Austin and Wilma de Jong (eds), *Rethinking Documentary: New Perspectives, New Practices*, Maidenhead: Open University Press, pp. 39–50.
Schäuble, Michaela (2011), 'All Filmmaking Is a Form of Therapy: Visualizing Memories of War Violence in the Animation Film Waltz with Bashir (2008)', in Maria Six-Hohenbalken and Nerina Weiss (eds), *Violence Expressed: An Anthropological Approach*, Farnham and Burlington VT: Ashgate, pp. 203–22.
Sobchack, Vivian Carol (1992), *The Address of the Eye: A Phenomenology of Film Experience*, Princeton, NJ: Princeton University Press.
Sobchack, Vivian (1999), 'Toward a Phenomenology of Nonfictional Film Experience', in Jane Gaines and Michael Renov (eds), *Collecting Visible Evidence*, Minneapolis: University of Minnesota Press, pp. 241–54.
Waldman, Diane and Janet Walker (1999), 'Introduction', in Diane Waldman and Janet Walker (eds), *Feminism and Documentary*, Minneapolis: University of Minnesota Press, pp. 1–35.
Zaatari, Akram (1995), 'Abbas Kiarostami Interviewed by Akram Zaatari', in *BOMB Magazine*, 1 January, <https://bombmagazine.org/articles/abbas-kiarostami/> (accessed 24 April 2019).

Filmography

Carri, Albertina (2003), *The Blonds [Los Rubios]*. Argentina (DVD: Woman Make Movies).
Flaherty, Robert (1922), *Nanook of the North*. US: Pathé (DVD: The Criterion Collection).
Flaherty, Robert (1926), *Moana*. US: Paramount Pictures.
Folman, Ari (2009 [2008]), *Waltz with Bashir*. Israel/Germany/France (DVD: Artificial Eye).
Maddin, Guy (2007), *My Winnipeg*. Canada: Documentary Channel (DVD: Soda Pictures).
Maysles, Albert, David Maysles and Charlotte Zwerin (1968), *Salesman*. US: Maysles Films Inc.
McCay, Winsor (1918), *The Sinking of the Lusitania*. US: Jewel Productions. Available at <https://www.youtube.com/watch?v=dyd2KhGFLZg> (accessed 24 April 2019).

Oppenheimer, Joshua (2013), *The Act of Killing*. UK: CREAM (DVD: Dogwoof).
Panh, Rithy (2013), *The Missing Picture [L'image Manquante]*. France/Cambodia: CDP/ARTE/Bophana Production (DVD: New Wave Films).
Rouch, Jean (1958), *Moi, un noir*. France: Films de la Pléiade.
Rouch, Jean (1959), *La pyramide humaine*. France: Films de la Pléiade.
Watkins, Peter (1964), *Culloden*. United Kingdom: BBC TV.

13. *REPENTED*: A CREATIVE INTERSEMIOTIC TRANSLATION

Agnieszka Piotrowska

In Edward Said's introduction to *Orientalism* (2003 [1978]) there is one particular scene, from the French writer Gustave Flaubert, which symbolises the encounter between the West and the subaltern, and, in broader terms, the encounter between the coloniser and the colonised. The scene features the Egyptian courtesan Kuchuk Hanem who may have been Flaubert's lover too. Said comments: 'He was foreign, comparatively wealthy, male, and these were historical facts of domination that allowed him not only to possess Kuchuk Hanem physically but to speak for her and tell his readers in what way she was "typically Oriental".' Said goes on brilliantly to construct an argument, using some of Gramsci's ideas, on hegemonic forces in culture and society, ascertaining that the West/East and West/South relations at that point in time rested on a strategy of 'flexible *positional* superiority, which puts the Westerner in a whole series of possible relationships with the Orient without ever losing the relative upper hand' (ibid.: 7) (emphasis in original). Re-reading the above quote today, what is very clear, almost embarrassingly blindingly clear, is that the colonisation taking place in the encounter between the prostitute and Flaubert is not only a colonisation of a subaltern non-Western subject by a dominant Western one, but it is also, or perhaps primarily, an intra-gender encounter of an all too familiar kind: a man buying a woman, penetrating a woman, taking things from her that he needs, including her voice which he then makes his own. Said's poignant point *equates* in some way a woman and the subaltern in the colonial encounter: and perhaps it is also true that a non-Western woman has been the most likely object of such a colonisation.

This chapter reflects on my own practice in Zimbabwe and in particular focuses on the issue of reclaiming the voice of a subaltern woman in colonial times. I focus on my practice research, which involves the adaptation of a theatre play by the award-winning Zimbabwean playwright Stanley Makuwe into an experimental film about colonial and post-colonial gender relations in a small mining town in Zimbabwe. The play deals with the painful legacy of colonialism: a black woman is the key recipient of discrimination and subjugation on the part of white colonisers but especially also on the part of her black lover. The chapter will map and analyse our joint attempt to create a different place/space in which to begin to build bridges across our different cultures and the painful historical legacy and trauma that still haunts Zimbabwe and other African countries. Through deploying theatricality on the one hand and the cinematic archive, treated as found footage, on the other, we attempted

Figure 13.1   The experimental film *Repented* (2019) was based on the play *Finding Temeraire* (2017), first performed at the Harare Arts Festival in May 2017.

to create what the feminist Donna Haraway (2016) calls a 'non arrogant collaboration'.

There is clearly a controversy in the heart of the project: the play is about a woman but is written by a man. The film is then directed by a woman but she is a European. Does it matter? In the post-colonial (de-colonial) context of southern Africa it does matter. The play by the Zimbabwean playwright Stanley Makuwe deals with life in a colonial mining settlement Mashava in Rhodesia and in the early independence years of the independent Zimbabwe. Mashava existed as an actual historical place but the intense engagement of the two characters in the play and in my film is of course fictional. The play, and later my adaptation of it, becomes also a mythical space in which the grand political narratives play out as the background to the profound intimate dramas in the foreground; the play is therefore about how the political and the historical affects the personal in the particular place. In this specific case it was not an issue of an adaption to screen – although it was that too – but rather, I would argue, it was indeed a translation, not just from the play onto the screen, but rather, from one semiotic system to another, from one way of thinking about the place and its meaning to another.

There have been very many works on cinema and adaption (for example: Andrew 1984; Cohen 1979; Corrigan 1999; Stam 2004) but here I am trying to focus in particular on the process of 'describing' and 'naming' a particular place and what it might mean in terms of some kind of notion of accuracy, both historical and geographical, and epistemological truth. I am also interested in the ability of writing to describe physical experience as a procedure which introduces order into chaos and is also an enabling procedure – enabling knowledge but also facilitating deep enjoyment, or psychoanalytical *jouissance* (of which more later). As we will see directly, there is controversy about the above and the question is indeed: is it true that the writing and naming enhances experience? Or does it take away from it, making it too concrete and obvious?

Umberto Eco's *Experiences in Translation* (2001) reminds us that in order to translate anything from one system of meaning to another there must be at least some points of convergence, some meta system of meanings that is accessible by all despite different ways of expressing it. He therefore makes the following point: 'If, in order to translate a text α, expressed in a language A, into a text β, expressed in a language B (and to say that β is a correct translation of α, and is similar in meaning to α), one must pass through the metalanguage X, then one is obliged first of all to decide in which way α and β are similar in meaning to a text γ in X and, to decide this, one requires a new metalanguage Y, and so on *ad infinitum*' (Eco 2001: 12). Roman Jakobson identified the type of translation that Eco discusses as interlingual translation ('an interpretation of verbal signs by means of some other language' (1971:

261)), which he distinguished from intralingual translation ('rewording ... of verbal signs by means of other signs of the same language') and intersemiotic translation ('an interpretation of verbal signs by means of signs of nonverbal sign systems' (ibid.) – in which we can include the translation of experience into language). The terms 'intralingual', 'interlingual', and 'intersemiotic' will be useful in the following discussion of translation.

Lawrence Venuti, the seminal scholar of translation, also advocates an infidelity to the original place from which the experience was initiated. He writes: 'a translated text should be a site at which a different culture emerges, where a reader gets a glimpse of a cultural order and resistency' (1995: 305).

The case study of my own work which I am using here is but one example. The questions asked have broader significance, also in terms of establishing the relationship between the experience and the description of it in a screenplay or other writings, and here the particular translation from one cultural circumstance to another, not in terms of where the play is set (as this does not change) but rather in the film's subsequent reception at festivals, conferences and events in the West. Here I reflect upon what might occur between the two, between author (and therefore the reader and the viewer) and the place and the experience described.

Finding Temeraire and Repented

Primrose, the main character of Stanley Makuwe's play *Finding Temeraire* which premiered first at the Harare International Festival of the Arts in May 2017 (directed by me) and was then performed in New Zealand where the Zimbabwean author now lives (directed by somebody else), is a deeply troubled but powerful woman. In an act of intersemiotic translation, I then adapted the play to the screen as a medium-length experimental film entitled *Repented* (2019). Here the issues have been plentiful, for a male Zimbabwean author wrote a strong female character and asked a European female director (me) to direct it. Makuwe wrote a very powerful female voice and asked me to direct the play in order, he said originally, to give the play the right emotional engagement with the material. The original work is a demonstration of how it is possible to develop a sense of a historical space without necessarily developing the physical sense of the place.

The play was written in English, and not Shona, the initial process of translation taking place in the writer's mind – as the characters lived in the colonial times it is possible that English was indeed their main shared tongue. Nonetheless, in my experience of Zimbabwe in contemporary times, people mostly would speak Shona to each other in intimate circumstances, despite English being one of the legal languages. Stanley Makuwe takes pleasure in his mastery of the English language but also confessed to me that writing in

A CREATIVE INTERSEMIOTIC TRANSLATION

Figure 13.2 The image is from the performance of *Finding Temeraire* at the Harare International Festival of the Arts in 2017, with Charmaine Mujeri (as Primrose) and Eddie Sandifolo (as Temeraire).

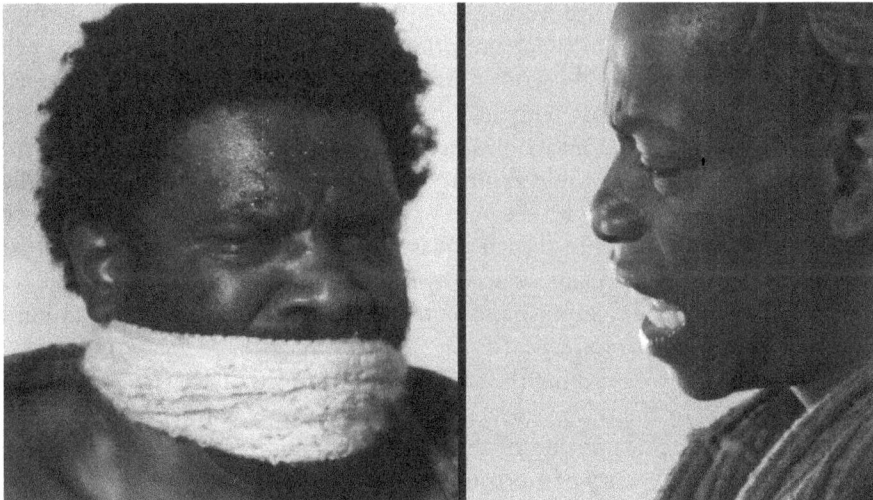

Figure 13.3 The same scene as adapted for the screen for *Repented* (2019) using the split screen technique with Charmaine Mujeri and Eddi Sandifolo.

English has given him a chance to create distance between himself and the trauma he was describing, a trauma which in part at least had its roots in an actual situation in the past.

Of course, I was excited and flattered to be asked to direct the play;

187

nonetheless, I was aware of some of the difficulties, particulary regarding gender.[1] In regard to *Finding Temeraire,* a male writer wrote a voice for a subaltern woman (= inter-gender, inter-lingual translation) and asked a European woman director to translate it for the stage and the film (intersemiotic translation). I was slightly anxious, but I considered the situation and was seduced by the beauty and strength of Makuwe's work, so I put other doubts aside. Between us, Stanley and myself that is, I think we managed to subvert and circumvent the inter-gender and intralingual issue of the female voice being written by a man.

Finding Temeraire takes place in a former mining village called Mashava. The play is a two-hander, consisting of a woman visiting an ex-lover for revenge. Primrose carries on long monologues about the past, before actually revealing her own identity as that of Temeraire's former lover and the mother of his son who, faced with his coldness and the indifference of the world, has a psychotic breakdown, murdering her baby soon after his birth. The play's construction is on the surface fragmentary as Primrose re-tells a number of short stories of their life in the pre-independence Mashava. It is interesting to consider that the process of finding her voice makes it possible for Primrose to find a different place for herself: through the words spoken at last she shifts from a crazy vengeful woman to a place of forgiveness. Makuwe lets his character create a space in which the words at last become an important speech act. How they are received becomes crucial to what kind of space is developed here: and so there is a possibility of it becoming a space of forgiveness instead of rage. The knowledge that we produce here together (the writer, the director, the film editor and the whole Zimbabwean crew and, last but not least, the astonishing actors) deals with the pain which is still mostly treated with silence in Zimbabwe and elsewhere because it is almost unbearable to consider: that the pattern of subjugation introduced by the colonisers vis-à-vis black people is replicated in intimate relationships, by the man objectivising the woman until she fights for her voice to be heard.

Without actually describing the settlement, Primrose offers vignettes which give the reader (or the theatregoer) a sense of the place, without describing it. These vignettes include stories of the whites-only club they all visited despite not being white, the story of a prostitute calling herself Dolly Parton who was the reason a great fight broke out in the club, the bizarre colonial couple of Baas and Madam Clipston (who had a large dog Madam Clipston got too fond of so Baas Clipston shot it), and other episodes.

These stories evoke the sense of the pre-colonial settlement with roles assigned and with no possibility of any fluidity whatever. In the play the stories have the role of preparing both the viewer and Temeraire for the revelations to come. Temeraire does not recognise Primrose as his former lover in the first instance – some twenty or even twenty-five years have elapsed since they were lovers and she has spent that time in prison, plotting her revenge. Even though Temeraire is the reason for her action and the core of her being, his role in the play is that of a listener and a passive responder; he too is a shadow of his former self. The play opens with a description of loneliness which leads into a story. The arrival of the woman is an intrusion, an unwanted visitor – on the surface, but in another way this is a deeply yearned-for interruption of the loneliness. Temeraire, who remains silent for most of the play, begins it this way: 'I am Temeraire, once the plumber of Mashava. It is like this. I am killing cockroaches when this woman comes to my house. At that time the afternoon sun is hot but not too hot … It is a long time since I spoke to someone *who knows the people and the places I knew*, so I just talk to her like I know her and I don't have to ask her who she is or where she came from' (Makuwe 2017: 1, my emphasis).

The stage direction after the first short introduction is 'a crumbling house' and the very first words uttered by Primrose relate to the settlement's state of decay, the Compound she calls it, now infested by cockroaches:

> Primrose
> When did cockroaches start coming to Mashava?
> Temeraire
> Every year they keep coming. We have seen more this year than any other time.
> Primrose
> There were no cockroaches in Mashava. Not in Westernlee. In the Compound one cockroach, all the houses would be scrubbed and sprayed. (Makuwe 2017: 1)

In the initial scenes, we also learn that his garden has grass and no flowers, as flowers are harder to grow 'and need a lot of water', continuing the theme of abandonment and decay. We also learn that many houses are empty – in the Compound, which presumably means where the white people used to live. Primrose asks straight out: 'where are all the white people?' and Temeraire just says 'They left'. But this is all the description Makuwe gives us about the actual physical place in which the dramas unfold: that the houses were cleaned and scrubbed under colonial times and that now they are infested and neglected. I will come back to the cockroach presence in the play, but for now let us just consider the character of Primrose and her long monologues both before she physically overwhelms Temeraire and afterwards. Her stated plan is revenge. Once she has tied him and gagged him, she appears to be preparing to hurt him further ('She circles him, like she wants to tear him apart' (ibid.: 11)). She enjoys taunting him too: 'Tell me, Temeraire. Are you afraid to die? Are you afraid of death? Do you fear hell?' (ibid.: 11), although she also appears to still consider whether a torture might be enough. ('Not so fast. Your type dies better in a slow cooker' (ibid.: 11)). And then: 'Temeraire, I am not here to kill you. I'm here to piss in your face' (ibid.: 13).

Crucially, before any of her torture can take place, she demands that he talk to her – for it appears he never really talked to her in the past:

> Primrose
> You don't want to talk.
>
> [She sharpens the knife.]
>
> Primrose
> Ooh, today you will talk. I swear, you will talk. (ibid.: 14)

The story Primrose tells Temeraire (as well as the audience) is that of an almost classic subaltern woman not only not being listened to by anybody but also really not knowing how to *translate* any of her experiences or emotions into words. In the past, as a very young woman she describes, she never learnt how to find pleasure in talking (never mind writing). This is reminiscent of the (post) colonial melancholy as Ranjana Khanna (2003) would say and its 'metaphorisation', that is indeed the ability to describe emotions, being the negative ones, which will lead to violence (of which I have written extensively elsewhere (Piotrowska 2017, for example)).

Psychoanalytically, we know that in order to develop a place for one's subjectivity, it is necessary to use words, to talk or to write – there is no other way. However, the only *jouissance* Primrose knew in her youth was a simple bodily pleasure – which, when corrupted, turned into a full psychotic episode and physical violence. There is nowhere to go and when she is abandoned by all with her unwanted baby son, she first strangles him with a scarf she shows Temeraire and then drowns the child in the white men's sewage pond.

Through her long speeches, she is able to develop her own place, which does not depend on violence – not even on her body this time, but on the language. This is the journey of describing, for the first time, perhaps, her emotions and her suffering, Primrose is able to arrive at a point when she is able to move beyond her despair and her fury – and eventually forgive Temeraire. When Primrose leads Temeraire to the sewage pond to look for their son buried there twenty-five years ago, clearly a metaphorical gesture of despair, she demands that he name him. Naming is crucial after all, for without naming the experience is meaningless and does not last. Words do matter: 'Do you have a name for your son, Temeraire? ... Name him. Name him now so that we call him by name. [She waits. He says nothing] When you call someone you call them by name. You can't just say, "hey you, hey you," as if you are one of those white people whose shit swallowed your son's dead body. There has to be a name,

A CREATIVE INTERSEMIOTIC TRANSLATION

Figure 13.4 We use different archive footage in a split-screen display to situate the love story in an actual historical moment in time. We re-claim the colonial footage to give it a different meaning.

Temeraire. This is your son, not your garden boy. You are the father. Name him' (ibid.: 22).

Temeraire, who by now has totally lost the power of speech, fails to name their dead son and the word he eventually enunciates is the one word which by now really matters to him: her name, 'Primrose'. In the epilogue, we learn that he found other words in the end, words of love, and that, somehow, Primrose and Temeraire are together again.

'Found Footage' in Translating, Adapting and Betraying

In her review article 'The Politics of Translation' (2018), Marina Warner argues that translation has always been a political issue, in terms of decisions made but also, more simply, who translates whom and why. She reviews a number of contemporary volumes on translation, including Mark Polizzotti's *Sympathy for the Traitor: A Translation Manifesto* (2018) and Mireille Gansel's *Translation as Transhumance* (2018). In general terms, Warner points out that:

> Two fundamental quarrels run through these books: the first over claims about fidelity and felicity, the second over cultural appropriation and consequent monolingualism (the continued expansion of the

Anglosphere). How to honour the character of the source of the language and its relation to cultural difference? Should a translator respond like an Aeolian harp, vibrating in harmony with the original text to transmit the original music, or should the translation read as if it were written in the new language? (ibid.: 22)

An adaptation might be a different matter, although perhaps not entirely different: we are still looking at two semiotic systems that need translating. Umberto Eco's most basic point about the possibility of a translation at all, is relevant here, for adaptation in Jakobson's terms is intersemiotic.

In his classic work on adaptation, Robert Stam defines adaptation as 'less a resuscitation of an originary word than a turn in an ongoing dialogical process. Intertextual dialogism, then, helps us transcend the aporias of "fidelity"' (Stam 2004: 24). Later in the volume, in his discussion of *Robinson Crusoe*, Stam quotes the author Salman Rushdie, who celebrates 'hybridity, impurity, intermingling, the transformation that comes of new and unexpected combinations of human beings, ideas, politics, movies, songs' (Rushdie, in Stam 2004: 362), and concludes, 'artistic innovation ... occurs on the transnational borders of cultures and communities and discourses', and 'it is only in the eyes of another medium ... that a medium reveals itself fully and profoundly' (Stam 2004: 364–5). It is beyond the scope of this chapter to review critiques of Stam's view and my case is very different – it was a collaboration with a Zimbabwean writer which in some ways was simple and respectful to the original. In other ways, particularly in the screen version, my work did take Makuwe's play into a slightly different direction, without, I hope, changing the spirit of his work.

My main innovation regarding the theatre production of *Finding Temeraire* was nothing out of the ordinary regarding the writer/director collaboration. Amongst other things, I lowered the ages of the main characters for reasons of my own – the actors Charmaine Mujeri and Eddi Sandifolo are my trusted collaborators and I had confidence they could pull off the difficult parts. I also thought it was possible to imagine the characters from twenty or twenty-five years ago as young rather than already middle-aged then – and in fact questioned in any event the initial suggestions of their ages as written by Stanley Makuwe. My vision was that Primrose would have been a very young woman indeed, naïve in her infatuation with Temeraire.

The key issue of the adaption/translation of Stanley Makuwe's play was indeed the additional of another level of intertextuality to the film (not the play) – and that was through the use of black and white archive footage not necessarily directly linked to the proceedings or rather linked thematically and conceptually but not in any way actually connected to the physical place of Mashava. This seems a very simple idea now and almost obvious but it was neither of these two things when I first presented it as a plan to the film's editor Anna Dobrowodzka. We have then experimented with introducing split screens to the film, both in order to offer different perspectives onto the narrative but also to translate the historicity of it onto the screen at times alongside the live action of the drama between the two main characters. All of the footage we used would have been shot during the colonial times in Rhodesia and in South Africa by those who were either supporting the oppressive regime or directly hired by representatives of it to obtain relevant footage. We felt that the introduction of the split screens and the archive footage not directly linked to the place in which the action occurred, offered in fact *more* the sense of place than any literal or faithful use of the actual footage could do – notwithstanding the fact that there was not any directly linked to Mashava. In addition, and very importantly, the colonial archive as 'found footage' in conjunction with the words uttered by Primrose were more successful at 'translating' her experience which is only partially spoken about in the play, namely the experience of a young black woman whose only currency is her bodily beauty and affective labour.[2] The concepts of intersectionality (Crenshaw 1989: 139) come to mind here also as within the hierarchy of the women in Mashava, and in many other colonial settlements, a woman like Primrose was really at the very bottom of the pile.

The final element of this discussion of translation is the notion of ethics and fidelity regarding using the archive as 'found footage' and also, more generally, the freedom a translator might have. In his essay 'The Ethics of Appropriation' (2014), Thomas Elsaesser reminds us: 'the origins of found footage films, as opposed to compilation films, are usually located within the Marcel Duchamp tradition of Dada and conceptual art, of Surrealism and the *objet trouvé*, the found object. The point of such a stranded object, left behind by the tide of time, is that it is made beautiful and special by the combination of a recent loss of practical use and its perishable or fragile materiality' (ibid.: 32).

The situation here is both different and similar: different because the archive and the split screens have a direct role to play in the film, which is not to do with beauty but rather to do with the truth and knowledge – and indeed the writing and description of what life may have been like in the past. However, this appears to be only part of the story: the characters in the play *Finding Temeraire* remember *the place* of Mashava as a good place. True, it is to do with them being young at the time but there is also a certain ambivalent and ambiguous nostalgia which they both seem to evoke and which Makuwe has captured in his play. Indeed, the nostalgia might be for the rigid, predictable and fixed, as opposed to the independence which has brought with it cockroaches – a most bizarre image in Makuwe's play which resonates uncomfortably with the known colonial insults towards the local population. Now, they stand for a dirty mess and lack of order – even as the order of the past was a denigrating and, in the end, a hated order. In our appropriating of the archive footage we also wanted to convey what it is that was being missed – as it was not just the profound injustice and oppressiveness of the place, it was also parties and dances and fun – almost as a gesture of defiance on the one hand but also, painfully, a re-enactment of the systematic inequality.

Polizzotti (2018) is adamant that it is good to abandon any idea of faithfulness to the 'original' or originating work: 'A good translation', he writes, 'offers not a reproduction of the work but an interpretation, a re-representation, just as the performance of a play or a sonata is a representation of the script or the score, one among many possible representation' (ibid.).

Marina Warner reminds us further also that 'many emigres have performed acts of translation themselves, going into voluntary exile from the demands – the oppression – of the mother tongue' (Warner 2018: 23). Was this also Makuwe's decision? Perhaps the fact that his beautifully written work was written in the language of the colonisers has given him a sense of power, in a way not dissimilar to our use of the 'found' footage and split screens. The philosopher Jacques Derrida in *Monolingualism of the Other* (1998) observes the power of language and reflects on his own position in it as a stranger and a master at the same time. He also brings forth the notion of the importance of language as the carrier of the law. His own position is precisely that of a colonised subject and as such he states that:

> all culture is originarily colonial ... Mastery begins, as we know, through the power of naming, of imposing and legitimating appellations ... First and foremost, the monolingualism of the other would be that of sovereignty, that law originating from elsewhere, certainly, but also primarily the very language of the Law ... The monolingualism imposed by the other operates by relying upon that foundation, here, through a sovereignty whose essence is always colonial, which tends, repressively and irrepressibly, to reduce language to the One, that is to the hegemony of the homogeneous. (ibid.: 39–40)

Derrida writes here as somebody whose supreme power of expression lies in the language which is in fact the language of the coloniser, as he was an Algerian child in Algeria going to a French school, and then on to higher education in France. There is no other language that he could in fact call his own any more – at the time of writing the words quoted, but also at any other time – French was not his mother tongue and his mother tongue was lost to him forever. His ability to write and name both his thoughts and ideas but also particularly emotions was his strength and our gift from him. As for the search for the truth, the psychoanalyst Jacques Lacan, who was Derrida's friend and an intellectual sparring companion, maintained that we cannot help but lie in our various translations in the name of the search for truth, and that the harder the story, the better it is to tell it as fiction for 'truth has a structure of fiction' (Lacan 2006: 684).

Any adaptation is a translation from one semiotic system to another and indeed any creative work at all is a translation of kinds – of the physical and bodily experience – of places we visit, people we love and histories we try to tell, looking for our place in the world. In creating *Repented* we all learnt many things about history and the painful legacy of colonialism but, perhaps more importantly, yet again it was re-affirmed that creative collaborations do help in building bridges even if some of the wounds have not yet healed.

NOTES

1. I have discussed the voice of a subaltern woman in Zimbabwe at length in my *Black and White* book.
2. Kimberlé Williams Crenshaw, an African American lawyer and thinker, in the late 1980s and 1990s famously pointed to the ineffectuality of Western (white) feminism and stressed different forms of discrimination converging often in an multi-fronted prejudice against women of colour in particular (Crenshaw 1989: 139). Prejudice is constituted by mutually reinforcing vectors of race, gender, class, ability and sexuality, has emerged as the primary theoretical tool designed to combat (feminist) hierarchy, hegemony, and other forms of exclusivity and dominance.

REFERENCES

Andrew, Dudley (1984), 'Adaptation', in *Concepts in Film Theory*, New York: Oxford University Press.
Cohen, Keith (1979), *Film and Fiction: The Dynamics of Exchange*, New Haven: Yale University Press.
Corrigan, Timothy (1999), *Film and Literature: An Introduction and Reader*, Upper Saddle River: Prentice-Hall.
Crenshaw, K. (1989), *Demarginalizing the Intersection of Race and Sex: A black feminist critique of antidiscrimination doctrine, feminist theory, and antiracist politics*, Chicago: University of Chicago Legal Forum.
Derrida, Jacques (1998), *Monolingualism of the Other: Or, the Prosthesis of Origin*, trans. P. Mensah, Stanford: Stanford University Press.
Eco, Umberto (2001), *Experiences in Translation*, trans. Alastair McEwen, Toronto: University of Toronto Press.
Elsaesser, Thomas (2014), 'The Ethics of Appropriation: Found Footage between Archive and Internet', Keynote address at the Recycled Cinema Symposium DOKU.ARTS.
Gansel, Mireille (2018), *Translation as Transhumance*, trans. Ros Schwartz, New York: Feminist Press.
Haraway, Donna (2016), *Staying with the Trouble: Making Kin in the Chthulucene*, Durham, NC: Duke University Press.
Jakobson, Roman (1971), 'On Linguistic Aspects of Translation', *Selected Writings, volume 2*, The Hague: Mouton, pp. 260–6.

Khanna, Ranjana (2003), *Dark Continents: Psychoanalysis and Colonialism*, Durham, NC: Duke University Press.
Lacan, J. (2006 [1966]), *Écrits*, trans. B. Fink, New York: Norton.
Piotrowska, Agnieszka (2017), *Black and White: Cinema, Politics and the Arts in Zimbabwe*, London: Routledge.
Piotrowska, Agnieszka (2019), *The Nasty Woman and the Neo Femme Fatale in Contemporary Cinema*, London and New York: Routledge.
Polizzotti, Mark (2018), *Sympathy for the Traitor: A Translation Manifesto*, Cambridge, MA: The MIT Press.
Said, Edward (2003 [1978]), *Orientalism*, New York: Vintage Books.
Stam, Robert (2004), *Literature Through Film: Realism, Magic, and the Art of Adaptation*, Malden, MA: Blackwell.
Venuti, Lawrence (1995), *The Translator's Invisibility: A History of Translation*, London and New York: Routledge.
Warner, Marina (2018), 'The Politics of Translation', *The London Review of Books*, 11 October.

NOTES ON AGNIESZKA PIOTROWSKA'S *REPENTED*

Thomas Elsaesser

(These are the key points of Thomas Elsaesser's introduction to the film in October 2018 at Gdansk University and then at the Essay Film Presentation at the cult bookshop in Amsterdam on 2 December 2018, <https://perdu.nl/nl/r/a-day-on-the-essay-film-visual-erosions-sprouting-words/>)

1. The opening magnificently builds up the blend of a contemplative-reflective-retrospective mood (Primrose in the boat), and a state of abjection and imprisonment (the somnolent and comatose Temeraire, staring straight at us from behind bars): this foreshadowing the tense psychological encounter between these two characters, clearly heading for a confrontation.

2. This human drama is set off against a serene, breathtakingly beautiful, but mercilessly indifferent natural landscape – a perspective to which the film returns at important moments: it gives us both relief from the tense drama, and it gives us the sense of a larger frame of reference, within which the heart-breaking tragedy of the woman and the abject state of the man are an insignificant blip.

3. In fact, the landscape translates into visual metaphor the enigma of Primrose's repeated phrase: 'I'm not your darling'. Nature, too, is not your darling: so that Primrose's gesture of forgiveness, grace and mercy (if that is what it is) is not the response of a weak woman, giving in, because she is needy for human

contact and male companionship at whatever cost, and instead, it is the result of her agency as woman who is also a 'force of nature'.

4. Charmaine delivers an extraordinary performance throughout. She really brings to life the meaning of this character and conveys the complexity of her actions: its ethical as well as political project. Endlessly watchable, she carries the film. Better even than she was in *Suitcase*.

5. Charmaine's spellbinding presence throws into sharp relief the fact that Eddie has failed to flesh out or develop his character. He is disappointing, especially if one knows his extraordinary performance in *Escape*, and his equally riveting play in *Suitcase*. This is a drunken, senile loser, unimaginable that he might once have consorted with the white elite, or that he had the women at his little finger. Once he is tied to the chair he does a better job, but that's not too hard.

6. Temeraire is supposed to be the framing narrator, a fact that one forgets for most of the film, and one is somehow shocked when his voice comes on again, and we see a quite different Temeraire, lovingly pouring water over Primrose's back. These final minutes are strong and sufficiently human to make one feel engaged with both characters.

7. Generally, the historical footage is brilliantly used, and quite amazing. It adds another perspective altogether. At first glance it seems to illustrate what Primrose is saying but it not only documents the colonial regime and its callous indifference to their black servants: it introduces another perspective, since these pictures were taken to celebrate colonial life, but now these images are eloquent witnesses for the prosecution, the colonial regime self-condemns itself in the footage. Congratulations!

8. What makes the use of the footage so interesting is that it is more ambiguous than I made it appear just now: for instance, the travelling shot gives an oddly nostalgic, sentimental tone to the film, almost as if regretting those colonial times when everybody knew their place, the streets were clean, and the people prettily dressed in white. Is this nostalgia not also ironic, in the light of the shocking decay and dissolution that the country has undergone since the whites left? Secondly, this feeling of nostalgia is reinforced by the shots of babies and kids, as if to evoke even more strongly not only the pain of a mother who killed her own son, but also the pain of a lost paradise of colonial order.

9. The film presents the viewer with the story of a strong woman, fighting for the memory of a loss that society has declared a crime. There is the problem of

an underdeveloped male character, upstaged at every turn by a brilliant performance from the female lead, but female anger as agency is well-conveyed.

10. Conclusion: a film of considerable force and with some well-scripted dialogue and a convincing domestic setting that combines physical squalor with the spiritual dignity of a space of transformation and moral cleansing. *These two people claw at, scratch and fight with each other, even in the knowledge that they are both victims. They only have each other as antagonists because the real villains and antagonists – the colonial regime, its legacy and the contemporary failed state – cannot be reached or confronted. In the shack these villains are out of the picture, but powerfully brought back in, through the found footage and shots of the ghetto that open the film.*

14. *HOW DO YOU SEE ME?* THE CAMERA AS TRANSITIONAL OBJECT IN DIASPORIC, DOMESTIC ETHNOGRAPHY

Nariman Massoumi

INTRODUCTION

How do you see me? (2017) is a thirty-minute observational documentary film about my mother focusing on her domestic life and relationship with my father. Filmed over a few months as my parents prepared to sell their house and move home, the documentary explores their everyday lived experience as elderly long-term immigrants, and my relationship with them, refracted through the intermediary of the camera. My family left Iran as refugees in the mid-1980s during the Iran–Iraq war to seek asylum in Britain.

The film was made as part of a practice research project which considered how diasporic experience can be examined through 'domestic ethnography' – Michael Renov's term (2004) for documentary films that engage the participation of a filmmaker's own family or kin as central subject. For Renov, domestic ethnography is a unique intersubjective mode of enquiry where 'self and other are simultaneously, if unequally, at stake' (2004: 219) as a consequence of the reciprocity and interplay entailed by the close family tie. Documentaries of this kind are not strictly ethnographic participant observations due to the intimate relations existing between the filmmaker and subject. Yet neither can they be simply defined as autobiographies, for some degree of separation still exists between the filmmaker and subject, self and other. Domestic ethnography is therefore distinguished from other documentary practices through its complex amalgamation of ethnography and autobiography where the ethnographer is intimately tied to the subject of inquiry and autobiographical self-knowledge is 'refracted' through a 'familial Other' (2004: 216). In this sense, domestic ethnography is both distinct from, and closely intermingled with, autoethnography.[1]

One of the central lines of inquiry in the research was to examine the practice of domestic ethnography – and, more specifically, the documentary encounter with a parent – in closer detail. How does the relationship between filmmaker, subject and viewer change in such intimate filmed encounters? What are the implications for the filmmaker, the subject and those in and outside the family circle? What are the commonalities, differences and boundaries between documentary domestic ethnographies and other established, everyday practices of family filmmaking such as the home movie or video?

These questions were also explored within the broader cultural history and context of a displaced family. Despite his thoughtful consideration of this mode of documentary, Renov does not examine domestic ethnographies made by migrants or diasporic subjects. For displaced people, however, the family household is a key cite in the experience of migration and resettlement, where cultural practices and histories are maintained and negotiated through personal, intergenerational relationships. By bringing the camera into the home, what insights could domestic ethnography provide into intergenerational experiences of diasporic displacement? What affect could it have on the family's understanding of its own personal and collective history and what are the implications for the visual records constituting the family archive?

How do you see me? was a creative practical exploration into these questions and followed on from two short films: one about my mother's homecoming journey to her hometown in Tabriz and another about my father's memories of arrival in Britain. Building on these works, the aim of the film was to focus on lived experience. It was shot over a period of about three months, during which I moved into my parents' home and filmed on a regular (sometimes daily) basis adopting an observational approach.

In the resulting film, the camera is static throughout, quietly observing intimate, occasionally banal aspects of my parents' lives and with a focus on the furnishings, corners and characteristics of their domestic space. There is a fragmented and accidental nature to the film, both in terms of the coverage of space and activity taking place, as well as the interactions between them and with me behind the camera. The film has no voice-over or music, lending precedence to the ordinary sounds emanating from inside the home.

The first half of the film focuses on my mother's daily routines, her struggle with her health and her relationship with my father. This is juxtaposed at different points in the film with a series of photographs from the family archives, taken before and after the Iranian revolution of 1979, which tell a personal backstory of displacement and social change.

Figure 14.1 The author pictured with his mother and sister in 1985.

About halfway through the film, my mother has an epileptic seizure followed by a second seizure the following day. After this point the film takes a self-reflexive turn, giving greater attention to my relationship with my parents through on- and off-screen conversations, some of which include discussions on the film's purpose. The title of *How do you see me?* is derived from one such (extensive) conversation with my mother towards the end of film where she posits this question to me directly. It prompted me to reflect deeply on my relationship to her vis-à-vis the camera and to ask myself some fundamental questions regarding the motivations and intentions underlying my lifelong obsession with watching (and recording) my parents through the lens. What lies behind this desire to continually capture their lives on screen? What am I seeking when I look at them through the frame of the viewfinder? What relationship, if any, might this have to our wider cultural experience and histories?

This chapter finds some answer to these questions by examining the psychological role played by the camera for me as the filmmaker in these intimate encounters. It focuses on the inner psychic activity taking place during the act of peering at a parent through the viewfinder, especially in the moment of witnessing a domestic trauma (in this case, my mother's seizures), and what bearing diasporic displacement could have on this. Drawing on the object-relations psychoanalysis of D. W. Winnicott, I posit the camera as a *transitional object* to identify the interconnections between the psychological processes underlying domestic documentary encounters and emotional anxieties resulting from displacement. While I focus on the specific context of filming my own parents, I consider the ideas put forward here to be potentially applicable and relevant to a wide range of other scenarios where filmmakers witness troubling or difficult material through the lens.

While psychoanalysis has had a long legacy in film studies, object-relations psychoanalysis has had limited application. However, as Catherine Grant (2015) has noted, the work of Annette Kuhn and other object-relations film scholars has provided a much-needed psychodynamic approach to cinematic experience and pleasures that moves beyond the Freudian and Lacanian 'frameworks of scopophilia and voyeurism' through 'their careful attention to time-based, conscious and unconscious, inside/outside interactions of cinematic spatiality, mobility, framing, proprioception, memory *and* play' (2015). But even this excellent work has, in the main, focused on cinematic spectatorship or criticism in relation to the film or media object. Piotrowska's book *Psychoanalysis and Ethics in Documentary Film* (2014) is unique in its exclusive focus on filmmaker–subject relations in the documentary encounter using psychoanalysis, but it still does so from a Lacanian perspective.

In fact, despite a now established interest in the contribution of psychoanalysis to documentary studies (Renov 2004; Cowie 2011; Piotrowska 2014), Winnicottian object-relations psychoanalysis remains rare, if not entirely absent.[2] Whereas Winnicott's ideas have been used as a framework in the creative arts, their potential relevance to creativity and authorship in the practice of documentary film production has been entirely neglected.

It is my contention, however, that Winnicott might offer a psychological contribution (or perhaps counterpart) to John Grierson's much-debated definition of documentary as the 'creative treatment of actuality' (1933: 8). I use Winnicottian object-relations to illuminate the connection between the creative act of framing, the intimate documentary encounter in the home and my own (childhood) displacement. The focus rests on the filmmaking *experience* and how peering through the viewfinder might be considered a kind of 'play' with one's external environment. I suggest that, through the dialectic of separation and attachment, the camera can function both as defensive strategy and creative vehicle (and that these are intertwined) for second generation filmmakers, like myself,[3] when negotiating personal and collective traumas in the home.

As the attention is on these internal preoccupations in the experience of making, with the view that their influence can often be overlooked and go unacknowledged, there remains little room to provide a detailed account or analysis of the film itself, nor to consider the range of other factors influencing the making of the film.[4] By the same token, in order to introduce Winnicott's psychoanalysis to documentary discourse and practice, his ideas are given precedence and discussed at some length in the overall balance of the chapter. It goes without saying, they do not represent the only means by which to frame and understand the film as a whole.

Transitional Objects

The transitional object is a term first introduced by Winnicott as an important part of the process in which human beings develop the correspondence between what they perceive objectively in the external world around them and what they conceive internally. Transitional objects become of first use in the earliest stage of development. For the baby, the 'first possession' is the breast, presented by the mother in response to the baby's need. By adapting to this need, the mother enables the infant to imagine the breast as something of its own creation, under their own 'magical control' – and therefore, with the illusion of their own omnipotence. Essential to Winnicott is an acceptance of this paradox: 'we never challenge the baby to elicit an answer to the question: did you create that or did you find it?' (1971: 89).

What follows is a process of disillusionment, aided by the mother or primary carer (in Winnicott's words the 'good-enough mother'). The baby interacts with other objects, perhaps accidently grabbing a thumb or the corner of a sheet perceived to be the breast, beginning a process of negotiation with external reality, between the 'me' and 'not-me' objects. As Kenneth Wright explains: 'a bit of blanket evokes, or re-presents a remembered experience of the mother's body – her warmth and softness – by reduplicating its sensory pattern within its structure, thus providing an image within which to "hold" the experience' (2013: 208).

Transitional objects are these first 'not-me' possessions, such as the teddy bear, a blanket or a rag that are external to the infant's body but are not entirely conceived as such. Rather they are invested with the illusionary association with the 'first possession' and therefore are a human being's first symbolic objects. It is in this intermediate state where individuals negotiate their inner world with their external life, where a 'reality-testing' takes place, 'between a baby's inability and his growing ability to recognise and accept reality' (Winnicott 1971: 3) and for the 'passage into objectivity to be smoothly negotiated' (Wright 2009: 33).

The emphasis on separation and attachment is dialectical in that separation is only possible through the security of attachment. A 'good-enough' holding or facilitating environment provides the belief or trust that the separation can be done safely. As Roger Silverstone explains, in order for an individual to 'see him or herself as separate from another' requires a recognition of their link with them:

> Independence involves dependence. The emergence of the individual as ontologically secure requires both a distancing and a closeness in his or her relationships with others and a complementarity of inner and outer

security. Inner and outer, the worlds of subjective and objective reality, have to be distinguished but also related. (1994: 9)

Winnicott suggests human beings are never free from this negotiation of reality-acceptance. Transitional objects operate in an intermediate environment, between the 'subjective object (the emerging him or herself) and the object subjectively perceived (the not-me or other)' (Silverstone 1994: 10), which Winnicott calls 'potential space'.[5] This liminal zone between the individual psyche and object environment forms the basis of childhood play, where objects and phenomena are put to the service of inner reality and fantasy and, for Winnicott, the foundation for cultural experience throughout our lives.

Our capacity to create and appreciate art, our feelings for religion, fetishism and ritual encompass the same dynamics of being absorbed in play. Suitable conditions (a 'good-enough' environment) are required within which we can have the confidence to explore our own individual ways of expressing and relating to the objects and others around us, enabling the 'endless possibility for discovering something in the world for oneself, for making it one's own and making it live' (Kuhn 2013: 5).

The environments in which we negotiate the 'not-me' phenomena outside our control is socially and culturally predetermined, our 'inherited tradition', defined by Winnicott as that which 'belongs to the common pool of humanity, into which individuals and groups of people contribute and from which we might draw if *we have somewhere to put what we find*' (Winnicott 1971: 99, original emphasis). Cultural experience in potential space thus involves bringing something of our inner world and something of the pre-existing external world together in a 'perpetual interplay ... of separateness and union' (Kuhn 2013: 5).

As we enter into the challenges presented by our social environment, transitional objects occupy an important role in developing our sense of identity, agency and individuality. This explains the intense emotional and mental energies children can invest in transitional objects at an early age, whether to assist sleep or as a source of comfort against the anxiety of separation. These investments in objects diffuse into other cultural activities or objects that engage our interest, although they might take renewed significance if 'deprivation threatens' (Winnicott 1971: 6).

Transitional objects thus help us accept difference and similarity by 'allowing the individual to learn to engage in the life-long process of starting, developing, and ending other object relationships' (Sabbadini 2011: 24).

The Camera as Transitional Object

Silverstone makes a convincing case for television functioning 'cathectically and culturally' as transitional object by entering into the 'potential space' left by 'teddy bears, blankets and breasts' (1994: 13). Hills (2013) suggests how new technologies, such as smartphones and web-based media, offer an equivalent in ontological security in a digital world. Wright has examined the creative process of the artist with reference to transitional objects and maternal mirroring (Wright 2009, 2013).

I want to put forward the idea of the camera functioning as transitional object in the framing of a documentary subject. At its most elementary, the act itself provides the filmmaker with a means by which to lend subjective meaning to their immediate and surrounding external reality. Framing an external object or another person allows the opportunity to perceive it or them 'anew' within the boundaries of a frame in the moment itself (regardless of the act of viewing the images later). In the act of framing, the person or object becomes a 'found object', a re-visioned version of themselves, a *'this is what I was searching for!'* (Wright 2013: 207, original emphasis) from the filmmaker's perspective. They have essentially not changed, but the frame allows the person or object to be re-discovered, to acquire a renewed focus and attention and a personal significance. Through the choice of frame, the filmmaker acquires a degree of subjective, creative control over what they see in front of them. The viewfinder enables creative perception through the possibility of putting phenomena of the external world within a boundary.

In fact, as Kuhn (2013) has shown, drawing on Madeleine Davis and David Wallbridge (1981), frames play an essential role for Winnicott in providing form and meaning to the dynamic between the inner and outer world and how they operate to contain, bound and give physical and mental shape and structure, both spatially and temporally, to processes and activities. This, I would argue, could be extended into the act of peering through a viewfinder or an LCD screen which facilitates an opportunity to bound and give shape to the world around us within a limited spatial enclosure.[6]

Creme (2013) applies Winnicottian psychoanalysis to argue the case for film viewing as playful, the continuation of make-believe in childhood games. The reality of the film on screen creates a potential space for creative play and underlying our engagement in a film is the crossing of barriers between offscreen and onscreen space. A shot can illicit the anticipation of what is happening beyond the frame and what will happen next. We get 'involved' in the action of the film by crossing the 'screen barrier' into the 'place of the screen-playing' (2013: 44).

This 'playing' can equally apply to what unravels within the frame or 'barrier' of the viewfinder in the documentary encounter, in the negotiation between what is taking place in front of the camera, what crosses into the vision of the frame and what is anticipated or hoped for or felt by the filmmaker, drawing on their inner reality/experience and precipitating an element or illusion of control over the unfolding external reality in front of them.

The psychoanalyst Andrea Sabbadini defines this psychological movement at the boundaries of the internal and external worlds as a 'bridge space' conceptualised in filmmaking as:

> that which spreads out in front of the filmmaker's eyes and separates him from the scene he is in the process of shooting – but, at the same time, also keeps him in contact with it. A territory that will soon no longer be occupied by the images framed by the camera, but is not yet occupied by the final product to be eventually projected on the screen. (2011: 20)

In this way, the viewfinder enables a separation from, and union with, the subject or objects that move in and out of the frame. The camera thus might be considered a particularly privileged kind of transitional object – one that enables a negotiation of multiple object relationships through the possibilities made available by looking and framing.

Camera as Transitional Object in *How do you see me?*

There are two central points I deduce from Winnicott's definition of the transitional object, which are relevant to my discussion. First, for the transitional object to acquire its meaning it is dependent upon creative apperception. The object can remain the same but is *seen* differently. As Wright argues, 'creative perception precedes creative activity' because the transformation of an object comes through the act of seeing the object afresh. This is the way the object 'becomes emotionally charged and a bearer of personal significance' (2013: 206).

The familiar details and characteristics of my parents and their movements become 'found objects' within the boundary of the frame in the act of filming. In fact, throughout the film, there is a detailed focus on my parents' bodies, their gestures and facial expressions in close-up as they inhabit the spaces of their home as if to declare and reiterate their existence: shots of my mother's hands as she washes up or when she takes her own blood pressure; my father's belly button revealed through his unbuttoned shirt; their faces and reactions while they watch and react to television news. Within the viewfinder, my parents' activities or their very being become objects of my imagination while they retain their integrity, not having essentially changed through the act of framing. They are the familiar, already existing primary objects, newly found.

Secondly, there is the role of the transitional object in managing or controlling loss, or, as Emma Wilson has suggested, a 'narrative of pain management' (2012: 45). For physical and psychological separation to be achieved safely and with confidence the child needs a way of representing and remembering the mother in her absence (Wilson 2012: 46). Furthermore, it follows that the management of loss and creative perception are interrelated. The transitional object offers a creative, imaginative vehicle for reproducing or holding or remembering an absent experience or bond that is in the process of being lost.

Many scholars and critics, not least André Bazin (2005), have drawn attention to this psychological need in photography and film *per se*, as a defence against time passing. For David MacDougall, a kind of 'grief' takes over in the separation of the signifier from the object in the moment of filming, because 'while a camera is always filming the present, the film it contains is always an instrument of the past' (1998: 34). In filming my parents this awareness is coupled with the acknowledgement of my parents' ageing bodies and the acceptance of (or perhaps resistance to) their soon-to-be absence. To that end, the creative impulse in filming them becomes a way to manage or acquire some sense of control over my impending loss of them.[7]

MacDougall also notes how the view of the subject through the viewfinder is 'ontologically' different from the resulting film image and different again from that which appears in the final film, for during filming it 'takes place in the ephemeral zone in which life has yet to accumulate meaning and a future' (1998: 29). Filmmaker and subject's existence are bound together as they occupy a shared space, surrounded by the same environment, breathe the same air and react to the same phenomena.

As discussed earlier, for potential space activity to take place productively it requires a secure and 'good-enough' facilitating environment. In a therapy session this facilitating environment might be the room, the couch, the allocated time and the confidence between patient and therapist for a relationship to develop over repeated sessions. In a documentary film encounter it is the presence of the camera, and the level of trust developed around it, that facilitates the interaction between filmmaker and subject. There needs to be a confidence on the part of the subject in order for them to share freely with the filmmaker their reflections, experiences, thoughts, memories, lived experience and aspects of their inner reality. Piotrowska (2014) suggests the subject in the documentary encounter can build a degree of trust in the filmmaker that is not unlike the psychoanalytical process of transference, where feelings from a previous relationship (such as a parent) are redirected toward the analyst.[8] If transference and counter-transference are indeed applicable to the filmmaker–subject encounter, then in domestic ethnography these processes are potentially magnified and in greater flux, more 'co(i)mplicated',[9] due to the parent–child relations between subject(s) and filmmaker. In other words,

THE CAMERA AS TRANSITIONAL OBJECT

the subject's projected feelings towards the filmmaker as parent/analyst are potentially reversed when the filmmaker is the child of the subject.

FILMING MY MOTHER'S SEIZURE

This is most evident when encountering my mother's epileptic seizure during the filming of *How do you see me?* My mother's seizures were one of the most traumatic aspects of my childhood experiences and usually came during periods of high stress or family conflict, amplifying those moments of tension. They happened quite unexpectedly, and seemed to possess her, contorting her face and her body. Her eyes would cloud over as though looking and entering into some imaginary state, her facial muscles would seize up, she would let out a cry and her body would writhe and fall to the ground. After a seizure, she would first moan and let out random mutterings before falling into a deep sleep.

Their sudden occurrence would cause enormous emotional distress for me throughout my childhood. As an adult, when they take place, the same feelings of insecurity and anxiety immediately resurface. For these reasons, when the seizure took place during filming, I initially avoided filming it and tried to help her. I also felt it to be exploitative to film her in this vulnerable moment.

However, as my father comforted her, I filmed some of the aftermath, from a distance, in which she was recovering with her unconscious moans and cries. Filming it calmed some of my anxieties and allowed a way of managing the situation, processing it and taking a semblance of control over it. I was able

Figure 14.2   A still frame from *How do you see me?* (2017)

to separate myself from the event, to adopt an outside position, witness from a distance and contain and reconnect with it through the boundaries (and the security) of the viewfinder frame.

My feelings are reflected in the way the event was filmed and framed. The camera is positioned low, at knee level, from inside the corridor into the living room with half of the frame taken by the door: a perspective demonstrating curiosity, as though spying or watching secretly from a safe distance. It is imbued with an element of risk or danger. There is an underlying desire to witness, but a fear and insecurity in encountering the event up close.

In fact, it is much like how I remember witnessing such moments as a child, as my father would encourage us to leave the room while he helped my mother recover to avoid adding to our distress. To that end, the positioning of the camera in the corridor and framing through the door recalls this childhood subjectivity: as a cautious but curious witness to a domestic trauma.

The ethics of witnessing pain or suffering and its mediation is a vexed issue, particularly in relation to the spectatorial distance (spatial and temporal) made possible by modern visual technologies (Sontag 2003; Saxton 2009: 64). For Libby Saxton, however, there is a tendency within criticism of mediated suffering

> to posit an opposition between eyewitnesses, whose look is legitimised by their presence at the injurious event and exposure to potential danger, and mediate witnesses, whose look is unlicenced because they remain at a safe remove, reliant on visual technologies. (Saxton 2010: 65)

In defining the camera as transitional object, I am suggesting the filming of the seizure blends these two modes of viewing suffering. On the one hand, my own ontological security is at stake as eyewitness to my mother's seizure, bringing up fearful childhood memories. Yet the filming of the event also enables a spectatorial distance which, while not equivalent to spatiotemporal remove for a distant viewer once it appears in the film, is nevertheless an act of mediated witnessing that is ontologically not dissimilar to watching the seizure on screen.

Furthermore, during my mother's seizures she often talks, sometimes nonsensically, in Farsi or her own native tongue *Azeri* (a Turkish dialect). In this particular instance, she repeated the word 'Allah' continually (despite not being religious). The act of filming it with a detached camera, of witnessing from the outside if you like, brought into a play an ethnographic distance that projects the experience of personal domestic trauma into wider cultural history of displacement.

CHILDHOOD DISPLACEMENT

In contrast to the act of filming the seizure from a distance, further below I explore the psychological effects (and ethical implications) of filming my mother's seizure in close-up. But first I want to briefly extend the discussion on childhood subjectivity within the film by considering the psychodynamics of filming my parents within domestic spaces.

The type of positioning of the camera during the filming of the seizure (through the doorway peering in) is not an isolated occurrence in the film. In fact, shots through corridors, doors, window frames and at the thresholds of domestic space are a recurring motif. For Winnicott, these in-between spaces and boundaries of the home are significant in early childhood development for the exploration of the familiar and unfamiliar – a 'prime site for the negotiation of inner and outer worlds' (Kuhn 2010: 85). Liminal spaces such as hallways, doors, corners, stairs, windows and edges increasingly become privileged sites for risk-taking as a toddler experiments with the physical boundaries of the inside and outside, familiar and unfamiliar. Spaces within the home become an extension of the separation-individuation process, as the infant or toddler starts to test their physical separation from the mother. The home's security and safety offer precisely the trust and confidence needed to be able to venture out, embark on such explorations and risk-taking, through the belief that it can be done safely.

Childhood games rehearse the separation and attachment from home through the going back and forth, between the thresholds of and boundaries of home – between the security of being inside and the wider open spaces of exploration, pushing the boundaries of risk, facing challenging, non-home spaces. Kuhn has noted how the distinctive nature of film for capturing space, time and motion with a set of bounded frames means it is a particularly privileged site for capturing the experience of transitional phenomena as seen in the *mise-en-scène* of films focused on home and childhood. Films like *Mandy* (Mackendrick, 1952), *Where Is the Friend's Home?* (Kiarostami, 1987) and *Ratcatcher* (Ramsay, 1999) all treat 'transitional phenomena of the child's world' in such a way as to project them 'into the realms of adult cultural experience' (Kuhn 2010: 88).[10]

In *How do you see me?* the filmed encounters from the spaces and boundaries of domestic space play a similar role. They separate and reinforce the relationship between inside and outside and give the film a viewpoint that is akin to (and recalls) early childhood experiences of looking and exploring spaces within and outside the home. I would argue these spaces take on an additional significance when the filmmaker comes from a cultural history of displacement. If childhood games are about exploring the boundaries and risks in and out of the domestic environment, they are dependent on the home as a refuge – that is, on the basis of a confidence and security in being able to *return*. The diasporic condition or experience is arguably defined by an ambivalent relation to home (as a physical entity and ideational construct) and often by the inability, or indeed the impossibility, of return across space and time.

For immigrant children, implications of displacement can be more complex as their experience of home as a secure place for forging their confidence and mental health is abruptly compromised by change at an optimal time of development. While the home is not the only facilitating environment and not always a secure or safe environment for every child, displacement from a home can mean a children's tasks become more complex as 'they must seek new spaces to serve as holding environments, and make sense of their lives between pre and post-migration' (Bursztyn and Bursztyn 2015: 86).

As a five-year-old, my own experience of displacement occurred precisely during this optimal period of childhood development, during the turmoil of the Iran–Iraq war. The facilitating environment of our home, the primary site for potential space activity and 'reality-testing', was disrupted by the insecurity and upheaval of war and migration. Not only did familiar people and places, systems of communication and cultural practices abruptly change, but the additional absence of my father for four years[11] meant the process of separation and attachment was essentially in flux. The rupture that took place at the height of this pivotal period in childhood undoubtedly has had some bearing on my motivations and obsessions with filming my parents in adulthood. By mnemonically restaging or re-presenting the experience of childhood looking and seeing, the snooping shots from the thresholds of domestic space appear to have their roots in those earlier disruptive infantile experiences.

Zeynep Turan has argued that for those who have experienced abrupt and often involuntary displacement, personal artefacts around the home can function as transitional objects, a means for repersonalisation offering continuity with their former material environment (2004, 2010). They enable individuals to feel safe in the host country by articulating a sense of cultural identity and as a defence against the insecurity of displacement. As such, they project the childhood dialectic of separation and attachment into the experience of resettlement. However, for second generation migrants the objects serve as a means for an imaginary attachment to their roots and as a means for dealing with the loss of their parents.

The filming of my parents in their home could be seen to be adopting a similar psychological process of repersonalisation. In one sense, the act of filming of domestic objects around the home (such as a *samovar*) or the integration of family photographs into the film can be viewed as a form of 'collecting' – in the same way that, say, the filmed material in Agnes Varda's *The Gleaners and I* (2000) is a form of gleaning. But more broadly, the camera itself becomes the privileged transitional object *par excellence* – a means through which this continuity with the former home can be recalled and reimagined as the threat of losing of my parents, my primary connection with this previous place and time, looms.

The Documentary Close-up and the Mirror Role of the Mother

It is worth recalling at this point that the consolation and management of loss through a transitional object is as much a process of frustration and disillusionment with the 'insult' of reality as it is about creative spontaneity and illusion. Indeed, it is through the latter (capacity for creativity) that the former (reality-acceptance) can be managed in the pursuit of independence. Central to this lifelong journey is the development of autonomy and control achieved through the security of a facilitating environment and the confidence to take risks safely. I have tried to suggest these elements are present in the activity of framing and peering through the viewfinder and how these are pronounced in the encounter with a parent in domestic space due to their relationship to childhood experience and subjectivity. In the first instance of filming my mother's seizure, the camera operates defensively as a kind of security blanket to manage and process impending loss by allowing a separation from the unfolding reality of the traumatic event. In this final section, I want to consider an instance where control is lost and where a filmmaker is confronted with an object they are unable to face directly – where the 'insult' of reality is too sudden or forthcoming. Such a moment occurred during a second encounter in filming my mother's seizures.

After the first seizure, when my mother had returned to consciousness, she expressed her disappointment with me for not having filmed the seizure in full for she wanted to see what she looked like when it happened. Her seizures usually come and go, but on this rare occasion she had another seizure the following day. Yet again I found it difficult to film, but eventually forced myself to film some of the recovery process to fulfil her request. In order to capture her expression, I filmed her face in close-up but never intended to use it. When I showed her the rushes, she encouraged me to use the footage in the film, telling me to be brave and saying there was nothing wrong with her disability. The inclusion of this scene in the film was thus intimately bound up with her intervention.[12] When editing it in the film, and watching it and reflecting on it with others, I was forced to consider in greater depth why seeing my mother's face during a seizure was so troubling.

In *The Mirror-role of Mother and Family*, Winnicott develops maternal identification and adaptive response into the realm of communication. As the baby makes the progress towards independence from the mother their feelings of insecurity and anxiety are alleviated by the mother's (or primary carer's) facial reflections, like a mirror of their emotional state. Winnicott proposes the mother's face as a precursor to the mirror in the emotional development of the self and acknowledges Lacan's mirror stage as a key influence. Unlike Lacan, Winnicott's mirroring in the mother's face is not based on misrecognition but as a way a human being forms a sense of self through the recognition reflected in the other. Aside from the holding, handling and object-presenting that supports the baby's development, Winnicott is interested in what the baby sees:

> What does the baby see when he or she looks at the mother's face? I am suggesting that, ordinarily, what the baby sees is himself or herself. In other words the mother is looking at the baby and *what she looks like is related to what she sees there*. (Winnicott 1971: 112)

The mother reflects the baby's mood by giving back, in her facial expressions, a mirror to what the baby is feeling. In this non-verbal feedback, 'the mother visually and iconically gives back or "presents" to the infant the "shape" (or "semblance") of his current feeling state' (Wright 2013: 209). The mother's face functions therefore as a kind of symbolic pattern and medium for self-realisation to take place. As Bassil-Morozow notes, this feedback-process is not a perfect reflection, but in the 'active interaction' of connection and reception that is human contact (2015: 198). The 'mirror' or reflection becomes an essential part of the process of forming one's own sense of identity:

> Naturally, as the child develops and the maturational processes become sophisticated, and identifications multiply, the child becomes less and less dependent on getting back the self from the mother's and the father's face and from the faces of others who are in parental or sibling relationships. (Winnicott 1971: 118)

Winnicott is offering a nuanced perspective on the emergence of the self, our emotional, mental and creative capacities in the interaction of looking, seeing and being reflected back through the recognition of another. What is key in Winnicott's mirroring is the reflection of one's emotional state, predicated on an internal rather than external identification. As Laurence Spurling (1991) suggests, the difference in the medium of the face over the glass in Lacan's misrecognition is significant. Narcissus gazes into a pool of water to see his own reflection. Whereas the glass of a mirror is rigid and fixed, water is a natural substance and therefore malleable. It can be touched causing ripples and physically responds to its environment. In Spurling's view, the reflection in the mother's face is, for Winnicott, more like the water of the pool than the glass of the mirror, 'for a face is alive, it is constantly changing, expressions play across it' (1991: 63). In this two-way process, in the struggle for recognition, as the reflection is not always there or absent, the infant gets settled into the idea that what is seen is the mother's face and, in the process, perception takes the place of apperception (1971: 113). This becomes the basis for creative looking and aesthetic experience. Only by being recognised in the responsive look of another does a self-identity emerge and thus the feeling of being alive (Wright 2009: 62). Winnicott views his own work in psychotherapy as a maternal mirroring, 'giving back what the patient brings' in a 'complex derivative of the face that reflects what is to be seen' (1971: 117). If he is successful then Winnicott thinks the 'patient will find his or her own self, and will be able to exist and feel real' (1971: 117). Winnicott refers to the portrait paintings of Francis Bacon, which he sees as an aspect of the painter's relationship to his mother:

> Francis Bacon is seeing himself in his mother's face, but with some twist in him or her that maddens both him and us ... Bacon's faces seem to me to be far removed from perception of the actual; in looking at faces he seems to me to be painfully striving towards being seen, which is at the basis of creative looking. (Winnicott 1971: 114)

How might this apply to the close-up of my mother recovering from a seizure? Drawing on Béla Balázs, Renov argues that the facial close-up in documentary film is the 'compositional choice best suited to strengthening the bonds of engagement and compassion that may arise from audio-visual testimony' (2012: 3). Words fail what the moving image can capture in the multimodal, 'polyphonic' expression of the face, and the complexity of affect on display. Film has a capacity to record the 'microphysiognomy' of facial movements and contours with great subtlety and detail. It can arrest our attention by isolating the face in time and space and deepen our gaze into an unconscious. For Renov, this means the documentary close-up provides the potential for a proximity to the other, for an understanding and thus an ethical encounter. In the ethics of Emmanual Levinas, the primacy of the self is displaced by the primacy for the other. We are obligated, responsible for and a 'hostage' to the other – ethics is primary. Renov proposes that the Balászian documentary close-up, through its naked exposure to another in proximity, meets the Levinasian ethical demand – and hence, this underlines the necessity of the close-up in audiovisual testimonies. Arguably, it is this very potential of the documentary close-up, of bringing us closer to the other, that can also render it in some contexts as exploitative. In contemporary popular television documentary, the practice of zooming in on a subject's face when he or she is displaying emotion or high levels of distress could exemplify this.

Levinasian ethics have had some weight in the study of the filmed encounter (Cooper 2006; Downing and Saxton 2010; Renov 2012; Piotrowska 2014), but also come under significant philosophical scrutiny, not least by Alain Badiou (2001).[13] There is little scope here to engage in a lengthy ethical discussion but it is worth briefly considering how Winnicott's mirror-role could present its own contribution to this debate. Like Levinas, Winnicott believes in the separation of the self and other. However, as C. Fred Alford argues, Winnicott brings the separation and connection together in 'holding', gratitude, concern, and not, *pace* Levinas, as a hostage being (Alford 2000: 243). The difference here is that for Winnicott human relationships 'can combine both separation and attachment in a single act, staying in tune with the needs of the other so the other can risk being alone – that is, risk being' (2000: 247). In other words, being held by the mother in our earliest experience or by a friend or partner, allows us the safety and security to be free. For Winnicott, the problem is our clinging, our dependency, our *need* for the other and not our obligation, our responsibility, our being held hostage to them. In Winnicott, then, we have 'attunement', being in emotional contact with another human being, where there is a 'subtle combination of otherness and identification' (Alford 2000: 246). We respond to a friend's feelings by being 'attuned' to their feelings even though we might not respond or reflect those feelings perfectly. With Winnicott our identification with a face of another is one of recognition, reflection and attunement rooted in our earliest formative experiences with the mother's face. This, I would argue, is the intersubjective power of the documentary facial close-up and if Bacon's faces 'maddens him and us' as Winnicott claims, then, so too does my mother's rolling eyes, her dribbling, her pain and her lack of consciousness as I desperately seek in her face a reflection or recognition of myself.

It should be noted, in the interplay of human communication, reflecting back includes a complex interaction of behaviours and gestures, where the voice and body are of equal importance. A mother rocking a baby or the sound of cooing or humming in her voice, for example, would arguably add positive value to the reflection and recognition of the face. In that sense, the sonic aspects of the seizures (the groaning and crying) were also a significant factor in precipitating feelings of stress for me as a child.

Seeing and hearing one's own mother or primary carer in pain mobilises intense feelings of agony linked to our self-existence. The anxiety of witnessing my mother's seizures could be attributed to the threat it posed to my ontological security rooted in my early childhood experiences, where the primary object through which my sense of self was formed momentarily faced the possibility of death. In filming the second seizure in close-up, the camera did not retain the sense of security enabled by the detached camera when filming from a safe distance during the first. The camera as transitional object is, therefore, not without risks.

Concluding Remarks

Drawing on the ideas of D. W. Winnicott, I have attempted to illuminate the psychological processes and motivations underlying diasporic, domestic ethnography by examining two separate instances of filming my mother's seizures during the making of *How do you see me?* In the first encounter, filmed from a distance, the act of filming my mother's seizure was a way of maintaining a separation from the profilmic scene while dealing with the actuality of an impending loss as it unfolded before me. Its framing and positioning through a corridor recalled (and re-presented) childhood experiences of witnessing my mother's seizures. In contrast to its role as a defensive tool, recording from a detached distance, the filming of the seizure in close-up, initiated by my mother's desire to see what she looked like, urged me to confront her condition and vulnerability directly, and exposed the psychological perils in doing so.

Both the distant observation and the intimate close-up can be determined by, and better understood through, the prism of childhood seeing and being seen. This subjectivity is elicited and reinforced by the film's construction from, and attention to, spaces and thresholds within the home. Winnicottian object-relations help explain the psychodynamic processes and attachments behind these intimate domestic encounters and their connection to the insecurities and memories of displacement and resettlement.

How do you see me? appears to combine conventions of observational cinema, *cinema vérité* and home video through the use of static camera, self-reflexivity and interactive, informal conversations in the home. This mixture of modes, drawing on autobiographical experience, might be considered to be an attempt to achieve a greater degree of authenticity in representation. By posing the camera as a transitional object I have sought to show an entirely different set of motivations underlying the creative choices and framing, rooted in my own internal preoccupations, shaped in part by social and environmental changes throughout my childhood and adult life. While I have made these points in relation to the very specific case study of my own filmmaking encounters with my mother, the ideas presented here are arguably applicable to a variety of other documentary contexts, not least the work of displaced filmmakers engaged in intimate familial subject matters.

Chantal Akerman's *No Home Movie* (2015), her final film before her tragic untimely death, is a case in point. Akerman films conversations and encounters with her mother in spaces around her mother's home, in her kitchen, in close proximity, from hotel rooms and over Skype. Observations of her mother's deteriorating health and ageing take place through corridors, thresholds and doorways in the home, as well as close-ups of the carpets, surfaces and edges. Throughout the film, the camera elicits a child's gaze, quietly examining the details of her mother's everyday lived experience, their intimate relationship and her mother's developing illness. As Pinkerton (2016) remarks in his review, the film 'achieves a surreptitious, snooping quality – we never cease entirely to be children in the company of our parents, and Akerman gives a sense of crossing the carpet on tippy-toes so as not to break the silence' (2016: 62). As a number of other critics have also remarked, the film's detached camera subtly links this childhood subjectivity to generational trauma.[14] Through the camera, the impending loss of her mother alongside Akerman's search for access to a collective history, is negotiated and managed in the private spaces of the home.

Winnicott's ideas help explain the role of the camera as creative vehicle and therapeutic tool for displaced generations of filmmakers, making sense of their past through encounters with their parents in the home. However, they could equally apply more broadly to the work of filmmakers dealing with a range of difficult, troubling, intimate, personal and/or traumatic material. One application of the camera as transitional object, for example, could be in instances where filmmakers or photographers document atrocities in violent conflicts, the psychological role the camera being a creative defence against this 'insult' of reality. As I have tried to suggest above, Winnicott's notion of maternal mirroring offers a new way of thinking about viewer identification and the ethics of the documentary close-up of a subject's face, especially when experiencing pain or distress. There is then, arguably, further potential for the application of Winnicottian object-relations to documentary practice and discourse as well as diaspora film studies.

Notes

1. I have argued elsewhere (Massoumi 2017) for the value in retaining the distinction between domestic ethnography and autoethnography (the term is oddly absent from Renov's discussion). While this distinction applies in relation to the documentary film, the chapter itself constitutes a form of autoethnographic scholarship as the arguments and insights put forward are based on a reflection on my own subjective experience.
2. In Piotrowska's volume on psychoanalysis and the cinema (2015), Winnicott is applied in Vicky Lebeau's chapter on mirror images with reference to Gerhard Richter's exhibition piece *Mirror* (1981) and in Helena Bassil-Morozow's analysis of maternal loss in Andrei Tarvoksy's *The Mirror* (1975).
3. Strictly speaking I am one of the first or the '1.5 generation', having arrived in Britain as a child.
4. Ultimately, the most fruitful engagement with the arguments in this chapter would be in conjunction with watching the film itself, which is available on request.
5. Also sometimes referred to as 'transitional space'. I have opted for Winnicott's original terminology in *Playing and Reality* (1971).
6. And, one might add, a temporal boundary in the act of starting and stopping the recording.
7. Piotrowska (2014) considers another important and neglected aspect of trauma and loss in the documentary encounter, where the filmmaker can act as substitute

and an embodied presence for the subject's longing for a lost beloved and how this can lead to intense emotional attachments.
8. The notion of a transference and counter-transference in documentary was first posited by Emanual Berman in Berman, Rosenheimer and Aviad (2003).
9. In the 'complexity and the interpenetration of subject/object identities' there is, according to Renov, '*co(i)mplication*'.
10. Catherine Grant's videographic essay *Interplay* (2015) juxtaposes scenes from some of these films and others to powerful effect in a visual exploration of the relationships between childhood and film space(s).
11. My father could not acquire a visa to Britain and therefore lived in Germany for four years before joining the rest of us in 1989. This became the subject of my short practice research film *Baba 1989* (2016) where my father recalls his experiences of arriving in Britain and his attempts at resettlement and reintegrating into the family. For a detailed discussion on the film and its making, see Massoumi (2017).
12. This was somewhat unexpected not least because my mother is not always willing to be filmed. *How do you see me?* includes negotiations taking place between us over what can or should be filmed.
13. See Piotrowska (2015) for discussion on Levinasian ethics and Badiou's critique.
14. For example, Hoberman (2017) and Mai (2017).

REFERENCES

Alford, C. F. (2000), Levinas and Winnicott: Motherhood and Responsibility, *American Imago*, 57:3, 235–59.
Badiou, A. (2001), *Ethics: An Essay on the Understanding of Evil*, London: Verso.
Bassil-Morozow, H. (2015), 'The Poetics of Maternal Loss in Tarvoksky's *The Mirror*', in A. Piotrowska (ed.), *Embodied Encounters*, Hove, East Sussex: Routledge.
Bazin, André (2005 [1967]), *What is Cinema?* London: University of California Press.
Berghahn, D. (2013), *Far-flung Families in Film: The Diasporic Family in Contemporary European Cinema*, Edinburgh: Edinburgh University Press.
Berman, E., T. Rosenheimer and M. Aviad (2003), 'Documentary Directors and Their Protagonists: A Transference/Countertransferential Relationship?' in A. Sabbadini (ed.), *The Couch and the Silver Screen: Psychoanalytic Reflections on European Cinema*, Hove: Routledge.
Bursztyn, A. M. and C. Korn-Bursztyn (eds) (2015), *Immigrant Children and Youth: Psychological Challenges: Psychological Challenges*, Santa Barbara: ABC-CLIO.
Caldwell, L. (2013), *Little Madnesses: Winnicott, transitional phenomena and cultural experience*, I. B. Tauris.
Cooper, S. (2006), *Selfless cinema? Ethics and French Documentary*, London: Legenda (Research monographs in French studies, 20).
Cowie, E. (2011), *Recording Reality, Desiring the Real*, vol. 24, Minneapolis: University of Minnesota Press.
Creme, P. (2013), 'The Playing Spectator', in A. Kuhn (ed.), *Little Madnesses: Winnicott, Transitional Phenomena and Cultural Experience*, London: I. B. Tauris.
Davis, M. and D. Wallbridge (1981), *Boundary and Space: An Introduction to the Work of D.W. Winnicott*, Routledge.
Downing, L. and L. Saxton (2010), *Film and Ethics: Foreclosed Encounters*, London: Routledge.
Grant, C. (2015), '*Interplay*: (Re)finding and (Re)framing Cinematic Experience, Film Space, and the Child's World', *LOLA*, 6.
Grierson, J. (1933), 'The Documentary Producer', *Cinema Quarterly*, 2:1, 7–9.

Hills, M. (2013), 'Recoded Transitional Objects and Fan Re-readings of Puzzle Films', in A. Kuhn (ed.), *Little Madnesses: Winnicott, Transitional Phenomena and Cultural Experience*, London: I. B. Tauris.

Hoberman, J. (2017), 'Motherless Brussels: Notes on Chantal Akerman's No Home Movie', *The Tablet* [online], <https://www.tabletmag.com/jewish-arts-and-culture/246459/chantal-akermans-no-home-movie> (accessed 31 January 2019).

Kuhn, A. (2010), 'Cinematic Experience, Film Space, and the Child's World', *Canadian Journal of Film Studies*, 19:2, 82–98.

Kuhn, A. (ed.) (2013), *Little Madnesses: Winnicott, Transitional Phenomena and Cultural Experience*, London: I. B. Tauris.

MacDougall, D. (1998), *Transcultural Cinema*, Princeton, NJ: Princeton University Press.

Mai, N. (2017), 'No Home Movie – Chantal Akerman', *The Art(s) of Slow Cinema* [online], <https://theartsofslowcinema.com/2017/10/02/no-home-movie-chantal-akerman-2015/> (accessed 31 January 2019).

Marks, L. (2000), *The Skin of the Film: Intercultural Cinema, Embodiment, and the Senses*, Durham, NC: Duke University Press.

Massoumi, N. (2017), 'Domestic Ethnography, Diaspora and Memory in Baba 1989' in B. Harper and H. Price (eds), *Domestic Imaginaries*, Palgrave Macmillan: Cham, pp. 169–89.

Pinkterton, N. (2016), 'Film of the Week: No Home Movie', *Sight and Sound*, July, pp. 62–3.

Piotrowska, A. (2014), *Psychoanalysis and Ethics in Documentary Film*, Abingdon: Routledge.

Piotrowska, A. (ed.) (2015), *Embodied Encounters: New Approaches to Psychoanalysis and Cinema*, Hove, East Sussex: Routledge.

Renov, M. (2004), *The Subject of Documentary*, Minneapolis: University of Minnesota Press (Visible evidence, vol. 16).

Renov, M. (2012), 'The Facial Closeup in Audio-Visual Testimony: The Power of Embodied Memory', *Preserving Survivors' Memories* [online], <http://www.preserving-survivors-memories.org/media/presentations/Michael_Renov_The_Facial_Closeup_in_Audio-Visual_Testimony.pdf> (accessed 31 January 2019).

Sabbadini, A. (2011), 'Cameras, Mirrors, and the Bridge Space: A Winnicottian Lens on Cinema', *Projections*, 5:1, 17–30.

Saxton, L. (2009), 'Ethics, Spectatorship and the Spectacle of Suffering', in *Film and Ethics*, Abingdon: Routledge, pp. 70–83.

Silverstone, R. (1994), *Television and Everyday Life*, London: Routledge.

Sontag, S. (2003), *Regarding the Pain of Others*, Basingstoke: Macmillan.

Spurling, L. (1991), Winnicott and the Mother's Face, *Winnicott Studies*, 6, 60–6.

Turan, Z. (2004), 'Personal Objects from the Homeland: Reconstructing Cultural and Personal Identities', *International Journal of the Humanities*, 1, pp. 314–29.

Turan, Z. (2010), 'Material Objects as Facilitating Environments: The Palestinian Diaspora', *Home Cultures*, 7:1, 43–5.

Wilson, Emma (2012), *Love, Mortality and the Moving Image*, Basingstoke: Palgrave Macmillan.

Wright, K. (2009), *Mirroring and Attunement: Self-realization in Psychoanalysis and Art*, Hove, East Sussex: Routledge.

Wright, K. (2013), 'Found Objects and Mirroring Forms', in A. Kuhn (ed.), *Little Madnesses: Winnicott, Transitional Phenomena and Cultural Experience*, London: I. B. Tauris.

Winnicott, D. W. (1971), *Playing and Reality*, London: Tavistock Publications.

Winnicott, D. W. (1990), *Home is Where We Start From: Essays by a Psychoanalyst*, New York: Norton.

15. 'SHUT YOUR HOLE, GIRLIE. MINE'S MAKING MONEY, DOLL': CREATIVE PRACTICE-RESEARCH AND THE PROBLEM OF PROFESSIONALISM

Roberta Mock

These are words that have come out of my mouth:

> Good evening. I'm ... a raconteur. A storyteller. Dirty stories. Clean stories.
>
> I'm also a *chanteuse*. [Are there any Jews in the house? Yeah?] That's French for *kurva*.
>
> I own a vibrator. A French poodle. And I went out and bought a roto-rooter. Ah that roto-rooter. I live it up with that roto-rooter. *Mechaya!* A long roto-rooter, I can lend it to two broads standing behind me.
>
> ... I like that one myself. Clever, isn't it?
>
> Definition of indecent: if it's long enough, hard enough and in far enough, it's in decent ...
>
> Definition of a cotton picker: a girl who loses the string of her tampax.
>
> Definition of a happy Roman: Glad-he-ate-her.
>
> Definition of a guy who manufactures maternity clothes. A mother-frocker.
>
> ... Honey, I got no talent. I got guts, [*baitzim,*] big balls. Get used to me, doll.[1] (Williams, 1962)

Almost all of them belonged originally to Pearl Williams (1914–1991) and appear on her live comedy record, *A Trip Around the World Is Not a Cruise.*

This album was recorded in 1961, when Williams was in her late forties, and lasts about forty minutes in total: just under twenty minutes per side. The first side features one of her 'midnight' shows at a club in New York; the second was recorded during her 'late late' set, presumably on the same night. Accompanying herself on the piano, and with a liberal sprinkling of Yiddish, Williams jokes about oral sex, vibrators, adultery, promiscuity, prostitution, ethnicity and class. She is working deep 'blue', throwing in a few belted song parodies and some vaguely liturgical Jewish popular classics. When it was released the following year, Williams's LP (an acronym for a 'long playing' album) had a warning on the cover that read 'For adults only' (see Figure 15.1), meaning that it was not considered suitable for radio airplay and that it was usually kept behind the counter in record stores. You had to ask for it. My grandfather had a copy and it was regularly played at my parents' house parties in the 1960s and 1970s. As Giovanna Del Negro has noted, 'party records' like *A Trip Around the World Is Not a Cruise* were often played during 'intimate gatherings in suburban Jewish homes', creating 'a semi-public context of performance in the heart of the domestic sphere' (2010: 188).

I have performed Williams's words in a number of different contexts, including as a way into academic presentations about performing them to another audience. There is usually a sigh of relief when I explain that they are not

Figure 15.1 Front cover of Pearl Williams's LP, *A Trip Around the World Is Not a Cruise* (1962)

actually *my* words, although, by this point, they have almost certainly become so. I imagine these academic audiences wondering if it is altogether *appropriate* for a speaker to open a research paper or conference keynote with a string of old school dirty jokes. I suspect that it makes even more of a difference that I'm a woman, perhaps even an older woman. It's somehow not very, well, *professional*. On the other hand, most people don't just wander into academic presentations; they are probably aware that I am a performance researcher. And so I then imagine them thinking, 'Oh those performance researchers. Never knowing where the boundaries are. Getting away with *anything* because they are supposed to have presence, charisma, talent ... Oh.' Because didn't I also say that I had no talent? Maybe that was a double bluff. 'Maybe what I' – by whom, of course, I now mean a kind of fictional audience member – 'intuited as, well, *unprofessional*, was actually professional *technique*. A professional technique that she' – by whom, of course, I now mean a kind of fictional me – 'just said wasn't even her own.'

And this fictional audience member would, conveniently, be pretty much on the money since this chapter swirls and settles around concepts of professionalism and technique and repetition and embodiment in creative practice-research. At its heart is reflection on my performance in January 2016, on the occasion of my fiftieth birthday, of Pearl Williams's album (rather than, as I may have implied, subsequent presentations *about* this performance). This makes it sound like I performed the entire record. I didn't, but I'll return to that later since, before launching into methodology, or even findings, one is expected to discuss research imperative.

Chickens and Eggs: Thinking about Research Imperatives

Two days before my first performance of *A Trip Around the World Is Not a Cruise,* as part of a cabaret that I organised and programmed, I produced a handout for audience members: a one-page document that was posted on the Facebook event page and was also printed and made available throughout the venue on the night. This document tried to emphasise – to anybody who bothered to read it – that I positioned what I was doing as practice-research. In many ways, in announcing in written form that my performance was practice-research, it effectively *became* practice-research (although only for those for whom that label is meaningful). On my handout, I outlined my three main aims: (1) to locate Pearl Williams's material in my body by finding a Jewish voice; (2) to interrogate her LP as an act of cultural memory; and, finally, (3) to interpret Williams's performance from the inside out.

Here is a probably-not-very-professional confession: these aims imply that I always knew why I wanted to make this performance and that I was clear about what I wanted to find out by doing it. I didn't and I wasn't. In fact, this wasn't even the case when I prepared the handout only days before. In retrospect, I *can* say that my aims crystallised in the act of their articulation and do indeed capture what I had been approaching for many years as a researcher – that is, the generation of insight that not only combines methodologically but is also *about* familial, aesthetic and cultural histories and genealogies; that interrogates how one prepares for intersubjective exchanges in moments of performance, characterised always as an event; and that acknowledges how the present always includes absence, what is no longer (or perhaps has never been). But we've been acculturated by dominant (practice-)research agendas to think we must be able to express research questions and aims – or at the very least, a problem that needs to be explored – in advance of actually doing a performance (if not in advance of starting to prepare it, or in its very conceptualisation). All I really knew was that I *had* to do this performance. I knew this about nine years before I got around to it, so you'd think I would have been better prepared when the time eventually came.

I am a product of what Rachel Hann (2015) has called the 'first wave' of practice-research in performance. I participated, for instance, in the hugely influential AHRB-funded Practice as Research in Performance (PARIP) project, led by Baz Kershaw from 2001 to 2006, as its South West Regional Coordinator.[2] Upon reflection, perhaps I need to acknowledge that I'm rather more than a product; perhaps I need to own the fact that my colleagues and I are responsible for many current expectations, however inadvertent or unexpected the consequences. Let me give you an example of these expectations. Every time I speak about *A Trip Around the World Is Not a Cruise*, I note that over the course of her career Pearl Williams sold over a million records, and yet she is barely remembered today. I have always had a not-so-secret agenda, one that wasn't expressed in my aims for the performance even when I was struggling to articulate them, because it doesn't fit with understandings of what comprises a research imperative. In particular, *drawing attention to* somebody or something in and of itself is usually considered a by-product (that is, 'impact') rather than an end product (that is, 'output') of research. And, in order to be valued as impact in, for example, the Research Excellence Framework (REF),[3] you need to not only evidence that it makes a difference that people are now aware of this somebody or something but *also* that this has effected change in some demonstrable way, *and* that your performance can be clearly identified as an 'internationally recognised' research output in itself – which seems to be a classic chicken-or-egg situation.

This was something we did not foresee – although perhaps we should have – in the heady days of first-wave practice-research. We were fighting to have our work recognised and valued in the academy. Like many lecturers in theatre departments, I was tired of being told that what I did was not serious, was not critical, was not structured and informed, was not … well, *research*. I was annoyed that my own PhD, started in the early 1990s, couldn't include practice and eventually felt completely separate from the collaborative, feminist, 'total theatre' work I was making in a company called Lusty Juventus Physical Theatre which I co-founded with my colleagues. (I was one of those fortunate people who was appointed to a full-time academic job at the same time I started my PhD – something increasingly rare in the current climate.) For our first four productions, between 1996 and 2001, Lusty Juventus was what we did in our spare time. It did not count in our workload modelling. It was not listed on our research returns to the REF-precursor. We received no kudos for hiring graduates or receiving Arts Council England (ACE) funding. There was no such thing as 'impact' then.

Now I wonder if we (and by 'we', I mean first-wave practice-researchers) didn't walk straight into the trap of neoliberalism; indeed, if we might not have unwittingly become poster children for the neoliberal university in our attempt to make equivalence and so compete with more traditional methodologies and their expression of findings. In our packaging and framing of the originality, significance and rigour of practice-research in certain multimodal ways (and here I'm referencing REF criteria and the infamous 300-word textual descriptors in which we point to having met them), have we not reified a market-driven, corporatised system of value and self-regulation which actually excludes many types of embodied knowledge generation? While this seems contradictory, one path to understanding how scholars like myself were able to reconcile the attraction and promise of practice-research with its grading and monetisation might be found in Michel Foucault's assessment of neoliberalism in the late 1970s.

Foucault believed, although not without reservations, that neoliberalism was able to offer a form of governmentality characterised more by incentivisation and so less through 'internal subjugation of individuals', producing an environment 'in which minority individuals and practices are tolerated' (Foucault in Dean, 2014: 436). Mitchell Dean and Daniel Zamora (2018) note the relationship between Foucault's thinking on neoliberalism and his advocacy of 'techniques of the self' through which people could 'subjectivate' themselves, thus inaugurating a line of critical radical thinking that coalesced around considerations of 'self-identity', 'reflexivity' and 'ethico-politics'. Coming of age as a researcher in the 1990s, in a discipline like performance studies that particularly valorises interrogation of and with these concepts (not to mention Foucault's contribution), it is perhaps no coincidence that they are central to my own extended project as a researcher working within a neoliberal environment, both disguising and making palatable some of its central tenets.

Paradoxically, fighting for the inclusion of (often feminist) research, located in and through and as lived experience of the body, has created a moebius strip of solutions and problems. As Sarah Burton observes in a chapter on writing for REF in Yvette Taylor and Kinneret Lahad's *Feeling Academic in the Neoliberal University*, this 'stems from the way that the value system of the neoliberal academy and the audit cultures it allows to thrive is driven by a patriarchal conception of legitimate knowledge production'; as a result, 'many of us simply end up working harder' in order to demonstrate that legitimacy (Burton, 2018: 132). Indeed, my experiences align with the overarching themes arising from Taylor and Lahad's collection – that is, the negotiation of privilege, risk, entitlement and even failure. This, for me, has much to do with competing types of professionalism, since what is professionalism if not self-regulation? Moreover, the environments that sustain and reward 'successful' professional academic researchers are not the same as those that sustain successful professional practitioners. The binding of performance practice to research therefore becomes, for many, a double bind.

Archives, Repertoires and Gynelineage

My performance of Williams's *A Trip Around the World Is Not a Cruise* was the first time I was able to bring together the two strands of my research: the making of performance with what I had been establishing and analysing for about a quarter of a century – that is, a female Jewish performance tradition which focused, in the twentieth century, on comedy and popular entertainment. Over this period of time, I became increasingly aware that my commitment to this performance tradition was associated with a growing respect for a professionalism which was (and continues to be) too often overlooked. This began, consciously, when I saw the comedian Joan Rivers live for the first time in 2002, mainly out of a sense of dutiful curiosity. What I encountered that night was a consummately *professional* performer, a woman who really knew the business of stand-up. In fact, I'll go further now – in the moment of performance, Rivers *was* stand-up, embodying its history and its cross-generational transmission. I began to understand *professionalism* – in this context – as the interarticulated manifestation of experience and performance mastery.

Simultaneously, I became aware of my own role as an 'expert spectator', the scholarly flip side of the professionalism of the performers whom I study. 'Expert spectator' is a term coined by Susan Melrose (2007) to describe those who are trained, or have trained themselves, not only to 'see what they can see' but also to imagine the rest in a way that has been 'carefully planned for and largely anticipated by the performance-makers'. When I finally performed stand-up myself via *A Trip Around the World Is Not a Cruise*, it was as somebody who learned it, not through doing (which is the standard route for professional performers), but through years of expert spectating.

I had referenced Williams's record repeatedly – and, frankly, quite superficially – when writing about Jewish women and performance over the previous twenty or so years. Mainly this was to position her historically in a self-conscious tradition of bawdy musical comedy by American women that starts with Sophie Tucker (1886–1966). To offer some sense of how this pivot works, in her homage to 'Soph' Tucker in the 1970s and 1980s, Bette Midler used to use one of Pearl Williams's response to hecklers: 'Shut your hole, honey. Mine's making money'– which, I think you'll agree, is the ultimate neoliberal put down (Williams herself tended to use 'girlie' and 'doll' rather than 'honey').[4] Tucker started in vaudeville, working originally in blackface during the first decade of the twentieth century, which was often the only mainstream performance option for 'plain', often Jewish, performers. As Maria de Simone has noted, this experience encouraged her to deploy 'racial, ethnic and character impersonation' as a 'business practice' predicated on vaudeville's dependence on novelty and audience demand (2019: 165). Tucker became a household name with a reputation as a raunchy comic entertainer through the use of *double entendre* and the explicitness with which she referred to sexual desire. As part of the package, she sang the blues as well as shmaltzy Yiddish ballads. Performers like Pearl Williams frequently acknowledged their debt to Tucker as well as a sense of lineage in generational terms. On the back cover of *A Trip Around the World Is Not a Cruise*, for instance, is an anecdote about Tucker popping up backstage like some kind of fairy godmother to tell Williams: 'You're me at your age, only better.'

Williams's closest professional associates were Patsy Abbott (1921–2001), who started her career as a vocalist, and Belle Barth (1911–1971), who billed herself the 'Hildegard of the Underworld' and the 'doyenne of the dirty line'. As Michael Bronski writes in a ground-breaking newspaper article about these three women: 'They were tough working-class cookies who used street language. Women were "broads," men were "guys," penises were schlongs or schmucks, vaginas were "knishes," and they have no problem using words like "bitch," "faggot," or "asshole"' (Bronski, 2003). Williams, Abbott and Barth were all raised in New York, performed on the same circuit at the height of their careers, and recorded for the same independent labels; Barth's album, *I Don't Mean to be Vulgar, but It's Profitable*, and Abbott's *Have I Had You Before?* were both recorded live in the same year as Williams's *A Trip Around the World Is Not a Cruise*. By the late 1960s, all three were located primarily in Florida where both Abbott and Barth ran their own clubs. After commanding a significant salary of up to $7,500 a week and headlining in Las Vegas, Williams spent the years leading up to her retirement, at age seventy, performing at the Place Pigalle in Miami Beach 'to houses packed with busloads of Jewish retirees from nearby condos' (Del Negro, 2010: 193–4).

Besides their use of song and Yiddish – the *mamaloschen*, or mother tongue, of smutty American urban humour – one of the things these comedians had in common was the way they foregrounded their own sexuality as ageing women.

Again, this starts with Tucker, who milked her 'Red Hot Mama' persona until her death in 1966 at the age of 79. In her song 'I'm Living Alone and I Like It', for instance, recorded in the 1950s, she suggests that she was happy to pay for some gigolo action: 'If I wanna have some fun, if I get bothered and hot, I phone one of those young tall dark handsomes that I've got. So it costs me a twenty or a fifty, so what?' I suspect that *this* (negotiating my own sexuality while ageing) is what really compelled me to return to this gynelineage as a performer. And I chose to explore Williams's album, in particular, because I remembered seeing it in the teak cabinet under the record player in our living room when I was growing up. In certain company, my mother used to perform some of Williams's jokes herself. For adults only. The voice of adult: a blur of my mother's and Pearl Williams's. The voice of having grown up.

Here is a second confession that will undermine my professionalism as a researcher: I had only consciously (that is, as an adult, within the previous forty years) listened to about two minutes of *A Trip Around the World Is Not a Cruise* before I started working on my own performance of it. To be clear, not only had I written about this album, which was sitting on my shelf as a kind of family heirloom, but this was a *very* long time after I announced that I would be performing it. I didn't have the record digitised until a month before I was scheduled to perform, which is when I started the process of transcribing. The short excerpt I *had* heard – some of which appears at the top of this chapter – represented the majority of what was then available of Williams's work online.[5] And when it came time to start working with her text in detail, it occurred to me that I was probably committing to a tremendous error of judgement.

It suddenly seemed like career suicide to attempt to make a performance six months into my new role as a research institute director (an institute that didn't exist yet, this was to be part of its launch), given that I had never performed stand-up before, that the audience certainly wouldn't understand most of the (at least) fifty-five-year-old jokes (especially with some of the punchlines in Yiddish), that I had only just heard the material for the first time and that some of it was 'problematic' to say the least. Here's an example (that I chose not to perform myself): 'D'ya hear about the fag, was brushing his teeth one morning and his gums start to bleed? He says, "Thank god, safe for another thirty days"' (Williams, 1962). In general, Williams's material is both accepting of and sympathetic to queer experience; although she married and divorced twice, she lived with a woman for years in what was widely rumoured to be a lesbian relationship (Bronski, 2003). While Williams acknowledged and gave voice to a wide range of sexual practices, this was expressed within the mores of the time and to largely straight audiences. As Del Negro has discussed, Williams tended to play to suburban, second generation immigrant, Jewish couples on their annual vacation 'who longed to escape the unquestioned blandness of their white collar existence and the climate of cultural conformity', in liminal, drunken, late-night venues that prepared them up to a point for her transgressions of gender and sexuality (2010: 204).

I did not feel I had the time to develop the confidence to knowingly quote and make sense of another space and culture, while remaining in the present as a performer. The fact that I am also not very good at memorising lines also contributed to my anxiety. So I decided that I only had to do five minutes of Williams's material – that, after all, is about the length of a standard open mic slot or first set on television. And here we can see the negotiation of professional tensions in action, a negotiation that acts as a smokescreen for real world compromise. Because even though I wasn't entirely sure *why* I was doing this performance in research terms, nor what precisely I would hear when I listened to the album in full, my methodological conceit up to that moment was that I would perform Williams's text in full. Failure had always been inevitable and in a split-second decision – one that I was choosing to understand as self-care – the nature of that failure changed significantly in that it became possible to succeed on different terms.

In the end, I performed a fifteen-minute set, comprising about twelve minutes from *A Trip Around the World Is Not a Cruise*, with the rest of the material sourced from a webpage that embedded a selection of very short audio files from Williams's other albums. The latter included her *Hava Nagila* medley, which I sang as a grand finale with the klezmer fusion band, Hazaar! The band was on stage for my entire performance and also played two extended dance sets that evening. One of its members is my ex-husband, Dave. You can see him in Figure 15.2, on the left (that is, stage right), playing the clarinet. In her sets, Williams's piano playing underlined punchlines. It was fundamental to her rhythmic structure and was part of her voice. (Williams entered the world of showbusiness in 1938 when, on her lunch break as a legal secretary, she agreed to accompany a friend at a singing audition; apparently, she was hired on the spot and went on stage as a professional pianist that night.) My piano playing was not up to the task, so I asked Dave to be my accompanist. We rehearsed once together and otherwise worked separately from Williams's LP and a script I sent him of the material I had chosen to perform. This was probably both brave and stupid (or, more generously, just what we could pragmatically manage living in different cities), given that timing and rhythm is almost everything when performing comedy (especially comedy featuring words that the audience is unlikely to understand). And we are *really* not what one could call a cohesive entity; in fact, we had never performed together before, ever, even when we used to be married.

In her book about the performance of cultural memory in the Americas, Diana Taylor identifies two modes of memory. The 'archive' represents 'supposedly enduring materials' such as texts, documents, bones, videos (Taylor,

Figure 15.2 Roberta Mock with Hazaar!, *A Trip Around the World Is Not a Cruise* (Plymouth, 16 January 2016). Photo: Benjamin Graham.

2003: 19) – or records like Pearl Williams's *A Trip Around the World Is Not a Cruise*. The other mode of memory discussed by Taylor is the so-called ephemeral repertoire of embodied practices and 'non-reproducible' knowledges such as dance, spoken word, ritual, gesture and so on. Once it starts flowing through real bodies, the repertoire is both changeable and unpredictable. We see this in Bette Midler's use of Williams's jokes as an alter ego inspired by Sophie Tucker. It is evident in the collaborative outcome arising from my need to perform some of those jokes with a musician – and not just *any* musician since together we relied upon and produced a very complex and intense network of personal memory associations. Whereas the archive tends to represent an accumulation of official viewpoints, the repertoire – through its 'constant state of againness' (Taylor, 2003: 21) – might be considered the domain of cultural process where new meanings are made. This is one of the reasons why I was adamant that my performance was not an 'impersonation' of Pearl Williams, which I associate with schmaltzy nostalgia acts that are live but not living. Rather, it was intended as an example of how the archive and the repertoire always exceed the limitations of the other and 'exist in a constant state of interaction' (Taylor, 2003: 21).

That there wasn't 'one' archive or 'one' repertoire at work in my performance-making does, of course, cast some doubt on the appropriateness of generically referring to 'the' archive or repertoire. The starting point was

Williams's record, of course, situated in a complex lineage of live performances and recordings. The closer you listen to it, the more you realise how edited it is, how much has been left out. There are also its flickering manifestations online which I had used to write about it in the past – transcriptions and descriptions of Williams's performance which deceive you through the power of linguistic sign-posting into believing in their accuracy. Then there are multiple pathways of repertoire that enact embodied memory – that is, the individual agency that 'requires presence', the participation in 'the production and reproduction of knowledge by "being there"' (Taylor, 2003: 20). These various strands of archive and repertoire are intricately braided in any specific moment of performance.

For the first part of my set, I was wearing my grandmother's fur coat, a fur like Williams wears on the front cover of *A Trip Around the World Is Not a Cruise*. Its removal (see Figure 15.3) was an homage to two moments expressing professional pride in accomplishment by women in their mid-seventies. The first was Aretha Franklin's dropping of her full-length fur to the floor during her Kennedy Center Honors performance a month earlier, in a tribute to Carole King's *Tapestry*. The second was an almost identical gesture by Sophie Tucker during the 1962 *Royal Variety Performance*. Removing her fur stole to reveal a glittery well-fitted evening dress, the autobiographical 'saga' that Tucker half sung/half recited to the Queen and Prince Philip (and British

Figure 15.3 Roberta Mock, *A Trip Around the World Is Not a Cruise* (Plymouth, 16 January 2016). Photo: Benjamin Graham.

television audiences watching at home) begins with her flinging 'fishes and knishes' in her mother's café while singing to any 'mamzer' she thought would proffer a tip, before ending up in New York, where 'to my surprise / I found there were guys / who idolize / gals oversize'.

There were also traces in my performance of my mother performing parts of Williams's album in the early 1970s, teaching me through example how to be a 'funny Jewish broad' (before I was sent to bed when things got raucous). *And* there were traces of my godmother in Jerusalem who explained to me that one of the song scraps I was performing from Williams's recorded set, which I couldn't understand, was from a Yiddish comedy album by the Barton Brothers (1947).[6] She sang it to me over Skype: 'Joe and Paul *ah fargeniggen.*' The joke was about how Jewish words sound dirty even when they're perfectly clean; *fargeniggen* means pleasure, joy, happiness. On top of all this, the last act of the evening – since I positioned my own set in the prime spot, second from the top of a cabaret bill – was my former student, Sally, who performs under the monicker, The Fantastic Miss Fanny. Her routine, which she devised independently, included some of the Sophie Tucker jokes that Bette Midler borrowed from Pearl Williams. Sally's own burlesque students were working the floor during the cabaret party as well.

Finding Voice

While, in numerous ways, the entire evening was a manifestation of archive and repertoire in interaction, coming at it from a different direction, my specific part in it was a crystallisation of almost all of my practice-research going back nearly fifteen years. In many different genres, the conundrum to which I have continually returned is how to 'act' (like or as) my 'self' in non-mimetic ways. This issue consciously emerged through the final Lusty Juventus production, *M(other)*, in 2002. When we embarked on it, the primary research enquiry circulated around the creation of non-essentialised representations of motherhood that resisted stereotypes of the maternal, as well as feminist methods of collaborative theatre-making.[7] What I ended up discovering, however, was more about how, in the transition from director to performer, I found the need to create a staged persona that acted as metaphor but did not simulate.[8] Nearly a decade later, in 2011, I performed some of my inaugural professorial lecture as an alter-ego, Bobby the Tel Twelve Mall Elf.[9] At the time of making it, I thought this piece was about the performance of material and metaphorical boundaries – and, in particular, about how the city of Detroit is constituted through and as performance. It was only some time later that I realised the extent to which it was about my negotiating the 'performing I' and 'represented I' through the tropes of autobiography and cultural memory while simultaneously working to destabilise them.

As in these previous performances, the word-based spoken text of *A Trip Around the World Is Not a Cruise* became the means through which I augmented my performative self spatially and temporally. This attempt to balance the demands of representing/acting and presenting/not-acting gave rise to complex processes of embodiment. In *The Jew's Body*, the Jewish cultural historian, Sander Gilman, identifies the voice as one of the key markers of Jewishness. This Jewishness – for which, read 'otherness' and 'difference' – is compounded when the voice speaks in Yiddish, the 'hidden' language of the Jews, one that exposes the impossibility of successful assimilation (Gilman, 1991: 34). My own grandparents, who emigrated to Canada as young people, both spoke Yiddish as their first language, but I never learned it myself. While Pearl Williams's use of it in her act did not seem foreign to me, it equally was not comprehensible as anything more than emotive sound.

Perhaps because I could only access Williams via her voice, my performance preparation focused almost entirely on my own voice. For the final month, I spent an hour or so a day stretching and then an hour or more doing vocal exercises. I then spent a few hours transcribing Williams's record, often having to listen to the same passage over and over again, and then speaking it back, again over and over again. Eventually I shaped the text and essentially rehearsed by reading it over Williams's voice. She speaks faster than me, uses her mouth and throat differently, and can sing (that is, in a way that others might find enjoyable). There was a period in which I contemplated moving between speaking Williams's words myself and lip-synching to the record. But, besides being technically very difficult to accomplish – since I would have needed to know and own the words I was ventriloquising just as well and there was also the matter of moving between live and recorded music – this would have created distance between myself and Williams, my body and the voice, between me and my Jewishness.

Still, ventriloquism and its theorisation start to point to how performance analysis might operate from the inside out – which, after all, was one of the stated aims of the project. As Steven Connor writes in his cultural history of ventriloquism, *Dumbstruck*, the voice is both a bodily process and a bodily production or residue. Although it issues from within, it crosses the border from bodily interior to exterior, out into the surrounding space, and only becomes sound through the presence of another body. In so doing, 'My voice defines me because it draws me into coincidence with myself, accomplishes me in a way which goes beyond mere belonging, association, or instrumental use' (Connor, 2000: 7).

One day, while I was working on my performance – that is, doing vocal exercises accompanied by YouTube videos – a Facebook message from my mother popped up on screen. She had a rehearsal tip for me.

Me: What's your suggestion?

My mother: You're a swan. Most of these women (Totie, Pearl, Sophie) were round chickens. When you're practising, cut the distance between your shoulders and the floor so that you feel shorter and rounder. And, while I can't explain it, you'll start feeling more Jewish, and funnier. I'm reaching back here. When I entertained a lot (informally of course) and when I too was a swan who stood and walked tall, it worked for me. Maybe it will help you. Hugs.

She was right, as mothers so often are. My mother drew attention (both then, in practice, and now, upon reflection) to the importance of technique, what Ben Spatz describes as 'the knowledge content of specific practices': 'Technique consists of discoveries about specific material possibilities that can be repeated with some degree of reliability, so that what works in one context may also work in another' (Spatz, 2015: 42). The process of making *A Trip Around the Work Is Not a Cruise* was effectively one of training my body over a period of twelve months (far beyond the time I spent working on the actual spoken and sung material) to produce a certain type of voice.

As Diana Taylor has noted, the body that does cultural memory 'is specific, pivotal, and subject to change ... The bodies participating in the transmission of knowledge and memory are themselves a product of certain taxonomic, disciplinary and mnemonic systems' (2003: 86). I *did* feel 'more Jewish' and better able to embrace Williams's material, not only when I imagined myself short and fat, but also when I concentrated on techniques practised during one of the training workshops I attended, in preparation to do so. This was led by Walli Höfinger and Christiane Hommelsheim, who are both Roy Hart voice teachers,[10] at the 2015 Giving Voice Festival at Falmouth University. What I wanted to learn from them was how to be positive and powerful in my voice – despite having a limited range (and ability to carry a tune) – to locate a voice with 'depth', one that was lower but still 'my own'. To this day, I refer to a little drawing I made on my phone during the workshop: a 'take away' reminder to sing and speak in alignment with my vagina as a means of remaining corporeally grounded. Konstantinos Thomaidis has noted that there are two strands of vocal training, each of which extend time and space beyond the moment of voicing. One attends to internality and the 'emergence of voicing in specific anatomical structures' such as pelvic muscles; this can be described as a 'listening-in'. However, the practice of a 'listening-out' that precedes sounding – which would include my repeated listening to Williams's recording and the voices of women such as my godmother – renders 'the emergence of vocal presence unequivocally intersubjective from the outset' (Thomaidis, 2019: 160).

LOCATION, LOCATION, LOCATION

When I first decided to perform *A Trip Around the World Is Not a Cruise*, it was not conceived as cabaret or a nightclub act. The original idea was that I would visit people's homes, upon invitation, and then eat a meal with their guests. During the course of this meal (which would include what my father used to call 'Jewish soul food', like *gefilte* fish and *kishka*, that nobody would actually eat), I would eventually perform all of Williams's album. I imagined myself as some embarrassing old aunt who makes a spectacle of herself, having drunk rather enthusiastically from the Manischewitz bottle. Eventually, after ten or so dinner parties across the country, I thought I would perform a (or rather, Williams's) nightclub set, much as I eventually did in the venue I always envisioned: the Duke of Cornwall hotel ballroom in Plymouth. (By the time this took place, it had been renovated and looked much more tasteful and corporate but still felt, to me, like the ballroom of a freshly painted Borscht-belt hotel or cruise ship.) This version of the project didn't happen for a myriad of reasons, but especially the impossibility of touring for an extended period of time while meeting responsibilities at my university. In fact, those responsibilities, as a Senior Manager, have become the defining condition of all elements of my research. It shapes both the trajectory of my performance practice-research and also the nature of specific projects.

Here we return to the incompatibility of professional expectations within the academy for practice-researchers, this time due to the extraordinary variety of modes in which we operate within higher education. I have shifted from company to solo work, from touring productions to film or one-off performances, not because it suits either the nature of my practice or my research enquiries but because it is all that is possible, unless you bring in sufficient external money to buy you time. And this is virtually impossible for those whose practice cannot easily be commodified or articulated as commodifiable either within the cultural sector or our highly competitive research economy. To be a professional academic forecloses on my having a professional creative practice in the field I research; and, being unable to develop that creative practice professionally means I will always struggle to meet measurable criteria of research quality. But I digress (sort of).

There are some interesting clues in my original plans to perform *A Trip Around the World Is Not a Cruise*. The first is that I associated it with the domestic, returning the spoken material to home environments where Williams's record was most often experienced. The second was that I imagined both myself, and Williams's words, as embarrassing and intrusive and inappropriate (as inappropriate at a twenty-first-century dinner party as at an academic conference). I was particularly interested then in how non-Jews, far removed temporally and geographically from the culture that produced

Williams's act, would react to it. Part of me expected *some* laughter, if only because of the recognition of rhythms and patterns of joke-telling that are now firmly embedded in the mainstream comedy industry. Part of me expected none. Silence. Or nervous, half-hearted but well-meaning, twitchy snickers.

But two things happened when the performance finally came to pass. The first is simply that rather than performing 'the Jew', out of place, in a non-Jewish environment, I intuitively felt compelled to create a party space in which the default position was Jewish – gloriously, over the top, outrageously and unapologetically – despite the fact that only about eight people in the entire room of about 170 were actually Jewish (and most of those eight people performed on stage that night). The latter included Marisa Carnesky, who performed a magic routine, and Lazlo Pearlman, who was the evening's compere and also acted as my 'outside eye' during final rehearsals.

The second thing that occurred, almost certainly connected to set and setting, was that I *killed*. Really. The audience ate it up. They laughed hard and a lot. It was an extraordinary experience from the stage, hitting me like a wave of energy. They *got it*, even when they didn't specifically understand all of the parts that made it. The roar when it was all over was not just relief that I hadn't died on stage. I can't prove this, of course. There is no video. That is deliberate. The performance was an exchange, which in itself is not something that can be captured on video; the combination of sound and vision seduces too many people into believing that they may read the encounter in similar ways to a live audience. I had originally planned to make an audio recording and to press a vinyl LP of it, returning my performance back to 'the archive', but that didn't happen. I'm okay with that, as I have to be, because I need to acknowledge that in not attending to the making of a high-quality recording – in leaving it to 'chance' – and here I must stress that there was *nothing* else about that evening left to chance, not the candy corn that was sold, not the tealight holders on the table – I was effectively deciding that I would not be submitting this performance to the next REF.

More specifically, in a manner that seems almost passive-aggressive, I ensured that it would not be available as an assessible primary research output – that is, in the mediated mode we describe as 'performance documentation'. And that is because, I knew – or else, I think I knew – even before doing the performance, that the research output itself was my body and that my research findings were manifest in and inseparable from its extended spatio-temporality. When I suggest that this is impossible to access via a 'document', it is not because I am romanticising what Spatz has called 'the *trope of excess*' but precisely because, as he observes, *'what we know* becomes *who we are*' (2015: 56; emphasis in original). What characterises embodied technique is a 'nonspatial, multiplicitous linearity' that represents 'epistemic depth and breadth', and knowledge can only be recognised through the aggregation of its elements 'as well as countless relationships among them and contexts in which they might be applied' (Spatz, 2015: 45, 46, 48).

Of course, there were audience questionnaires designed to determine what networks and potentials might have been recognised, hard copies of which were on tables in the venue; electronic versions were posted on the Facebook event page the day before the performance and I sent a reminder out the following day as well. I never really expected that many would be returned. Despite some very thoughtful and thought-provoking responses on the twelve questionnaires that I got back, what really struck me was the number of people who told me less formally (frankly, they *blurted* it out) that, because of this performance, they looked at me in a new way. Many assumed that deep down I had been harbouring a desire to tell filthy jokes – in short, that I was co-extensive with the material I was speaking – despite the fact that many had known me for twenty years and had never heard me speak or behave in this way before. It is one of the ideas in my previous writing about comedy – and women's comedy in particular – that was made evident for me on that night. That is, audiences laugh when they believe that *that* body, with *that* history, is capable of saying *those* words in *that* way.

I have often wondered why this is the case and now think that, again, ventriloquism might offer a way forward. As Connor notes, 'Voices are produced by bodies but can also themselves produce bodies' (2000: 35). He refers to these bodies as 'vocalic' and they are created, shaped and sustained through the oscillating operations between the speaking object and speaking subject. While technique underpins what might have been heard, or translated, the performances produced by such bodies are, for me, as significant for their expression of what can *not* be heard. I had always thought of performance research outcomes as embodying what cannot be expressed in the writing about them, but I am now starting to wonder about the ways and whys that performance research might express what is not there: in my case, for instance, the choices *not* to tell Williams's jokes that I felt were (intentionally or not) racist or homophobic or that asked us to laugh about rape in uncomfortable ways. Or how I cut jokes that I thought were too far removed from contemporary experience and re-ordered others so they built like a current stand-up set.

The day after my performance of *A Trip Around the World Is Not a Cruise*, I got a call from my friend Mark. Among other things, he's kind of a promoter and he phoned to tell me he had some gigs for me. I honestly didn't know what he was talking about. 'Doing what?' And he said, 'Stand-up.' And I said, 'But I'm not a comedian.' And he said, 'Yes, you are. I saw you doing comedy last night.' And I said, 'But that was all I have. Those were my fifteen minutes. And they weren't my jokes. And I wouldn't know what to do if somebody heckled.' And he said, 'So you make up another fifteen minutes. There's money involved.' But it was impossible. When is a comedian not a comedian? When she's a practice-researcher.

Doing It Like a Pro

In the opening episode of the television series, *The Marvelous Mrs Maisel* (2017), set in the late 1950s, the title character's 'natural' ability as a comic (sharpened by her close observation and note-taking during gigs) is contrasted with her soon-to-be ex-husband who gets on stage and performs routines that he has copied from a Bob Newhart LP.[11] Like his wife, we the audience dismiss him because he is not original. This means he is not a 'real' comic. He is an amateur – which parallels the way originality is the central criteria for 'real' researchers (just think about how we understand professional postdoctoral scholarship in contrast, for instance, with what is expected of undergraduate students). To be a professional stand-up – here conflated with 'paid' – in this historical moment, means writing or co-writing your own words. There is no way, ethically, that I could continue to perform Pearl Williams's act as my own. And yet, I have also found no way – so far – of taking it further as practice-research. I'm not convinced repeating my fifteen minutes with different audiences would reveal any significantly different or deeper insights. And the other alternative – to do the material that I cut – would be at odds with my knowledge and intuition as an expert spectator. This is something I discovered as a result of the professional interference that prevented me from performing the whole album in the first place.

While it may seem blindingly obvious to me now, practice-research in comedy has to operate like any comic practice – in other words, it does actually need to make people laugh. Or try to. You can't generate significant insight into making people laugh, or what it feels like to make people laugh, unless you make people laugh. Otherwise, you produce insights into how *not* to make people laugh. Of course, it is possible to learn an enormous amount from disastrous processes and spectacular aesthetic failure. In one of the most memorable journal articles I have encountered, Martin Welton provocatively argued that practice-as-research is producing a plethora of appropriately theorised practice that is either 'bad' or 'boring' (2003: 349). Like Welton, I'm saying that the professional standards and intentions of creative practice and creative practice-research are not always compatible. And I'm going to stretch my neck out and say that perhaps, sometimes, they need to be.

Having said that, sometimes, creative practice and creative practice-research can speak to each other in profoundly revealing ways. One of Williams's jokes always made me laugh when I said it out loud, both in rehearsals (which, I should probably remind you, were almost always only attended by myself) and on stage in front of others. This was not laughing as professional strategy, or what Tony Allen calls 'timing the corpse' – that is, a technique used to engage the audience in the 'now' by 'shifting from one seemingly authentic emotional state to another' (Allen 2002: 29–30). I can do that too, but here I mean simply that I 'really' laughed because I was and remain able to recognise my body, its history and its present working conditions in the neoliberal academy, in these words: 'Oh boy, am I a nut! If I were normal could I work like this? Never in a million years. My mother doesn't know what I do for a living. She thinks I'm a whore in Chicago.'

And so I end, close to where I began, with the concept of professionalism, both my own as an expert spectator and also in respect of what became increasingly striking about Pearl Williams as I learned to embody her words. This time I am referring not only to style and technique but also to content. Williams always played with the two associations of being a 'pro' – that is, both a hard-working, disciplined entertainer who knows her craft and business, and also a prostitute. One of the first things Williams tells us on the album is that she's 'a *chanteuse*' which is 'French for *kurva*.' Her audiences were expected to know that *kurva* means 'whore' in Yiddish. It was a line I decided to keep in my own performance, with some heavy gestural signalling.

But there was one particular line I felt I had to remove from my performance text, despite the fact that it explained the title of the show (and the album), because I didn't feel I could easily help my audience to understand it: 'Polly Adler wrote a book: *A House is Not a Home*. I'm writing a sequel: a trip around the world is not a cruise' (Williams, 1962). Perhaps you recognise the title of the book, published in 1953, from the Burt Bacharach and Hal David song of the same name. The song was actually written for a film version (which bombed) of the book, which was a ghost-written autobiography of a Jewish madam. Adler's 'house' was a brothel, a frequent setting for Williams's jokes. This chain of connections makes me think about how my own vocalic body is situated within a repertoire, as well as Marjorie Garber's description of Jewishness as 'spectral visibility' – that is, 'the visibility of the ghost' (1999: 99). For me, it's a ghost located in the auras created when archives and repertoires, pasts and presents, merge and eclipse each other at the intersection of professional cultures.[12] And if there's one thing we know about ghosts, pinning them down is always something of a challenge.[13]

NOTES

1. In Yiddish, *kurva* means prostitute; *mechaya* means pleasure; and *baitzim* (which I inserted in this text, although Williams uses the term elsewhere) means testicles or balls. Roto-rooter is an American plumbing service; Williams was presumably referring to an industrial device used by the company to clear blocked drains.
2. The Arts and Humanities Research Board (AHRB) preceded the formation of the

AHRC (i.e. Council) in the UK. The Practice as Research in Performance (PARIP) website is archived at <https://www.bristol.ac.uk/parip/>.
3. The Research Excellence Framework (REF) is a national exercise in the UK for assessing the quality of research at departmental and institutional levels. It is used to determine the distribution of government funding for research.
4. Although it appears on *A Trip Around the World Is Not a Cruise*, Giovanna Del Negro attributes this line to Belle Barth (2010: 213); however, she also notes that Barth and Williams attended each other's shows, referred to each other on stage and discussed their relationship on their LPs (191). It is therefore not unlikely that they shared effective put downs for hecklers.
5. You can still listen to these two minutes and twenty seconds of *A Trip Around the World Is Not a Cruise* at <https://www.youtube.com/watch?v=Md0KBVTs5IM> (last accessed 10 February 2019). For a few weeks in the year prior to the performance, the entire album was available on YouTube, but it just as mysteriously disappeared again before I began rehearsing. This, in itself, says a lot about the permanence of the seemingly ubiquitous digital 'archive', and perhaps 'archives' more generally.
6. In another example of repertoire in action, the Barton Brothers learned this act from hotel staff in the Catskills, where it had been originated by Red Buttons.
7. Lusty Juventus's *M(other)* project is included in Ludivine Allegue, Simon Jones, Baz Kershaw and Angela Piccini (2009: 2018 and accompanying DVD).
8. The reason for my transition into performing, at that particular stage as a practitioner, was entirely due to professional considerations – that is, because our EU funding would only cover the costs of a certain number of people to tour to Greece where the show was to premiere.
9. For more about this performance, see Roberta Mock (2017).
10. Roy Hart (1926–1975) was an actor, theatre-maker and voice teacher who developed extended vocal techniques that were originally conceived as psychotherapeutic tools.
11. *The Marvelous Mrs Maisel* takes some significant liberties in terms of historical veracity, including the fact that Bob Newhart's record didn't come out for another three years. Even more relevant in this context, there were simply no women working it like Midge Maisel in the late 1950s; you had to look to comics like Pearl Williams and Belle Barth, who was fairly regularly arrested for obscenity, to find any form of equivalence and their material was really rather different, especially from the perspective of class. Mrs Maisel is performing stand-up for a twenty-first, rather than mid-century, audience, not unlike I was trying to do while preserving Williams's actual words in my performance *A Trip Around the World Is Not a Cruise*.
12. Elsewhere I have argued that a powerful triangle of association that connects the prostitute, actress and stereotype of the Jewess has haunted the careers of Jewish women performers since the mid-nineteenth century (Mock 2007: 10).
13. Sometimes it takes a ghost to find one. The day after my performance, my mother (who wasn't there) sent me a message to say that my grandfather (who died over fifteen years earlier) enjoyed it very much: 'He started to cough and had trouble catching his breath, at one point. Do you remember how that used to happen when he laughed too hard and too long?'

REFERENCES

Allegue, Ludivine, Simon Jones, Baz Kershaw and Angela Piccini (eds) (2009), *Practice-as-Research in Performance and Screen*, Basingstoke: Palgrave Macmillan.

Allen, Tony (2002), *Attitude: The Secret of Stand-up Comedy*, Glastonbury: Gothic Image Publications.
Barton Brothers, The (1947), *Joe and Paul (Based on themes by Rumshinsky & Secunda)*, New York: Apollo Records, 138, 78 RPM.
Bronski, Michael (2003), 'Funny Girls Talk Dirty', *The Boston Phoenix*, 15–21 August, at <http://www.bostonphoenix.com> (accessed 20 September 2005).
Burton, Sarah (2018) 'Writing Yourself In? The Price of Playing the (Feminist) Game in the Neoliberal University', in Yvette Taylor and Kinneret Lahad (eds), *Feeling Academic in the Neoliberal University: Feminist Flights, Fights and Failures*, London: Palgrave Macmillan.
Connor, Steven (2000), *Dumbstruck: A Cultural History of Ventriloquism*, Oxford: Oxford University Press.
De Simone, Maria (2019), 'Sophie Tucker, Racial Hybridity and Interracial Relations in American Vaudeville', *Theatre Research International*, 44:2, 153–170.
Dean, Mitchell (2014), 'Michel Foucault's "apology" for neoliberalism', *Journal of Political Power*, 7:3, 433–42.
Dean, Mitchell and Daniel Zamora (2018), 'Did Foucault Reinvent His History of Sexuality Through the Prism of Neoliberalism?', *Los Angeles Review of Books*, 18 April, <https://lareviewofbooks.org/article/did-foucault-reinvent-his-history-of-sexuality-through-the-prism-of-neoliberalism> (accessed 1 May 2018).
Del Negro, Giovanna P. (2010), 'From the nightclub to the living room: gender, ethnicity, and upward mobility in the 1950s party records of three Jewish women comics', in Simon J. Bronner (ed.), *Jews at Home: The Domestication of Identity*, Oxford: Littman Library of Jewish Civilization.
Garber, Marjorie (1999), *Symptoms of Culture*, London: Penguin.
Gilman, Sander (1991), *The Jew's Body*, New York and London: Routledge.
Hann, Rachel (2015), 'Practice Matters: Arguments for a "Second Wave" of Practice Research', <https://futurepracticeresearch.org/2015/07/28/practice-matters-arguments-for-a-second-wave-of-practice-research/> (accessed 4 November 2016).
Melrose, Susan (2007), 'Introduction', at <https://www.sfmelrose.org.uk/> (accessed 1 December 2018).
Mock, Roberta (2007), *Jewish Women on Stage, Film, and Television*, New York and Basingstoke: Palgrave Macmillan.
Mock, Roberta (2017), 'Preface: Being T/here', in Luisa Greenfield, Myna Trustram and Eduardo Abrantes (eds), *Artistic Research: Being There, Explorations into the Local*, Copenhagen: NSU Press.
Spatz, Ben (2015), *What a Body Can Do: Technique as Knowledge, Practice as Research*, London and New York: Routledge.
Taylor, Diana (2003), *The Archive and the Repertoire: Performing Cultural Memory in the Americas*, Durham, NC and London: Duke University Press.
Thomaidis, Konstantinos (2019), 'The Always-Not-Yet/Always-Already of Voice Perception: Training towards vocal presence', in Mark Evans, Konstantinos Thomaidis and Libby Worth (eds), *Time and Performer Training*, London: Routledge.
Welton, Martin (2003), 'Against inclusivity: A happy heresy about theory and practice (Challenging some of the new orthodoxies of theatre studies)', *New Theatre Quarterly*, 19:76, 347–51.
Williams, Pearl (1962), *A Trip Around the World Is Not a Cruise*, Los Angeles: After Hours Records. LP (LAH-70).

16. FEMINIST 'PENSIVE-CREATIVE PRAXIS' AND IRIGARAY: A POROUS, DIALOGICAL ENCOUNTER

Judith Rifeser

In this chapter, I draw on my own feminist audiovisual essay film practice to showcase the importance of practice for theory. I propose a novel reading of Luce Irigaray's philosophy of the caress and in particular her notion of the space in-between that shares concerns with film-philosophical theories and debates around creative practice research. Jennifer M. Barker's (2009) film-phenomenological work on porosity is particularly useful in this context. My central contention is that the metaphor of the 'pores' can serve as a catalyst to explore the embodied creative research process as an object of study and the role as researcher/ practitioner in this process. Said differently and for the purpose of this chapter, porosity allows me to consider three key ideas: permeability, imperfections and the potential that can arise from creative practice research – moving beyond traditional patriarchal scholarship towards what I term 'feminist pensive-creative praxis'. I argue for an embodied methodology, drawing on Laura Mulvey's (2006) work as well as making use of Robin Nelson's (2013) understanding of 'praxis' as 'theory imbricated within practice', to suggest that this approach foregrounds the dialogical and creative interplay of the porous, dialogical encounter, as well as its political intent.

Pores and their 'Clogging'

Pores are small openings in the skin that allow for sweat or oil to come to the surface, but they do not have muscles, so they cannot actively open or close.

For Jennifer M. Barker (2009), pores manifest the notion of permeability, acting as a gateway to the very inside of the body, as well as the idea of the border of self and other. Above all, pores remind us of touch that is not just felt here or there but also in the spaces in-between. She notes: '[T]ouch is not just skin-deep but is experienced at the body's surface, in its depths, and everywhere in between ... to a state of "total immersion"' (Barker 2009: 2). This conceptualisation of touch that permeates the pores of the skin and which is felt both outside as well as deep inside the body is key for this chapter to foreground my understanding of creative practice research as a deeply bodily, sensual and sense-evoking experience. Parallels can be established between Barker's work and Luce Irigaray's philosophy of the caress (henceforth the Irigarayan caress) that have to date been overlooked for film-phenomenological research and creative research practice. Irigaray's establishment of the space in-between allows the conceptualisation of the pores as gateways between the inside and outside of our body, buttressing the entanglement of the body for creative practice research. The application of Irigaray's work to creative practice requires broaching a new territory (Rifeser 2017), which I propose here as feminist 'pensive-creative praxis'. My own creative practice project was born out of the curiosity to grasp the Irigarayan concept of the caress and, related to this, Irigaray's notion of 'I love to you', and to explore these concepts in my own embodied audiovisual practice research. The piece I discuss here was my first ever practice piece: a three-minute long stop-motion animation short entitled *A Letter of Love to You* (UK, 2016) that premiered at the London Feminist Film Festival 2016 and was subsequently showcased at a number of other events across the UK.

The central question of this chapter, then, is to what extent one can map out the connections between theoretical accounts on touch and the caress with one's own experience as researcher/practitioner in the creative practice process. This project enriches film-philosophical debates and their interrogation into creative research practices furthermore, by showing how Irigaray's work – which has, to date, been overlooked – might add something fruitful to the debate. I argue for the value of reading film-philosophical ideas alongside contemporary outlooks into creative research practice and my own practice, to imagine an in-between space for a porous, dialogical encounter. Prior to this endeavour is the understanding of the importance of considering creative practice on a par with theory. A crucial question that arises then is: How does creative practice research offer a valuable contribution to scholarship by contributing to knowledge and ultimately a betterment of our world? By reflecting on my own practice, this chapter seeks to explore the value of creative practice research for theory, and the importance of the researcher/practitioner in this process, via the metaphor of the 'pores'.

Pores are openings in the skin that allow for a gateway between the outer layers of the skin and the visceral parts of the body thanks to the surfacing of fluids of oil and sweat. What is perceived often as a negative part of human bodily activity, is, however, an important process to maintain a healthy body. When this process is disturbed, it might show in the form of a clogged pore that in turn allows for bacteria to cause inflammation, resulting in what is more commonly known as a pimple or spot, or in an in-grown hair, or it might not show at all and just be felt underneath the skin. First, the clogged pore reminds us of the imperfection of our skin, our body and, by extension, as researchers of the imperfection of the research process. Imperfections draw our attention to the need for cleanliness. The emphasis on 'hygiene' in the research process has been a point of critique of traditional scholarship by creative practice researchers (Haseman and Mafe 2010), who recognise the relevance of the imperfections and the learning that can emerge from them, as I shall explore later on in this chapter. My findings resonate with the broader aim of this anthology by foregrounding the need for film studies to engage with the importance of practice for theory and the embodied presence of the researcher/practitioner entangled in this process. Moreover, the imagery of the 'clogged pore' serves as a metaphor for 'feminist film praxis' by calling out the affront or disfiguration of patriarchy and its scholarship. In other words, the 'clogging' brings fore through the irritated skin the need to challenge the status quo of patriarchal scholarship and the need to consider other modes, methods and methodologies. Before turning towards my creative practice, it is necessary to briefly consider how this project sits within the wider field of my research. I therefore begin by considering the Irigarayan caress and how it might yield something useful for creative research practice.

The Gateway via the Irigarayan Caress

The Irigarayan caress shares concerns with contemporary film-phenomenological research that is interested in the bodily, sensual and sense-evoking aspects of the cinematic experience and embodied spectatorship even though most studies draw predominantly on the work of Maurice Merleau-Ponty (Cooper 2013; Lindner 2012; Barker 2009; Sobchack 2004, 1992), Gilles Deleuze (Rizzo 2012; del Rio 2008; Marks 2000, 2002; Shaviro 1993), and more recently Jean-Luc Nancy (McMahon 2012). While there are works that propose the usefulness of Irigaray's thought for film phenomenology (Bolton 2015; Lehtinen 2014; Quinlivan 2012; Vasseleu 2002), much of this never moves beyond textual and philosophical engagement with her ideas, some of which is also psychoanalytical (Bainbridge 2008). The usefulness of the Irigarayan caress for creative practice research has to date been overlooked, and this chapter suggests that by paying attention to themes of embodiment and porosity in Irigaray's writings, new perspectives on feminist film praxis can be developed.

Formally, Irigaray's notion of the caress allows us to build a bridge between the focus on touch in phenomenological film scholarship as embodied (Sobchack 2004; 1992), visceral (Barker 2009), textured (Fife Donaldson 2014), or grounded in closeness (Marks 2002; 2000) or distance (McMahon 2012), and Irigarayan film feminist scholarship that mobilises psychoanalytical (Bainbridge 2008) and film-phenomenological tropes (Bolton 2015; Quinlivan 2012).

The Irigarayan caress is perhaps best understood through what it is not. In Irigaray's philosophy, the meeting with the other in the desire-fuelled caress is not a merging with the other. As Irigaray highlights that '"[t]he touch of the caress" is a gesture that embraces but at the same time maintains the sense of oneself' (Irigaray 1993: 186). The precondition and condition of this peaceful and respectful meeting rests upon the necessity for maintaining this sense of self (Irigaray 1993; 2000). Furthermore, '[i]n this double desire, "you" and "I" always remain active and passive, perceiving and experiencing, awake and welcoming' (Irigaray 2000: 29). In other words, Irigaray's philosophy of the caress is unique in revealing the value of paying attention to *both* presence and absence, closeness, *as well as* distance; touch *and* its absence, activity *and* passivity, self-affection *and* respect and love for the other in difference, the singular I *and* the multiple. Crucial for the conceptualisation of the Irigarayan caress is the space-in between in which the respectful meeting with the other can take place; that is, an imagined space where the subjectivity of each individual is respected. This, as I argue below, invites reflection on the role of porosity as described above. As I explore later on, the entanglement of the practice of making film with the body of the researcher/practitioner is key to this process. Before turning to this, I shall briefly introduce my own creative practice research.

ATTEMPTING/PRACTISING THROUGH PRACTICE: *A LETTER OF LOVE TO YOU* (UK, 2016)

In this chapter, I want to discuss a piece of experimental work that forms part of my creative research practice, and more specifically, my use of stop-motion animation. In *A Letter of Love to You*, I filmed small, white, square pieces of paper on a floor, evoking the idea of the pieces coming into dialogue with each other to discuss the words: 'I love you' through the influence of Irigaray's conceptualisation of the phrase 'I love to you' (Irigaray 1993; 1996). Essential here, for Irigaray, is the insistence on the 'to' for seeking to make the loved one not an object but rather as an independent subject.

My stop-motion piece starts with a single square on the floor with the word 'I'. The paper moves slowly into the frame in a staccato-motion, purposely not completely giving into the illusion of movement but rather rightly playing with

Figure 16.1   *A Letter of Love to You* (UK, 2016) (00:00:18)

the idea of stillness and movement. This sensation counteracts the voice-over which engages in a monologue on the notion of love, the usage of the words 'I love' in our everyday life, and the experience of loving someone and trying to make sense of it. The idea to use stop-motion animation did not initially arise from Barker's (2009) theoretical work on touch in relation to stop-motion animation. Instead, this technique arose out of the need to translate the sensual, sense-evoking and deeply moving experience of proclaiming love to someone, into a cinematic experience. To me, stop-motion was sensed as this immediate sensation of contact, of touch both with the content as well as with the medium itself before I could make sense of the practice as object of study. In the process of reflecting upon my practice, elements of Barker's work strongly resonated with my initial experience through creative research practice and helped me make sense and articulate my own experience. 'Stop-motion entices the viewing body with materiality and textures that beg to be touched', Barker (2009: 137) notes, supporting what I had experienced in my practice. Attempting to understand the Irigarayan addition of the 'to', required an initial examination of the usage of the words 'I love'. As I recount in my audiovisual work, I spent a month counting the times in which the words 'I love …' were used around me: 152 times. Central to all the affirmations of love was a longing or desire for touch, the evocation of a sensation or experience.

According to Barker (2009), more than any other type of film, stop-motion evokes desire. Stop-motion 'addresses itself first and foremost to the fingertips, provoking our desire to touch, caress, squeeze, and scrape the image before us'

(Barker 2009: 137). Similarly, Irigaray (1993) notes that desire is also essential for the caress as the meeting between two is born out of (sexual) desire. A sense of intimacy is established that 'invites our fascination with the border between movement and stillness, in a way that evokes sexual desire' (Barker 2009: 144). Barker's argument here allows us to draw a parallel to the Irigarayan caress as the latter is driven by sexual desire and continuously negotiates movement/stillness. Breathing offers an initial sensation of the Irigarayan caress, by foregrounding the spaces of inner and outer (Quinlivan 2012). Drew Leder refers to this notion of 'absorption' and feeling 'in-spired' in the cinematic experience. He notes: 'I feel in-spired, 'breathed-in' ... The boundaries between inner and outer thus become porous' (Leder 1990 as cited in Barker 2009: 147). The cinematic experience can offer unique moments of becoming deeply absorbed (Barker 2009: 147) and creative practice research can offer a heightened sensation of this process. An aspect that needs to be considered then in the course of this chapter is then not only one's role as researcher/practitioner but also the how the creative practice research process affects us. In the process of creating my stop-motion animation piece I felt 'in-spired', absorbed in the process of touching and the sensation of feeling touched, deeply engaged in this porous dialogical encounter both as practitioner and researcher.

The embodied creative practice of making this stop-motion animation piece was an attempt to grapple with the Irigarayan philosophical concept audio-visually, recalling the term 'practitioner'. The term 'practitioner', often used to refer to someone engaged in practice research, echoes the idea of 'practising' which implies the incompleteness of not having yet acquired a specific skill and the continuous effort to 'attempt' a given task in order to learn or to achieve a given aim. It is worth noting here just briefly that the essay film format in which my wider creative practice is presented shares a similar concern in that the term 'essay' from the Old French 'essayer', meaning weighing up or trialling (Alter 2007: 45), is a synonym for attempting. Rather, I want to suggest that creative practice research, like the essay film and non-cinema is porous as well as 'ethical because it acknowledges its imperfections' as well as its 'essayistic' quality' (Brown 2018: 3). As I will show in the course of this chapter, the recognition of the imperfections or what I refer to as a 'clogged pore' are just as important as the gateway that creative practice research provides for bridging the gap between theory and practice. We shall consider the embodied work of the researcher/practitioner imminently. However, before we do so, it is first necessary to consider the relationship between theory and practice as well as the term used in the title of this chapter, namely 'praxis' and its relation to creative practice.

The Gateway between Practice and Theory

The term 'praxis' should be understood as 'theory imbricated within practice' (Nelson 2013: 5). As I argued elsewhere (Rifeser 2017), this definition is useful as it challenges the commonplace Western tendencies to separate out theory and practice, as observed in film phenomenological research on the distinction between writing about film and making film, leading to a 'gap that exists between our actual *experience* of the cinema and the *theory* that we academic film scholars construct to explain it' (Sobchack 2004: 53). Drawing on Karen Barad's (2007) idea of 'entanglement', the term 'praxis' asserts the deep imbrication of theory and practice, instead of seeing practice or theory as an 'add-on'. The concept of 'entanglement' acknowledges that we are humans in this world and that, just as we influence the world, so it also influences us (Brown 2018: 2–3). Building on this, what I propose is that using the term 'praxis' serves like pores as a gateway towards another space, a space in-between that opens up a dialogical space for new research practices, echoing Irigarayan ideas about the function of the caress in the meeting with the other. What happens, though, when this gateway is disturbed by a clogged pore?

Disturbances to the Whole: Broaching a New Field of Research

The bridging of theory and practice unsettles many of the conventional strategies and procedures that remain deeply embedded in our traditional research structures (Haseman and Mafe 2010; Nelson 2013), an aspect I hinted at earlier in mentioning the clogged pore and the need for cleanliness. In relation to thinking about creative practice research as a body and about the process for the researcher/practitioner as an embodied experience, notions of cleanliness in relation to the body and the process of 'appearing clean' are required (Haseman and Mafe 2010). The imperfections or disturbances that arise in the research process are applicable to any discipline. However, in creative research, the process is further complicated by the reality of professional protocols and regulations that urge the practitioner to set out a research question from the outset without taking due account that the actual creative practice research process might reveal unanticipated research questions and therefore shape the research in unexpected ways. Furthermore, there is often a need to 'guarantee a methodological "hygiene"', often before the research is undertaken, without taking into due consideration the non-linearity, 'messiness and dynamism of the process of inquiry' (Haseman and Mafe 2010: 212).

The nature of creative practice research is permeable in that it aims to create a dialogical space that allows for a meeting between two: practice and theory. The process of making *A Letter of Love to You* affected not only the direction my research took but also mobilised my need to consider myself as feminist researcher/practitioner, and the tacit knowledge (Nelson, 2013) residing inside me. In other words, I needed to consider my role as researcher/practitioner, that is my body, a body that touches, senses, perceives, feels that is deeply entangled in the creative research process and which in turn resonates with feminist methods and methodologies (Ramazanoğlu and Holland 2002; Lykke 2010). The emphasis on the embodied experience of the creative research process supports also, particularly relevant for this chapter, Irigaray's call for an embodied methodology as a 'a way to disrupt the phallogocentrism of existing language' (Lykke, 2010: 102–3). The Irigarayan caress shifts from an ocularcentric and logocentric investigation to a focus on that body that touches, senses, perceives and feels. That body, which for Irigaray is particularly a feminine body, wants to be considered in its entirety as a 'whole', rather than as a 'hole', in order to 'speak for the singularity of each woman in her multiplicity' (Bolton 2015: 45). It is crucial to consider the notion of the 'whole' to buttress the entanglement between theory and practice. Each of these conceptual frames provides a useful grounding for understanding the scholarly power of creative practice as a form of research, and especially as a form of research practice that is inscribed in the feminine. Is it important for creative practice research to be acknowledged in the 'Western intellectual tradition ... [not] as the negative "other" of privileged theory' (Nelson 2013: 22; also see Nelson 2006). The continuous drive to perceive the 'whole' speaks to the continued effort of creative research practices to confront the complexities of methodologies and methods that challenge the existing canon and to seek out epistemological innovations in the West and beyond.

A Third Strand: Starting from Practice

Creative practice research can create a place for disruption that can be appropriated to transgress borders (Biemann 2017: 262). Pushing this idea a step further, in order for creative practice research to be conceived as an independent whole and thus not an 'add on' of theory, we have to consider the notion of crossing borders beyond the imperfection of a clogged pore, beyond the instilled cleanliness of traditional research regulations, in order to perceive the (Irigarayan) in-between, that is the space in which a fruitful dialogue between theory and practice can emerge. Creative practice research might then 'be perceived as a third type of research that ... is in fact a very different strand' (Haseman 2010: 150). For as practice arises 'from the need of practice [itself] and practitioners' (Gray 1996 as cited in Haseman and Mafe 2010: 213), so does the starting point of research shift to being within the realm of practice, as opposed to being a theoretical problem. The process is then turned upside down in that, starting from embodied practice, 'the practice becomes theory generating' (Bolt 2010: 33; Scott 2016), rather than theory generating or explaining the practice. This has important consequences for understanding the broader relationship between research as a form of practice and its engagement with theoretical and conceptual ideas and raises questions about the role of the researcher/practitioner. Let us now turn to a question I signalled earlier, namely: How does the creative research process affect the researcher/practitioner?

Imperfections that Move the Researcher/Practitioner

Studies in creative practice coincide in that '[t]he nature of such research is that it shifts, and in doing so it moves the researcher with it' (Scott 2016: 21; also see Nelson 2013; Haseman 2010). In other words, encountering practice as a researcher/practitioner is a fluid process located between doing, thinking and reflecting, and the researcher is part of this ever-moving process that recalls the Irigarayan space of the in-between. The deeply embodied experience of the researcher/practitioner incorporates '*all* the activity an artist/creative practitioner undertakes. Researcher/practitioners think, read and write as well as look, listen and make' (Haseman and Mafe 2010: 214).

As in the Irigarayan meeting amongst two people, in order to enter into dialogue, one must embrace the opportunity to move outside one's own borders. Simultaneously, it also means living with seemingly contradictory impulses. The imagery of the Irigarayan caress offers a means of continuously negotiating the space in-between. If, as observed before, we consider film as a body (Sobchack 1992), I contend that, in the creative practice process, the body of the researcher/practitioner is continuously moving in dialogue with the body of the creative practice research, creating a creative form of Irigarayan caressing engagement that brings life to the in-between space of the praxis. In other words, in the sphere of praxis, the relation of theory to practice is also continuously negotiated in an attempt to find a space in-between where they can meet, conjuring up again the space in-between of the Irigarayan caress. How can the researcher/practitioner use the creative practice and the knowledge that emerges from the process to inform or indeed generate theory?

As discussed above, the metaphor of the clogged pore evokes messiness, a tension that challenges the status quo which is useful for feminist research practices. Emphasis is placed on reflexivity as a key strategy in the creative practice process (Scott 2016; Nelson 2013; Haseman and Mafe 2010) which is also a method often adopted within a feminist framework (Ramazanoğlu and Holland 2002; Lykke 2010). Similarly, debates about creative practice research in film studies often tap into debates about reflexivity, which is often understood as the personal, singular enunciator directly linked to the author (Rascaroli 2009). In creative practice research, the researcher/practitioner is engaged in the reflexive process with the aim to organise and articulate the findings of the research as author in a clear and coherent way. Of course, the tension and complexity is not unique to creative practice research. However, in creative practice research, there are multiplicitous forces to be negotiated, such as the connections and tensions between practice/theory, the range of methodologies and methods employed in the process, the position of the researcher/practitioner, and, finally, the articulation and presentation of the findings and the negotiation of the spaces and formats in which this is to happen (Haseman and Mafe 2010: 218). The process of reaching the final step is porous and, I suggest, full of creative potential perhaps precisely because of being non-linear and messy and constantly moving.

Feminist film theorist and practitioner Laura Mulvey (2006) highlights that technology now allows us to still the moving image, highlighting its 'aesthetics and the illusion of movement' (Mulvey 2006: 185). Referencing her essayistic audiovisual practice engaging with the extended shot of Laura Turner at the start of *Imitation of Life* (Douglas Sirk, USA, 1959), Mulvey describes this experience as bringing forth a 'sense of wonder' that moves her, causing an e-motive responsive in this 'extended pause on a still frame' (Mulvey 2006: 184). Using stop-motion as a creative research output intensifies the feeling of frustration by foregrounding not only movement but the illusion of such movement that is really stillness made to feel like movement. In a sense then, 'stop-motion animation indulges both our passionate tenderness and morbid, destructive curiosity about the nature of the machine, both cinematic and human' (Barker 2009: 144). It offers us a porous dialogical encounter by offering a gateway to think not only about the film but about the cinematic apparatus, and that which it usually hides, hence revealing its imperfections.

Debates about creative practice research evoke the metaphor of the pore by often tapping into the thematic of imperfections and its integral role in shaping the lived experience of creative practice research. In particular, the term 'refractiveness' borrowed from film theory (Mullarkey 2009; Corrigan 2011) resounds in the emphasis placed on the relationship between making and unmaking, between failure and abjection, evoking again the term 'essaying' or 'attempting'. Such ideas are helpful in considering the non-linear, messy processes involved in the kind of creative practice used to produce an essay film, where imperfections often play a dominant role. As I suggested earlier, creative practice is constantly moving and moving the researcher/practitioner in the process. Whilst this process provides a gateway to various possibilities, the continuous movement also creates anxiety and frustration (Haseman and Mafe 2010) due to its instability and unpredictability for the researcher/practitioner in today's capitalist environment.

For Irigaray, in order for the meeting between two to happen, a space in-between for dialogue must be established. She emphasises the importance of stillness in the process: this is crucial for being with oneself and for listening to the other, allowing a space for questions to arise for a fruitful dialogue. The need for stillness then offers a respite from the messiness and frustration of the process that, in my own experience, has been a crucial element to develop my own practice further and to generate new connections to theory. The Irigarayan in-between space here offers a reassuring form of containment by providing space for movement and stillness, allowing for the creative practice research to unfold despite the refractive experience that could be framed as failure.

Film studies has long debated the relation between stillness and movement. If, after Sobchack (1992), we perceive cinema as a body that expresses itself back to us, and if cinema gives to us the illusion of movement as discussed previously through the work of Mulvey, then the format of stop-motion animation, as used in my practice, is 'the illusion of the illusion' and is thus 'a metaphor for cinema itself' (Barker 2009: 136). Perhaps then, stop-motion animation resembles, in this way, non-cinema, creating a point 'where aesthetics meets politics … where we examine the ideology of cinema as a form' by examining what cinema might 'exclude or occult' (Brown 2018: 2). Stop-motion animation entices the viewer to reflect upon the illusion of movement and the stillness that the moving image tries to occlude. Stop-motion then reveals an imperfection. But simultaneously, it also evokes the notion of play and a sense of curiosity about the cinematic apparatus, offering a way to engage overtly with what is usually hidden through editing techniques. Stop-motion animation then engages the viewer in critical reflection, an aspect that is key to the creative research process. Movement and stillness in the creative research process evoke, as previously argued, on the one hand the sensation of feeling 'in-spired' by the creative practice process, and, on the other hand, the importance of stillness to reflect upon oneself as researcher/practitioner, as well as the creative research and the creative research process as object of study itself. Thinking about the process, as Nelson highlights, 'demands a rigorous and iterative process' (Nelson 2013: 44). Raymond Bellour's (1987, 2012) thinking on what he calls the 'pensive' spectator proves useful in this context, in particular for moving image creative practice.

According to Bellour, the photograph is the most visible and memorable means by which the spectator can be pulled out of the cinematic experience. It is through experiencing the photograph or what he terms the 'photogram', namely the moment in which a moving image is stilled, 'that makes the spectator of cinema, this hurried spectator, a pensive one as well' (Bellour 1987: 10). It is a spectator that is halted, pulled out of the narrative, the continuous movement of the visuals to think, to reflect upon the image. Moreover, the 'pensive spectator' is thus able not only to reflect upon the stilled image but more broadly on 'the nature of cinema itself' and this opportunity to reflect upon the cinematic experience is not lost even once the film returns to movement (Mulvey 2006: 186). She further asserts that it is both a 'literal delay' of 'repetition and return', showcasing the 'relation between movement and stillness as a point at which cinema's variable temporality becomes visible' (Mulvey 2006: 182). This is crucial, given the 'difficulty of articulating the cinema's varied relation to time, the sense of being beyond verbal language' (Mulvey 2006: 182). These considerations draw attention to the difficulty of articulating through language and by extension through writing the creative research and its process(es). What Nelson (2013: 36) terms 'complementary writing', that is, writing that is not a 'translation' of the practice into words but rather supports the research by showcasing the investigative process that took place, provides the opportunity to share the creative research process not only with like-minded practitioners in a specific field. Instead, the complementary writing accompanies the creative research by explicating its context(s) and by buttressing the contribution to scholarship of the work, supporting the sharing of the new knowledge acquired with the wider community (Nelson 2013). The term 'pensive', then, is useful as it allows a bridging of the 'reflexive' and the 'refractive' by acknowledging both the position of the researcher/practitioner and their continuous, porous entanglement with their body of work in practice and theory.

By acknowledging the entanglement of theory and practice, this praxis also turns towards the borders, limitations and imperfections of ourselves, cinema, practice research, and our world. It is a pensive research/practitioner who recognises the porosity and thus the gateway as well as the messiness and imperfections of the process, the struggle between movement and stillness, between one's own creative research and creative research practices more generally. The embodied experience of the research process returns us to the inherent perseverance to explore that which is hidden, to attempt, to practise – to 'essay'. It is here that a 'pensive-creative praxis' comes to life: it is a practice and theory that 'is not constrained to the abstract and propositional but embraces embodied passions' (Nelson 2013: 82). This ignites again the concept of a deeply embodied, porous encounter that evokes the Irigarayan caress and provides a space in-between that embraces the gateway, the imperfections and the opportunities that arise from within. The Irigarayan caress is driven by desire and I contend that likewise creative practice research is driven by desire. Like the spectator in film, the researcher/practitioner is driven by a desire to understand, to perceive, to know. The practitioner scholar is engaged in navigating a permeable space, that is, a constant negotiation between practice and theory that might start with practice, rather than taking theory as a starting point for the research enquiry. Earlier I noted the etymological root of the term 'practitioner' that denotes the idea of 'attempting'. The term 'creative', in turn, stems from the Latin '*creatus*', meaning to 'create, to bring forth', conjuring up the creative practice process of 'doing-thinking' (Nelson 2013: 29), that seeks to move from doing to thinking, 'from action to thought' (Ryle 1986 as cited in Nelson 2013: 62), from practice to theory. To acknowledge the role of the practitioner/researcher and the 'clogged pores' within the research process, and to embrace and engage with potential contradictions, messiness and disparate elements, offers the potential for creative practice research to have a profound impact on our knowledge and our ever-moving and shifting globalised world.

Feminist 'Pensive-creative Praxis' in Action

As discussed above, stop-motion animation entices the viewer to reflect upon the illusion of movement and the stillness that the moving image tries to occlude. Stop-motion then reveals an imperfection. But simultaneously, it also evokes a sense of curiosity about the cinematic apparatus, offering a way to engage overtly with what is usually hidden through editing techniques. Stop-motion, then, offers a space for 'pensive-creative praxis' that becomes praxis for me not only through the merging of theory but also due to its political intent. It is here that I experienced a moment in which something emerged out of the practice that I later came to understand as a political gesture.

In my short film, and in engaging with the proclamation of love, I found it necessary to engage with the voice as it is often the main tool used to confess love for someone. Of course, in film studies, the voice and its relation to the visual have been the subject of much debate, most prominently perhaps within the realm of psychoanalytic theory (Chion 1999; Dolar 1996). Inspired in particular by feminist theorisations of the voice and the voice-over in relation to Irigaray's work (Silverman 1988), and the potential of the disembodied woman's voice (Doane, 1980), I sought to explore these ideas in my practice. I did not want to use only my own voice but rather to evoke the sense of a multiplicity and to emphasise – even within my humble means – the fact that love is a concern of human beings, independent of gender, race, ethnicity, age, religion or class. In my voice-over, I modified the pitch and speed of my own voice to evoke a voice that would purposely not be easily categorised as 'feminine' or 'masculine'. In my attempt to audiovisually explore the Irigarayan understanding of love, and to simultaneously record the creative practice process, I reflected again on the Irigarayan caress. In this porous space, between practice and theory, the notion of the 'clogged' pore arose again. As I returned to Irigaray's work, I came to understand how my practice had become theory-generating in that it exemplified to me the complexity of and contradiction embedded within Irigaray's theory of the caress for the lived experience of embodied subjectivity. Irigaray's philosophical concept of the caress remains within the dualistic heterosexual woman/man paradigm, an element she later confirmed in the Irigaray seminar 2017, and an element which is critiqued in research on Irigaray's work more broadly in relation to race, gender and intersectionality (Ingram 2008; Bloodsworth-Lugo 2007). My exploration of the Irigarayan caress through research practice took on an important gender-political stance. Indeed, my broader project was shaped by what my creative research practice revealed: namely, the need to engage with these contradictory elements rightly in order to move beyond this limiting theoretical framework for my practice and into a space of embodied, feminist, intersectional praxis.

I understand feminist 'pensive-creative' praxis as a space to seek out in order to challenge and subvert traditional patriarchal scholarship. Feminist 'pensive-creative praxis', as argued in this chapter, offers a framework to foreground its political potential where existing perceptions are interrogated, borders are collapsed and new connections as well as new ideas are formed. Forging links between theory and creative practice research is central to these endeavours, propelling the political intent engrained in the notion of praxis. The embodied experience of the researcher/practitioner is central to this creative research process. This opens a space in-between where practice and theory meet and where the embodied experience of the researcher/practitioner is recognised, buttressing the importance of embodied creative practice research that, like a pore, is permeable, imperfect because at times clogged, and offering great potential.

Note

This research was undertaken with the financial support of the University of Roehampton Vice-Chancellor Award; additional funding was awarded by the Dean of Southlands College and the Dean of Digby Stuart College, University of Roehampton to attend the Irigaray seminar 2017.

References

Alter, N. (2007), 'Translating the essay into film and installation', *Journal of Visual Culture*, 6:1, 44–57.
Bainbridge, C. (2008), *A Feminine Cinematics: Luce Irigaray, Women and Film*, Basingstoke: Palgrave Macmillan.
Barad, K. (2007), *Meeting the Universe Halfway: Quantum Physics and the Entanglement of Matter and Meaning*, Durham, NC: Duke University Press.
Barker, J. M. (2009), *The Tactile Eye: Touch and the Cinematic Experience*, Berkeley: University of California Press.
Bellour, R. (1987), 'The Pensive Spectator', *Wide Angle*, 9:1, 6–10.
Bellour, R. (2012), *Between-the-Images*, Zurich: JRP/Ringier.
Biemann, U. (2017), 'Performing Borders: Transnational Video', in N. M. Alter and T. Corrigan (eds), *Essays on the Essay Film*, New York and Chichester: Columbia University Press, pp. 261–8.
Bloodsworth-Lugo, M. K. (2007), *In-Between Bodies: Sexual Difference, Race, and Sexuality*, Albany: SUNY Press.
Bolt, B. (2010 [2007]), 'The Magic is in Handling', in E. Barrett and B. Bolt (eds),

Practice as Research: Approaches to Creative Arts Enquiry, London and New York: I. B. Tauris, pp. 27–34.

Bolton, L. (2015 [2011]), *Film and Female Consciousness: Irigaray, Cinema and Thinking Women*, Basingstoke: Palgrave Macmillan.

Brown, W. (2018), *Non-Cinema: Global Digital Filmmaking and the Multitude*, New York: Bloomsbury.

Chion, M. (1999 [1982]), *The Voice in Cinema [La Voix au cinéma]*, trans. Claudia Gorbman, New York: Columbia University Press.

Cooper, S. (2013), *The Soul of Film Theory*, London: Palgrave.

Corrigan, T. (2011), *The Essay Film: From Montaigne, After Marker*, Oxford: Oxford University Press.

Del Rio, E. (2008), *Deleuze and the Cinemas of Performance: Powers of Affection*, Edinburgh: Edinburgh University Press.

Doane, M. A. (1980), 'The Voice in the Cinema: The Articulation of Body and Space', in *Yale French Studies, No. 60, Cinema/Sound, pp. 33–50*.

Dolar, M. (1996), 'The Object Voice', in R. Salecl and S. Žižek (eds), *Gaze and Voice as Love Objects*, Durham, NC and London: Duke University Press, pp. 7–31.

Fife Donaldson, L. (2014), *Texture in Film*, Basingstoke: Palgrave Macmillan.

Haseman, B. (2010 [2007]), 'Rupture and Recognition: Identifying the Performative Research Paradigm', in E. Barrett and B. Bolt (eds), *Practice as Research: Approaches to Creative Arts Enquiry*, London and New York: I. B. Tauris, pp. 147–58.

Haseman, B. and D. Mafe (2010 [2009]), 'Acquiring Know-How: Research training for Practice-led Researchers', in H. Smith and R. Dean (eds), *Practice-led Research, Research-led Practice in the Creative Arts*, Edinburgh: Edinburgh University Press, pp. 211–28.

Ingram, P. (2008), *The Signifying Body: Toward an Ethics of Sexual and Racial Difference*, Albany: SUNY Press.

Irigaray, L. (1993), *An Ethics of Sexual Difference*, London: Athlone Press.

Irigaray, L. (1996), *I Love to You. Sketch of a Possible Felicity in History*, trans. A. Martin, New York: Routledge.

Irigaray, L. (2000), *To Be Two*, London: Athlone.

Lehtinen, V. (2014), *Luce Irigaray's Phenomenology of Feminine Being*, Albany: SUNY Press.

Lindner, K. (2012), 'Situated bodies, cinematic orientations: Film and (queer) phenomenology', in S. Ba and W. Higbee (eds), *De-Westernizing Film*, London: Routledge, pp. 152–65.

Lykke, N. (2010), *Feminist Studies: A Guide to Intersectional Theory, Methodology and Writing*, New York and London: Routledge.

Marks, L. U. (2000), *The Skin of the Film: Intercultural Cinema, Embodiment, and the Senses*, Durham, NC: Duke University Press.

Marks, L. U. (2002), *Touch: Sensuous Theory and Multisensory Media*, Minneapolis: University of Minnesota Press.

McMahon, L. (2012), *Cinema and Contact: The Withdrawal of Touch in Nancy, Bresson, Duras and Denis*, Oxford: Legenda.

Mullarkey, J. (2009), *Refractions of Reality: Philosophy and the Moving Image*, New York: Palgrave Macmillan.

Mulvey, L. (2006), *Death 24x a Second: Stillness and the Moving Image*, London: Reaktion Books Ltd.

Nelson, R. (2006), 'Practice as Research and the Problem of Knowledge', *Performance Research*, 11:4, 105–16.

Nelson, R. (2013), *Practice as Research in the Arts: Principles, Protocols, Pedagogies, Resistances*, Basingstoke: Palgrave Macmillan.

Quinlivan, D. (2012), *The Place of Breath in Cinema*, Edinburgh: Edinburgh University Press.
Ramazanoğlu, C. and J. Holland (2002), *Feminist Methodology*, London: Sage Publications.
Rascaroli, L. (2009), *The Personal Camera: Subjective Cinema and the Essay Film*, New York: Wallflower Press.
Rifeser, J. (2017), 'Luce Irigaray's Philosophy of the Caress: A New Horizon for a Dialogical Encounter with Practice-as-Research', in *Working with Luce Irigaray*, <https://workingwithluceirigaray.com/previous-seminars/the-seminar-2017/judith-rifeser-luce-irigarays-philosophy-of-the-caress-a-new-horizon-for-a-dialogical-encounter-with-practice-as-research/> (last accessed 23 December 2018).
Rizzo, T. (2012), *Deleuze and Film: A Feminist Introduction*, London and New York: Continuum.
Scott, J. (2016), *Intermedial Praxis and Practice as Research: 'Doing-Thinking' in Practice*, London: Palgrave Macmillan UK.
Shaviro, S. (1993), *The Cinematic Body*, Minneapolis: University of Minnesota Press.
Silverman, K. (1988), *The Acoustic Mirror: The Female Voice in Psychoanalysis and Cinema*, Bloomington: Indiana University Press.
Sobchack, V. C. (1992), *The Address of the Eye: A Phenomenology of Film Experience*, Princeton: Princeton University Press.
Sobchack, V. C. (2004), *Carnal Thoughts: Embodiment and Moving Image Culture*, Berkeley: University of California Press.
Vasseleu, C. (2002), *Textures of Light: Vision and Touch in Irigaray, Levinas, and Merleau-Ponty*, London and New York: Routledge.

17. THE PATHS OF CREATION, OR HOW CAN I HELP MY DYBBOUK TO GET OUT OF ME?

Isabelle Starkier

For a long time, I have been maintaining some sort of schizophrenia, divided between my artistic work, and my research and teaching theatre at University. As long as I can assault theatrical works or literary works to adapt, sometimes translate, and even play when it's possible, but always direct, my artistic gesture has been and will remain for me an art of living. This is the only way I can assume my human condition. I shaped my identity in this artistic gesture: first as a daughter (my father was an architect and my mother an actress in her youth), as a woman, as a Jew, as a citizen, and also – but it took me a long time to realise it – as a university researcher. My artistic creation accompanied me at all times, at all stages of my life, drawing an evolutive path that the research at the University could help me to write down.

Would we say, as Pablo Picasso did in 1926: 'I don't search, I find' (2014) or on the contrary in theatre: 'I don't find, I search'? Nobody can ever say in theatre that he has found; we are always searching. However, creation is not research and of course research is not creation. Research is feeding creation which is feeding research. So we will try to follow the paths of creation, full of sound and fury, of laugh and work, to try to answer the essential question: 'Was the chicken before the egg or the egg before the chicken?'

This is a fundamentally circular question that gives to research and creation, to both of them, an absolutely wonderful status of uselessness in our neoliberal society – to integrate the subject – while this uselessness is really a beginning of hope: the soul supplement that we need in order to live and not only to survive. Let's say that we are the cherry on the cake – as art could be perceived – but the cherry gives its flavour to the cake, gives the real taste of it.

The second point that comes after uselessness is the ability in creative practice research to give objectivity to our totally subjective artistic point of view. Let's ask how research, in the area of creative practice research, might be necessarily autobiographic. This objectification of our artistic subjectivity could be what Paul Claudel calls 'co-naissance': the new 'born with' of the artist, a new birth to the world will show us how to follow the path through creation to reach knowledge.

Theatrical Adaptation of Novels: A Gesture of (Re) writing

What happens between knowledge as know-how and knowledge as practice and research? The first step would be to understand what to catch, what to snatch, what to extract on these paths of creation to make it and transmute it into knowledge. Creation means intuition and research means analysis. In creative practice research, we take the risk of not knowing, following our own intuition. *It* is, or *something* is searching during the process of creation more than we are searching voluntarily – a little bit like during a psychoanalytic cure. We are going to a mysterious end, far away from the limited date of the production submitted to the market law of the market: we follow the path of our project.

And because my own material could only be autobiographic, I will take as an example of my creative practice research the intuition that made me lean on the novel for a theatrical adaptation, or more precisely how to transfer great mythological characters of the novel's repertoire into theatre, into theatrical shapes or scenic writings.

I began with *Scrooge* – from Charles Dickens's *A Christmas Carol*. I wrote an adaptation for one actress and fourteen characters. The costume set (because her gigantic dress was the set in which every puppet and object was hidden) was representative of the Book, from where all the characters of the novel magically appeared as in a dream or a nightmare. The main character wasn't Scrooge but the Book itself. The words were becoming shapes, characters, incarnations. To integrate my explanations and because once more our material in creative practice research is our own plays and directions, I refer to the video.[1] Here, the narration was becoming theatrical in using dialogue between the different parts of the story that were told by the actress. I just kept very few sentences of the tale to get into a playing with the metaphorical incarnation of the characters (the employee is only represented by his muffler and a candle).

The second step of my path was the creation of *Quichotte*. I began once more with the set as an opening Book to create the whole world of the play,

Figure 17.1 *Scrooge*, Scrooge, Charles Dickens, adaptation and direction Isabelle Starkier, with Anne Mauberret-Thunin, Avignon 2006 (Scrooge with the employee and the mask of the niece)

Figure 17.2 *Quichotte*, Cervantes, adaptation and direction Isabelle Starkier, with Eve Castro, Paris 2009 (Quichotte as a puppet which goes out of the actress's costume of Sancho Pança).

but this time the two main characters were Don Quichotte and Sancho Pança as two faces of the same mythological figure. As Franz Kafka said: 'Sancho Panca, who has never boasted about it, succeeds over the years, devouring stories of brigand and novels of chivalry during the nights and evenings, to completely divert his demon entirely from himself. He did so well that he – whom he later called Don Quixote – threw himself now and again into the wildest adventures' (1975, 132; my translation). In contrast to *Scrooge*, there was no more storyteller because it was no longer a tale. Here, we entered into the book but everything was seen through Quichotte's eyes first and Pança's eyes in the second part, except for the Countess, who is the repulsive character that judges Don Quichotte as a foolish and distractive jester, that makes fun of him and seems to be the external look of the reality, of the 'reasonable' materialism.[2]

The third step was my adaptation of *Alice in Wonderland* and *Alice Through the Looking Glass* called *Du côté d'Alice*, in reference to the famous Proustian book *Du côté de chez Swann*.

I tried to manufacture the theatrical writing as the story itself seemed to be manufactured. I wanted the spectator to see how this unbelievable and mysterious, mystical story of Alice was built. It is not a tale, it is like a puzzle. So I did it as if I was inventing the story with two Lewis Carroll – one was writing with the sounds (a musician) and the other with the drawing (a painter). So that I could write directly on stage, in the space with my words – my spatial, flesh words – the signs of Carroll's writing.[3]

Figure 17.3 *Du côté d'Alice*, adaptation and direction Isabelle Starkier, with Angélique Zaïni, Avignon 2012 (Alice and the magic bottle).

The fourth step in my creative practice research was *Un gros grand gras Gargantua*. Here my point of view was different because I wanted to rewrite in a modern area the keys that let us understand these mysterious and metaphoric Rabelais novels, full of symbols and fables (I chose to mix different books such as *Gargantua*, *Pantagruel*, *Le Quart Livre* … around the main character of Gargantua). So I began to take the keys of my own vision as a director: what I saw in the narrative story as the way men eat or think, the way we feed ourselves just to fulfill our emptiness and, on the contrary, how to taste and feel the life nourishing our brain and our body – as humanism can teach

Figure 17.4 *Un gros grand gras Gargantua*, François Rabelais /Pascale Hillion, direction Isabelle Starkier, with Pierre-Yves Le Louarn, Avignon 2015 (Alcofribas reading?)

us. That was, of course, my reading of what gigantism could represent in our imaginations and instead of writing this new story only with the actor's bodies and the space, I decided to mix the original parts I chose with a new (re)writing by a French playwright.[4]

My next step will be a play about a more contemporary character, Mangeclous, extracted from Albert Cohen's novels. The main interest will be to work on a literary character speaking about other literary characters (Anna Karenina) as too literary! A book in a book, a sort of directing the deconstruction of a writing process.

All these theatrical adaptations are working on the 'subground' (between the subconscious and the underground) of the writing process: the invisible part we have to make visible if we want to allow the artistic gesture to appear, this mysterious moment of creation that underlies the final 'product'.

'FULL OF HINTS FOR THE WORKERS IN THEATRE'

If I come back to the link between intuition and analysis, research does not kill creation as all artists fear about. There is a very common fear among artists that visiting a shrink will lead to understanding our process of fantasy, the main background of our creation, which will put a stop to our creative ability. On the contrary, knowledge, and in this case our own knowledge of ourselves, digs the furrow of our creation which stays always mysterious and invisible. Research is drawing this mysterious way of creation to a conscious path – which helps to create and transmit.

Grotowski spoke wonderfully about 'robbed transmission' in a 'robbed film'.[5] And Grotowski tells us that we can't teach or give an artistic personal gesture, but only technical tricks and – more important and more invisible – the way to re-do it, to re-do the visible part of creation becoming at this point research: creative practice research.

Edward Gordon Craig did say the same when he asked his pupils to draw, to take notes as the best mean to *know* how to grab: 'You have only a school now. Let no public see this grim "revival" – lovely here and there – full of hints for workers in theatres – no more'.[6] In my point of view, these 'full of hints for the workers in theatre' are the best definition of creative practice research. Research goes with the creation, step by step. It allows us to know how to re-do what intuition just did.

Research helps us to glimpse what is absolutely invisible in creation. Art is digging the mysterious hole of the world, the matrix hole of human condition, deep as inferno and glowing as paradise.[7] We can't see inside (who could see the hinted face of God?), we can just turn around, hear voices that we can reinterpret, give shapes to these voices so that they could become visible. And as in alchemy where science and mysticism go together to search the philosophical stone, made of material and immaterial, or as in ancient Greek theatre, at the origin of Western theatre, where sacred rituals become the foundations of democracy, research helps us to find the way of turning around the black hole of our own human mythology. It allows us to stay, as a tightrope walker, in a delicate balance between intuition and cleverness, emotion and structure, Dionysus and Apollo.

And before coming back to my own creative practical research, let's assert that it is the best way, in our hopeless neoliberal society, to avoid falling into fascism or fundamentalism which is the religious way *not to know* about mystery but to fall in fear, trying to think (or precisely not to think!) about the incomprehensible world. We want, on the contrary, to know the way to turn, as in antique chorus, around the matrix hole and agree that consciousness and knowledge are part of our creation and of the creation's mystery. We don't fall in the dark deep hole, we are allowed to think about the hole, to imagine it which is yet conceptualisation, to think about its infinite deepness as Pascal did with the infinitely small and the infinitely big. And when Pascal gives as a philosopher an answer – or a non-answer – about God, I personally think that he gives us the answer as a poet, which means: the path of thinking our inability to think is creation, which is what philosophical rationalised thinking can't afford.[8]

So, after a long time, suffering from being between research as a lecturer and creation as an artist, I resolved, as I said at the beginning, this schizophrenic pathology with creative practice research. When I tried to put words to my actions – and acting too – to follow the steps of my intuition, of my emotion like through 'a conscious diary', it was like reversing internal knowledge in external knowledge, transforming an artistic gesture in ideas: an 'Ideas Theatre' as Antoine Vitez called it (1991: 271), putting words in his artistic way, as Peter Brook or many others did. Many of those whom we could call 'Masters' are writing on their creation as it is a part of their creation process.

How Did I Let my Own Dibbouk Get Away?

Could we agree with Valere Novarina telling us that the thought is made, is manufactured in the mouth? I would say yes, as Marcel Proust does, when he offers us a kind of methodology for creative practice research with his 'madeleine'. The sensation comes first in the narrator's mouth eating a madeleine, and intuition arrives to open and let you just follow the path of your knowledge – which is exactly the path of creation. It makes Marcel Proust one of the major artists working as a searcher about his sensations, his intuition. Once more, Apollo builds shapes on the drunkenness of Dionysus: reason gives frame to spontaneous gushing of our artistic intuition.

Creation would be to let the vision emerge (and not only the hearing) of God's voice[9] or, in other words, to dig the mysterious matrix hole of the world, this invisible universe that we make visible in creation. Research would be to interpret, as Nietzsche could speak about: 'The being as being interpreted'. Research will be the interpretation of these interpretations of the world – which is creation. Antoine Vitez, one of the greatest directors in the 1980s, said that 'art has to let us hear what can't be heard, show what can't be showed and tell what we can't tell' (1991: 271). He also said: 'I think that everybody will not understand immediately what is in the play. Doesn't matter. When a tale is sufficiently exemplary, if it is sent in the public with enough violence, it stays in the memories and gives us the ability to *think*, and understand *after*. I send ideas, like punches' (1991: 63–4).

Research helps to create our Dibbouk and gives him the ability to get out of ourselves. I speak about Dibbouk because it is for me the perfect metaphor of theatre and what is acting (possession, exteriorisation …). *The Dibbouk (or Between Two Worlds)*, a play written by Shalom An-Ski in 1917, was the first step in the creation of a Hebrew theatre in Russia when it was directed by Vakhtangov. It is also the starting point for all my academic research on Jewish theatre. I wrote my PhD thesis on the prohibition of making images: what could constitute a theatre with an absolute prohibition on making images?

Figure 17.5 *Kafka's dance*, Timothy Daly, direction Isabelle Starkier, with Anne Le Guernec (Paris 2006) (the fiancée with Kafka's puppet).

That is probably what brought me, consciously and unconsciously, to work in my plays on the grotesque in theatre.

My artistic gesture mixed identity and creation in the grotesque – as we can see how it is manufactured in Yiddish theatre, which so influenced Kafka, and at the same time it allowed me to understand expressionism from an internal point of view. As a director and as an actress, I had to experiment with the difference between caricature and stylisation in expressionism. Expressionism is not over-acting as it could seem to be. It is the body's writing in the space as if the actors' bodies were like letters on the white page of the stage. I had to experiment with the way to drive an actor to essentialise his gesture, to stylise it so as to use his own body as a sign and not as full of sense – as psychology can give to an actor's performance. So working with the actors on what could be expressionism in Yiddish theatre helped me in my knowledge, as a reader at University, to transmit the meanings of expressionism, the operation that gives its aesthetics. This research went from 'Kafka's dance' to 'The man in the attic', two plays written by Timothy Daly, a famous Australian playwright.[10]

My main tracks in this last play were:

- How the grotesque can allow re-playing the 'big' History in a small history, which would be the transposition in a stylised tale of the philosophical features that are underground.
- How to tell History from an internal point of view, which could be metaphorical: full of signs and not giving sense (interpretation).
- How the fable, told through this small world enclosure in the infernal circle between the Neighbour, the Man, the Woman and the Jew, allows us to understand how barbarity happens, locating the step where man falls into inhumanity. So the play was a sort of long-scale going from an historical process to the internal human being.

I did some of the same work during my last creation 'The tango of wandering stars', which is musical theatre about Yiddish tango in relation to the twentieth-century migration of Jewish people from Poland to the United States and Argentina.[11]

This is not only a way to undertake therapy (letting others pay for it!) but once more transforms my own story into a universal tale – which gives us the definition of art.

IN CONCLUSION: HOW TO OPEN THE DOOR ...

In conclusion, creative practice research allows us *to name the doing*, to name what is acting. Research in creative practical research would be to think the creation, I mean the process of creation so that we would be able to transmit neither creation which is invisible, neither the technics of creation – which is the way we teach theatre in practical classes – but to transmit the process of creation, the visible paths that bring us to creation, as Antoine Vitez, Peter Brook, Jacques Lassalle, Edward Gordon Craig and so many others did in essays on their theatre – trying to understand the way they create so they could be 'robbed' by their pupils, as Grotowski said.

Research puts distance between us and our intuition, our emotion; not to leave them but, on the contrary, to follow them in a visible, readable and clear way even if we don't know what is behind the door. Kafka tells the story of a man walking all his life to reach a door behind which he sees the truth of the light. At the end of his path, he arrives exhausted at the door, where light is more and more brilliant, and asks the guard in front of the door to allow him to enter at the end of his life to see the truth behind these doors. And the guard refuses, answering that the truth is not behind the door but is the path that the man did all his life to reach the door ... (in Kafka 2000: 1054–6).

This philosophical and poetical tale is also my creative practice research's personal path, working in my creation on the process of creation itself. Working on the great figures of literature's mythology as Scrooge, Don Quichotte, Alice or Gargantua: all these characters are following an initiatory trip to reach at the end ... the understanding of their own path. Scrooge understands that his real life is only the metaphor of a philosophical process about human being. Alice tries to interpret the puzzle of her growth and her femininity, jumping from one mystery to another, just to accept that her growing is puzzling and enigmatic. Gargantua is the tale of an initiatory travel in his own body, which is the world and Quichotte, in particular, beginning to travel at fifteen,[12] and going on the world's paths to give sense to his life; returning at the end, on his deathbed, he tells Sancho Pança that all his apparently crazy paths led to the discovery that: 'I am who I am'(soy quien soy).

Charles Dullin could be the final reference transmitting what is fundamental to this creative practice research: 'Past gives you examples. It doesn't say: "Imitate to do as perfect as possible what I did". But he says: "Do as I do, search as I searched, work"' (Dullin 2011: 61). In that sense, creative practice research is at the perfect contrary to our society, built on uselessness, consumption, efficiency, far away from the time of research. We eat the cake, but we don't have any more the essential flavour of the cherry: it is a stodgy cake, without any colour and flavour.

To know is to do in creative practice research: research is the path to get inside our own creation and to question it. Not to answer but to ask question ... As a rabbi said to his pupils: 'I got the answer! I got the answer! ... But who have the question?'. Creative practical research is the research of the truth revealed by creation, the horse hidden in the stone that the sculptor lets appear with his work. In the doing is the process of knowing – coming back to the incredible Grotowski's definition of transmission about the 'ignorant master' and the 'robbed talks'. 'Art is path', said Paul Klee, and that sums up what creative practice research has to be.

NOTES

1. <https://vimeo.com/118144784>
2. <https://vimeo.com/7556354>
3. <https://vimeo.com/75768948>
4. <https://vimeo.com/174277583>
5. Grotowski said:
   > There are two things in your question, there are two things. One thing: can we take ownership of someone else's practices? Obviously, we can, if we have a special guide who … in truth it's like history: can we rob a Master? The great Master, indeed, he makes his disciple elected all the possibilities of robbing him. But he does not give it, no, he lets the other go rob, that's what's essential. He's a very bad teacher, if I can say teacher who … (makes the gesture of giving) no, no … create the conditions when he sees that we put something in the hat, a hidden rabbit, and we do not do not give him that rabbit, and leave the hat on the table. It's like when everyone who has the real job, he has a secret behind. This secret is never disclosed. So, we just rob him. We try the burglary. It is one of the most essential filiations, it is burglary. But yes, but it's not stealing the secret outside, it's like stealing things related to sources, secret processes, not the ones we see.'

   'La parole de Jerzy Grotowski: légende', Jerzy Grotowski talking during one of the Action of the Académie Expérimentale des Théâtres: 'Le laboratoire d'acteur. Des origines au commencement avec Jerzy Grotowski', 3–5 April 1996 at the Workcenter of Jerzy Grotowski and Thomas Richards at Pontedera (Italie). Vidéo by Pierre-Henri Magnin. Document from the Académie Expérimentale des Théâtres at the Institut des Mémoires de l'édition contemporaine (Imec). Thanks to Pascale Butel-Skrzyszowski, head of the archive division of the funds at Imec et of the funds of Académie Expérimentale des Théâtres and thanks to Michelle Kokosowski.

6. Gordon Craig, Edward, 'A note on sanity in stage production of Shakespearean plays', quoted by Le Bœuf Patrick, 'Attention!(ce n'est qu'une) école', in *Faire théâtre sous le signe de la recherche*, sous la direction de Losco- Lena Mireille (2017), Presses Universitaires de Rennes.

7. Victor Hugo said that 'The sublime is down' – speaking about literary creation.

8. Mais si notre vue s'arrête là, que l'imagination passe outre ; elle se lassera plutôt de concevoir, que la nature de fournir. Tout ce monde visible n'est qu'un trait imperceptible dans l'ample sein de la nature. Nulle idée n'en approche. Nous avons beau enfler nos conceptions au-delà des espaces imaginables, nous n'enfantons que des atomes, au prix de la réalité des choses. C'est une sphère infinie dont le centre est partout, la circonférence nulle part. Enfin, c'est le plus grand caractère sensible de la toute puissance de Dieu, que notre imagination se perde dans cette pensée.

   (Blaise Pascal (1951), *Les Pensées*, Luxembourg: Lafuma, fragment 199.

9. As it is told in *The Bible*: 'Tout le peuple voit les voix' (Exodus 20:22).
10. <https://vimeo.com/174277910>

11. <https://vimeo.com/233634431>
12. Kabbala is studied only after reaching fourteen years of age, which seems to mark the beginning of understanding our own mysteries.

References

The Bible (1989), translated into French by André Chouraqui, La Flèche: Éditions Desclée de Brouwer.

Dullin, Charles (2011), *Introduction, choix et textes*, Mayenne: Editions Actes Sud.

Gordon Craig, Edward (2017), 'A note on sanity in stage production of Shakespearean plays', quoted by Le Bœuf Patrick, 'Attention! (ce n'est qu'une) école', in *Faire théâtre sous le signe de la recherche*, sous la direction de Losco- Lena Mireille (2017), Presses Universitaires de Rennes.

Kafka, Franz (1975), *La muraille de Chine*, trans. Jean Carrive et Alexandre Vialatte, Mayenne: NRF Gallimard.

Kafka, Franz (2000), *Récits, romans et journaux*, trans. Marthe Robert, Paris: Classiques modernes, Librairie Générale Française, La Pochothèque.

Pascal, Blaise (1951), *Les Pensée*, Luxembourg: Lafuma: fragment 199.

Picasso, Pablo (2014), *Je ne cherche pas, je trouve – Écrits et pensées*, Paris: Éditions Cherche Midi.

Vitez, Antoine (1991), *Le théâtre des Idées*, Saint-Amand: Éditions Le Messager Gallimard.

18. 'WE WANT TO KILL BOKO HARAM': REFLECTIONS ON THE PHOTOGRAPHIC REPRESENTATION OF CHILDREN IN A DISPLACEMENT CAMP

Tunde Alabi-Hundeyin

This chapter reflects on my visual ethnography and participatory photography practice in the context of displacement. It is a scholarly exploration of my creative process in photographically constructing children living at the Internally Displaced Persons (IDP) Camp in Durumi, Abuja, Nigeria's capital; and the contemporary photographers from whose representational practices I have drawn inspiration. Additionally, I reflect on my practice as a form of advocacy and on humanitarian photography as a subset of the documentary photography form.

Background

Seventh in the world's most populous nations ranking (around 198 million people), Nigeria also has an estimated '1.7 million IDPs in over 321,580 households across six states of northeast Nigeria with 40 per cent residing in camp-like settings in urban areas plus 1.4 million returnees' (Vanguard 2018). The majority of these people were displaced following the insurgency by the Boko Haram terrorist group in northern Nigeria. According to the Global Terrorism Index (GTI), the West African nation is the third country most impacted by terrorism globally, though the number of people killed in 2018 reduced by 5,950/80 per cent compared to the peak of terrorist deaths in 2014 (Institute of Economics and Peace 2018).

Boko Haram, whose ideology is predicated upon anti-Western education, has abducted hundreds of schoolgirls and killed thousands of people (Delman

2015). Okoli and Iortyer (2014: 44–5) cite public insecurity, livelihood crisis, humanitarian abuses, population displacement and refugee debacle, and human casualty/fatality as the humanitarian consequences of the Boko Haram insurgency. 'The plight of these displaced people in their various places of refuge can be best described as critically threatening' (p. 45), having been dislodged from their families, social capital bases, and thrown into a serious humanitarian crisis. I have therefore produced a documentary photography project, which focuses on the survivors, particularly the children living in the Durumi displacement camp, adopting visual ethnography and participatory photography (photovoice) methods. The objective of the project was to create a counter-narrative to the normative form of media representation of distant suffering.

Most of everyday news and images of Africa in the global media are thematically narrow and negative, focusing disproportionately on violence, war, famine and disease (Scott 2017: 40-41, Schwittay 2015: 7). This creates a negative impression of issues regarding the continent and, as observed by Tallon (2008: 4), causes long-term damage – through stereotypes of the people and countries misrepresented via 'poster child' images – for short-term gains of successful charity fundraising. Also, it perpetuates 'chronic underdevelopment by reinforcing the impression that the entire African continent is a hopeless case' (Wright 2017:148). Wright cites Lugo-Ocando (2015) who argues that aid organisations are guilty of using stereotyped and de-contextualised images of Africa and that without the mass media these organisations cannot disseminate their appeals and images (Cottle and Nolan 2007: 863).

Participation and Photography

In action research, participation democratises power as the 'object of study' becomes 'the subject' (Fals-Borda and Ordóñez 2007:11), hence, creating a multiplicity of knowledge and ideas. McTaggart (1997: 28–9) suggests that participation implies the enabling of ownership and agency in the creation of knowledge, while Kemmis and McTaggart (2005: 563) construct it as a social and educational process of interrogating and reconstructing social practices. Participatory photography uses the photovoice methodology to document issues that under-represented people can mainstream to policymakers, thereby initiating social change. Participants are given cameras to capture images that voice their own realities; their narratives validate pluralist local knowledge and disrupt existing hierarchies and power relations (PhotoVoice 2016: 5). The democratisation of power in a participatory photography exercise empowers the participants better to take responsibility and initiate key decisions than in visual ethnography, which is more open to subjectivity.

The photovoice methodology is a powerful tool for representation, a process encapsulating a range of decisions and protocols involving marginalised subjects. 'Representation is concerned with the subject of the image, where the image is seen, how it is seen, in what context, with what other images and information; by whom it is seen' (PhotoVoice 2016: 34). It is a painstaking process of gaining access to participants, creating mutual understanding and respect, earning trust, and getting informed consent. These decisions and protocols carry risks that can potentially frustrate the project objectives or outcomes. These could include identity, emotional, political, exclusion or security risks – on issues surrounding the association of subjects with difficult experiences leading to stigma, discrimination, marginalisation or vulnerability.

PHOTOGRAPHING THE CHILDREN

International aid agencies and the media tend to utilise disempowering photos of helpless and passive children from the Global South for fundraising appeals and various other purposes, while vulnerable Western children receive a more privileged representation; showing them positive, active and empowered (Cottle & Nolan 2007: 863; Wilson 2011: 316–17; Schwittay 2015: 6). The visual ethnography was designed to adopt the latter representational practice.

Moreover, in *Utopia*, I planned to document twenty children within the ambience of their family units. Since the research attempts to combat stereotypes where only children (sometimes children and women) are portrayed by these relief organisations and the media, I intended to, where possible, show their parents. The images would be 'to camera' posed portraits of the children with their relatives, and observational (documentary) style photos of regular daily tasks such as studying, recreation, etc. The images would be taken within their immediate surroundings where they are comfortable. Humanity, dignity and agency were to be at the heart of the photographic construction – not suffering, and devoid of 'visual drama' (Friend 2007: 94), what Friend (2010: 3) regards as 'ordinariness'.

In negative representations of vulnerable children by aid agencies and the media, there is a tendency to create a shock effect with poverty porn with a view to satisfying the audience's expectations. The news and visuals of the suffering other is, therefore, a 'form of entertainment' in the media (Moeller 1999: 33). Sontag agrees that:

> The hunt for more dramatic (as they're often described) images drives the photographic enterprise, and is part of the normality of a culture in which shock has become a leading stimulus of consumption and source of value ... How else to get attention for one's product or one's art? How else to make a dent when there is incessant exposure to images, and

overexposure to a handful of images seen again and again? The image as shock and the image as cliché are two aspects of the same presence. (2003: 23)

Power Imbalance

Explaining the power imbalance subsisting between a photographer and a child, McIntyre and White (2002:12–13) illustrate how some press photographers were invited by an aid organisation to a refugee camp to photograph children who had been displaced by war. All the images captured showed weeping children. On further investigation by the NGO press officer, it was discovered that the children cried because they assumed that the long camera lenses were guns and that the photographers were soldiers.

Power imbalance unintentionally might create a space for exploitation. Depending on age, exposure and circumstances, a child will react in excitement or fear at the sight of a camera. In creating safe spaces for children to be photographed, a photographer has a responsibility to make them feel comfortable and understand the import of the image-taking. I developed a cordial working relationship with each child, enabling them to exercise their agency and liberty.

However, by allowing the children to freestyle their poses, I noticed some creative body postures by two female subjects, which highlights gender influence in photography. In a bid to 'please' a male photographer, teenage girls tend to present more submissive poses with heads to the side, rolled eyeballs, subtle, symbolic movements (of hips), and/or playing with their hands around their heads or faces.

In Figures 18.1 and 18.2, Hauwa Ali and Fatima Umoru's body postures exhibit subtle gendered relations of looking, regarded as *the male gaze*. In her research, *Visual Pleasure and Narrative Cinema* (1975), Laura Mulvey argues about women's objectification in the Hollywood movies produced by men in the 1970s and that the pleasure of looking belongs to the menfolk, while women play the passive role of being the image to be gazed at (p. 11; Wells 2003a: 324). The spectator of the image identifies with this male gaze through the screen. The internalised male gaze regulates women's bodies and subjectivities, such that anticipating a male gaze or posing before a male photographer's gaze triggers a stylised body posture. According to the objectification theory, the internalisation of the sexually objectifying male gaze is regarded as self-objectification (Calogero 2004:16).

Even among conservative, veil-donning Muslim women, as is the case with Hauwa and Fatima, self-objectification is a practice. According to Glapka, who terms it 'the hijab and the repertoire of gaze' (2018: 221), 'the emphasis on veiling specifically the female body in Islam imply that apart from dictating

Figure 18.1 Hauwa Ali (Photo: Tunde Alabi-Hundeyin).

Figure 18.2 Fatima Umoru (Photo: Tunde Alabi-Hundeyin).

how the body should look when visible to the male heterosexual spectator, the male gaze regulates the extent of the body's visibility' (p. 218). While standing aloof to preview the photographs of the other children that I had taken, Hauwa approached me, quizzing, 'Will you not take my photo?' Moments later, after the shoot, in a mischievous voice, Fatima whispered to me: 'Uncle, Hauwa says she likes you!' This mild drama further strengthens the argument that the male gaze influences women's subjectivities and representation in creative practice, confirming that power relations might trigger 'complicated unconscious mechanisms' (Piotrowska 2013: 88).

In addition, Fatima's posture speaks volumes about the male gaze. Her deliberate hand-crossing is a conscious effort to display her *henna* tattoo. Although henna tattoo is a staple of bridal adornment in the local Hausa culture, it is also very popular among the women. Her *lalle*, locally made black dye used as nail polish, serves the same purpose as the *henna* tattoo.

Power imbalance also influences the process of obtaining consent for image capture and use. Informed consent suggests that permission to capture an image is given without pressure and that the subject has the capacity to understand all information, including the risks involved in doing so (PhotoVoice 2016: 56). I therefore obtained informed verbal consent and signed written consent from the parents and the children in addition to information sheets, explaining the import of the project. Non-literate parents who only spoke Hausa were spoken to through an interpreter. They thumb-printed the information and consent sheets. One of the participants, on signifying her disinterest, was subsequently allowed to pull out of the workshop with no questions asked. In cases where the children were too eager to be photographed without their parents' consent, they were not captured.

Practice Framework

I assess my practice in the project, *Utopia*, within the parameters designed by Warren Buckland (2018), focusing on form, technology, style, aesthetics and interpretation.

Photography is the *form*, specifically humanitarian photography as a subset of the documentary genre. The project adopts portraiture and participatory photography to communicate its narrative. Regarding the *technology*, I used a full-frame digital SLR camera and shot in colour. The *style* of the photographs is a positive representation, showing agency and the humanity of the subjects, while fixed, wide angle, telephoto lenses were used to frame the shots in portrait and landscape formats. *Aesthetically*, the use of ambient lighting is consistent in all the images; there is a deliberate effort to create an environmental context with the shallow depth of field (DOF). The subjects adopt natural, relaxed poses. The *interpretation* will be deciphered by the audience, but all the photographs are intended to present an empowering representation of the photographed individuals.

My body of work, *Utopia*, departs from the stylisation of images in Sebastião Salgado's monograph, *The Children: Refugees and Migrants* (2000) in different ways. Salgado adopted portraiture in monochrome portrait format throughout, most likely shot on film. He is inconsistent with ambient lighting in the interior exposures, though he may have used reflectors or speed light, and DOF is absent in many of them. The children look straight into the camera lens in natural poses, although it's not obvious from the photographs that they were taken as a measure to give the photographer a breather from the children, who were milling around him for snapshots.

Publishing the book about these refugee and migrant children in different continents was accidental. Salgado recalls that when he finally looked at his collection on these children, he saw the humanity and dignity through their appearances, poses and expressions, though they had experienced suffering in their short lives (pp. 7–8).

In Vanessa Winship's *Sweet Nothings* (2008), she photographs schoolgirls living along the borderlands of Turkey. Her intent was, through the photographs, to enable the voices of the schoolgirls who were, with the support of the government, increasingly breaking tradition to enrol in schools. Similar to Salgado's account of photographing the children, the recipient of the prestigious Henri Cartier-Bresson prize (2011) recalls experiencing mixed emotions during the shoots. 'I was touched by the gravity in their demeanour at the moment in front of the camera, their fragility, their simplicity, their grace, their closeness to one another, but most of all I was struck by their complete lack of posturing.' Winship gave the girls agency in choosing their poses. Having been shot by a female photographer, the male gaze is absent in the monochromatic images of the preteen and teenage Turkish girls, unlike my work, *Utopia*. Her head-to-toe framing style shows her subjects in their full regalia of uniform, socks and boots.

We are Congo (2010) is an Oxfam-sponsored coffee table book that focuses on the people displaced by the war in the Democratic Republic of Congo. The celebrity photographer, Rankin (John Rankin Waddell), a British fashion and portrait photographer, undertook the task of capturing 'the spirit of the [Mugunga Refugee] camp's inhabitants – not as victims, but as people – highlighting their essential humanity and strength' (p. 3). Rankin departs from the quintessential photography practice in the other case studies previously discussed, having shot subjects against a white background and studio lights, his standard approach in his commercial photography practice. He notes that his objective was to make viewers notice and connect to the 'expressions in their eyes and on their faces – their humanity' (p. 9).

Created by Fati Abubakar as a response to the growing need for an objective representation of her home state, Borno, the epicentre of Boko Haram's theatre of death, @BitsofBorno on Instagram and Facebook regularly shows Fati's photographs and stories of resilient Borno people who have survived the insurgency. Fati recalls how in the heat of the crisis, while studying in London, she kept seeing horrifying news reports emanating from her home state. She would ring her parents to assess the situation and they would always assure her that they were safe. The impression she got from the media, however, was that the entire state was on fire and that everyone was displaced.

> I decided that I was going back to Borno to show the good, the bad, and the ugly. I would talk about my community as I see it. Do I see resilience or do I see sadness? I keyed in on resilience because that's what I wanted to highlight. We are not all traumatised. But it's the trauma you get shown in mainstream media. The representation that Africa is poor and diseased – true, we've got those but there are also great things. Essentially my work started out of anger, to be honest. Pure anger that we are not represented the way we should be. (Abubakar 2018)

Bits of Borno has earned Fati global acclaim for her approach to the representation of the victims of Boko Haram's terrorist activities and subsequent displacement. It has provided the world with an alternative source of information on the true state of affairs in Borno, Adamawa, and Yobe – the three states most affected by the crisis. Between 2014 and 2016, when the insurgency was at its peak, the region became a no-go area for many journalists and aid workers but Fati's images assured her audience that families, individuals and children stood resilient and strong – in their homes or in displacement camps. Her photo stories, shot in street portrait style, give children agency and power, depict everyday life in Borno and have been published by global media organisations like the BBC, Reuters, The New York Times, CNN, Voice of America and Newsweek Europe. Humanitarian organisations including UNICEF, Oxfam and International Alert have also commissioned her to shoot projects.

From the bodies of work reviewed, Salgado, Winship, Rankin and Fati clearly departed from the infantilisation of (socio-cultural) difference popular in humanitarian photography. Their art deployed positive imagery with a bias for the children's agency and dignity. Positive images are believed to be 'more representative of the truth than negative ones' (Lidchi 2015: 291).

Photovoice

I selected ten of the oldest twenty children photographed to engage in a participatory photography workshop where they were taught visual storytelling skills and given cameras as tools for self-representation and advocacy. I gave them the freedom to choose how they would be pictorially represented and what they would like to show the world about their own lives. Some of their friends who were not selected for the project – ethnography and participatory – showed keen interest; they were relentless in their efforts to listen in on the lessons by the classroom windows to the extent of distracting the class intermittently. The selection of the twenty children was done with help from Gola Umaru, my chaperone and spokesperson of the IDPs. Umaru helped in identifying families who would be willing to participate in the project.

The objectives of the photovoice were to enable the voices of misrepresented children, introduce them to basic camera skills, build their confidence in the use of cameras, and promote their agency in taking self-representation photographs with compelling narratives. Further objectives include: encouraging the participants to engage with each other's photographs, correcting media stereotypes of children of colour, and contributing to research data creation and collection. Hopefully, the exhibitions of the photographs generated through ethnographic and participatory methods will provide the opportunity for a counter-narrative approach to representing the 'Other' and reduce the infantilisation of difference by international non-governmental organisations (INGOs) and the media.

The photovoice workshop introduced the children, aged between ten and fifteen, to visual literacy and covered areas including aesthetic elements of a photograph, a photographer's decision making *in media res*, and photo reading tips. Photo dialogues focused on the techniques, themes and perspectives in photographs that make them communicate. The camera handling session was the most exciting for the children as they learned framing, focusing, and lighting a scene using a compact digital (point-and-shoot) camera.

The first treasure hunt task was to capture images of *three things I like and three things I dislike*. Other exercises included *my house/neighbourhood*, *photos that tell a story* and *a day in my life*. The images produced during the hunt reveal the children's thoughts. They advocated for better shelters/life, and a better environment. Also, they highlighted relationships and communal life in the camp, their support systems, the dignity of labour, the lives of the working mothers, and the invisible working fathers. Reminiscing on their pre-displacement experience in the comfort of their parents' homes, they formulated a utopia and envisioned a future where they would be free to live in bigger houses with better facilities.

However, the downside to the quality of photos captured was that there weren't enough cameras to go around the children; they were then paired up and made to share. While the files were being transferred onto my laptop, some of the children in the second group spied on the content of shots created by

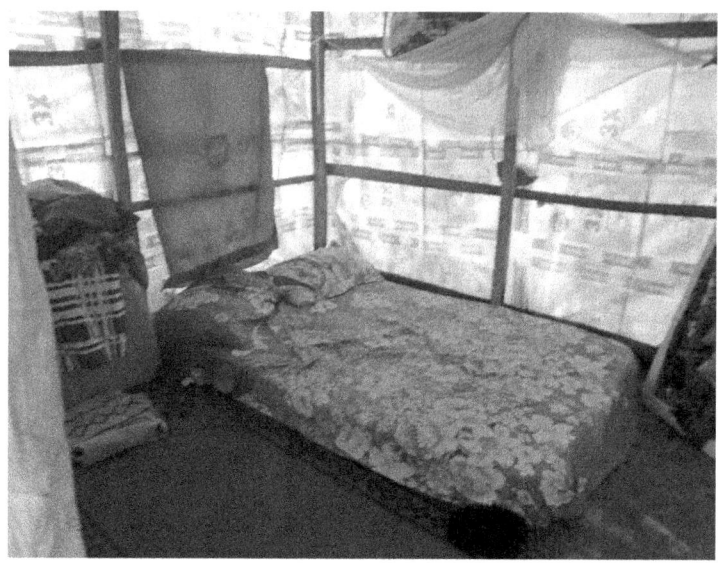

Figure 18.3   Photo Credit: Fatima Umoru – 'I share this mattress with four of my siblings. Back in Gwoza, all of us had 3 bedrooms to share. *I'm Fatima Umoru, 10 years old. I've had the first position in class twice and I want to be a teacher in the future because I love children.*'

Figure 18.4   Photo Credit: Suleiman Nuhu – 'This house is near our camp shelter. It is beautiful, and I'd like to live in it. In the future, I want to own something like this. *My name is Suleiman Nuhu, 15. I'd like to join the Army because I want to defend my country. I don't love the way we were displaced from home and I don't want it to happen to anyone else.*'

CHILDREN IN A DISPLACEMENT CAMP

Figure 18.5 Photo Credit: Maimuna Umoru – 'Star Boy, my pet cat. *Maimuna Umoru is my name, 12 years old. I will join the Nigerian Army in dealing with Boko Haram for killing my uncle, Mohammed.*'

their contemporaries, coming back with similar compositions. Having enough cameras would be necessary for a more unbiased and qualitative narrative.

'WE WANT TO KILL BOKO HARAM'

Among the photovoice participants, 75 per cent shared with me their aspiration to become soldiers in the Nigerian Army. Their reason: 'We want to kill Boko Haram because they killed our relatives and displaced us.' From his interaction with the refugee children he photographed worldwide, Sebastião Salgado argues that they 'also carry wounds that are harder to heal than the trauma of physical dislocation' (2000: 9).

One of the photovoice participants, Yinusa Abubakar, aged 13, recounted witnessing the killing of his elder brother Adamu four years before. Three Boko Haram terrorists had entered their house in Gwoza and shot nineteen-year-old Adamu many times because he refused to be radicalised. 'I want to be an air force pilot because I want to kill Boko Haram for killing my brother', swore Yinusa. In a similar fashion, Zarau Ali, aged 10, declared, 'As a soldier, I want to defend my people against Boko Haram because they killed my father when we lived in Gwoza.' She could have become a suicide bomber if the deadly group had abducted her like hundreds of other schoolgirls kidnapped across the terrorised territory. According to the United Nations Security Council, the insurgents abducted 4,000 women and girls and used children in 135 suicide attacks in 2017 (UN Security Council 2018: 3).

NEOLIBERAL HOPELESSNESS

According to the Charity Commission, there were 183,855 registered charities in England and Wales as at 30 September 2018, with a collective income of £77.07 billion (Charity Commission 2018). This situation triggers competition for donor income among aid organisations, proven by their business-like approach to marketing, alliances with commercial organisations, and development of products unrelated to charitable activities (Bennett 2003: 335). However, as a result of the United Kingdom government's austerity measures, the public sector – educational and health institutions – also competes with charities for funds (Hibbert 1995: 7). Competition in the industry leads to the compromising of ethical standards and priorities (Orgad and Seu 2014: 23–4; Cooper 2015: 79–80) and a presentation of narrow images of poverty, malnourishment, devastation and despair in the Global South (Lidchi 2015: 276). Clashes regarding ethical and artistic concerns often occur between INGO communication managers and photographers commissioned to execute projects for charity organisations (Nissinen 2015: 298–307).

Issues surrounding exploitative practices, representation, captioning, framing and informed consent may flare tensions. Pressure also arises from artistic asphyxiation – photographers' struggle to retain their own artistic impressions in their creative work. Working for established institutions exposes their work to stricter analyses than personal projects where they have a greater control of the creative process and the output. I recall a child protection issue that I had with a UNICEF communication chief while working on a sensitive project. I was criticised for inadequately anonymising the identity of a child whose face I had hidden from the camera's gaze. The official wanted a tighter framing of the photographic subject, where the child was less recognisable, and I had to negotiate for more desirable techniques of constructing the child without making lacklustre images. Nissinen (2015: 300) argues that 'Photographers struggle with how to position their work and maintain their reputations within the framework of NGO's ethical and institutional guidelines.'

Humanitarian photographers have to either conform to or negotiate the requirements and demands of donor organisations who are burdened by the exigencies of raising scarce funds in an austere environment through what film critic and scholar, Thomas Elsaesser (2020) calls 'tactical compliance'.

Recounting her experience of being under pressure for certain kinds of images from INGOs, Fati Abubakar maintains that she always rejects the requests to produce shocking images. An INGO proposed to commission her for some images of street children. She declined to take up the project due to its objectification approach – the organisation requested images of children seated in a heap of trash. Referencing veteran photographer Don McCullin, who has been regarded as 'a conscience with a camera', she argues that photographers have the huge moral burden of objective representation (Abubakar 2018).

Aid and media organisations' sources of funding play a major role in influencing their key decisions, including communications. A humanitarian organisation that puts its marketing team under pressure for funds is more likely to use shocking, stereotyping and oversimplifying images in its fundraising drive. A senior UNICEF official in Nigeria blames the objectification of children on smaller NGOs with lesser reputations who struggle for funds. He reveals that the multilateral organisation receives its larger share of funds from institutional donors and, as such, doesn't require negative imagery to raise funds. The Hiroshima generation in Japan, who were assisted by UNICEF during their crisis, constitute the bulk of these institutional donors. He adds that the wealthiest man in Africa, Aliko Dangote, requires no photo evidence to be convinced to donate. 'UNICEF's global reputation has marked it out for huge funds and it can survive without the use of negative images' (UNICEF Official 2018).

Daily Trust newspapers and the News Agency of Nigeria (NAN) are large media organisations in Nigeria. While the former is privately owned, NAN is a federal government news reporting agency providing text, photographs and videos to other media organisations. Based on their differing funding sources, both organisations differ on policies regarding the representation of displaced persons, even though both function within the same context of the Nigerian media law. On the representation of IDPs, Yakubu Abubakar, *Daily Trust*'s photo editor submits that 'We show them the way they are – but not if they are naked. There was a photograph we published of children in an IDP Camp, sitting on the ground, waiting for food supplies that were not forthcoming. The next day after it was published, government officials visited the camp to resolve the issues based on our report' (Abubakar 2018).

On the other hand, Bamidele Jones, NAN's chief photojournalist suggests the 'piper notion', saying, 'He who pays the piper calls the tune'. He continues: 'Issues that can aggravate the situation in the country or issues that can make people take up arms against the government are not reported … we are supposed to stand with the government to inform, educate and entertain the people. In reporting IDPs' conditions in the camps, we have been objective' (Jones 2018). The sponsor regulates the agenda-setting and shapes representation, determining whose voice is heard, how, and what is heard. As INGOs grapple with their fundraising challenges and issues of executing sponsors' needs, commissioned photographers should reconcile with the thoughts of Thomas Elsaesser, who suggests that 'Creative practice research in the era of neoliberal hopelessness, has to be a creativity *after* neoliberalism, but also *after* resistance and *after* authorial autonomy.' He further argues that a creative has to negotiate authorship, learning processes, and be flexible to adapt to the requirements of creative practice, including 'tactical compliance' and 'tactical attentiveness' to the external forces that appeal to the sensibilities, of not just the creative, but others (Elsaesser 2020).

These challenges, therefore, present opportunities for humanitarian photographers to learn reflexivity, flexibility and defiance – as the situation requires. The global economy is governed by neoliberal forces, including, to a large extent, in the third sector. Tactical compliance and tactical attentiveness resolve the complex dilemma and drama between art and cash.

Conclusion

Utopia promoted the humanity and the dignity of the Durumi Camp children in the way they were posed, presented and represented. It highlighted their agency and enabled their voices through participatory photography, allowing them a freehand to voice their own realities, express their concerns and their utopia. They advocated for better shelters, improved living conditions, increased supplies, and a greater support system. The children constructed their own narratives through photography – their own photography. I stumbled on their career aspirations through serendipity, while having dialogues with them about their images. To the question, 'What would you like to be in future?' I had expected a default response of 'I want to be a doctor/pilot/engineer/lawyer', only to be shocked by my first interviewee (and subsequently the others) who wanted to become a soldier for reasons previously expressed. For children who had often been spoken for in the media, *Utopia* provided a platform for self-narrativisation.

Though guided by the ethics of photography, my representational practice was devoid of institutional interference, corporate politics and neoliberal concerns. This provided liberty from artistic asphyxiation similar to Salgado, Winship and Fati's referenced projects. In Rankin's work for Oxfam, he expressed his agency in constructing his Mugunga camp subjects as people, not victims – despite being an institutional commission. Artistic liberty, even within the ambience of neoliberal forces, grants photographic subjects a greater agency and humanity. While Salgado and Fati's photographs reflect humanity and dignity, Winship's girls had agency in the choice of poses and they experienced no male gaze. However, the male gaze influenced my outcomes in *Utopia*. I also adopted Salgado and Rankin's style of facial expressions, oscillating from smiling to natural, as opposed to dead-pan portraiture visible in Winship's book.

The case studies that have been engaged with in this chapter reflect aesthetics, agency, and dignity as contemporary approaches to representing vulnerable people encountering negative situations. Such images are empowering and confront normative poverty porn and suffering stereotypes of marginalised children. I attempted to confront stereotypes, and created empowering images with my project, *Utopia*.

Documentary photographers must see themselves as witnesses and mediators of reality. Gender, cultural background, age, experience, choice of camera/lenses and distance all influence the mediation of reality. Relying on the knowledge of journalism, art, sociology and history, the documentary genre investigates certain social phenomena with the possibility of social change (Price 2009:69). Contemporary documentary photography must continue to challenge the status quo in a stereotype-perpetuating commodification culture – which Susan Moeller suggests has become 'intrinsic to the marketing of the media' (p. 34). Some of these 'hegemonic constructs' surround concepts relating to 'race, gender and class' (Ramamurthy 2009: 228).

REFERENCES

Abubakar, F. (2018), *Doctoral Research Interview*.
Abubakar, Y. (2018), *Doctoral Research Interview*.
Apps.charitycommission.gov.uk (2018), *Charities in England and Wales 30 September 2018*, [online], <http://apps.charitycommission.gov.uk/showcharity/registerofcharities/SectorData/SectorOverview.aspx> (accessed 31 March 2019).
Bennett, R. (2003), 'Competitor analysis practices of British charities', *Marketing Intelligence & Planning*, 21:6, 335–45.
Buckland, W. (2018), 'Teaching Film Analysis from a Filmmaking Perspective: Reassessing the Work of Vlada Petric', in Creative Practice Research in the Age of Neoliberal Hopelessness Conference, Luton: The Research Institute for Media, Arts and Performance, University of Bedfordshire.
Calogero, R. (2004), 'A Test of Objectification Theory: The Effect of the Male Gaze on Appearance Concerns in College Women', *Psychology of Women Quarterly*, 28:1, 16–21.
Cooper, G. (2015), 'NGOs, Media, and Public Understanding. 25 years on: an interview with Paddy Coulter, former Head of Media, Oxfam', in S. Cottle and G. Cooper (eds), *Humanitarianism, Communications and Change*, New York: Peter Lang.
Cottle, S. and D. Nolan (2007), 'Global humanitarianism and the changing aid-media field: "Everyone was dying for footage"', *Journalism Studies*, 8:6, 862–78.
Delman, E. (2015), *The World's Deadliest Terrorist Group*, [online] The Atlantic, <https://www.theatlantic.com/international/archive/2015/11/isis-boko-haram-terrorism/416673/> (accessed 14 May 2018).
Elsaesser, T. (2020), 'Creativity and Neoliberalism: Between Autonomy, Resistance and Tactical Compliance', in A. Piotrowska (ed.), *Creative Practice Research in the Age of Neoliberal Hopelessness*, Edinburgh: Edinburgh University Press.
Fals-Borda, O. and S. Ordóñez (2007), 'Investigacion Accion Participativa: Donde Las

Aguas Se Juntan Para Dar Forma a La Vida. Entrevista Con Orlando Fals Borda', *Revista Internacional Magisterio* 26:11.
Friend, M. (2007), 'Homes and Gardens: Documenting the Invisible', *Home Cultures*, 4:1, 93-100, DOI: 10.2752/174063107780129699.
Friend, M. (2010), 'Representing Immigration Detainees: The Juxtaposition of Image and Sound in "Border Country"', Vol. 11, No. 2, Art. 33, May 2010 FQS, <http://www.qualitative-research.net/> Forum Qualitative Sozialforschung / Forum: Qualitative Social Research (ISSN 1438-5627).
Glapka, E. (2018), 'Lost in Translation: The Male Gaze and the (In)visible Bodies of Muslim Women – A Response Article', *Journal of International Women's Studies*, 19:2, 215–29, <http://vc.bridgew.edu/jiws/vol19/iss2/14>
Hibbert, S. (1995), 'The marketing positioning of British medical charities', *European Journal of Marketing*, 29:10.
Institute of Economics and Peace (2018), *Global Terrorism Report 2018: Measuring the impact of terrorism*.
Jones, B. (2018), *Doctoral Research Interview*.
Kemmis, S. and R. McTaggart (2005) 'Participatory Action Research. Communicative Action and the Public Sphere', in N. K. Denzin and Y. S. Lincoln (eds), *The SAGE Handbook of Qualitative Research*, 3rd edn, Thousand Oaks, CA: Sage Publications, p. 1210.
Lidchi, H. (2015), 'Finding the Right Image: British Development NGOs and the Regulation of Imagery', in H. Fehrenbach and D. Rodogno (eds), *Humanitarian Photography: A History*, New York: Cambridge University Press.
McIntyre, P. and A. White (2002), 'Child Rights and the Media – Putting Children in the Right', *International Federation of Journalists (IFJ) Journal*, p. 13.
McTaggart, R. (1997), 'Guiding Principles for Participatory Action Research', in R. McTaggart (ed.), *Participatory Action Research: International Contexts and Consequences*, Albany: SUNY Press, pp. 25–9.
Moeller, S. (1999), *Compassion Fatigue*, New York: Routledge.
Mulvey, L. (1975), 'Visual Pleasure and Narrative Cinema', *Screen 16/3 Autumn*. Widely reprinted including her (1989) *Visual and Other Pleasures*, London: Macmillan.
Nissinen, S. (2015), 'Dilemmas of Ethical Practice in the Production of Contemporary Humanitarian Photography', in H. Fehrenbach and D. Rodogno (eds), *Humanitarian Photography: A History*, New York: Cambridge University Press.
Okoli, Al. C. and P. Iortyer (2014), 'Terrorism and Humanitarian Crisis in Nigeria: Insights from Boko Haram Insurgency', *Global Journal of Human-Social Science: F Political Science*, 14:1, Version 1.0.
Orgad, S. and I. Seu (2014), 'The Mediation of Humanitarianism: Toward a Research Framework', *Communication, Culture & Critique*, 7, pp. 6–36.
PhotoVoice (2016), Participant Training Handbook: A comprehensive introduction to participatory photography.
Piotrowska, A. (2013), *Psychoanalysis and Ethics in Documentary Film*, London: Routledge.
Price, D. (2009), 'Surveyors and Surveyed: Photography out and about', in L. Wells (ed.), *Photography: A Critical Introduction*, 4th edn, London: Routledge.
Ramamurthy, A. (2009), 'Spectacles and Illusions: Photography and commodity culture', in L. Wells (ed.), *Photography: A Critical Introduction*, 4th edn, London: Routledge.
Rankin (2010), *We are Congo*, London: Oxfam.
Salgado, S. (2000), *The Children: Refugees and Migrants*, New York: Aperture.
Schwittay, A. (2015), *New Media and International Development: Representation and effect in microfinance (Rethinking Development)*, London: Routledge.

Scott, M. (2017), 'How Not to Write about Writing about Africa', in M. Bunce, S. Franks and C. Paterson (eds), *Africa's Media Image in the 21st Century. From the 'Heart of Darkness' to 'Africa Rising'*, London: Routledge, pp. 40–51.

Sontag, S. (2003), *Regarding the Pain of Others*, New York: Farrar, Straus and Giroux.

Tallon, R. (2008), *The Image Dilemma*, The Global Education Centre, New Zealand.

UNICEF Official (2018), Doctoral Research Interview.

United Nations Security Council (2018), *UN Documents on Boko Haram-affected areas: Security Council Meeting Records*, 22 March 2018, S/PV.8212, [online] New York: United Nations (UN), p. 3 <https://www.securitycouncilreport.org/un_documents_type/security-council-meeting-records/?ctype=Boko%20Haram-affected%20areas&cbtype=boko-haram-affected-areas> (accessed 3 March 2019).

Vanguard (2018), *NPC puts Nigeria's population at 198m*. [online], <https://www.vanguardngr.com/2018/04/npc-puts-nigerias-population-198m/> (accessed 8 April 2018).

Wells, L. (2003a), 'The Photographic Gaze', in L. Wells (ed.), *The Photography Reader*, New York: Routledge, pp. 323–26.

Wells, L. (2003b), 'Words and Pictures: On reviewing photography', in L. Wells (ed.), *The Photography Reader*, New York: Routledge, pp. 428–34.

Wilson, K. (2011), 'Race, Gender and Neoliberalism: Changing visual representations in development', *Third World Quarterly*, 32:2, 315–31.

Winship, V. (2008), *Sweet Nothings*, London: Foto8.

Wright, K. (2017), 'It Was a "Simple", "Positive" Story of African Self-Help (Manufactured for a Kenyan NGO by Advertising Multinationals)', in M. Bunce, S. Franks and C. Paterson (eds), *Africa's Media Image in the 21st Century. From the 'Heart of Darkness' to 'Africa Rising'*, London: Routledge, pp. 147–57.

19. BETWEEN 'COUNTER-MOVEMENT' (INGOLD) AND 'LIVING WITH GHOSTS' (DEMOS)

Mischa Twitchin

It might, perhaps, seem paradoxical to offer an academic essay about creative research, as if one had already supposed what might be required of an essay, rather than seeing it as a matter of and for such research itself. Is there, for instance, a risk that the expected conventions of such an essay (addressing what Adorno called the 'academic guild' (1991: 3)) might occlude the very question of research that it is intended to explore? This concerns not so much 'form and content' as, rather, the way in which de- and re-contextualisation (regarding citations or examples) resonate with the creative work being discussed. If that work concerns a medium other than discursive writing – and is not itself engaged in creative writing (but, nonetheless, in the work of essaying knowledge) – how might this be evidenced in an article such as this? How might the understanding of an essay engage with a film montage, for example, to explore questions of research in terms, precisely, of its own creative practice? What new knowledge might derive from the relation between montage (at least, in its concept) and its elaboration in prose; in the relation between essay and film? Rather than an essay on or about film, then, what if the research in question concerns, precisely, the practice of essay-film?

Besides the already cited discussion by Adorno, my reflections here could also be introduced with reference to Whitehead and Ingold – as examples of and for thinking through relations between science and art; not least (with the Ingold example), at a time when research within universities is often obliged to attend to evaluative criteria that leave little scope for what could be called creative. In terms of a manifesto, Ingold writes: 'What I have witnessed, over these decades, is the surrender of science to the forces of neoliberalism. And to find a counter-movement in the contemporary world, we have to turn not to science but to art' (Ingold 2016: 10). The 'two cultures' environment, in which science and art are conceived of separately (especially in the ways by which they are funded), finds a powerful contrast in the evocative prose of Whitehead: 'The creativity of the world is the throbbing emotion of the past hurling itself into a new transcendent fact' (Whitehead, 1967: 177). What both authors express is a *concern* with knowledge as a creative practice distinct, for example, from an institutional one. While I will return to the vital sense of concern in research, I wish to begin with the question of essay-film and consider, first, the easily overlooked figure of the hyphen, as this might offer a clue to the current situation for thinking about creative research practices and the potential correspondence between forms and faculties.

* * *

The quarrel – that was already 'ancient' in Plato's account of it (*Republic*, X, 607b5–6) – between sense and the senses (or between aesthetics and science, pathos and logos) has been rather displaced by appeal to the hybrid realities admitted by inter-disciplinary uses of the hyphen. Distinct from the supposed conflict between practice and research, for example, we now have the idiom of 'practice-based research', institutionally validated (however problematically) even by the award of PhDs. Whether the hyphen holds together two fields in tension, sublates them both, or still serves to define one in terms of the other, remains an open question, however; where practice often appears as a supplement to, rather than an actual shift in, conceiving the supposed means and ends of research. After all, creative and academic practice, or artistic and scholarly research, are not necessarily the same thing; still less are they all equally communicable in terms that would make them either simply comparable or commensurate. The latent hyphens in the designation 'practice as research', for example, are meant to obviate the familiar distinction between 'theory and practice', where theory supposedly justifies the claims of practice to be recognised as research. This returns us to the opening considerations about the conventions of an essay: what kind of theory (or essay) is entailed by a particular research practice (or example) – not least, when it is conceived of in creative terms; where (in Adorno's account) 'transitions repudiate conclusive deductions in favour of cross-connections between elements, something for which discursive logic has no place' (1991: 22)?

With the conjunction of essay-film (as my example of creative practice here), it might still seem that research is implicitly ascribed to the essay and practice to the film, as if the hyphen made no difference to understanding these terms in their connection. Instead of recognising a mixed genre, the designation 'essay' remains typically aligned with the critical-factual and that of 'film' with the creative-fictional. Indeed, writing (as here) about an example of essay-film – about how a particular instance might evidence a mode of knowledge production – perhaps runs the risk, therefore, of re-inscribing the very separation of terms (as if between 'showing and telling') that it is meant to avoid. As will hopefully become clear, the relation between creative practice and appropriation (or between imagination and citation), in this example of essay-film, enables a theoretical fiction marked by this use of a hyphen.

Distinct from simply supposing the category of 'practice-as-research' or 'practice-based' research, this example (as an instance of such practice) highlights the way in which the hyphen signifies a creative tension in meaning. Here, the audio-visual medium – in a film diptych entitled *Phantom Europe* (discussed below and freely accessible on Vimeo (Twitchin: 2016)) – offers not so much a composite as an instance of parataxis between the two poles of this hyphenated relation. Writing an article with this example engages with the relation between the 'arts of understanding' and the 'arts of presentation' (*ars intelligendi* and *ars explicandi* (Geertz, 1989: 46)) – as explored by the film itself (addressing a particular exhibition) – to try and avoid simply reproducing the supplementary logic in which artistic research is standardly reconceived by and for scholarly review. Still following Adorno, the potential of the essay form is that it 'suspends the traditional concept of method', where 'thought's depth depends on how deeply it penetrates its object, not on the extent to which it reduces it to something else' (1991: 11). What kinds of narrative, or expository form, then, might elaborate – rather than 'reduce' – the research practice in question? After all, if there is a question *of* creative research, this must surely also be a question *for* creative research.

* * *

The sense of practice being appropriated 'as research' by institutional criteria, which claim to define its value in their own terms (particularly in the context of neoliberal governance), is indicative of concerns that do not necessarily correspond to either research or practice as such, but rather to the amalgam of power-knowledge. This is especially the case where research is instrumentalised in terms of its grant-value, rather than being recognised for its reflexive value as a practice. Of course, research is rarely (if ever) 'pure' and its partiality (in every sense) is always open to monetisation. But the sense that grant-value, in the neoliberal academy, functions as an institutional surrogate for research seems evidenced in it often being an explicit part of academic job descriptions. The sense of attracting, rather than creating, institutional research value mirrors expectations in funding applications where the proposed research, all too often, has to appeal to what is already defined by existing disciplinary criteria, rather than admitting to what might be as yet undefined. The specific temporalities of humanities research – respecting the dynamics of intuition and speculation, for example – are foreclosed by what is effectively a system of payment by results (or prescribed 'outputs'), in which the bindweed of 'excellence' leaves little space for creativity. In this context, the description of 'blue-skies thinking' seems to become increasingly pejorative, being typically denigrated as 'unrealistic' in order to forestall any actual testing of 'reality'.

The question of time in Humanities research is exemplified by Bergson's comparison between painting a picture and assembling a jigsaw puzzle, cited here by Tim Ingold:

> For, as Bergson insisted, the artist's invention is inseparable from the progress of his work. If he is painting a picture, the picture is not already created before the painting begins. This is what makes painting different from solving a jigsaw puzzle. With the puzzle, the result is already given; 'to obtain it requires only a work of recomposing and rearranging – a work that can be supposed going faster and faster, and even infinitely fast, up to the point of being instantaneous.' With painting, by contrast, 'the time taken up by the invention is one with the invention itself. It is the progress of a thought which is changing in the degree and measure that it is taking form. It is a vital process, something like the ripening of an idea.' (Ingold 2007: 47; Bergson 1911: 359–60)

To misapply the terms of a discussion by Kirsten Hastrup concerning creativity and agency, institutional funding culture is oriented by concepts of intention rather than anticipation (distinguishing between individually and socially oriented concepts of temporality): 'As distinct imaginative modes, anticipation and creativity work upon different temporalities: the first relates to perceived continuities; the second hinges on discontinuity' (2007: 204). The demand to predefine outcomes, for example, supposes a view of both research and researcher (in the temporality of their relation) that is still bound to a Lockean framework of individuals and their work(s).

The idea of the autonomy of research, like that of creative practice (or, indeed, of art), might seem naïve, or even retrograde, in the current environment. But just as 'the theoretical intimacy of relations between claims for autonomy in art and politics' (Osborne 2018: 61) needs critical attention, so does that between art (or creative practice) and research – especially when claims to autonomy (that is, claims concerning a specificity distinct from the 'values' of marketisation in higher education) are subject to extraneous auditing. The imposition of evaluative criteria that are indifferent to particular research interests – in the name of 'social impact', 'knowledge transfer', 'relevance' (especially to particular policy issues) and institutional 'strategic aims'

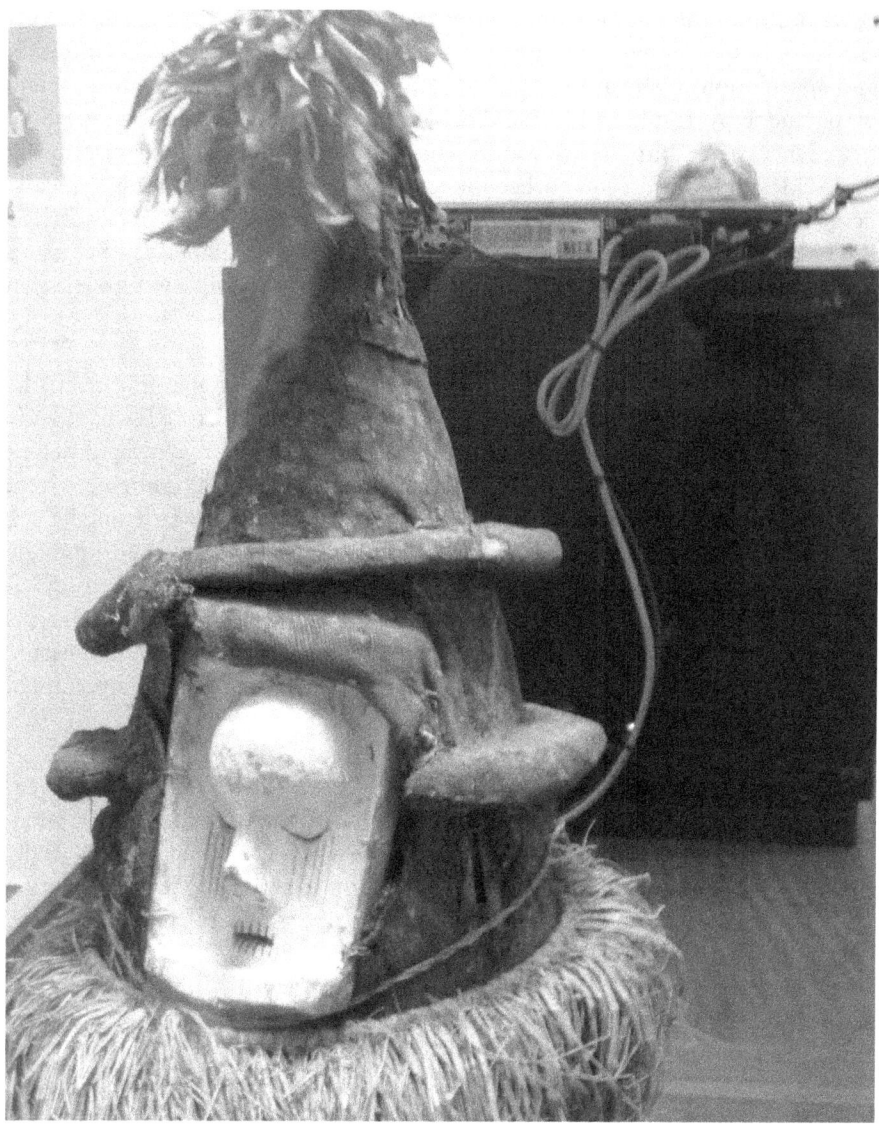

Figure 19.1   Photo taken (29.12.16) by Mischa Twitchin at the 'European Ghosts' exhibition (curated in collaboration with the Royal Museum of Central Africa, Tervuren) held at the Kunstmuseum aan zee, Ostend (www.muzee.be).

– redefines the freedom of that research's conception and modes of enquiry. Indeed, this is often explicitly framed in terms of 'value for money', as an administrative surrogate for intuition and imagination.

The relation between the creative and the autonomous here touches upon a familiar distinction, where the freedom *to* pursue creative research entails a degree of freedom *from* the requirements of institutional recognition (especially through funding). That the promise of (at least, relative) autonomy is precisely what distinguishes creative research in the first place becomes a matter of 'concern', rather than 'fact', when reconsidering its institutional situatedness.[1] Reflecting on the emotional understanding (or value) of knowledge (as of its occasion), Whitehead writes:

> I contend that the notion of mere knowledge is a high abstraction, and that conscious discrimination itself is a variable factor only present in the more elaborate examples of occasions of experience. The basis of experience is emotional. Stated more generally, the basic fact is the rise of an affective tone originating from things whose relevance is given. Thus the Quaker word 'concern', divested of any suggestion of knowledge, is more fitted to express this fundamental structure. The occasion as subject has a 'concern' for the object. And the 'concern' at once places the object as a component in the experience of the subject, with an affective tone drawn from the object and directed towards it. (1967 [1933]: 175–6)

The point here is not to separate concern from 'mere' fact (or data) – or, indeed, affect from concept (in Deleuze and Guattari's terms (1994)) – as if it were simply a question of inverting the standard power-knowledge ratio. Rather it is to engage in a sense of the 'correspondence' between subject and object, to use a poetic term (from both Goethe and Baudelaire) that sounds anachronistic in today's target-driven research culture. The value of an emotional correlation is discounted by research metrics, deforming the possibilities not simply of creative research but, as Whitehead suggests, the sense of knowledge as such.

For Tim Ingold, correspondence (with respect, precisely, to its untimely associations with poetics) is one step towards a 'counter-movement' in today's destructive conditions of and for shared understanding. Indeed, in his advocacy of a research practice emanating from a 'crucible of mutual involvement', Ingold suggests that the 'vitriolic repudiation of what we could call a science of correspondence coincides in a way that is not accidental with the colossal expansion, over the last four decades, of globalisation and the political economy of neo-liberalism' (2016: 10) – not least, of course, in the demands now made by funding bodies upon universities. How, though, might the question of this political economy itself return in an example of such 'correspondence'? How might it appear as a haunting theme in such work itself?

*   *   *

Taking an example from my own 'creative' essay-film projects, what becomes conceivable as, or for, research in this medium, concerning the entwined heritage of colonialism and capitalism, under the title of *Phantom Europe*? As already mentioned, this film diptych takes as its subject an exhibition (which was held in Ostend, 2016). With new commissions from contemporary artists and also loans from the Museum of Central Africa in Tervuren (during its closure for renovation), the exhibition was concerned with the changing representation of African art in European contexts, under the title of *European Ghosts*; or, in its French title, *L'Europe fantôme*.[2] I have written elsewhere about this exhibition as a research project (Twitchin 2017), but here I wish to explore the approach of the essay-film as an instance of creative research specifically, where its subject concerns the very idea of its medium (in every sense of the word). Amongst the many questions raised – questions that can be posed not only *to* the film, but which are already posed *by* it – one theme seems to me to be essential. This concerns the memory of what is not perceived until recognised in images afterwards, as reflected upon by both Walter Benjamin and, with respect to film specifically, Jacques Derrida. This scenario concerning perception is also evoked by Bénédicte Savoy (referencing Benjamin again) in her inaugural Collège de France lecture, in which she describes herself seeing, as it were 'for the first time', a statue of Champollion in the college's courtyard – the iconography of which had been there to be seen all along, but which only now became visible, understood as an instance of the 'return of the colonial repressed' (2017: 44).

In this context, broaching the unconscious of contemporary knowledge, the creative research of *Phantom Europe* can be elaborated in retroactive terms through such questions as the following: How does the filmmaking bring into focus, as it were, or refract, a subject that might not otherwise be apparent? How might one elaborate what Benjamin famously called the 'optical unconscious' here, as a question of – but also for – creative practice research? What kind of knowledge (as mediated by film) may, indeed, be understood as phantomatic in this retroactive version of the exhibition? In relation to the genealogy of essay-film (with André Bazin's suggestion of its 'new montage … from ear to eye' (1958)), how does voice haunt the image, reproducing (or echoing) a split between the verbal and the visual? How does this engage the ostensible difference between addressing an image and addressing the viewer in the film? What new possibilities of and for knowledge arise in the acousmatic split between de-contextualisation and re-contextualisation – as, precisely, a question of montage? How does this question become itself possible where there is no deictic sound in the film image, and therefore no apparent difference (except for one that might be imagined) between either material or conceptual senses of foreground and background? How does this field of and for critical reflection arise from a paratactic practice of montage, distinct from the synchronised modalities expected of documentary filmmaking and the associated conventions of continuity editing? How does this montage create a potential for discovery, as a question of its very medium, in and for the research – addressing (in this particular case) the relation between ideas of the ethnographic and of art in European museums? And how does this expand the film's concern – as that of its particular subject – with the hauntological conditions of colonial representability?

These questions indicate what follows from the example of the creative practice, as a crystallisation of intuitions that remain contingent but which (through such experimental reflection, testing its possibilities afterwards) take on a seeming necessity, which could not have been known in advance. The retroactive potential of and for experiment (rather than the testing of an abstracted hypothesis supposed in advance) generates a research subject that is specific to its own medium; at least, until new questions arise, which might expose the assumptions of the film as uncritical (if not fallacious). Such questions, and the interpretations they entail, might themselves offer a further creative development in the knowledge being invoked (if not actually invented) in the form here of the essay-film as a research practice.[3] What relation, then, might be discovered between the medium of the exhibition and its subject ('European ghosts'), as exposed by the relation of the film (as a medium) and its ostensible subject (the exhibition)?

Occurring in a particular time and place, the exhibition is evidence of its curators' own research project, which in this case concerns 'European Ghosts'. Transposed into a mobile medium, that research becomes accessible in new terms – typically, for example, as a catalogue publication; or, in its montage of de- and re-contextualisation, through filmmaking. In my own example, the creative practice of essay-film engages its medium with an implied or latent research concept, which concerns modes of knowledge production (or, perhaps, its reproduction) in the apparatus or chronotope of European ethnographic museums, as indeed a citation of its 'ghosts' (or the phantomatic).[4]

* * *

To speak *of* ghosts is, supposedly, more credible than to speak *with* ghosts (the former may be deemed research; the latter, superstition), and yet much of film or photographic culture offers precisely such a dialogue between technique (or art) and experience (or conscience). This is succinctly expressed in an inspired improvisation to (and, indeed, for) the camera, by Jacques Derrida: 'cinema + psycho-analysis = the science of ghosts' (McMullen 1983); or, as we might gloss this formula: 'the photographic + the unconscious = hauntology'. Echoing Benjamin's sense of what comes to be known in memory that was not 'originally' perceived, Derrida speaks here of a 'memory of the past that

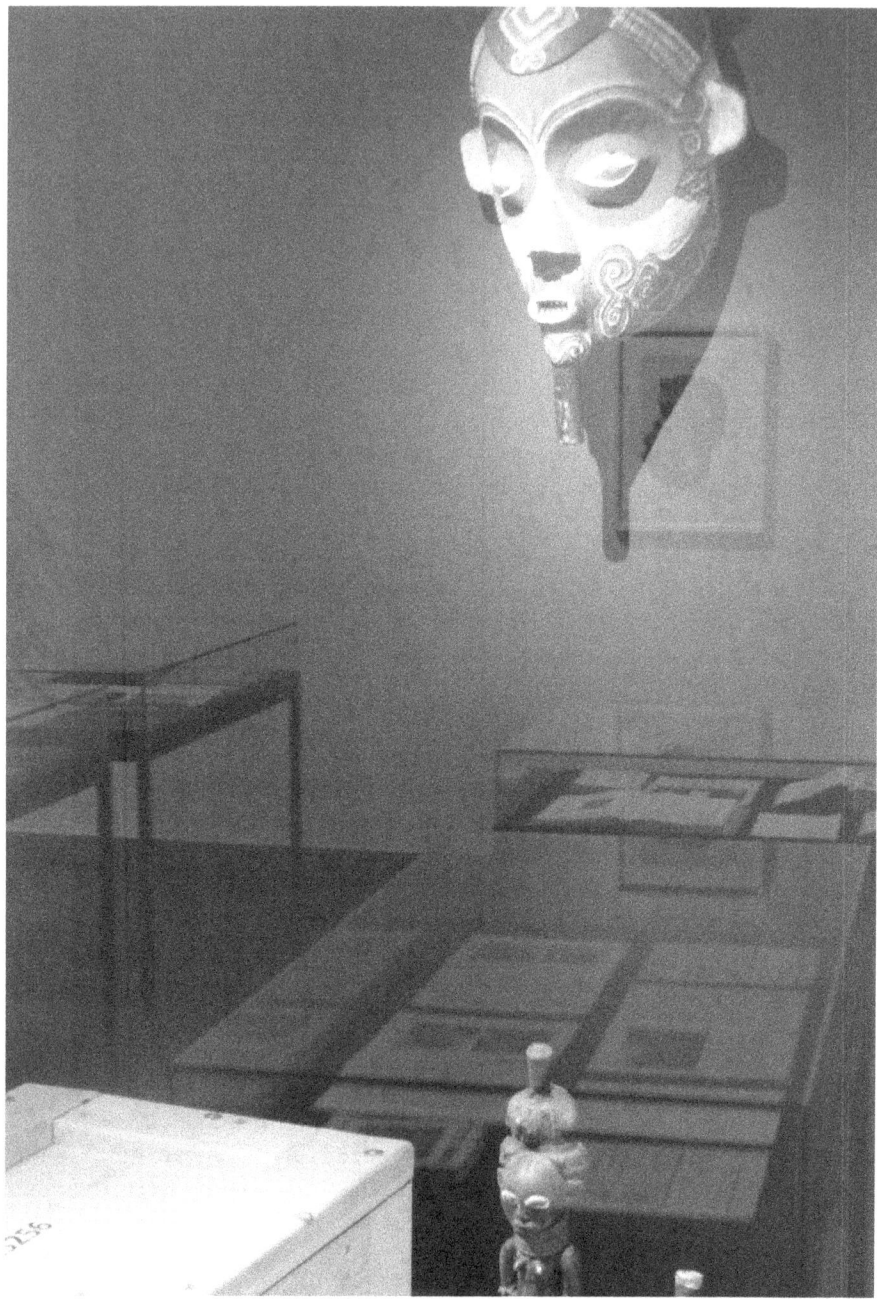

Figure 19.2 Photo taken (29.12.16) by Mischa Twitchin at the 'European Ghosts' exhibition (curated in collaboration with the Royal Museum of Central Africa, Tervuren) held at the Kunstmuseum aan zee, Ostend (www.muzee.be).

has never taken the form of the present' (McMullen 1983). The notion of a 'hauntology' is further elaborated by Derrida (1994: 10) in his reading of the ghost of Shakespeare in Marx, with which he proposes a mode of cultural enquiry that unsettles proleptic, rather than analeptic, claims to knowledge.[5] This also displaces any residual sense of the photographic as simply offering a research medium in terms of the 'verifiable' and 'objective'.

Standard research funding applications, however, are oriented by a forward-looking linearity, for all their rhetoric about methodological innovation. This latter term is not intended to offer a change in the supposed premise of the research but rather a 'new' interpretation of that premise – adding to knowledge rather than transforming it. Most research funding prefers facts to phantoms; or, in Whitehead's terms, abstractions to concerns. In the very title of *Phantom Europe* there is an echo of hauntology and its 'occult language' – concerning 'the real and the imaginary', 'objective positivism and subjective belief', 'modern science and pre-modern animism' (Demos 2013: 8) – as it addresses the 'post-colonial' production (and reception) of critical and creative research between two sites of exposition: the museum apparatus and the photographic medium, in the example here of an essay-film.

We might note a haunting precursor of this essay-film idea in Stephen Heath's combinatory displacement of 'screen images, film memory', with its citation of montage as a concept in common between cinema and psychoanalysis (in the theory of drives), as well as shared concepts of the 'terminable and interminable' and 'secondary revision'. In Heath's suggested comparison between screen memory and film image, the dynamic relation in montage between de-contextualisation and re-contextualisation (as a mode of knowledge or research), and between dis-possession and re-possession (as a mode of phantasy or creation), resonate together (echoing both Derrida and Leiris) in the phantomatic. Producing its own 'object' of investigation concerning museum ethnography, the film broaches a set of questions (as discussed above) that evidence the potential of creative research. In contrast, for example, with writing a review of the exhibition – at least, one that would be publishable in a 'relevant', or 'appropriate', scholarly journal, fulfilling prescribed disciplinary criteria from which concern would be largely abstracted – the retroactive effect of the film creates its own prospective possibility of and for research.

* * *

At first sight, *Phantom Europe* offers a set of tourist photographs read in light of an essay that has no necessary relation to them (although the source of the essay by T. J. Demos does in fact appear in one of the images). This tourism is not simply that of a physical journey from 'home' to somewhere else – in this case from London to Ostend. It also concerns a mental or conceptual journey, made visible in that photographic displacement, as then figured in the possibility of revisiting the film (now that the exhibition is long over) – as, indeed, I am doing in this very article. This possibility creates a new mode of learning with respect to the museum project's 'ghosts', as evidence of relations between an optical and conceptual unconscious concerning the subject of the research; that is, of 'phantom Europe'.

Rather than being concerned with 'visitors and voyeurs on the one hand and commodified actors or targets of strangers' fantasies on the other' (as Lucy Lippard evokes it (1999: 4)), this tourism becomes the theoretical fiction of the film itself, as something that holds the future in its own past through photographs put into a montage as a 'film memory', articulated in relation to fragments of the text by Demos that is quoted in it. This sense of the photographic, in which 'the future nests so eloquently that we, looking back, may rediscover it' (Benjamin 2005: 510), is a dimension of that 'other nature' that, according to Benjamin, the camera – rather than the eye – discovers: the optical unconscious (Benjamin 2005: 512). This allows us to conceptualise the creation of percepts, rather than their simple registration; where what is recorded by the camera is not registered by the eye/ I of the museum visitor, or tourist, except retroactively – as a question of this creative practice. It is only through the montage that these percepts become manifested, precisely, as a work of memory or (with Whitehead) of affective concern. Between the fictional and the real, the film's journey with the camera-eye, as a form of autoethnography on screen, exposes the paradoxical necessity of the contingent (Twitchin 2019d), as that which could not be known in advance, but only afterwards. In the pre-digital age, this could have been a journey through a photo album, or a slide show, accompanied by a commentary composed of personal recollections. In this essay-film, accessible online, there is a theoretical reflection accompanying images that offers, rather, an impersonal 'recollection'.

The montage composes an illusion of continuity and correspondence between images that themselves promise the fabled indexical relation with the 'documented' journey to see – and to make visible – a particular exhibition in Ostend. These illusions – which are standard in any reference to film – gloss the realities of fragmentation and parataxis involved in the impossible pursuit of documenting 'being there', which the reproducibility of the photograph allows us to reconceive. The past appears to be recorded as it was, while becoming open to being revisited, as if in its enduring, but discontinuous, present. Between the theory and the practice, the screen memory and the film image, a new experience emerges that is not reducible to the one or the other. Abstracting from the moving, bustling, jostling world, the film produces its own time of and for reflection, which is not that of its ostensible object (which was itself a deliberate construction of visibility through juxtaposing stillness and movement by means of the apparatus, or technology, of an exhibition).

In this 'phantomatic' context, the contrast of silent stills and syncopated soundtrack (with voice and music) allows for an experimentation through parataxis – where there is no sound-time in the image itself. The visual sequence – with its animation of still photographs through cut, fade, or dissolve – appears in relation to the syncopations of an autonomous soundtrack, which predetermines the film's duration. The logic of the edit is thus free from the relations between sound-images that are supposed in continuity editing, based on filmed movement with synchronised sound. The creative push and pull between form and content – as between sound and image (as if between the arts of understanding and presentation) – generates new resonances between each register. As an instance of creative practice, the work of editing concerns discovering the mutual implication of word and image in exposing the subject of the research; not least, in the phantomatic experience of the film's apparent continuity.

And what of the voice in this relay of 'showing' what is shown, with regard to what is said? The voice is not identified with any particular image but, perhaps, with the screen (distinct from the photograph) – playing with the fact that the arbitrary appears necessary in the habitual expectations of film viewing. But is it the image or the viewer that the voice addresses? Or is it the site of a split between the two? A near distance, perhaps – given that no narrative or diegetic sound here offers an imagined difference between background and foreground? This acousmatic dimension of the essay-film (to adopt a theorisation made with respect to feature films by Michel Chion (1999)) is a key to its hauntological conditions as a medium of and for research. The sense that the image becomes visible through the words (whether critically or metaphorically), or the words become imaginable through the photographs, would be simply reductive were the film's medium conceived of in terms of an application of one sense to the other. Fundamentally, the essay-film poses a question of its own making: what becomes representable by means of its specific montage, as indicated by the hyphen that haunts the designation of its medium? It is in this echo of its autonomy that we return to the creative difference that such a practice might make for its own conditions of research.

* * *

Curiously, there are resonances with questions of political economy even in Hans Richter's initial formulation of the term 'essay-film' (in 1940), where he searches for a vocabulary that would distinguish its ambition from the documentary. Richter's example is precisely that modern spectre, 'the stock exchange as a market' – where apparently invisible forces wreak their havoc on peoples' lives. The sense that capitalism is a form of war against society is manifested today in the manifold consequences of neoliberalism, not least in the 'assault on universities' (Bailey and Freedman 2011). The lie of so-called 'small government' is demonstrated by the use of legislation to undermine the understanding of higher education as a public good and to engineer a marketisation of university activities. The redefinition of research, through the criteria of the so-called Research Excellence Framework (REF), with the ever-increasing value of 'impact', is now also informing the subsequent Teaching Excellence Framework as an instrument for allocating funding. As Nick Couldry suggests: 'The *point* of the REF is to remove core research funding from "research units" whose research lacks demonstrable impact (that is, "impact" defined primarily by reference to the economy and policy-making). So it is hardly surprising that core *teaching* funding is now to be withdrawn from institutions except where they teach in certain priority areas: priorities not for society, but for the national economy, in other words economic sectors where jobs cannot be filled' (2011: 42).

The phantomatic, like Spinoza's soul (Berardi 2009: 21), is, after all, embodied; it possesses or animates both material and immaterial 'things'. The essay-film, in Richter's view, offers an example of this:

> The essay film, in its attempt to make the invisible world of imagination, thoughts, and ideas visible, can draw from an incomparably larger reservoir of expressive means than can the pure documentary film. Since in the essay film the film maker is not bound by the depiction of external phenomena and the constraints of chronological sequences, but, on the contrary, has to enlist material from everywhere, the film maker can bounce around freely in time and space. (Richter 2017 [1940]: 91)

Being able to move 'freely in time and space' is the creative possibility of both the essay-film and ghosts – where the photographic and the phantomatic correspond in the evocation of an ethnography of modernity, not least in its colonial 'possessions'. To draw out a concern from T. J. Demos's text *Return to the Postcolony*, with which *Phantom Europe* inscribes its own commentary on method, how does the phantomatic – 'living with ghosts' – invite reflection on the hauntological conditions of colonial representability? This was the very theme (at least, partially) of the exhibition shown, as it returns in the filmmaking. Whatever is made visible in this second degree of representational technology, however, is due not simply to the framing of the photograph. Besides the optical unconscious there is also a conceptual unconscious at work, where the commentary proposes its own questions as to what is visible, albeit not referring to *these* images – save in the 'screen memory' of their particular montage.

The concern of 'living with ghosts' is a question of the photograph in its specifically modern relation to the spectral or phantomatic. This technology of research also concerns its politics (a medium, after all, is never neutral) and, therefore, of 'living with ghosts justly', as Demos says (echoing Derrida). With respect to neoliberalism, this engages with that 'counter-movement' advocated by Ingold in the introduction to this essay. Reflecting on *Phantom Europe*, as an instance of creative practice, further questions arise: how might questions of justice inform those of research in the age of neoliberalism? How are the living seen to be haunted by the legacies (or ghosts) of colonial injustice? Indeed, what hope is there for 'creative practice' to participate in decolonising research? Such questions no more invite a conclusion than creative research invites audited 'outcomes'. As Ingold notes (echoing examples from both Bergson and Alfred Gel): 'The meaning of the pattern, therefore, can be grasped only by an intuition that enters into it, or that follows its trails, rather than by an intellect that, in contemplating the finished work, attempts to reconstruct the puzzle from its solution' (2007: 49). To return to the dynamic of the hyphen in this essay – with Adorno's sense of the essay, that it 'co-ordinates elements instead of subordinating them' (1991: 22) – one could say here that creative practice is concerned with what remains open-ended.

Notes

1. This distinction between concern and fact, drawn from the vocabulary of the Quakers, is advocated by Whitehead and has been more recently adopted by Bruno Latour, framing a renewed reflection on the distinction between objects and things in the name of what he calls a 'new respectful realist attitude' (Latour 2004: 231 and 244).
2. The French version, which is anglicised in my film's title, refers to Michel Leiris's account (2017 [1933]) of the French colonial-ethnographic expedition 'from Dakar to Djibouti' in the early 1930s, in which he participated, written up as *L'Afrique fantôme* [*Phantom Africa*]. I have now also made a series of films exploring the self-representation of the newly re-opened Tervuren museum, which are also freely accessible on Vimeo (Twitchin 2019a–c).
3. This non-prescriptive relation to discovery through research, with its relative autonomy from the demands of institutional 'discipline', was made possible by a British Academy Post-doctoral Fellowship, for which I am profoundly grateful.
4. I have further developed this in a series of films with the subtitle of the 'Museum of World Culture', exploring the sense of this idea in the counterpoint of images from the Stockholm Ethnographic museum and fragments of essays by Karl Marx, Édouard Glissant, Michel Leiris, Wyatt MacGaffey, and W. T. J. Mitchell (see <http://vimeo.com/user13124826/videos>).
5. Similar concerns have been recently returned to in terms of the 'virtual' by Kader Attia in his film *The Medium is the Message* (2019), presented at the Haus der Kulturen der Welt's opening *New Alphabet* project (with a short essay, 'Countering Virtual Dispossession', in the accompanying booklet (2019)).

References

Adorno, Theodor (1991), 'The Essay as Form', trans. Shierry Weber Nicholsen, in *Notes to Literature*, Vol. 1, New York: Columbia University Press, pp. 3–23.

Attia, Kader (2019), 'Countering Virtual Dispossession', in Bernd Scherer and Olga von Schubert (eds), *The New Alphabet*, Berlin: Haus der Kulturen der Welt.
Bailey, Michael and Des Freedman (eds) (2011), *The Assault on Universities*, London: Pluto Press.
Bazin, André (1958), *André Bazin on Chris Marker*, trans. Dave Kehr, article accessible on the Chris Marker website: <http://chrismarker.org/andre-bazin-on-chris-marker-1958/>.
Benjamin, Walter (2005 [1931]), 'Little History of Photography', trans. Edmund Jephcott and Kingsley Shorter, in Michael Jennings, Howard Eiland and Gary Smith (eds), *Selected Writings*, Vol. 2, Pt 2, Cambridge, MA: Belknap Press of Harvard University Press, pp. 507–30.
Berardi, Franco (2009), *The Soul at Work: From alienation to autonomy*, trans. Francesca Cadel and Giuseppina Mecchia, Los Angeles: Semiotext(e).
Bergson, Henri (1911), *Creative Evolution*, trans. A. Mitchell, London: Macmillan.
Chion, Michel (1999), *The Voice in Cinema*, trans. Claudia Gorbman, New York: Columbia University Press.
Couldry, Nick (2011), 'Fighting for the University's Life', in Michael Bailey and Des Freedman (eds), *The Assault on Universities*, London: Pluto Press, pp. 37–46.
Deleuze, Gilles and Guattari, Félix (1994), *What is Philosophy?*, trans. Hugh Tomlinson and Graham Burchill, London: Verso.
Demos, T. J. (2013), *Return to the Postcolony*, Berlin: Sternberg Press.
Derrida, Jacques (1994), *Spectres of Marx*, trans. Peggy Kamuf, London: Routledge.
Geertz, Clifford (1989), *Works and Lives*, Cambridge: Polity Press.
Hastrup, Kirsten (2007), 'Agency, Anticipation and Creativity', in Elizabeth Hallam and Tim Ingold (eds), *Creativity and Cultural Improvisation*, Oxford: Berg, pp. 194–206.
Heath, Stephen (1977), 'Screen Images – Film Memory', in *Cine-Tracts*, Vol. 1, n. 1, pp. 27–36.
Ingold, Tim (2007), 'Introduction' to Part 1, in Elizabeth Hallam and Tim Ingold (eds), *Creativity and Cultural Improvisation*, Oxford: Berg, pp. 45–54.
Ingold, Tim (2016), 'From science to art and back again: the pendulum of an anthropologist', in *Anuac*, Vol. 5, n. 1, pp. 5–23.
Latour, Bruno (2004), 'Why has critique run out of steam? From matters of fact to matters of concern', in *Critical Inquiry*, Vol. 30, pp. 225–48.
Leiris, Michel (2017 [1933/1981]), *Phantom Africa*, trans. Brent Edwards, Calcutta: Seagull Books.
Lippard, Lucy (1999), *On the Beaten Track*, New York: The New Press.
McMullen, Ken (1983), *Ghost Dance* (film).
Osborne, Peter (2018), *The Postconceptual Condition*, London: Verso.
Richter, Hans (2017 [1940]), 'The film essay: a new type of documentary film', trans. Maria Alter, in Nora Alter and Timothy Corrigan (eds), *Essays on the Essay Film*, New York: Columbia University Press, pp. 89–92.
Savoy, Bénédicte (2017), *Objets du désir, désir d'objets*, Paris: Fayard.
Twitchin, Mischa (2016), *Phantom Europe* (film diptych accessible at <https://vimeo.com/181630585> and <https://vimeo.com/181043313>).
Twitchin, Mischa (2017), 'Sites of Research, or "No Layers of the Onion": Phantom Europe', in *Oxford Artistic and Practice Based Research*, Vol. 1 (<https://www.oarplatform.com/sites-research-layers-onion-phantom-europe/>).
Twitchin, Mischa (2019a), *Tervuren 1*: <https://vimeo.com/322368836>; <https://vimeo.com/322369544>; <https://vimeo.com/322370195>.
Twitchin, Mischa (2019b), *Tervuren 2*: <https://vimeo.com/333637888>; <https://vimeo.com/336828479>.

Twitchin, Mischa (2019c), *Tervuren 3*: <https://vimeo.com/333638698>.
Twitchin, Mischa (2019d), 'What chance failure?' in Tony Fisher and Eve Katsouraki (eds), *Beyond Failure*, London: Routledge, pp. 37–54.
Whitehead, Alfred North (1967 [1933]), *Adventures of Ideas*, New York: The Free Press.

20. *SCREEN MEMORIES:* A VIDEO ESSAY ON *SMULTRONSTÄLLET/ WILD STRAWBERRIES*

Catherine Grant

[*Screen memory*]: a recollection of early childhood that may be falsely recalled or magnified in importance and that masks another memory of deep emotional significance.

(*Merriam-Webster Dictionary*)

Screen Memories is a short split-screen video that began as a piece of free-associational audiovisual exploration. Rather than an explicit work of scholarly exposition, explication or argumentation, it is an instance of creative practice as a mode of enquiry:[1] a concise compilation made to perform or frame a new audiovisual encounter – in this case turning on a technique of gentle defamiliarisation (*Ostranenie*) – in order to engender new material thinking and feeling. As film historian and theorist Pam Cook has noted, in relation to her own practical exploration of videographic film and television studies, audiovisual forms like this

> can produce a 'writerly' experience à la Roland Barthes in which viewers / readers / essayists generate their own meanings. The video essay constitutes an event; it transforms existing material to fashion an open-ended process of re-reading and re-writing. (Cook 2014)

Given this open-endedness, what follows is a written exegesis and contextualisation of the video that aim to expand on its central topic and to make more manifest its audiovisual methodology. I provide this in order to situate the

SCREEN MEMORIES

Figure 20.1 *Screen Memories*, A Video Essay.

video even more clearly as practice-led *research*, that is as a work attempting to produce new knowledge, both through its particular form and through the reflections generated by this.

Screen Memories is one of a number of videographic works of spatial montage that I made about Ingmar Bergman's films to be screened at events to mark the one-hundredth anniversary of the Swedish director's birth on 14 July 1918. Each of these works uses its multiple-screen form in the service of a poetic analysis through synchronous performance, a playing together of cinematic motifs, similarities, repetitions or variations that would otherwise only be meaningfully apprehended as such *sequentially* in the audiovisual time-based medium.[2] In their double unfolding, across screens, of the already 'profuse simultaneity of signifiers' (Burch 1981: 29) in any single collection of frames from Bergman's cinematic sequences, these videos also explore, as a compositional principle, art historian and theorist Roger Cardinal's notions of the 'haptic mosaic' in pictorial culture (Cardinal 1986: 127). They issue an invitation to the 'mobile eye' of the viewer to engage in intensified processes of 'peripheralized attention' (Cardinal 1986: 124, 114), in an accretional method of meaning-making through 'seesaw scanning of the text, compelled by the very duality of the signs' (Rifaterre 1980: 165–6).[3] As Cardinal argues, such 'decentered scanning can constitute a refreshing alternative register of filmic experience' (1986: 112). I will return to reflect on these aspects, but first will offer some notes on the production method of the video.

In the *Screen Memories* montage, the sequence of shots that comes to be shown in the left-hand screen is taken from the beginning of the first of two

305

daydream *cum* 'flashback' scenes in Bergman's 1957 film *Smultronstället/Wild Strawberries*. I silenced the soundtrack and slowed down the image track. The right-hand screen sequence plays out, in its entirety, the later of the two *reverie* scenes, the one that takes place at the end of the film. While reproduced in its original duration, this sequence is also partially silenced, with source sound only at its beginning – some contextualising voiceover from the film's protagonist Isak Borg (played by Victor Sjöström) – and at its end, when we hear Isak's relaxed breathing followed by some chords played, extra-diegetically, on a harp, in the film score, after the screen turns black. The juxtaposed film sequences are seemingly anchored in directorial biography by my addition, in the middle part of the video, of an extract from an audio recording of Bergman's comments about the conception of his film, which I sourced during the making of the video from an online copy of Melvyn Bragg's 1978 *The South Bank Show* interview with the Swedish director.[4] The video montage is accompanied for most of its length by my doubling of a short melodic, looping musical track by digital composer and artist Podington Bear, which I also encountered online during the making of the video.[5] As that music concludes, the harp cadence from the original soundtrack of *Wild Strawberries* sounds out (its source the sequence in the right-hand screen), accompanying (in the left-hand screen) the shot of Isak slowly making eye contact with the camera/audience/ us, breaking the 'fourth wall'. At the same moment (and while Isak's image, with its direct stare, slowly fades to black), in the other screen space, the viewer is finally presented (before the credits sequence) with some manifest scholarly thinking in the form of an epigraph – a free-floating quotation from the 1899 essay which lends its title to the video, Sigmund Freud's 'Screen Memories': 'It may indeed be questioned whether we have any memories at all *from* our childhood' (Freud 1899: 322). It only becomes clear that Freud *is* the source of these words, though, as the first entry in the credits sequence appears. The viewer may otherwise confuse them with discourse issuing directly from *Wild Strawberries* given that their presentation mirrors the style of subtitling of Isak's speech earlier in the video. Freud's culminating words are intended to work as a kind of retroactive prism, or belated framing device, through which to *re-view* what has preceded them. With their contradiction of the video's other verbal content, they may prompt a moderate re-examination of (at least) the *naturalness* of the 'screen memories' that we have just experienced, and possibly even a challenge to their apparent 'truthfulness' and the comfort they may have generated.

The second part of Freud's sentence from which the climactic quotation is taken, which doesn't appear in the video, reads: 'memories *relating to* our childhood may be all that we possess' (1899: 322). This presents, possibly even more clearly than the first part, the radical challenge of Freudian thinking on 'screen memories'. That perhaps before a certain age, and perhaps after that, too, *none* of what we remember is reliable or straightforward, even if it appears to be – an unsettling notion in many ways.

Although I had certainly come across Freud's concept before encountering film scholar Elizabeth Cowie's book chapter on *Wild Strawberries* in 2003, I don't recall ever properly *comprehending* its radicalness, which might explain why reading her analysis and arguments, in which she connects this concept to Bergman's film for the first time, provoked my interest to such an extent.[6] Cowie refers to this concept by name in relation to the film on two occasions in her chapter, each focusing on my favourite sequences (the ones I gather in my video), one early in the film and the other, as I have said, its closing moments:

> Early in this journey [from Stockholm to Lund, the film's protagonist Isak Borg] revisits his family's summer home where he spent his childhood holidays, and where he experiences a strange reverie whereby 'the clarity of the present shaded into the even clearer images of memory'. Although prompted by memory, he was never in fact present at the scenes he now witnesses; they are in fact imagined, or a screen memory. (Cowie 2003: 192)

> These interactions motivate a sense that Isak has in some way redeemed himself in that, through the course of the past twenty-four hours, he has acquired a self-knowledge and also a new concern for others in his acceptance of his responsibility for the unhappiness of others. As a result we can enjoy with Isak the film's concluding restitutive scene in which, as he lays down to sleep, Isak daydreams an encounter he has returned to many times, he tells us, although it appears to be a screen memory: he is again back at the summer house with the strawberry patch. (Cowie 2003: 195)

My appropriation of these sequences in order to juxtapose them in a video can be viewed *manifestly* as a work of scholar-fandom: I wanted to bring together these beguiling segments in a lyrical and hopefully captivating, synchronous two-screen montage in order both to pay homage to them, as well as to understand them even better in the light of Cowie's discussion of them – but not without *transforming* them in the process. In some ways, even as a transformative work attempting to free-associate audiovisually from the feelings and memories attached to what it compiles, *Screen Memories* turned out nonetheless to be a very literal-minded piece of remembering, repeating and working-through of its sources. One of the readings that it offers up is quite straightforward: the video presents us with the similarities, in its spoken verbal content, between what both writer-director Bergman, in his 1978 interview, and his 1957 film protagonist Isak thought from the perspective of their respective locations about the conscious recall of childhood memories as a form of comfort or escapism – a pacifying *technique* (to use Bergman's choice of word in the interview) for use in times of anxiety and insecurity. The video might itself *appear* comforting or escapist as it showcases this technique in action in a lyrical way that chooses not to depart (very much) from the tone, or affect, of the film's 'happy ending'. Nonetheless, as I worked on the editing, I realised that I actually regarded the emerging audiovisual form as a kind of mini 'mind-game film' (Elsaesser 2009), a *rebus* ('Freud's epithet of the dream', as Cowie puts it (2003: 199)). I understood materially that I was producing a collection of found elements not simply to enjoy, but to *puzzle over*, and potentially also to generate forms of belated or deferred understanding, especially in the light of the element (central to its mix, for me) from which I *don't* explicitly quote: Cowie's reading of these recollections possibly as 'screen memories' in the psychoanalytic sense.

As fellow film theorist Mary Ann Doane writes of Freud's concept of 'falsely recalled or magnified in importance' *cover* memories,[7]

> The screen memory is a detail, a contingency, which is nevertheless richly vivid and sensuous in its cognitive opacity. It stands out in a scene and constitutes itself as the marker of specificity itself. Screen memories are characterized by their intensity; they are, in Freud's words, recollected '*too* clearly'. (Doane 2002: 166; quoting Freud 1899: 305).

A memory recollected '*too* clearly' echoes *Wild Strawberries* protagonist Isak's verbal evocation of his first piece of childhood remembering on his journey in the film, prompted by revisiting the wild strawberry patch of his family's summer house: 'the day's clear reality dissolved into the *even clearer* images of memory that appeared before my eyes with the strength of a *true stream of events*' (my emphasis). This voiceover segment was substituted (silenced) in my video, as I have described above, by the deployment of an extract from a recording of Bergman's own voice recounting (in a late 1970s British television interview) his frequently repeated story of how the origins of *Wild Strawberries*' script resided in noting his ability to summons detailed – '*almost photographic*' – childhood memories of his grandmother's Uppsala apartment as a calming technique at times of anxiety and insecurity. This origin story was always presented as 'true', in auteurist dialogues with Bergman, until later in the Swedish director's life when he revised it rather bluntly:

> In [my earlier autobiographical interviews gathered in *Bergman on Bergman*, 1973], I relate in some detail an early morning trip by car to the city of Uppsala. How ... I wanted to visit my grandmother's house at

Trädgårdsgatan. How I stood outside the kitchen door and, for a magical moment, experienced the possibility of plunging back into my childhood. That's a lie. (Bergman 1994: 21–2)

When I came across the recording of the Bergman interview episode of the 1978 *The South Bank Show* episode online, I was fascinated by the hesitations in the Swedish director's account of this teleology of the film on which he had been drawing – possibly, '*too* clearly' – for twenty years.[8] These pauses (inarticulacies, uncertainties?) 'invited and disturbed my understanding in terms of symbolization', to use Cowie's words about 'hesitation in relation to' dream-work images (2003: 199). In my video editing process, I began to notice and explore more fully a number of vivid or sensuous details, or contingencies, to use Doane's understanding of cover, or screen, memories. Of these, one of the most striking (also discussed by Cowie) is, of course, the placement of old man Isak *in* the childhood memory, not only as an aged bodily presence, impossibly witnessing an event at which he wasn't in attendance,[9] but also as a vocal observer (and *guarantor*) of the scene. My video associates from this to Bergman's own ageing voice, which I now placed in the scene as an equally overdetermined, authoritative presence, evoking not only his actual 1978 age of sixty, or the fictional child self of whom he speaks, but also the younger man who made the film at thirty-eight, now speaking over the images of Isak/ Sjöström as an eighty-year-old grand/fatherly avatar in the film[10] (as well as over the images of fictional cousin Sara (Bibi Anderssen)) – all the while discussing, in this new context *opaquely*, his real-life grandmother.[11]

With these moves, my video may be re-performing something that Cowie has compellingly noted of Bergman's film itself:

> The continuous reworking of parallels and symbolism in *Wild Strawberries* through reversals, transformations and doublings which dissolve into differences produces an unintelligible interconnection, that is, its sense-making is only for the moment, for in the next it is disrupted by another, associative, connection. The imposition, or discovery, of causal logic is made problematic so that no unified subjectivity – either of the son or the father, of Isak or Ingmar, can be discovered behind the imagery. In the gap between Bergman as Isak the father, and Bergman as Isak the son, lies the navel of the dream and which the film and its crafted dreams both point to and dissemble. (Cowie 2003: 198)[12]

Aside from the detail, or contingency, of Isak's presence in his 'memory', the other element of these scenes which is 'nevertheless richly vivid and sensuous in its cognitive opacity' (Doane 2002: 166) are the textural aspects of Bergman's *mise en scène*.[13] In my videographic processing of these sequences, the synchronous side-by-side placement of them enabled me to experience these aspects afresh, as did my kaleidoscopic play with slowing down (in the left-hand screen) the black and white cinematography and editing choices: the beautiful shots and dissolves of the sky, the dappled light, the trees, the branches, twigs, stalks and blades of grass, and the strawberry patch itself. I was fascinated by the continuity of the patterning across the two screens in the finished video.

In his study of the benefits (and pleasures) of peripheralised spectatorship and its consequent generation of a fresh space in which to pause over details, Cardinal discusses the distinction that emerges between two 'divergent strategies of viewing': a 'literate' mode, which is drawn to the 'obvious *Gestalt* or figure on offer' – as directed by the intention of the artist or by our familiarity with classical image conventions – and a 'non-literate' or haptic mode that 'instead roams over the frame, sensitive to its textures and surfaces – to its *ground*' (Cardinal 1986: 124).[14] One of Cardinal's most compelling sets of examples (the one that immediately follows the above assertions) is cinematic: 'a kind of inchoate, tangled sampling' of undergrowth and other flora stirred by the wind in a number of Tarkovsky films. He continues:

> I find the phenomenal density of such passages of film to be strangely alluring ... They appeal to the non-visual senses as much as they appeal to the eye, to the extent that the gaze seems capable only of dyslexic fumblings in search of a secure *Gestalt*, falling instead into a kind of euphoric, unfocused swoon. (Cardinal 1986: 125)

In *Screen Memories, Wild Strawberries*' phenomenal density is doubled, and potentially defamiliarised as a result. But this shifting of perspective back and forward between Figure (the conventionally significant or meaningful aspects of an image-based text) and Ground (a background or context we might more usually take for granted, and not read for meaning) is also played out in other aspects of my video. As an *audio*visual essay it became an experiment in the anchoring or persuasive effects of music and sound (and other verbal content) in the multiscreen audiovisual experience.[15] Even though, as Ian Garwood writes in his brilliant study of sound in the multiscreen film (2008), '[a]dvances in soundtrack technology such as Dolby Stereo and Dynamic Digital Sound also allow sound to circulate within and around the frame in new ways', I chose not to use any spatialising techniques in the soundtrack design of this video. There is, thus, no spatial distinction between the sound sourced from the material in either of the two screens and the other sounds I added to the video.[16] Sonically, the video works as a single-screen experience. The voiceovers (both Isak's and Bergman's) most likely operate 'centrally' and *conventionally* – as Figure – to help stabilise (and contain) the dense and ever shifting visual content of the video, drawing us back – on semantic track—from an 'unfocused swoon' (Cardinal 1986: 125), and working together with the (semically complementary) music as an additional form of 'sonic glue' (Garwood 2008). This may be why Freud's climactic words, casting doubt on the veracity of what we have heard *if not seen*, may come as a (not altogether pleasant) surprise at the end of an otherwise comforting audio-viewing experience.

In her examination of Freud's 1899 'Screen Memories' essay, and especially in her treatment of the flowers and meadowland imagery in the case-study he analyses in that work (which turned out to have been his *own* memory), literary theorist Naomi Schor writes,

> Because of their hyperclarity and signification these details ... act to blind the reader, hypnotizing her so as to prevent her from noticing other equally important details, in particular (all) those that might reveal the identity of this talented patient [Freud himself]. (Schor 1987: 89)

> Freud's floral disguise, his rhetorical flowers, are a *mimesis of the falsification-work* which repression carries out on childhood recollections: by a process of mise en abyme, Freud has produced a true-false cover-memory, or better yet has re-forged an already counterfeit childhood memory. (Schor 1987: 90, my emphasis)

This phrase, the *mimesis of the falsification-work*, describes very well, it seems to me, what is (re-)performed in my video *Screen Memories – re-performed* because my video discovers, or posits, that this kind of mimesis of a cover memory is what may be being performed in the original sequences from *Wild Strawberries* themselves (the ones I have appropriated). If not an exact copy, my associative remix is an exploration (in miniature), a 'dreaming again', of Bergman's film's intrinsic deceptiveness, its temporal and semantic displacements (to paraphrase Doane 2002: 166).

As Cowie writes of Bergman's film's dream-work, and, in a *deferred* way, of my video essay,

> The dream is 'dreamt' again as a hermeneutic requiring not the recovery of meaning hidden in the dream, but the discovery of the meaning of the dreaming, of the selection and juxtaposition of elements, the transpositions – the work of the displacements and condensations. The dream-work is not a distortion of a message or meaning fully formed prior to and discoverable behind and before its deformation, but a process or encounter involving a production in which a symbolizing representation emerges. (Cowie 2003: 188)

Notes

1. 'Creative Practice as a Mode of Enquiry' is the subtitle of a 2018 book on this scholarly area by Craig Batty and Susan Kerrigan. *Screen Memories: A Video Essay on Smultronstället/Wild Strawberries*, by Catherine Grant, is available online: <https://vimeo.com/251838111>. The video and this reflection on it were first published by the journal *Cinergie: Il Cinema e le altre Arti* in 2018 under a Creative Commons Attribution 4.0 International Licence (Grant 2018). Thanks to the guest editors of that issue, Chiara Grizzaffi and Andrea Minuz for their work.
2. See, for example, *Lesson* (Catherine Grant, 2018), online < https://vimeo.com/257277668>; and *Persona Non Grata Sonata* (Catherine Grant and Amber Jacobs, 2018), online <https://vimeo.com/251331908>. *Screen Memories* is online here: <https://vimeo.com/251838111>. I am currently working on a monograph about these and many other works of spatial montage, in the context of digital cinephilia (forthcoming 2020), which will expand on some of my earlier written reflections on this topic (e.g. Grant 2013; Grant 2015).
3. Aylish Wood has usefully posited the notion of 'distributed attention' (Wood 2007: 11), following the work of phenomenologists such as Vivian Sobchack, to discuss digital interface culture, including multiple screens. Wood's book has been important in my general research into spatial montage, but I won't discuss it here as she doesn't refer to the art-historian, semiotician and communications studies research context that I am foregrounding in the particular video method under discussion (e.g. the work of Cardinal, Burch, Rifaterre, and van Leeuwen, among others).
4. Ingmar Bergman on *The South Bank Show*, with Melvyn Bragg, 1978, uploaded to YouTube by user FilMagicians, <https://youtu.be/CLVLKQ8Nh_A>.
5. From the Free Music Archive online at <http://freemusicarchive.org>.
6. Cowie's chapter is one of quite a large number of studies of *Wild Strawberries* that foreground its related, prominently figured acts of dreaming (including Arlow 1997; Bach 1975; Botz-Bornstein 2007; Coates 2010; Extence 2008; French and French 1995; Greenberg 1970; Petrić 1981; Steene 1965; and Williams 2012). Yet it was the first work to argue for the relevance of Sigmund Freud's concept of 'screen memories' in analysing Bergman's film. Beyond what Cowie writes, very helpfully and informatively, in her specific passages on this concept, and in her general, very suggestive treatment of the repressions, displacements and condensations of dream-work which, by extension, clearly echo those of 'screen memories', she doesn't completely define for her reader what these kinds of memories 'screen memories' might be, or what Freud said about them, specifically. Neither Freud's 1899 essay 'Screen Memories' nor his later revisions of the concept in subsequent work (for example: Freud 1900; 1914; and 1920) are discussed directly.
7. To cite again part of the dictionary definition with which I opened, <https://www.merriam-webster.com/dictionary/screen%20memory>.
8. Including in Bergman's *The Magic Lantern: An Autobiography* (1988).
9. In the first reverie, old Isak is actually in the place he dreams of, or revisits in memory – the *smultronstället* (wild strawberry patch); in the second reverie, he wills his virtual return from his bed back in Stockholm.
10. Another presence in this intersubjective relay for me is the eighty-four-year old Ingmar Bergman of 2003, the year of publication of Cowie's chapter and also when I first read this work by her. Bergman died in 2007. Victor Sjöström died in 1957 shortly after making *Wild Strawberries*.
11. The grandmother of whom Bergman speaks in the *South Bank Show* interview is the only family character (corresponding or not to Bergman's own family) not

directly figured in the reveries. Isak does visit his mother on his journey, which somehow recalls Bergman's anecdote about his grandmother.

12. A further excellent point about doubling was suggested to me by the first of the two anonymous peer reviewers of my video and article, to whom I am indebted: 'The projective elements of the dream-memory addressed in *Screen Memories*, in their function both as revelation and concealment, can be found in many other doublings in the film: the simultaneous presence of past and present, external and inner reality, lies and truth. On these aspects there are copious references: by way of example, one could mention ... Jacques Aumont (2003:158), according to whom in Bergman this doubling game is necessary in order to express what otherwise would be neglected.'
13. For reasons of space I won't refer directly, in any detail, to Lucy Fife Donaldson's brilliant 2014 book-length study of texture in film, except to recommend it strongly to anyone thinking through these kinds of questions.
14. I first came across Cardinal's work through its citation and exploration in Christian Keathley's groundbreaking 2006 book *Cinephilia and History, or The Wind in the Trees*, to which my present study is also heavily indebted.
15. In this respect, my video took up some aspects of Ian Garwood's compelling application to multiscreen works of certain insights from the work of Dutch-Australian scholar of multimodal communications Theo van Leeuwen in which the latter identifies the positions of *figure, ground* and *field* as crucial to the creation of aural perspective (Garwood 2008; van Leeuwen 1999).
16. In fact, only the right-hand screen material has any sync sound; the material in the left-hand screen has been silenced, as I indicated earlier.

References

Arlow, Jacob A. (1997), 'The end of time: a psychoanalytic perspective on Ingmar Bergman's *Wild Strawberries*', *International Journal of Psycho-Analysis*, 78: 595–9.

Aumont, Jacques (2003), *Ingmar Bergman. 'Mes films sont l'explication de mes images'*, Paris: Cahiers du cinéma.

Bach, Seldon (1975), 'Discussion of Greenberg's Article', in S. Kaminsky and J. F. Hill (eds), *Ingmar Bergman: Essays in Criticism*, London: Oxford University Press, pp. 194–201.

Batty, Craig and Susan Kerrigan (2018), *Screen Production Research: Creative Practice as a Mode of Enquiry*, Basingstoke: Palgrave Macmillan.

Bergman, Ingmar (1973), *Bergman on Bergman: Interviews with Ingmar Bergman*, New York: Simon and Schuster.

Bergman, Ingmar (1988), *The Magic Lantern: An Autobiography*, Chicago: University of Chicago Press.

Bergman, Ingmar (1994), *Images: My Life in Film*, London: Faber & Faber.

Botz-Bornstein, Thorsten (2007), *Film and Dreams: Tarkovsky, Bergman, Sokurov, Kubrick and Wong Kar-wai*, New York: Lexington.

Burch, Noël (1981), 'How We Got into Pictures', *Afterimage*, 8/9, 29.

Cardinal, Roger (1986), 'Pausing Over Peripheral Detail', *Framework* 30: 112–30.

Coates, Paul (2010), 'Doubling and Redoubling Bergman: Notes on the Dialectic of Disgrace and Disappearance', *Scandinavian-Canadian Studies/Études Scandinaves au Canada*, 19: 186–99, <http://scancan.net/coates_1_19.htm>.

Cook, Pam (2014), 'Word vs. Image: Making *Mildred's Kiss* (2013)', *The Audiovisual Essay: Practice and Theory of Videographic Film and Moving Image Studies*, <https://reframe.sussex.ac.uk/audiovisualessay/reflections/intransition-1-3/pam-cook/>.

Cowie, Elizabeth (2003), 'The Cinematic Dream-Work of Ingmar Bergman's *Wild Strawberries* (1957)', in Andrea Sabbadini (ed.), *The Couch and The Silver Screen: Psychoanalytic Reflections on European Cinema*, Hove: Brunner/Routledge, pp. 181–203.
Doane, Mary Ann (2002), *The Emergence of Cinematic Time: Modernity, Contingency, the Archive*, Cambridge, MA: Harvard University Press.
Elsaesser, Thomas (2009), 'The Mind-Game Film', in Warren Buckland (ed.), *Puzzle Films: Complex Storytelling in Contemporary Cinema*, Oxford: Wiley-Blackwell, pp. 13–41.
Extence, Gavin (2008), 'Cinematic Thought: The Representation of Subjective Processes in the Films of Bergman, Resnais and Kubrick', PhD thesis, University of Sheffield, Department of English Literature.
Fife Donaldson, Lucy (2014), *Texture in Film*, Basingstoke: Palgrave Macmillan.
Fluck, Winfried (2003), *Film and Memory. In Sites of Memory in American Literatures and Cultures*, ed. Udo J. Hebel, Heidelberg: Universitätsverlag C. Winter, pp. 213–29.
French, Philip and Kersti French (1995), *Wild Strawberries*, London: BFI.
Freud, Sigmund (1899), 'Screen memories', *Standard Edition 3*, London: The Hogarth Press, pp. 299–322.
Freud, Sigmund (1900), *The Interpretation of Dreams, Standard Edition 4 and 5*, London: The Hogarth Press.
Freud Sigmund (1901), *The Psychopathology of Everyday Life, Standard Edition 6*, London: The Hogarth Press.
Freud, Sigmund (1914), 'Remembering, repeating and working-though', *Standard Edition 12*, London: The Hogarth Press.
Freud, Sigmund (1920, 1962), *Three Essays on the Theory of Sexuality*, trans. James Strachey, New York: Basic Books.
Freud, Sigmund (1952), 'Medusa's Head', *Collected Papers*, 5, 105–6. London: The Hogarth Press.
Garwood, Ian (2008), 'Sound and space in the split-screen movie', *Refractory: A Journal of Entertainment Media*, 14, <http://refractory.unimelb.edu.au/2008/12/27/garwood/>.
Grant, Catherine (2013), 'Déjà viewing?: videographic experiments in intertextual film studies', *Mediascape: UCLA's Journal of Cinema and Media Studies* (Winter), <http://www.tft.ucla.edu/mediascape/Winter2013_DejaViewing.html>.
Grant, Catherine (2015), 'Interplay: (Re)Finding and (Re)Framing Cinematic Experience, Film Space, and the Child's World,' [Video and text] *LOLA*, 6, <http://www.lolajournal.com/6/interplay.html>.
Grant, Catherine (2018). 'Screen Memories: A Video Essay on *Smultronstället/Wild Strawberries*', *Cinergie: Il Cinema e le altre Arti*, No. 13, <https://doi.org/10.6092/issn.2280-9481/7914>.
Greenberg, Harvey R. (1970), 'The rags of time', *American Imago*, 27:1, 66–82. Reprinted (1975) in S. M. Kaminsky with J. F. Hill (eds), *Ingmar Bergman: Essays in Criticism*, London: Oxford University Press.
Jonte-Pace, Diane (2001), *Speaking the Unspeakable: Religion, Misogyny, and the Uncanny Mother in Freud's Cultural Texts*, Berkeley: University of California Press.
Karpf, Ernst, Doron Kiesel and Karsten Visarius (eds) (1998), *Once Upon a Time...: Film und Gedächtnis*, Marburg: Schüren.
Keathley, Christian (2006), *Cinephilia and History, or The Wind in the Trees*, Bloomington: Indiana University Press.
Petrić, Vlada (1981), *Film and dreams: an approach to Bergman*, South Salem, NY: Redgrave.

Rifaterre, Michael (1980), *The Semiotics of Poetry*, London: Methuen.
Schor, Naomi (1987), *Reading in Detail: Aesthetics and the Feminine*, London: Methuen.
Steene, Brigitta (1965), 'The Isolated Hero of Ingmar Bergman', *Film Comment* 3:2, 68.
van Leeuwen, Theo (1999), *Speech, Music, Sound*, Basingstoke: Macmillan Press.
Williams, Daniel Ellis (2012), 'The Role of Imagination in Bergman, Klein and Sartre', PhD thesis, Department of Film and TV, School of Arts Brunel University, <http://citeseerx.ist.psu.edu/viewdoc/download?doi=10.1.1.426.5203&rep=rep1&type=pdf>.
Wood, Aylish (2007), *Digital Encounters*, Abingdon: Routledge.

INDEX

Note: illustrations are indicated by page numbers in **bold**

Abbott, Patsy, 227
abjection, 77, 197, 251
Abubakar, Fati, 277–8, 283, 284
Abubakar, Yakubu, 283
accelerationism, 62–3, 77, 78
access-for-all films, 72, 74–6, 79
Act of Killing, The (2013), 169, 176–7
activism, 5, 55, 90, 126, 128, 155–6
adaptations, 88, 184–95, 259–63
Adcock, Mike, 115
Adler, Polly, 239
Adorno, Theodor, 12, 54, 59, 65, 288, 289, 290, 301
advertising, 53, 85, 110
aesthetic apparatuses, 52–3
aesthetic normalization, 52–3
aesthetic practices, 52
aesthetic sociality, 51
aesthetics, 16, 26–7, 31, 51–3, 54, 74, 120, 125–6, 130, 143–4, 146, 157, 251, 252
agency, 60, 61, 75, 95, 97–9, 104, 198, 199, 205, 272, 273, 277–9, 284–5
agnotology, 54–5
Ai Weiwei, 128
aid agencies *see* charities
Akerman, Chantal, 123, 217–18
Alabi-Hundeyin, Tunde, 12, 271–85
Alam, Shahidul, 109
Alford, C. Fred, 216

algorithms, 46, 60, 87
Alice in Wonderland (Carroll), 261
Alice Through the Looking Glass (Carroll), 261
Allen, Tony, 239
alt-right groups, 53, 58
Anderson, Benedict, 86
Anderson, Leon, 8
Andrews, Giuseppe, 157, 159
anger, 26–7, 28, 199
animation, 86, 153, 156–7, 167, 169, 170–1, 243, 245–7, 251, 252, 254
An-Ski Shalom, 265
anthropology, 6, 8, 96–7
appropriation, 51, 56–7, 59, 191, 193, 290
Arcadia (Pears), 88
architecture, 13, 47, 49, 61, 70–1
archive footage, 14, **191**, 191–4, 198
Aristotle, 134–5, 136, 137–8, 139, 146
Arnheim, Rudolf, 144
art *see* visual art
artificial intelligence (AI), 87
Aryan aesthetics, 26–7
Astruc, Alexandre, 120
Atakav, Eylem, 11, 19–33
attachment, 203, 204–5, 211–12, 216
audiences, 24, 30, 61, 66, 72, 115, 160–1, 222–3, 235–7; *see also* spectatorship
auteurism, 58–9, 66, 75, 120

316

INDEX

authority, 95, 109
authorship, 6–7, 58–9, 65, 66, 74, 85, 86
autobiographical material, 6, 8, 10–11, 24, 99, 125, 176, 200–1, 232, 259
autoethnography, 6, 7–9, 11, 16, 34, 94, 98–9, 201, 298
automation, 46, 60, 87, 89, 109, 112, 117
autonomy, 46, 59–60, 66, 94–5, 104, 125, 213, 284, 291–3
avant-gardes, 51, 117

Bacharach, Burt, 239
Bacon, Francis, 215, 216
Badiou, Alain, 216
Baker, Sean, 158
Balázs, Béla, 215
Barad, Karen, 248
Barker, Jennifer M., 242, 243, 246–7
Barrett, Jenny, 11, 94–106
Barth, Belle, 227
Barthes, Roland, 12–13, 16, 110, 304
Barton Brothers, 232
Bassil-Morozow, Helena, 214
Basu, Ambar, 94, 102–4
Baudelaire, Charles, 293
Baudrillard, Jean, 73, 76
Baxandall, Michael, 139
Bazin, André, 208, 294
Belli, Alessia, 97–8
Bellour, Raymond, 252
Benchley, Peter, 140
Benjamin, Walter, 109, 112, 294, 295
Benning, Sadie, 156
Bergman, Ingmar, 12, 305–11
Bergson, Henri, 291, 301
Berlant, Lauren, 53
Berliner, Alan, 123
Best Job in the World, The (2013), 35
Bhabha, Homi, 94, 96, 104
Birri, Fernando, 155
Bits of Borno (Abubakar), 277–8, 284
Blouin, Michael J., 54
Boal, Augusto, 157–8, 161
Bochner, Art, 8
Boko Haram, 12, 271–2, 278, 281–2
Bollywood, 124
Bolt, Barbara, 153
Bragg, Melvyn, 306
brands, 85, 86
Brazil, 158–9
Breathing Still (2018), 20, 31
Brecht, Berthold, 108, 112, 115, 165
bricolage, 31
Britain *see* United Kingdom
Brock, Bazon, 59–60, 61, 75
Broken Manual (Soth), 109
Bronski, Michael, 227

Brook, Peter, 265, 268
Broszat, Martin, 72
Brown, Wendy, 53
Brown, Will, 11, 14, 70–9, 150–61
Browne Report, 105
Bruner, Jerome, 88
Bruns, Axel, 152
Buckland, Warren, 3, 133–47, 276
Buddhism, 125
Burnat, Emad, 156
Burton, Sarah, 225–6
Butler, Bill, 140
Butler, Judith, 53, 97, 98

Cahiers du cinéma, 36
Calvino, Italo, 89
caméra-stylo, 120, 129
cancer, 22, 23, 30
capitalism, 20, 50–1, 60, 62–3, 76–9, 101–3, 158, 294, 299–300
Cardinal, Roger, 305, 310
caress, 12, 242–55
Carnegie, Andrew, 85
Carnesky, marisa, 236
Carroll, Lewis, 261
Case History (Mikhailov), 109–10
Casebier, Allan, 165, 177
Castoriadis, Cornelius, 170, 172
Cervantes, Miguel, 259–61
Chang, Heewon, 8
charities, 272, 273–4, 278, 282–4
Chen, Kuan-hsing, 124
Cheng, Andrew Y.-S., 156
child development, 204–5, 208, 209–18
child images, 272, 273–4
Children: Refugees and Migrants (Salgado), 277, 284
Children's Village (2012), **127**
Chile, 100–2
China, 12, 16, 119–30, 156
China's can Goghs (2016), 119–20
Chion, Michel, 299
Chomsky, Noam, 89, 138–9
Christmas Carol, A (Dickens), 259
cinéma vérité, 165, 167, 217
cinematic strategy, 133, 134, 143–6
citizen journalism, 86
Clancy, Tony, 12, 107–17
Claudel, Paul, 259
cleanliness, 244, 248
close-ups, 207, 211, 213–18
Cohen, Albert, 263
Cohen, Jeremy Jerome, 113
collaborative practice, 5, 12, 25, 184–95, 225, 229–30, 232
colonialism, 27, 95–8, 100, 102–4, 124, 159–60, 183–95, 198–9, 294–5, 300–1

317

comedy, 11–12, 22, 221–39
commodification, 27, 38, 51, 83, 85, 100, 102–4, 110, 113, 285
Comolli, Jean-Louis, 35–9, 40
Conformist, The (1970), 78
Confucianism, 122, 124–5, 126
Congo, Anwar, 176
Conman with 14 Wives, The (2007), 35
Connor, Steven, 233, 237
consent, 36, 38, 273, 276, 282
Constructions in Analysis (Freud), 173–6
consumption, 50–1, 127
Conrad, Joseph, 61
Convergence, 82
Conway, Steve, 82
Cook, Pam, 304
copy painting, 119–20
Couldry, Nick, 300
counter-movement, 289, 293
Cowie, Elizabeth, 7, 167, 168, 307, 308, 309, 311
Craig, Edward Gordon, 264, 268
creative classes, 50
creative industries, 50–1
Creative Practice Research conference, 1, 4, 46, 70, 78, 82, 107
creativity dispositif, 51–3, 56, 60
Creme, Phyllis, 206
Criticising China (2008), 122, 128
Crossfire (Alam), 109
Csíkszentmihályi, Mihaly, 88
Cuarón, Jonás, 155
Cuba, 155
cubism, 139–40
Culloden (1964), 165
cultural memory, 223, 229–31, 232, 234
Cultural Revolution, 125
curricula, 25, 32–3, 82, 105, 133

Dada, 193
Daily Trust newspapers, 283
Daly, Timothy, 267
Dane, Clemence, 894
Daniels, Jill, 11, 19–33
Daoism, 125, 130
David, Hal, 239
Davidi, Guy, 156
Davis, Madeleine, 206
de Beauvoir, Simone, 10
de la Cruz, Khavn, 156
de Simone, Maria, 227
Dean, Mitchell, 225
decolonisation, 32, 102, 150, 157, 160, 185, 301
Deconstructing Zoe (2016), 11, 94–106
deconstruction, 54, 95
de-contextualisation, 288, 294, 295, 297

defamiliarisation, 117, 304, 310
Del Negro, Giovanna, 222, 228–9
Deleuze, Gilles, 62–3, 244, 293
democracy, 54, 121, 264
Democratic Republic of Congo, 277
Demos, T. J., 297, 298, 300–1
Derrida, Jacques, 10, 54, 173, 194, 294, 295–7
deterritorialisation, 63
Devereux, Paul, 115
Dibbouk, The (An-Ski), 265
Dickens, Charles, 259
Diderot, Denis, 110
Different Bodies conference, 22, 28
digital media, 24, 25, 37, 60, 86–90, 120, 150, 152–4, 161
digital photography, 108, 279
direct cinema, 165–6, 169
disability, 23–4, 157
Disparition, La (Perec), 159
displacement, 201–3, 210–13, 217, 271–85
dis-possession, 297
disruption, 28, 30, 53
distribution, 19, 66, 152
Disturbing the Peace (2009), 128
Doane, Mary Ann, 308, 309
Dobrowodzka, Anna, 193
docu-fiction, 167
documentaries
  animation in, 167, 169, 170–1
  close-ups in, 207, 211, 213–18
  consent of subjects, 36, 38, 273, 276, 282
  direct cinema approach, 165–6, 169
  domestic ethnography, 200–3, 207–18
  dream sequences in, 167, 169, 170–2
  and ethics, 7, 12, 14–16, 105–6, 193, 210, 215–16, 218, 282–4
  fictive elements, 7, 164–78
  filmmaker/subject relationship, 7, 35, 37–44, 200–3, 208–10
  first-person documentaries, 119–30, 167–8, 176, 177
  funding, 20, 30, 48, 61
  history of genre, 165
  and knowledge, 6–7, 57, 98–9
  and objectivity, 6–7
  photographic, 271–85
  and psychoanalysis, 12, 35–44, 168, 172–7, 202–18
  re-enactments in, 166, 167, 177
  and reflexivity, 165, 177, 202
  and subjectivity, 7, 24, 48, 57, 98–9, 167–8
dogme 95 movement, 155
domestic ethnography, 200–3, 207–18
Don Quixote (Cervantes), 259–61
Dong Chongshu, 125
dream sequences, 167, 169, 170–2, 306–11

Drndić, Daša, 27
Du côte d'Alice (Starkier), 261, **262**
Duchamp, Marcel, 193
Dullin, Charles, 268
Dunne, Joseph, 135
Dutta, Mohan J., 94, 102–4
Dzhangal (Mendel), 109

Eadie, Bruce, 12, 164–78
Ecker, David W., 146
Eco, Umberto, 185–6, 192
editing, 13, 28, 29, 32, 48–9, 61, 64–5, 98, 141–5, 153, 165–6, 252, 254, 299, 309, 310
education *see* curricula; teaching
Eisenstein, Sergei, 110, 111, 144, 154
Elcott, Noam, 57
Ellis, Carolyn, 8, 99
Elsaeser, Hans Peter, **62–4**, 71, 73
Elsaesser, Liesel, 13–14, 71, 79
Elsaesser, Martin, 13, 47, 49, 61, 70–1, 73–4, 79
Elsaesser, Thomas, **9**, 9, 12–17, 46–67, 70–9, 90, 117, 193, 197–9, 282, 284
embodied knowledge, 5–6, 99, 225, 236–7, 250
emotion, 3, 22, 34, 39, 87–90, 127–8, 190, 194, 205, 209, 213–15, 264, 268, 293
empathy, 23, 24, 88–9, 90
employability, 25, 32, 81–2, 105
Enlightenment, 9, 62, 120, 123
entanglement, 245, 248, 249
epistêmê, 134–5, 139
Espinosa, Julio García, 155
essay-films, 12, 14, 19, 20, 46, 48, 66, 71, 126, 129, 152, 247, 251, 288–90, 294–301, 304–11
ethics, 7, 12, 14–16, 105–6, 120, 124–6, 129, 193, 210, 215–16, 218, 282–4
ethno-fiction, 99
Etruscan smile, 61, 65, 75–6
Eurocentrism, 95, 157
'European Ghosts' exhibition, **292**, 294–301, **296**
European Union, 51
experience economy, 51
expert spectatorship, 226, 238, 239
expertise, 138–43, 146, 147
expressionism, 267
Ezcurra, Polgovsky, 112

fables, 84, 88, 267
Facebook, 89, 152, 223, 233, 237, 278
facticality, 170, 172
factuality, 170
fake news, 54

family, 11, 13–16, 23, 41–4, 47–9, 65, 71–5, 84, 122, 124–7, 200–3, 207–18; *see also* fathers; mothers
Family Phobia (2009), 127
fascism, 73, 74, 76–8, 264; *see also* Nazism
fashion, 21, 51
fathers, 23, 40, 41–4, 65, 202, 209–10, 212; *see also* family
Federico, Fabrizio, 157
Felman, Shoshana, 10
femininity, 6, 10–11, 27, 249, 254, 268
feminism, 20–1, 22, 25, 32, 53, 185, 225, 232, 242–5, 248–51, 254–5
fiction films, 6, 7, 20, 89, 167
fiction literature, 13, 84, 86, 88, 101, 125, 159–60, 259–63
film *see* documentaries; essay-films; fiction films
Filming Othello (1978), 76
filmmaking manuals, 134, 140–3, 146
Finding Temeraire (Makuwe), **184**, 184–95, **187**
Finnegans Wake (Joyce), 159–60
first-person narratives, 3, 5, 8, 10, 11, 34, 50, 119–30, 167–8, 176, 177
First World War, 89
Five Broken Cameras (2011), 156
Five Obstructions, The (2003), 76, 154–5
Flaherty, Robert J., 6, 166, 167
Flaubert, Gustave, 183
Fleifel, Mahdi, 155
flexibility, 5, 53, 60
Flickr, 108–9
flow, 88
folk tales, 84, 86, 89
Folman, Ari, 169, 170–2
Fong, Rosa, 11, 94–106
forced marriage, 20, 22–3
form, 143–4, 146, 276
Foucault, Michel, 51, 60, 117, 225
found footage, 31, 152, 153, 156–7, 184, **191**, 191–4, 198
found objects, 193, 206, 207
framing, 29, 31, 48, 108, 206–7, 210, 211, 213, 217, 282, 300
France, 12, 28–9, 36, 43, 124
Frankfurt School, 50, 54
Franklin, Aretha, 231
Freakstars 3000 (2004), 157
freedom, 38, 54, 60, 103, 104, 292–3
Freiburg School, 54
Freire, Paolo, 157–8
French New Wave, 123
Freud, Sigmund, 35, 65, 173–6, 178, 203, 306–8, 311
funding
 for charities, 272, 273, 282–4

funding (*cont.*)
  for education, 105, 300
  for filmmaking, 20, 30, 48, 61
  for research, 83, 290–3, 297, 300
  for theatre, 225
Funke, Cornelia, 88
Furtado, Jorge, 159

game-playing, 81–90, 206, 211
Game Studies, 82
Gansel, Mireille, 191
Garber, Marjorie, 239
Gargantua and Pantagruel (Rabelais), 262–3
Garwood, Ian, 310
gatekeepers, 160–1
Geertz, Clifford, 6
Gel, Alfred, 301
gender
  and agency, 95, 97–9, 104, 198, 199
  gendered expectations, 126
  gendered knowledge, 10–11
  gendered looking, 274–6, 277, 284
  and the impacts of colonialism, 183–95
  and the impacts of neoliberalism, 53
  performance of, 94–104
  and power relations, 22–3, 96–7, 126, 274–6
  stereotypes of, 95, 96–8, 104
  and subalternity, 183–91
  and subjectivity, 11
  transgenderism, 11, 94–106
  and voice, 11, 39, 94–5, 183–4, 188, 254
  see also femininity; masculinity
generative grammar, 138–9
German expressionism, 123
Germany, 7, 13–16, 27, 31, 47–8, 61, 62, 65–6, 70–9
Ghana, 116
ghosts, 89, 239, 294–8, 300–1
Giardina Papa, Elisa, 53
Gilman, Sander, 233
Girl Power (1992), 156
Giroux, Henry A., 105–6
Giuseppe Makes a Movie (2014), 159
Glapka, Ewa, 274–6
Gleaners and I, The (2000), 212
globalisation, 120, 157, 159, 293
Glyn, Elinor, 85
Go Fish (1994), 156
Godard, Jean-Luc, 167
Goethe, Johann Wolfgang von, 293
González, Melissa M., 100, 101–2
Gottlieb, Carl, 140
Gottschall, Jonathan, 88
Gramsci, Antonio, 96–7, 183

Grant, Catherine, 3, 12, 203, 304–11
Greenberg, Clement, 59
Grierson, John, 167, 168, 169, 203
Gros grand gras Gargantua, Un (Starkier), 262–3, **263**
grotesque, 267
Grotowski, Jerzy, 264, 268, 269
Growing Up Married (2016), 19, 21, 22–3, 24, 26, 28, 30–1
Guattari, Felix, 62–3, 293
guerrilla fiction, 101
guerrilla filmmaking, 11, 150–61

Haggis-Burridge, Mata, 90
hallucination, 108, 114, 167, 169, 170–2
Hamlet (Shakespeare), 173–6, 178
Hann, Rachel, 224
Hara Kazuo, 127
Haraway, Donna, 5–6, 9, 185
Harrod, Mary, 11
Hastrup, Kirsten, 291
hauntology, 295–7, 299, 300
Hava Nagila (Williams), 229
Haynes, Todd, 156
Heath, Stephen, 297
hegemony, 81–2, 95, 97, 104, 183, 194, 285
Heidegger, Martin, 54, 170
Hesse Film Foundation, 48, 49, 61
high theory, 5, 12, 54, 103
Hill, Napoleon, 85
Hills, Matt, 206
Hitchcock, Alfred, 141–3
Hitler, Adolf, 7, 15
Hitler: A Film from Germany (1977), 62
Höfinger, Walli, 234
Hollywood, 20, 58, 70, 72, 74, 75, 77, 141, 274
Holocaust, 21–2, 27–8, 48, 72, 73, 75, 79, 172
home movies, 13, 24, 47, 48, 64, 66, 71, 201, 217
Home Video (2001), 126
Hommelsheim, Christiane, 234
homophobia, 100, 237
homosexuality, 23, 100–1, 156, 228
honour killings, 20–1, 23
How do you see me? (2017), 200–3, 207–18, **209**
Hu Xinyu, 127
Hugo, Pieter, 116
humanitarian organisations *see* charities
humanitarian photography, 271–85
hunger, aesthetic of, 155
Hwang, David Henry, 94, 96–7
hybridity, 96, 98, 192

I Beat the Tiger when I was Young (2010), 128
identity formation, 75, 94–106, 205, 214–16, 225
I'm In Heaven (1989), 20
image manipulation, 108
image writing, 126, 129
imagined communities, 86
Imitation of Life (1959), 251
immersion, 87–8, 90
impact narratives, 23, 26, 30, 83–4, 224, 291, 300
imperfect cinema, 150, 155, 161
imperfection, 154–7, 160, 161, 242, 244, 247, 251, 253, 254
Impressionism, 139
India, 102, 103, 123, 124
individualism, 3, 54, 60, 120, 125
infantilisation, 278, 279
Ingold, Tim, 288–9, 291, 293, 301
Inkheart (2008), 88
Inkheart trilogy (Funke), 88
Innes, Vari, 40–1, 43
Instagram, 89, 152, 278
intellectual property, 86–7
interactive fiction (IF), 86, 88
interactive selfhood, 126, 128–9
interdisciplinarity, 53, 119, 289
internally displaced persons (IDPs), 271–85
interpretation, 143–4, 276–7
intersectionality, 193, 255
intuition, 146, 236, 238, 259, 263–5, 268, 291, 295
invisibility, 6, 7, 23–4, 156, 264
Ionesco, Eugene, 111
Iortyer, Philip, 272
Iran, 156, 200–1, 212
Iran–Iraq War, 200, 212
Ireland, 159–60
Irigaray, Luce, 12, 242–55
Islam, 20–1, 274–6
Island of Flowers, The (1989), 159
Israel, 26–7, 156, 170–2
Italian neo-realism, 123, 167

Jakobson, Roman, 185–6, 192
Jameson, Fredric, 61–2
Japan, 31, 124, 125, 283
Jaws (1975), 140
Jenkins, Henry, 161
Jia Zhangke, 156
Jones, Bamidele, 283
jouissance, 185, 190
journalism, 26–7, 32, 86, 278, 283, 285; *see also* media
Journey to the South (2017), 29
Joyce, James, 159–60

Judaism, 11–12, 15, 20–2, 27, 48, 62, 71, 75, 221–3, 226–39, 265–7
Jung, Carl, 89

Kafka, Franz, 261, 267, 268
Kafka's Dance (Daly), **266**, 267
Keaton, Buster, 110–11
Keats, John, 139
Kemmis, Stephen, 272
Kern, Irmgard, 65
Kershaw, Baz, 224
Kershaw, Justine, 40, 41–2, 44
Kessel, Erik, 108–9
Khanna, Ranjana, 190
Kid Icarus (2008), 155
Klee, Paul, 269
know-how, 134, 135–8, 146, 259
know-that, 134, 135–8
knowledge
    and documentaries, 6–7, 57, 98–9
    embodied knowledge, 5–6, 99, 225, 236–7, 250
    epistêmê, 134–5, 139
    expert knowledge, 138–43, 146, 147
    and film, 3, 5, 133–4, 140–7
    gendered nature of, 10–11
    knowing-how, 134, 135–8, 146, 259
    knowing-that, 134, 135–8
    measurement of, 3, 4, 81–4, 290–3, 300
    non-reproducible, 230
    and objectivity, 2–3, 6–9, 57, 259, 297
    patriarchal models of, 2, 5–6, 10, 226
    and power, 57, 272–3, 290, 293
    praktikos, 134–5, 141, 144, 146
    production of, 2, 14–15, 34, 50–1, 83, 99, 105, 122–3, 259, 264–5, 289–97, 305
    scientific models of, 2–3, 6
    situated knowledges, 5–6, 293
    and storytelling, 3, 84–7, 90
    and subjectivity, 2–3, 6–9, 50, 57, 259, 297
    technê, 3, 134–5, 137, 141–6
    transmission of, 84–7, 90, 146–7, 234, 264, 267–9
Kondo, Dorinne K., 94, 96–7
Kuhn, Annette, 203, 206, 211

Lacan, Jacques, 35, 39, 41, 96, 168, 173, 194–5, 203, 214
Lacombe, Lucien (1974), 78
Lahad, Kinneret, 226
Lanzmann, Claude, 73
laojia (the old home), 122, 126–7
Lassalle, Jacques, 268
late work, 13
Latour, Bruno, 53–4
Lebanon, 156, 170–2
Lebow, Alisa, 168

321

Leder, Drew, 247
Leiris, Michel, 297
Lemebel, Pedro, 95, 100–2, 104
Leow, Zoe/Chowee, 94–106
Leth, Jørgen, 76, 154–5
Letter of Love to You (2016), 243, 245–7, 246, 248–9, 254
Lévi-Strauss, Claude, 31, 84
Levinas, Emmanual, 215–16
Liang Qichao, 125
lieux de mémoire, 72
Lindsay-Abaire, David, 88
linguistics, 138–9
Lippard, Lucy, 298
live streaming, 122, 126, 128–9
Locke, John, 9, 291
London Diaries (2009), 121
Loretoni, Anna, 97–8
love, 35, 38–41, 44, 78, 243, 245–6, 254
Lovers in Time (2015), 14
low-budget filmmaking, 150, 153–4, 155, 157
Lucariello, Joan, 88
Luhmann, Niklas, 52
Lusty Juventus Physical Theatre, 225, 232
Luxemburg, Rosa, 20

M. Butterfly (Hwang), 94, 96–7
McCullin, Don, 283
MacDonald, Ian, 89
MacDougall, David, 208
machinima, 156–7
McIntyre, Peter, 274
McLaughlin, Carl Bird, 155
McTaggart, Robin, 272
Madama Butterfly (Puccini), 96, 97
Maddin, Guy, 177
Mai, Nicola, 99
Makuwe, Stanley, 12, 184–95
Malaysia, 95–6
male gaze, 274–6, 277, 284
Man in the Attic, The (Daly), 267
Mandy (1951), 211
Mao Zedong, 125
Married to the Eiffel Tower (2008), 7, 12, 34–5, **35**, **36**, 39–44
Marvelous Mrs Maisel, The (2017), 238
Marx, Karl, 59, 63, 297
Marxism, 83, 101
masculinity, 11, 254
mash-ups, 152
Mass Observation archive, 85
Massoumi, Nariman, 11, 200–18
May, Teresa, 27
May Fourth Movement, 125
Maysles brothers, 166
measurement, 3, 4, 81–4, 235, 290–3, 300

media, 20–1, 25–7, 32, 55, 86, 160, 272–4, 278–9, 283, 285; *see also* journalism
Meiselas, Susan, 109
Mekas, Jonas, 123
melodrama, 72, 124
Melrose, Susan, 226
memory, 20, 28, 44, 47–8, 58, 65–6, 72–3, 123, 170–2, 174, 223, 229–31, 234, 294–8, 304–11
Memory of Home (2009), 121, **121**
Mendel, Gideon, 109
mental health, 24, 212
Merleau-Ponty, Maurice, 244
#MeToo movement, 26, 38
Metz, Christian, 107, 108, 113, 114, 115, 168
Midler, Bette, 227, 230, 232
Migge, Leberecht, 13–14, 64, 71
Mikhailov, Boris, 109–10
Millard, Kathryn, 86
Miller, Nancy K., 10
mirroring, 60, 206, 213–16, 218
Mirtahmasb, Mojtaba, 156
Mr. Klein (1976), 74
Mitscherlich, Alexander, 15
Mitscherlich, Margarete, 15
Moana (1926), 166
Mock, Roberta, 11–12, 221–39, **230**, **231**
modernism, 59, 73
Moeller, Susan, 285
Mondomanila (2010), 156
montage, 56, 108, 288, 294–5, 297–301, 305–7
Morley, Carol, 123
Morrison, Toni, 105
M(other) (2002), 232
mothers, 65, 202, 204, 208, 209–10, 213–18, 232, 233–4; *see also* family
Moulin, Le (2015), 124
mourning, 15, 26–7, 28, 42–4, 79
Mujeri, Charmaine, **187**, 192, 198
Mulvey, Laura, 154, 168, 242, 251–3, 274
Mumblecore movement, 155
Muncey, Tessa, 7–9
music, 89, 114–15, 222, 227, 229–30, 299, 306, 310
Musset, Alfred de, 77
My Family Tree (2008), 127
My Winnipeg (2007), 177
myth, 84, 89, 107, 112–13, 264

Nancy, Jean-Luc, 244
Nanook of the North (1922), 6, 166
narcissism, 75, 78
Nash, Robert J., 8
nationalism, 20, 58
naturalism, 108
Nazism, 7, 15, 48, 66, 71–4, 79

negative capability, 139
Negroponte, Nicholas, 86
Nelson, Robin, 242, 252, 253
neoliberalism
  and accelerationism, 62–3
  and automation, 60
  and creativity, 4–5, 46, 50–8, 60, 66–7, 116–17, 258, 264, 284
  disintegration of, 20
  and filmmaking, 19, 61–7, 75–9, 95
  gendered impacts of, 53
  and photography, 109–10, 112, 282–4
  resistance to, 4–5, 39, 43, 56, 58, 77, 95, 116–17, 284
  and subalternity, 94–5, 101–5
  and tactical compliance, 61–7, 75–9
  and the university, 4–5, 53, 55–6, 95, 105, 158, 225–6, 288–9, 290, 293, 299–301
News Agency of Nigeria (NAN), 283
Nichols, Bill, 6, 169
Nietzsche, Friedrich, 265
Nigeria, 157, 271–85
Night Will Fall (2014), 21–2
Nightingale, Not the Only Voice (2000), 126
Nissinen, Sanna, 282
No Home Movie (2015), 217–18
Nollywood, 157
non-cinema, 153–4, 247
non-reproducible knowledge, 230
nostalgia, 126–7, 193, 198, 230
Nostalgia (2006), 127
Novarina, Valere, 265
novels *see* fiction literature

object-relations psychoanalysis, 202–18
objectification, 274–6, 283
objectivity, 2–3, 6–9, 57, 204–5, 259, 297
October, 35
Off the Page event, 89–90
Okoli, Al Chukwuma, 272
Olson, Jenni, 156
120 Says of Sodom, The (1975), 76
Ong, Walter, 87, 89
Oppenheimer, Joshua, 169, 176–7
oppression, 58, 158–61, 193, 194
optical unconscious, 294, 298, 300
oral tradition, 84, 85–6, 87, 88, 89
Orientalism, 95–9, 183
Ostitto/Existence (2012), 21
ostranenie, 117, 304
otherness, 94–5, 97, 102, 103–4, 215–16, 233, 245, 249, 279
Ott, Mike, 155
Owen, Jean, 34

Palestine, 26–7, 155–6, 172
Panahi, Jafar, 156

participatory photography, 272–3, 278–81, 284
Pascal, Blaise, 264
Pasolini, Pier Paolo, 76
patriarchy, 2, 5–6, 10, 97–8, 126, 226, 242, 244, 255
Pearlman, Lazlo, 236
Pears, Iain, 88
pensive-creative praxis, 242, 243, 253–5
pensive spectatorship, 252–3
perception, 112, 207–8, 215, 294, 298
Perec, Georges, 159, 160
Perfect Human, The (1968), 154–5
performance documentation, 236
performance studies, 223, 224–6
performativity, 31, 77, 78–9, 84, 94–104, 128
Permanent Error (Hugo), 116
persistence, 70, 72, 74–5, 79
Petrić, Vlada, 133, 134, 144–6
Phantom Europe (2016), 290, 294–301
phenomenology, 168, 244–5, 248
Philippines, 156, 160
photography, 12, 31, 71, 107–17, 125, 201–2, 208, 252–3, 271–85, 295–301
photomontage *see* montage
photoshop, 108
photovoice methodology, 272–3, 278–81
Picasso, Pablo, 139–40, 258
Pinkerton, Nick, 218
Pinochet, Augusto, 100, 101
Piotrowska, Agnieszka, 1–17, **2**, 34–44, 46, 78, 82, 115, 154, 168, 173, 183–95, 197–9, 203, 208
Pisters, Patricia, 119
Plate Spinner, The (Clancy), 107, 110–12, **111**, 116
Plato, 289
playing *see* game-playing
Podington Bear, 306
Polizzotti, Mark, 191, 194
Poole, Stephen, 88
porosity, 242–4, 245, 247, 251, 253
Portrait of the Artist as a Young Man (Joyce), 159
postcolonialism, 2, 11, 95–104, 185, 297, 300
postmodernism, 59, 73, 123
poststructuralism, 56, 167, 172
post-traumatic stress disorder (PTSD), 172
poverty, 110, 273–4, 282, 285
power relations, 22–3, 96–7, 126, 128, 272–3, 274–6, 290, 293
practical knowledge *see* know-how; *praktikos*; *technê*
Practice as Research in Performance (PARIP) project, 224
praktikos, 134–5, 141, 144, 146
praxis, 242, 243, 244, 247–8, 250, 253–5

precarious employment, 5, 53, 76
Preselli Hills, Wales, 115
print culture, 84, 85, 86, 87, 90
production, 13–14, 19, 48–50, 58, 61, 64–6, 152
produsage, 152–4
professionalism, 13, 158, 223, 226, 228–9, 235, 238–9, 248
propositional knowledge, 136–8, 141, 146
Propp, Vladimir, 84, 89
prostitution, 183, 188, 222, 239
Proust, Marcel, 261, 265
psychoanalysis, 10, 12, 35–44, 75, 108, 168, 172–7, 190, 194–5, 202–18, 244–5, 254, 297, 306–8
Psychoanalysis and Ethics in Documentary Film (Piotrowska) 34–5
public selfhood, 126, 127–8

Quichotte (Starkier), 259–61, **261**

Rabelais, François, 262–3
racial performance, 94–104
racial stereotypes, 95, 96–8, 104, 272, 279
racism, 27, 104, 237
radio, 85–6, 222
Rancière, Jacques, 157
Rankin Waddell, John, 277, 284
Ratcatcher (1999), 211
Reading Experience Database, 85
Ready Player One (2018), 77
Real Toy Story, The (Wolf), 109
Reckwitz, Andreas, 51–3
re-contextualisation, 288, 294, 295, 297
Reed-Danahay, Deborah, 8
re-enactment, 166, 167, 177
reflexivity, 7, 31, 48, 53, 165, 177, 202, 225, 250–1, 253, 284
refractiveness, 251, 253
refugees, 109, 153, 155–6, 157, 271–85
Reifarth, Dieter, 48–9
Rein, Boaz, 170–2
Reisz, Karel, 134, 141–3
Renoir, Jean, 145
Renov, Michael, 7, 15, 74–5, 168, 200, 201, 215
Repented (2019), 12, 184–95, **187**, **191**, 197–9
repertoire, 230–1, 232, 239
repetition, 37, 73, 112, 223, 253
re-possession, 297
Research Assessment Exercise, 83
research auditing, 82–4, 290–3, 300
Research Excellence Framework (REF), 1, 3, 6, 81–4, 224–6, 236, 300
resistance, 4, 5, 11, 50, 52, 56, 58–61, 66, 76–9, 104, 117, 128, 284

reterritorialisation, 124
Rexroth, H. G., 65
Rich, Adrienne, 10
Richter, Hans, 299, 300
Riefenstahl, Leni, 7
Rifeser, Judith, 12, 153, 242–55
Rigg, Marlon, 123
Rivers, Joan, 226
Rocha, Glauber, 155
Roehampton Guerrillas (2011–2016) (2017), 160
Romanticism, 51, 112, 139
Rope (1948), 141–3
Roth, Philip, 61
Royal Road, The (2015), 156
Rudd, Amber, 27
Rughani, Pratap, 7
rule-changing, 139–41, 143
rule-following, 139, 140
Rules of the Game (1939), 145
Rushdie, Salman, 192
Russia, 109–10, 116, 124, 265
Ryle, Gilbert, 135–6, 137, 138, 1146

Saatchi Gallery, London, 109–10
Sabbadini, Andrea, 207
Said, Edward, 95, 97, 183
Salesman (1968), 166
Salgado, Sebastião, 277, 281, 284
Sandifolo, Eddie, **187**, 192, 198
Savoy, Bénédicte, 294
Saxton, Libby, 210
Schindler's List (1993), 73
Schlingensief, Christoph, 78, 157
Schor, Naomi, 311
scientific knowledge models, 2–3, 6
Sconce, Jeffrey, 157
screen memories, 297–8, 300, 304–11
'Screen Memories' (Freud), 306–8, 311
Screen Memories (Grant), 304–11, **305**
Scrooge (Starkier), 259, **260**
Second World War, 13–16, 21–2, 27–8, 48, 66, 71–5, 79
Segal, Naomi, 34
Seig, Katrin, 98
self-expression, 119–30
self-objectification, 274–6
self-portraits, 125
selfhood, 51, 75, 78, 86, 95–7, 103, 119, 124–30, 214–16, 225, 245
semiotics, 113, 185–6, 192, 195
separation, 203, 204–5, 208, 211–12, 213, 216
sexual violence, 22–3
sexuality, 39, 41, 44, 221–2, 227–9, 247, 274–6
Shakespeare, William, 173–6, 297

Shanghai Panic (2002), 156
Sherlock Jnr (1924), 111
Shlovsky, Viktor, 112, 116–17
shocking images, 110, 112, 273–4, 283
Shu Haolun, 127
Silverman, Kaja, 11
Silverstone, Roger, 204–5, 206
Singapore, 103
situated knowledges, 5–6, 293
smartphones, 89, 109, 116, 128, 150, 152–3, 158, 206
Smith, Patrick Milling, 87
Sobchack, Vivian, 70, 72, 168, 169, 252
social class, 101, 285
social constructivism, 53–4
social media, 25, 60, 86, 87, 89, 108–9, 116, 120, 126, 128–9, 152, 278
socialism, 20, 124
socialist realism, 124
Softley, Iain, 88
Sontag, Susan, 273–4
Soth, Alec, 109
space in-between, 242, 243, 245, 248, 249–52
Spatz, Ben, 234, 236
spectatorship, 37, 115, 203, 210, 226, 238, 239, 244, 252–3, 310; see also audiences
Speed (1994), 77
Spielberg, Steven, 73, 77
Spinoza, Baruch, 300
split screens, 26–7, **187**, **191**, 193–4, 304–7, 310–11
Spurling, Laurence, 214
Stam, Robert, 192
Stanley, Jason, 134, 136–8, 146
Starkier, Isabelle, 12, 258–69
state subsidies, 50–1
stereotypes, 32, 95, 96–8, 104, 232, 272, 273–4, 279, 283, 285
Stern report, 83
Stewart, Gavin, 82
Steyerl, Hito, 55–7, 61
stills, 31, 107, 109–10, 114–15, 155, 251–3, 299
Stone Ghosts (Clancy), 107, 112–16, **114**
Stonehenge, 113, 115
stories-within-stories, 173–6
storytelling, 3, 11–12, 25, 81–90, 99, 143, 146, 221, 278–9
Strachey, Alix, 65
Strachey, James, 65
style, 143–4, 146, 276–7
subalternity, 94–5, 101–4, 128, 183–91
subjectivity, 2–3, 6–9, 11, 24, 48, 50, 57, 98–9, 167–8, 190, 204–5, 259, 297
submission, 96–7, 98, 104, 274
subversion, 7, 12, 52, 53, 100, 101–2, 126

suffering, 113, 190, 210, 272, 273–4, 285; see also trauma
Sun Island, The (2017), 13–16, 46–50, 58, 61–6, 70–9
Superstar: The Karen Carpenter Story (1988), 156
surrealism, 111, 124, 193
Sweet Nothings (Winship), 277, 284
Syberberg, Hans Jürgen, 62
systems theory, 52

tableaux, 110
tactical compliance, 4, 12–17, 58, 61–7, 70–9, 90, 282–4
Taiwan, 124
Tallon, Rachel, 272
Tang Danhong, 126
Tangerine (2015), 158
Tango of Wandering Stars (Starkier), 267
Tarkovsky, Andrei, 154, 310
Taylor, Diana, 229–30, 234
Taylor, Yvette, 226
teaching, 20, 21, 24–5, 32–3, 81–4, 133, 146–7, 150–61, 300
Teaching Excellence Framework (TEF), 81–4, 300
technê, 3, 134–5, 137, 141–6
Technique of Film Editing (Reisz), 134, 141–3
technology, 143–4, 146, 276–7
television, 4, 14, 28, 39–40, 48–9, 61, 66, 86, 206, 215, 238
Tengo miedo totero (Lemebel), 101
terrorism, 271–2, 278, 281–2
textual analysis, 143–6
theatre, 12, 115, 184–95, 225, 232, 258–69
Theatre of the Oppressed, 158
theoretical knowledge see *epistêmê*; know-that
They Are Not the Only Unhappy Couple (2000), 126
Third World liberation theory, 158
This Is Not a Film (2011), 156
Thomaidis, Konstantinos, 234
Tian'anmen Square incident, 121
time, 37, 47, 48, 88, 107, 111, 116, 139–40, 291
Tioseco, Alexis, 160
Tokyo Compression (Wolf), 109
Tolstoy, Leo, 110
total theatre, 225
touch, 175–6, 243, 245–7, 249
tourism, 50, 52, 113, 297–8
transferable skills, 32, 53
transference, 7, 35, 37, 39, 208–9
transgenderism, 11, 94–106
transitional objects, 202–18
translation, 12, 124, 185–8, 191–5

'trash' films, 157
trauma, 15, 39, 40, 58, 65, 73, 75, 109, 167–78, 184, 187, 202–3, 209–10, 213, 218, 278, 281–2
Trip Around the World Is Not a Cruise (Williams), 221–39, **222**
Troche, Rose, 156
Trump, Ivanka, 26–7
Tucker, Sophie, 227, 228, 230, 231–2
Turan, Zeynep, 212
Turkey, 21, 23, 30, 277
24 Hours in Photos (Kessel), 108–9
Twitchin, Mischa, 12, 288–301

Uganda, 157
Ulysses (Joyce), 159
Umaru, Gola, 279
Under the Mask conferences, 82
underdevelopment, 155
underground films, 156
UNICEF, 282, 283
United Kingdom, 20–1, 27, 95–8, 103–5, 109–10, 115, 120–1, 151, 157–60, 164, 200–1, 282
United States, 26–7, 105, 221–2, 227–8, 267
urbanisation, 121, 122, 125, 126–8
Urrutia, Alejandro, 100, 101
Utopia (Alabi-Hundeyin), 273–81, **275**, **280–1**, 284–5

Vakhtangov, Yevgeny, 265
Van Gogh, Vincent, 120
Varda, Agnes, 212
vaudeville, 227
veiling, 274–6
Velody, Rachel, 11, 19–33
ventriloquism, 233, 237
Venuti, Lawrence, 186
Verma, Priyanka, 1, **2**
Vertov, Dziga, 111, 169
video diaries, 121, 122
video essays *see* essay-films
Villa, Pancho, 154
'Villager Documentary Project', 128
violence, 22–3, 26–7, 164, 190, 218, 271–2, 281–2
virtual reality (VR), 87–8
visibility, 11, 22, 159
Visible Evidence series, 165
visual art, 31, 119–20, 125, 130, 139–40, 165, 193, 215, 291, 294–5
Vitez, Antione, 265, 268
voice, 11, 20, 22–3, 28, 39, 94–5, 100–4, 153, 160, 183–4, 188, 223, 233–4, 237, 254, 299

voiceover, 66, 71, 74, 153, 166, 246, 254, 299, 306, 310–11
von Trier, Lars, 76, 154–5

Wakaliwood, 157
Wallbridge, David, 206
Waltz with Bashir (2009), 169, 170–2, **171**
Wang Fen, 126
Warner, Marina, 191–2, 194
Watkins, Peter, 165
We are Congo (Rankin), 277, 284
Weedon, Alexis, 3, 81–90
Weimar Republic, 66
Weiss, Peter, 56
Welles, Orson, 76
Welton, Martin, 238
West/non-West dichotomy, 20, 56, 95–8, 120, 122–4, 183
Where Is the Friend's Home? (1987), 211
White, Aidan, 274
Whitehead, Alfred North, 288–9, 293, 297, 298
Wild Strawberries (1957), 12, 306–11
Williams, Pearl, 11–12, 221–39, **222**
Wilson, Emma, 208
Winnicott, D. W., 202–7, 211, 213–18
Winship, Vanessa, 277, 284
Wisdom, Stella, 89–90
Wolf, Michael, 109, 112
Woolf, Virginia, 10
World Not Ours, A (2012), 155
Worthington, Andy, 105
Wozencroft, Jon, 115
Wright, Kate, 287
Wright, Kenneth, 204, 206, 207
Wright, Tom, 140
Wu Haohao, 127–8
Wu Wenguang, 128, 156

Xue Jianqiang, 127, 128

Yan Yunxiang, 125, 129
Yang Lina, 126
Yang Pingdao, 127
Year of the Nail (2007), 155
Yiddish, 222, 227–8, 232, 233, 239
yingxiang xiezuo, 129
Yoshimi, Takeuchi, 124
YouTube, 152, 153, 233
Yu, Kiki, 12, 119–30

Zamora, Daniel, 225
zero-budget filmmaking, 150, 153–4
Zhibo, 122, 126, 128–9
Zimbabwe, 12, 35, 184–95
Zionism, 27

EU representative:
Easy Access System Europe
Mustamäe tee 50, 10621 Tallinn, Estonia
Gpsr.requests@easproject.com

www.ingramcontent.com/pod-product-compliance
Lightning Source LLC
Chambersburg PA
CBHW052050230426
43671CB00011B/1859